Palgrave Macmillan Studies in Banking and Financial Institutions

Series Editor
Philip Molyneux, Bangor University, Bangor, UK

The Palgrave Macmillan Studies in Banking and Financial Institutions series is international in orientation and includes studies of banking systems in particular countries or regions as well as contemporary themes such as Islamic Banking, Financial Exclusion, Mergers and Acquisitions, Risk Management, and IT in Banking. The books focus on research and practice and include up to date and innovative studies that cover issues which impact banking systems globally.

Daniele D'Alvia

The Speculator of Financial Markets

How Financial Innovation and Supervision Made the Modern World

palgrave
macmillan

Daniele D'Alvia
Queen Mary University of London
London, UK

ISSN 2523-336X ISSN 2523-3378 (electronic)
Palgrave Macmillan Studies in Banking and Financial Institutions
ISBN 978-3-031-47900-7 ISBN 978-3-031-47901-4 (eBook)
https://doi.org/10.1007/978-3-031-47901-4

Cover illustration: Alex Grimm/getty images

This Palgrave Macmillan imprint is published by the registered company Springer Nature Switzerland AG
The registered company address is: Gewerbestrasse 11, 6330 Cham, Switzerland

Paper in this product is recyclable.

To my parents, Claudia and Fabrizio

Contents

List of Figures

CHAPTER 1

Introduction

Alexandre Cabanel was a French academic and classical painter born in the city of *Montpellier* in 1823. When he was twenty-four years old, he painted the Fallen Angel in 1847 as an academic oil on canvas that is currently stored at the *Musée Fabre* in France. The Fallen Angel or *L'Ange Déchu* is perhaps one of the most popular works of art ever created. Behind fixed arms, a winged nude hides his face. The seductive angel appears, Lucifer. His brows arch over red-rimmed eyes and a tear of rage as his mane of hair breaks in the wind. His physique is flawless. Although his posture seems relaxed, each muscle is tensed and ready to fire. This is the last moment before he is cast out of paradise, and it all began here, with an angel with fiery eyes. It was written in the Bible in Isaiah 14:12 (King James Version):

> How art thou fallen from heaven, O Lucifer son of the morning!

The passage goes on to say that Lucifer tried to raise his throne above the stars and become like the Most High, but God cast him down to the depths of the pits[1] as a mere man (Isaiah 14:13–15). Lucifer[2] was the most beautiful cherub angel of God, and he became the King of Babylon. Everything about Lucifer's appearance was a gift from God, yet the gift inspired his rebellion, and since then other angels followed him.

D. D'Alvia, *The Speculator of Financial Markets*, Palgrave Macmillan Studies in Banking and Financial Institutions,
https://doi.org/10.1007/978-3-031-47901-4_1

This book claims that the story of finance and speculation, and the same figure of the speculator has always been a story of rebellion too. Since the time of Galileo Galilei, the discoveries of new lands in the sixteenth and seventeenth centuries, the Protestant Reformation meant more than just a change in humanity's relationship with God. By eliminating the confessional, it warned people they would have to walk on their own and would have to take responsibility for the consequences of their directions. Human beings could not remain passive in the face of an unknown and uncertain future. They had no choice than to make decision over a far wider range of circumstances. For these reasons, the sixteenth and seventeenth centuries were a time of geographical exploration, confrontation with new lands and new societies, and experimentation in art, poetic forms, science, architecture, and mathematics. The secret mysteries of nature and science were deeply explored beyond traditional teachings. Since then, human beings necessarily started to act against God, because the freedom from dogmatic, absolute, and accepted truth was synonym to be empowered and to lead societies towards scientific and economic progress and development. In other words, the figurative image of Lucifer is not negative per se, and it represents and symbolises the story of human beings who are struggling to take control of their destiny in a new era where progress is determined by individual choices, and it is connected to the very idea of taking risks and facing uncertainties, two separate and distinct activities that I deeply examine in Chapter 4 of this book from an economic, philosophical, and historical prospective.

Despite the existence of many forms of speculation that might give rise to several species of speculators such as short sellers, moneylenders, bankers, and non-bank financial intermediaries, this book is still using a singular unique definition of 'speculator' rather than 'speculators' to further highlight its deep symbolic meaning. To this end, the definition of the 'speculator' of financial markets is not dogmatic and static, but fluid, flexible, and ontologically connected to the same existence of human beings (see Chapter 4). For these reasons, I have associated the figure of the speculator to the symbol of Lucifer to further maximise figuratively the idea of rebellion and to provide readers with a better explanation of the speculator's innate instinct to pursue and seek profit in any investment decision. In fact, the book is providing a subjective view of financial markets through the eyes of the speculator rather than an objective illustration based on financial regulation and the views of the regulators.

Nonetheless, as I will further illustrate in Chapters 2, 3, 5, and 6, in more than 2,000 years of financial history, human beings have developed several forms of speculation and financial innovation. Since the beginning of modern financial crisis (see Chapter 5) as well as starting from contemporary economic crises such as the Global Financial Crisis of 2007 (see Chapter 6) and the March Madness of 2023 (see Chapter 7), the need for a definition of speculation and—in particular—for a definition of the speculator has become a compelling need both from a theoretical and practical point of view in order to reduce or at least try to mitigate the negative outcomes of speculation *tout court*. Nonetheless, this book claims that speculation is a trigger to progress, creativity, and financial innovation. In light of this, the figure of the 'speculator' of financial markets is providing a unique reading key to variegated forms of speculation that—as I will illustrate—might occur in different markets as well as having different subject matters (from artistic works to houses and even perishable items).

To face uncertainty in the form of Hell, one must be prepared to manage risks in rational ways, at least from an actuarial prospective, under the laws of probability. Alike the descendant of Lucifer to the depth of the pits of Hell, the 'speculator' made his entrance into the financial stage since the time of the Glorious Revolution in Britain and the birth of Wall Street. Speculators have often been defined as smart individuals, opportunists, and schemers, whose main job is to second-guess the opinions of other investors to take advantage of the market information and its fluctuations. Evil individuals or entities, as it can be seen. Sometimes academics or policymakers have also defined financial markets as a gambling casino or casino capitalism where speculators play the part of the gamblers (see Chapter 4). I believe this is not entirely correct, and it might be misleading, although the qualification of gambling in relation to crypto finance—for instance—might be appropriate especially if one takes into consideration in those days the 'crypto winter' that has been occurred since 2022 (see Chapters 5 and 7).

Specifically, in Chapters 2, 3, and 4, I illustrate such perception by which early investors of financial markets were defined as 'gamblers'. Speculation has often been perceived in terms of gambling, and to accumulate fortunes has never been a promising activity because many times this might have triggered a negative stigma from society at large. It is human nature to accuse others of causing one's misfortunes, and speculators are often accused due to the nature of their business. Indeed, this book is showing how speculators and gamblers had sometimes to pay the price of their risky activities in 'human flash', prejudice, and discrimination. Think of Knights Templar, the Jewish merchants in Venice, and the Medici Bank in times when usury and the charging of interest were condemned as a sin (see Chapter 2) or the unjustified critiques that the accuser with the pseudonym of 'Satan' posed to the House of Rothschild, and in particular to Nathan Mayer Rothschild and his possible speculation on the London Stock Exchange in the immediate aftermath of the Battle of Waterloo (see Chapter 5). In other words, the fact of being promoters and owners of a concentration of assets and riches has never been an easy task, and sometimes it has also signified an actual curse. For example, Margaretha Hönin had a bad reputation. Even though she lived in the late sixteenth century, we know that her neighbours, the people of Coburg in Thuringia, despised her for being a *parvenu*[3] and a money-grabbing miser. Hönin was also said to be a witch, who met regularly with a dragon. For her neighbours, her economic behaviour was clearly linked to the visits from the dragon. But today, the connection between her miserliness and her witchcraft is obscure. Why was the link so obvious to her contemporaries? What was the relationship between economic behaviour and accusations of witchcraft? When investigating witchcraft, one needs to differentiate between real and imaginary magic in the early modern period. If one wants to understand the connection between the imaginary magic of the witches and economic behaviour, one needs to deal with the connection between the economy and the real magic practices by 'common' people.

In pre-industrial Europe, magic was a part of everyday life, very much like religion. People did not just believe in the efficacy of magic, they actively tried to use magic themselves. Simple forms of divination and healing magic were common, as was magic related to agriculture. The peasant household used divination to find out if the times was right for certain agricultural activities. Charms were supposed to keep the livestock in good health. Urban artisans and merchants also used economic magic to increase their wealth. Of course, the shadow economy of gambling and lotteries was obsessed with magic well into the twentieth century. Of all the forms of magic, magical treasure-hunting[4] had the greatest economic significance. Separate from these real forms of magic, there was the imaginary magic of the witches. Nobody was ever (or could ever be) guilty of witchcraft in the full sense of the word, which was defined by the late Middle Ages as a crime that consisted of five elements: a pact with the devil; sexual intercourse with demons; the magical flight (on a broomstick or a similar device); the witches' dance (often referred to by the anti-Semitic term 'witches' *sabbath*'); and malevolent magic. Early modern Europe and Britain treated witchcraft as a capital crime.

At first glance, the relation between the economy and the imaginary magic of the witches seems to be entirely negative. Witches were often accused of attacking livestock. They magically made frost, storm, and hail, and thereby caused crop failure. Indeed, their weather magic was said to endanger the economy of entire regions. Still at least in the majority of the witch trials on the European continent, the witches did not profit from their magic. Whether magic especially looked like a strange form of auto-aggression because the hailstorms the witches supposedly conjured up damaged their own fields as well. As a rule, the pact with the devil as it appears in trial records was not a contract like that of Goethe's Faust, which was mostly about the wishes of the magician. Rather, it started simply that the witch submitted to the will of the demon. She did what a demon told her and became the instrument of the demon's abyssal hatred of all creation. Witchcraft was mostly about destruction for destruction's sake, not about the personal interests and wishes of the witches, let alone their economic advantage.

However, there were exceptions. When Martin Luther wrote a short survey of economic magic, he began the discussion with a reference to the 'brides of the dragon'. At first glance, this might seem like an allusion to the Biblical allegory of Satan as a dragon.[5] However, Luther had a very specific form of witchcraft in mind: the witches that were said to be in contact with a dragon. Even though the belief in this form of witchcraft was widespread in early modern Germany, eastern Central Europe, and the Baltics, it was, to the best of my knowledge, virtually unknown elsewhere. The dragon in question was not the giant monster of medieval epics but rather a household spirit. Everything the dragon brought its master had been stolen from somebody else. Dragon magic was about magical theft. Indeed, the dragon seems to be an embodiment of transfer magic, that is, any kind of magic that takes some good, including fertility or energy itself, out of one context and transfers it into another context. The milk witch who conveys the milk from her neighbours' cows to her own livestock, or the vampire that takes life energy itself away from others would be good examples of transfer magic. And the dragon delivered not only various kinds of produce. It brought money. The very idea of the dragon had adapted to the rising market economy. The household dragon was feared and probably coveted by people living in the vast area between Bavaria and Estonia. The house dragon was mentioned not only in trial records from witch hunts, but in very different sources too: some early modern Scandinavian and German scientists at least knew the rumours about household dragons and commented upon them. They provided an alternative explanation for the dragon sightings. For them, *draco volans*—the spirit that looked like a burning beam with a thick head in the night sky—was clearly a meteorite. Others insisted that the phenomenon mistaken for a dragon was really a cloud of burning gas that was somehow attracted to the sooty smoke emerging from the chimneys of houses where they burned too much green wood. This would make the dragon a pre-industrial smog phenomenon. Most people saw the dragon simply as a demon, just another shape the devil could take on.

Women and men said to own a dragon were all fairly affluent. What distinguished them in the eyes of their neighbours, though, was that they had a uniformly bad reputation for reckless profit seeking, usury, and even fraud. Their fellow villagers considered these people greedy and highly aggressive. The accused replied that they were the victims not just of slander, but of envy. So the rumours about dragons were really attacks on profit seeking; the speculator was on trial. The rural ambassadors of the rising market economy were denounced as immoral and greedy, reviled as dragon owners. The state did not protect them.

The most prominent example of a dragon witch is probably Margaretha Ramhold from Coburg whom Johann Matthäus Meyfart mentioned in his witchcraft treatise. The Lutheran theologian Meyfart published his criticism of the witch hunts *Christiliche Erinnergun* in 1635, seven years after Ramhold's death. Ramhold came from a family of modest artisans. However, by tapping two new sources of income—they sold beer and milk even though they owned only one cow—Ramholds became relatively affluent. In time, the family began lending money on interest. Rumours of witchcraft quickly followed, focusing on the mistress of the household, and the authorities were duly informed that there was a dragon in the Ramholds' house. Margareta Ramhold was executed in 1628.

The 'rich witches' were rumoured to be the most powerful and most aggressive disciples of Satan. And indeed, there is a relatively high number of affluent people among the defendants of early modern German witch trials. Rich witches were *parvenus*, who had profited from the agrarian crises in the sixteenth and seventeenth centuries. Dr. Diederich Flade was a sixteenth-century German official, who was executed in 1589. He was a notorious money lender. Flade seems to have specialised in small loans he gave to the peasants from the impoverished villages surrounding the relatively well-off town of Trier. He became fabulously rich (and influential) in only a couple of years. Then came his sudden downfall. At least twenty-eight called witches denounced Flade in their confessions: they presented him as a demonic figure presiding over the *Sabbath*. When the prince elector of Trier explained why, after months of hesitation, he finally decided to have official charges brought against Flade, he said that Flade was 'notoriously avaricious'. The prince elector accepted the idea that Flade's economic behaviour indicated that he was in league with Satan. Another rich witch was Martin Gerber, a merchant and burgomaster of the Swabian small town of Horb. After having made a fortune in trade, Gerber took up brewing. When he purchased large quantities of barley to brew beer, he not only displaced small-scale brewers but also triggered such a substantial price increase for barley that the price of bread became inflated too. The people of Horb felt that Gerber's behaviour was especially objectionable because, instead of supporting his poor fellow townspeople with his money, he sought further profit and thereby rendered them poorer still. From 1597 onwards, suspicions of witchcraft developed not against Gerber himself, but against his wife and his daughter, who had vociferously supported him. Gerber's daughter was arrested and tortured. Even though she never confessed and was eventually released from prison, she fought against accusations of witchcraft for the rest of her life.

As it can be seen, a concentration of assets necessarily gives rise to a concentration of risks that in turn generates anxiety in the case of human beings (see Chapter 4), and in some other instances related to financial regulation, it might cause a 'regulatory activism' on the side of financial regulators in order to save the world from systemic risk and in the name of financial stability (see Chapter 7). And sometimes when such 'excess' of regulatory initiative or regulatory activism is focused either on one specific industry or on a determined financial instrument, this can also give rise consequently to a proper witch-hunting phenomenon alike the witch trials that I have just pointed out.

In Chapter 2, I will also illustrate, *inter alia*, how the negative accounts in relation to the speculator have even more ancient origins than witch trials. Specifically, such origins can be traced at the time of Ancient Rome and the *Forum Romanum* more than two-thousands years ago when the financing of voyages by sea was the equivalent of high finance performed by hedge funds in our contemporary idea of capital markets. Nonetheless,

Moses Finley, an influential historian has argued that wealthy Romans rarely engaged in financial innovations. He portrayed wealthy Romans as complacent landowners who mostly bought land, made interest-free loans, and spent their money on luxuries. By contrast, this book will argue and defend the idea that Ancient Greeks and Romans were excellent capitalists. They set up banks that invested in real estate, and extended credit facilities to people and businesses, with branches spanning the known world. For example, Ancient Greeks founded around 680 BC the Epizephyrian Locris—also called Locri—on the Italian shore of the Ionian Sea, near modern Capo Zefiro. This was one of the most celebrated of the Greek colonies in this part of Italy. It was a colony, as its name implies, of the Locrians in Greece, but there is much discrepancy as to the tribe of that nation from which it derived its origin. Strabo affirms that it was founded by the Locri Ozolae, under a leader named Euanthes. Unfortunately, Polybius, who had informed himself particularly as to the history and institutions of the Locrians does not give any statement upon this point. But we learn from him that the origin of the colony was ascribed by the tradition current among the Locrians themselves, and sanctioned by the authority of Aristotle, to a body of fugitive slaves, who had carried off their mistresses, with whom they had previously carried on an illicit intercourse (Polybius 12, 5, 6, 10–12). Locri was the first Greek community to have a written code of laws, given by Zaleucus (660 BC), and specifically it was the place where it was located the sanctuary of Olympian Zeus. As for all major Greek sanctuaries, the Locrian sanctuary of Olympian Zeus owned farmland, artisan workshops, and collected products and resources from the territory, which fed, together with offerings, the rich treasure of the sanctuary, to which the *polis* drew with loans, as in a bank. Bronze tables found in Locri confirm the origin of the loan amounts and provide us with a direct evidence of the 'loan' functions that were performed by sanctuaries. Loans were drawn for agricultural purposes (to farm cereals and barley) or for financing naval construction and carpentry works that were in high demand in Locri. Other loans mentioned the price of iron, which was another precious resource of the Locrian territory. As it can be seen, the sanctuary had an important and key role in Ancient Greece, but also within Ancient Romans. The sanctuary was not only a place of offerings to Gods, but one of the earliest banks of our civilisation. For instance, the sanctuary of Artemision in Ephesus, in modern Turkey, was one of the seven wonders of the ancient world, as well as a banking institution honoured by conquerors as diverse as Croesus, Xerxes, Alexander, Caesar, and Augustus. The secret of its longevity was the proximity to great wealth, combined with a banking culture that blended trust with fear. This was a holy sanctuary and to miss the repayment of a loan was to act against the Gods. Furthermore, Ephesus was well-positioned at a crossroad of the Mediterranean. A wealthy clientele of kings, aristocrats, and governors valued the security that the sanctuary provided and deposited their wealth there, out of the reach of enemies. The Artemision began as a place to deposit wealth under the protection of the temple's deity. However, it evolved over time into a much more sophisticated regional and international financial institution, operating not only as a reserve and depositary bank, but also undertaking fiduciary and mortgage business. The accumulation of earnings and reserves were of such magnitude that it became known as the Bank of Asia. Three lessons from the Artemision's extraordinary longevity and the sanctuary of Locri can be inferred. Firstly, the sanctuary had a higher purpose. Secondly, its sophisticated banking functions were always carried out in the sacred service of a goddess with a strong ethical code. Similarly, banks today need a guiding purpose that looks beyond financial performance and provides a clear and sustainable framework (see Chapter 7).

Banking was just one of many other financial innovations. Specifically, Ancient Romans had proto-corporations known as *societias*, for which Romans pooled money to provide government services or collect taxes (in the case of shipping, these transient organisations usually dissolved by the end of the voyage, when all parties received payment). They developed some forms of life insurance. They even established a single grain market that extended across the Mediterranean, and Romans were also innovators of maritime insurance. Historians estimate that the population of Ancient Rome peaked at between five-hundred-thousand and one million people (Storey 1997). At that size, the city could not survive without regular shipments of grain by sea. Peter Temin, an economic historian, has estimated that it would have taken two-thousand to four-thousand ship voyages each year to feed Rome at its peak. It was a sophisticated process. Roman agricultural products would be processed by machines, packed in amphorae, shipped in freighters, and distributed by inland waterways and roads. Such a large trading system required a financial ecosystem to fund and insure each voyage. Every voyage was a feat of financial engineering, with multiple financial interests at play.

Hence, I firmly believe that financial innovations have always been rooted in human creativity to increase competition and face uncertainty in the name of progress and profit seeking activities. To this end, Chapters 2 and 3 are tracing an old-new portrait of the speculator and financial innovations pointing out an intimate conflict of views: on the one hand, some celebrate speculators as engines of progress and prosperity; on the other hand, others argue that they recklessly pursue profit at the expense of us all. Chapter 2 and Chapter 3 are telling the story of the speculator of financial markets as a human story, about a diverse group of merchants, bankers, and investors that have over time come to shape the landscape of our modern economy. Its central characters include both the brave, powerful, and ingenious and the conniving, fraudulent, and vicious. At times, these characters have been one and the same. While speculators have not always behaved admirably, their purpose is a noble one. From their beginning in the Roman Republic, speculators have been designed to promote the common good. By recapturing this spirit of civic virtue, I argue that speculators and financial innovations can help craft a society in which all of us—not just shareholders—benefit from the profits of enterprise.

Furthermore, this book would like to investigate—for the first time—the subjective nature of financial markets through the eyes of the speculator. In fact, common wisdom associates the birth of modern financial markets or international finance to the liberalisation policies, the Bretton Woods system and its collapse, the petrodollar system, and the diversification of financial risk by investment banks through cross-border transactions. This is only one way through which financial risk is privatised, and finance is globalised, but still does not explain how financial markets have been shaped in their modern form. By contrast, the iconic and symbolic figure of the speculator does provide an account for this remarkable formation, and at the same time it opens up the discussion on whether the law itself must eventually admit to its limits when it comes to regulating subjective and immaterial desires that are sometimes based on irrational investment decisions and pure sentiment (see Chapters 2, 3, 4, 5, and 6).

Even financial crisis cannot be simply conceived as the product of markets' inefficiencies or de-regulation: markets are firstly the product of financial operators, and among them speculators have played a vital role. As I said, speculation is not necessarily a negative feature of financial markets per se, but the trigger of financial innovations despite speculators being often vilified in the press and associated with financial scandals. In light of this, one very vivid image of the importance of speculation as a sociological phenomenon and about its economic function has been provided by Victor Niederhoffer, a leading hedge fund manager in the 1980s and 1990s, who defines speculation in his book 'The Education of a Speculator' as follows:

> I am a speculator, and my daily bread depends on reversing big moves. In economic terms, my function is to balance supply and demand. I sell when prices are high and buy when prices are low. When prices are too high and consumers want to exchange cash for goods, I take their cash and let them have their goods. I prevent shortages by pushing prices down so consumers do not have to pay up. Conversely, when prices are down and producers want cash badly for their goods, I give them cash and take their goods. In these bad times, I keep producers from going broke, and prevent waste and spoilage by bringing prices up. I am like a dynamic refrigerator, or a captain rationing food on an unexpectedly long voyage. (Niederhoffer 1998, pp. vii–viii)

This short extract can directly prove that speculators play a role in society, and possibly serve a 'common good'. Speculators provide the other side of the bet in the game of supply and demand. If the majority believes that the outcome will be heads, it is the speculator who takes the bet that it will be tails. They are essential in providing liquidity, and sometimes even efficiencies to financial markets by regulating prices through the art of balancing demand and supply and thus facilitate the capital formation process which involves the transfer of savings to investment through the movement of capital from savers to borrowers. This process occurs in financial market venues, and these markets provide businesses with the ability to expand and grow, creating economic growth for society. By assuming risk, the speculator provides liquidity and helps the markets to function more efficiently. In many respects, all investors and businessmen are speculators. By definition speculation—in general terms—is a business risk with the hopes of a gain or profit. The person who runs a business and assumes the risk to be in business is essentially a speculator because the outcome is uncertain. Chapter 4 will amply explain the economic, philosophical, and essential role of uncertainty, which underpins rather than undermines any money creation processes. The investor that provides capital to business or the government in exchange for a return above inflation is also a speculator. The businessman, the investor, and the professional trader are all speculators who facilitate economic expansion. The capital formation process could not occur without speculation, but it is the professional trader, through the assumption of risk, who provides the balance of supply and demand as well as liquidity and efficiency in the markets that move capital. Speculators provide liquidity in the secondary markets because so many of them are willing to buy and sell what the market has to offer. The more buyers and sellers there are for a commodity or security, the easier it is to convert the investment to cash. Liquidity encourages investment, thus promoting the capital formation process. According to Austrian economist Murray Rothbard, author of 'Man, Economy, and State' (2000), speculators help to achieve market efficiency and price stability.

When markets are moving upward and everyone is making money, no attention is drawn to the speculator. The speculator by nature in today's terms is bearish, always betting against the majority. This is unpopular in a society that at least tendentially would like to believe in optimism. Because speculators reap financial gains when betting against the majority, the average investor feels that speculators do not contribute to the welfare of the world but only to their own pockets. It has always been like this especially when speculators are not right all of the time, which can lead to shortages or gluts in supply causing panic such as the South Sea Bubble in London in 1720 and various other market crashes over the centuries (see Chapter 5). For example, Dickson in his study on the financial revolution in Britain identified the key change as the rise of Parliament's power vis-à-vis the King in Britain with the accession of William III and Mary to the throne during the Glorious Revolution of 1688. The instrument of Parliament's power then became the Bank of England, serving as a bureaucratic 'delegated monitor' of the government's servicing of the ever-accumulating government debt. This idea of the Bank of England as a 'delegated monitor' has been attacked by Stephen Quinn. Indeed, beyond the formal role of the Bank of England, the real financial innovation was the secondary market for government securities, construed as an organisational innovation that served as a commitment mechanism. While the stock market in government debt developed rapidly after 1688 in London, the government's success in maintaining the marketability of the South Sea Company's securities after the collapse of the South Sea Bubble in 1720 (see Chapter 5) was the defining moment for this innovation in government debt. The refinancing of government debt by the South Sea Company in 1720, its speculative bubble, and then its re-organisation in 1723 were the key developments for England's successful financing of the subsequent wars of the eighteenth and nineteenth centuries. As it can be seen, even if speculation can give rise to financial distress or credit bubbles sometimes, it still matters in terms of progress and financial innovation.

The same can be claimed on the other side of the Atlantic, in the United States. In 1855 Wall Street's so-called promoters—analysts, CEOs, and traders alike—sold stocks beyond all reasonable valuations, trading mostly in infrastructural development in a rapidly industrialising and optimistic US. Growth boomed in the decades following the War of 1812, but trouble was brewing. These traders had little idea of what a balance sheet looked like, or the effects their wildly swinging stock prices had on the companies involved. The latest bull market rallied around stock in the Erie Railroad, but one trader was sceptical and started short selling Erie: Jacob Little, who is portrayed by Edwin Lefevre in 'Reminiscences of a Stock Operator'. Little was the first short seller in the history of Wall Street, or at least the first of any prominence. The tactic has since made fortunes for generations of speculators that I further illustrate in Chapter 6 of this book. And while short sellers today tend to bet against overvalued companies based on sophisticated data, in Little's day it was on the basis of rumour. Information in financial markets is key. Not unlike famous short sellers Joseph Kennedy in the Great Depression or even John Paulson during the 2008 Global Financial Crisis, these were people inside the industry who heard that a lot of the stuff that was being sold out there was worthless. This was the same information that Little worked on. Like Little, Daniel Drew was also a notorious speculator during Wall Street's early years, around the time of the Civil War. He earned his notoriety through truly stunning feats of insider trading. Americans who have lived through the greatest series of Wall Street scandals since the crash of 1929, would find him a familiar figure. This is also where the future generations of speculators and short sellers got a bad reputation for years to come (see Chapter 6).

Speculation has not only been a synonym of human progress and financial innovations, but sometimes speculation has been interpreted and qualified as a skill or even as a game. For instance, in 1688, Joseph de la Vega also known as Joseph Penso de la Vega and by other variations of his name, was a prolific writer and a successful businessman in the seventeenth-century Amsterdam. He was from a Spanish Jewish family, and he provides a very lucid picture of stock trading and speculation in his book titled 'Confusion of Confusions'. The book describes a market that was sophisticated but also prone to excesses, and de la Vega offers advice to his readers on such topics as the unpredictability of market shifts, and the importance of patience in investment. The book is very interesting especially in relation to four basic rules that de la Vega considers as landmarks in investment practices:

> The first rule in speculation is: never advise anyone to buy or sell shares. Where guessing correctly is a form of witchcraft, counsel cannot be put on airs. The second rule: accept both your profits and regrets. It is best to seize what comes to hand when it comes, and not expect that your good fortune and the favourable circumstances will last. The third rule: profit in the share market is goblin treasure, at one moment, it is carbuncles, the net it is coal; one moment diamonds, and the next pebbles. Sometimes, they are the tears that Aurora leaves on the sweet morning's grass, at other times, they are just tears. The fourth rule: he who wishes to become rich from this game must have both money and patience.

He describes speculation as a game, without using the word gambling (see Chapter 4 for further remarks on gambling). By contrast, de la Vega is depicting securities markets as a venue where an informed investor with patience and money can profit from them. To this end, speculation is rational activity and not something necessarily negative if one can recognise that to invest money in securities can also entail a total loss. In the end, speculators pay out of their own pockets when making a mistake, as opposed to the politicians and lawmakers who are not held personally liable. Who is more likely to learn from a mistake? This is why speculators are necessary in the marketplace. Amsterdam's growth in the seventeenth century as a financial centre can be a self-evident example, also when it survived the tulip mania of the 1630s, in which contracts for the delivery of flower bulbs soared wildly and then. In the end, the first six-hundred years of securities trading were filled with booms and busts, crises and wars, as I illustrate in Chapter 5. However, securities markets have a profound resilience and tenancy, bouncing back from problems by rebuilding credibility and confidence. That lesson from distant history is noteworthy in the present troubled time.

Finally, one of the most remarkable lessons that I have learnt by writing this book, it is that in the history of finance, any object can become the centre of speculative attention from artworks (see Chapter 3) and even perishable items. For instance, between 2022 and 2023 food speculation has grown due to extreme spikes in the cost of energy and food. This is due to Russia's war on Ukraine (a major wheat exporter), the effect of extreme weather on harvests, and pandemic-era supply chain bottlenecks that are still being felt. The staple food crops, such as wheat, have increased by more than thirty percent since the beginning of 2021. While soaring food prices threaten food security globally, large food trading firms are profiting. These companies bet on the direction of food prices by storing or trading substantial amounts of goods—making big financial gains as a result. It is not physical goods that are traded. Financial markets see producers and consumers alongside banks, brokers, and investors, trading in commodities such as food. Sometimes called paper trading because it involves the use of future contracts rather than actual crops, this activity happens on commodity exchanges around the world. Traders can buy (being long) or sell (being short) on these exchanges, and most contracts end before the delivery date so a trader does not have own or receive the goods to benefit—or not—from price changes. Similarly, traders only have to place a deposit with an exchange, from which gains and losses are added or taken. They do not have to put down the full value of the crop they are buying or selling via the commodity exchange unless they take delivery of the physical item at the end of the contract. While this can of course promotes speculation, commodity exchanges also help producers and traders in physical food commodities to manage their risk. For instance, a farmer might take a short position (essentially betting that prices will fall) on the price of wheat via a contract that ends (or matures) close to the time of harvest. If prices fall while the crop grows, the contract gains in value and makes up for the farmer's losses if the actual crops are worth less. It is similar to an insurance policy that enables the farmer to plan ahead at the time of planting the crop. This is a further example of how an apparent speculation phenomenon can turn out to have positive outcomes on the side of farmers, although sometimes this is true only for privileged classes and castes of farmers who have access to the 'means of speculation' such as in the cultivation of onions in India (Matthan 2022).

Speculation can also include novel crops or livestock that, at least for a moment, seem transformational. For instance, in the middle of the nineteenth-century breeds of chicken unfamiliar in the West were examples of such novel product, kicking off a speculative episode called the 'Hen Fever'. There were three people most responsible for kicking off the speculative mania that was Hen Fever. They were Edward Belcher, Queen Victoria, and George Burnham.

Queen Victoria and Prince Albert were fascinated by chickens and many breeds of chicken now living in Britain can be traced back to Queen Victoria's love of exotic birds. Prince Albert and his brother had grown up with their own aviary and Albert had brought ornamental birds with him to England when he married Victoria in 1840. Two years later he remodelled the royal aviary at Home Park, east of Windsor Castle, to house chickens, doves, bustards, storks, and pheasants, including a sitting room for Victoria. The Queen's fascination with chickens grew over the following years and began to attract public attention. In 1842, her biological assemblage was blessed with a gift of seven exotic chickens from the Far East known as Cochin-China Fowl. Victoria's menagerie led to an explosion in breeding and exchanging birds, a so-called 'hen fever', which was mirrored across the Atlantic in the United States (Burnham 1855).

Victorian English cities were home to a menagerie of animals, both exotic and domestic. Elephants, tigers, and lions were regular captive animals in circuses, and cities like London still had free-roaming cattle, pigs, and sheep, while chickens were homed in backyards. London was home to the world's largest livestock trade, and the Victorian middle classes were enamoured with chickens following Victoria and Albert's remodelling of the Aviary at Windsor Park. Importing, breeding, and exchanging exotic chickens, valued for their beauty over their meat or eggs, became a past-time of the wealthy.

Queen Victoria was gifted fowl from across the world and the middle classes across the country were swept up in the craze for importing fowl from China and India. However, many of these breeds did not fare particularly well in the British climate. Specifically, Cochin-China, a large domestic chicken native to China had arrived in England during the hen fever thanks to Captain Edward Belcher, who left England for circumnavigation of the world in 1836. He was interrupted by the First Opium War in which Belcher participated, commanding two ships and seizing the port of Hong Kong. On his return to London, Belcher collected flora and fauna from the region for the British Museum. Belcher thus introduced Cochin-China chickens to England in 1842. He gifted five hens and two roosters to Queen Victoria. The Queen gifted offspring to relatives abroad and sent a pair of Cochin-China chickens to the Dublin Cattle Show in April 1846. This was in the midst of the Irish famine; the gesture was a hopeful one, anticipating that the larger birds could solve hunger. While these chickens did not solve the famine, interest in the animals grew. In Britain, Cochin-China chickens increasingly sold for high prices in the late 1840s and early 1850s. Around 1849, the birds were imported to the United States. There, speculative mania for Cochin-China and other breeds of fancy chickens took hold from 1850 to 1855. George Burnham, a Massachusetts newspaperman and poultry breeder, was particularly important to the bubble. He got into the trade in 1849, the same year the unfamiliar breed was introduced at the first ever 'Exhibition of Fancy Poultry' in Boston's Public Garden. In the United States up to then, raising chickens was largely done on a small scale for eggs, mostly in New England. There was no large-scale industry raising chicken for meat. Not only farmers but also miscellaneous professionals like doctors and lawyers paid a visit to these exhibitions; middle class sorts not usually involved in agriculture seem particularly involved in the speculation that was getting underway. By 1851, Burnham was raising over a thousand birds; his buyers were poultry fanciers elsewhere. The craze had spread from Britain to the North-eastern US and was now spreading from the Northeast to virtually every other part of the United States. Prices for Cochin-China rose to one-hundred dollars (USD) per pair, or over three-thousand dollars (USD) in today's money. In Britain, prices were similar. Unfortunately for Burnham and other fanciers with commercial interest in the birds, public fascination with exotic poultry waned in the middle of the decade and prices fell, particularly in 1855. It was no longer profitable to bring new birds from Asia and local breeders were stuck with unwanted chickens. The mania triggered by the avian interests of Edward Belcher, Queen Victoria, and George Burnham may have seemed, by 1860 to have been a terrible folly. However, the events did give rise to a new industry, and a new diet in a large part of the world. Hen Fever illustrates the unexpected but fruitful outcomes of seemingly disorderly events like speculative episodes. It is indeed with this spirit of new discoveries and beyond personal prejudice or bias that this book should be read. In other words, I invite the readers to reflect beyond human emotions and fragilities, and to be able to truly understand the immense gifts of financial innovations and the vital role that the speculator plays despite the series of boom and bust, rise and fall, and market catastrophes. In the end, it is the same story of humankind to be a story of fall and rise, also because sometimes it is only by falling down to the depths of the pits—in the dark—that oneself might find the light.

Notes

1. In the Old Testament the word 'pit' frequently denotes a place of burial or a prison (Ps 28:1, 30:1, Isaiah 24:22, 38:18; Jeremiah 37:16; Ezekiel 31:14; Zechariah 9:11). The context in Isaiah 14 likewise demonstrates this usage.
2. The word in Hebrew is *hêlêl*, coming from the verb 'to shine' and meaning 'bright one' or 'daystar'. Essentially, the word Lucifer is the Latin translation of this word that mean 'light-bearing' from *lux*, namely light and *fero*, namely to bear.
3. One that has recently or suddenly risen to an unaccustomed position of wealth or power and has not yet gained the prestige, dignity, or manner associated with it.
4. Treasure hunters drew on a vast magical arsenal. They had spell books of any description, divining rods available in any kind of wood, amulets to protect them against evil spirits, and lead tablets etched with magical signs. Most treasures were thought to be watched over by some kind of spirit, and treasure hunters tried hard to come into contact with these. To the utter horror of the ecclesiastical authorities, they invoked angels and saints. Treasure hunters talked to ghosts. Some of them even tried to conjure up demons. Treasure hunting came close to being a magical mass movement. There were thousands of treasure hunters in early modern Europe and almost all of them tried to use magic. However, only a tiny minority was ever accused of witchcraft. As a rule, treasure hunters simply had to pay a fine or do some penal labour for a couple of days. Common people simply did not see treasure magic as witchcraft, and most of the judges agreed. It is telling that the strictest law ever enacted against treasure hunting, Henry VIII's so-called Witchcraft Act of 1542, was quickly abolished and does not seem to have had much of an impact on the local level, at least as far as treasure magicians were concerned.
5. From the twelve book (XII) of Revelation or the Apocalypse of John in the New Testament of the Christian Bible: 1. And a great sign appeared in heaven: a woman clothed with the sun, with the moon under her feet, and on her head a crown of twelve stars. 2. She was pregnant and was crying out in birth pains and the agony of giving birth. 3. And another sign appeared in heaven: behold, a great red dragon, with seven heads and ten horns, and on his heads seven

diadems. 4. His tail swept down a third of the stars of heaven and cast them to the earth. And the dragon stood before the woman who was about to give birth, so that when she bore her child he might devour it. 5. She gave birth to a male child, one who is to rule all the nations with a rod of iron, but her child was caught up to God and to his throne. 6. And the woman fled into the wilderness, where she has a place prepared by God, in which she is to be nourished for 1,260 days.

Bibliography

Burnham G P, *The History of the Hen Fever* (James French and Company 1855)

Cole A H, 'Agricultural crazes. A neglected chapter in American Economic History' (1926) 16 (4) The American Economic Review 622–639

Davies O, *The Oxford Illustrated History of Witchcraft and Magic* (Oxford University Press 2017)

Dickson P G M, *The Financial Revolution in England: A Study in the Development of Public Credit 1688–1756* (Macmillan 1967)

Grinder B, Cooper D, 'How hen fever led to chicken of tomorrow (Part 1: Hen Fever)' (2015) Financial History 9–11

Matthan T, 'Speculative crops: gambling on the onion in rural India' (2022) 130 Geoforum 115–122

Niederhoffer V, *The Education of a Speculator* (Wiley 1998)

Rothbard M N, Man, *Economy, and State: A Treatise on Economic Principles* (Ludwig Von Mises Inst 2000)

Rude E, 'The forgotten history of hen fever' (5 August 2015) National Geographic

Storey G R, 'The population of ancient rome' (1997) 71 (274) Antiquity 966–978

CHAPTER 2

The Speculator and Financial Innovations: An Old Portrait

I wish somebody would give me some shred of evidence linking financial innovation with a benefit to the economy. Paul Volcker, former Chairman of the Federal Reserve.

2.1 Introduction

This chapter introduces the reader to the iconic and sometimes also symbolic figure of the speculator, who is a modern risk-taker as further explained in Chapter 4. Often investors as well as financial regulators and policymakers ignore the important role that the speculator has played in shaping the contemporary features of financial markets. This chapter provides an old portrait of the speculator that starts with Ancient Rome and the important role played by *publicani*, which were public contractors who erected or maintained public buildings, supplied armies overseas, or collected certain taxes, particularly those supplying fluctuating amounts of revenue to the state (eg tithes and customs). Under the early empire (after 27 BC) the publicans' business was curtailed; they were more tightly controlled, and the government forced them to accept unprofitable contracts. The system fell into disuse in the late empire. For centuries, Europe witnessed nothing that resembled Rome's *publicani*.

D. D'Alvia, *The Speculator of Financial Markets*, Palgrave Macmillan Studies in Banking and Financial Institutions,
https://doi.org/10.1007/978-3-031-47901-4_2

This changed around 1600 when new business forms emerged to challenge the might of Spain and Portugal: it was the Dutch East India Company (see Chapter 3).

This chapter will also examine the 'sin' of usury. In 1290, all Jews were to be expelled from England, and allowed to take only what they could carry; the rest of their property became the Crown's. Usury was cited as the official reason for the edict of expulsion; however, not all Jews were expelled; it was easy to avoid expulsion by converting to Christianity. Many of these forced converts still secretly practised their faith. Christians in Italy adopted the same approach and by the eighteenth century the papal prohibition on usury meant that it was a sin to charge interest on a loan. As set forth by Thomas Aquinas in the thirteenth century and even before by St. Augustine in 426 CE, money was invented to be an intermediary in exchange for goods. Hence, it would have been unjust enrichment to charge a fee to someone after giving them money. As I will show even Dante in his Divine Comedy places usurers in the inner ring of the seventh circle of hell. Interest on loans, and the contrasting views on the morality of that practice by Jews and Christians are central to the plot of Shakespeare's play 'The Merchant of Venice'. Those literature works read in conjunction with the main sources of the Church Fathers will serve as a direct evidence of historical events that place usury as a forbidden and sinful activity. In light of this, I will also examine the equivalent prohibition of charging interest under Jewish law to highlight how against common wisdom, Jews too were condemning the charging of interest and they were conscious of the immorality of taking advantage of those in need. Nonetheless, *Heter Iska* was and it is still in Israel an indirect form of charging interest within the Jewish community. Similar *escamotages* were possible in Christianity too. For instance, the bill of exchange is a direct evidence of the Medici family playing a vital role in the expansion of this commercial practice (*Arte de Cambio* or Moneychangers' Guild). Essentially, Medici were foreign exchange dealers. Furthermore, the *commenda* was another contract that could serve the purpose of disguising interest, but the most powerful religious orders of the Catholic Church did not need indirect ways of charging interest: the Knight Templars were powerful lenders and bankers. Temple Church across fleet street in London is not only a Medieval Church, but it is the first banking house in existence in Europe. Nonetheless, lending to monarchs will eventually cause the dismantlement of the religious order.

Finally, this chapter will look at the *Monte di Pietà* that is a charitable institution which lends money to those in need at modest interest rates, on the security of gold, silver, or other precious articles given in pawn. Pawned valuables would be sold by auction after one year if the owner failed to pay back the money including the interest. Those institutions were originally formed in Italian cities in the mid-fifteenth century, and they are considered as the predecessors of the modern credit union, but also of modern banking due to the symbolic activity of depositing valuables through the *Monte di Pietà* and lending at interest.

2.2 Humble Beginnings in Rome

Financial speculation from Latin *speculum*—mirror as opposed to investment is based on a subjective belief in order to become profitable. Yet *speculator* in Latin describes a sentry whose job was to look out for trouble, and the financial speculator in Rome was named *quaestor* which means seeker. Sometimes speculators were identified as *Graeci* or Greeks probably because of Hellenic origins (Chancellor 1999).

A possible historical origin of speculation can be found in the Republic period in ancient Rome.[1] Within this historical context when Rome is extending its influence across the Mediterranean Sea, the commercial transactions between *cives romani* (the Roman citizens) and *peregrini* (foreigners) are growing in importance. Indeed, even before the preclassical period the interactions between *cives romani* and other populations, namely the *Latini* in Italy gave rise to the fundamental question of how to guarantee a peaceful coexistence between Romans and foreigners. With international relationships an important role was played by the *fides* that had a broad meaning, ancient origins, and was known even before the period of the early Republic (D'Alvia 2018). The main legal instrument to regulate the relationships between the Romans and *peregrini* was the treaty. In light of this, in the first international treaty of the Roman legal history between Rome and Cartago there was a specific mention of *publica fide* (the public good faith). It is stated there that the commercial transactions entered into by Roman merchants and the Carthaginians should be concluded by virtue of a public transaction, involving a *grammateus*, essentially a public notary, in order for the transaction to be protected by the *publica fide*. Commercial transactions were rendered trustworthy by means of *publica fide*. Trust is the fundamental feature to grant protection to those relationships.

Then at the end of the first Punic war in 242 B.C., Rome imposed the creation of a new *praetor*, the so-called *praetor peregrinus*. His jurisdiction was extended either to the disputes arising between foreigners as well as between Romans and foreigners (respectively *ius dicere inter peregrinos* and *ius dicere inter cives Romanos et peregrinos*). This can provide evidence of the growing importance of disputes between Romans and foreigners. The *bona fides* between Romans and foreigners was a binding principle and the Roman magistrate, namely the *praetor peregrinus,* recognised this binding nature in order to give legal effect to the commercial transactions.

It is important to highlight how this phase of the history of Rome is characterised by a high international involvement, and a cosmopolitan feature that is informed by the flourishing of commerce and the opening of new commercial routes in the Mediterranean Sea. Later on such international vocation will inform the birth of international law under the name of *ius gentium* (the law of nations), a sort of codification of such universal principle of good faith that was at the centre of any relationship in ancient Rome. A principle of trust and confidence that is not so different from modern financial markets where any financial transaction shall be informed—at least in theory—by trustworthy contractual parties. Nonetheless, financial markets and the selling of financial instruments have always provided room for schemes or frauds (see Chapter 5).

From a political point of view, the Republic is also seen as a period of territorial expansion presided by a government that was designed to represent both wealthy and poor citizens of ancient Rome. It was one of the first modern democracies of the ancient world. This has been possible—*inter alia*—by the application of good faith to inform international relationships between Romans and foreign populations. Yet with commerce and new opportunities, speculation started to grow. The Roman financial system had by the time of the Republic already developed many of the characteristics of modern capitalism. We know that Romans loaned money to each other with great frequency (Kehoe 1997), and sometimes they engaged in speculation by lending money to underwrite ships. At least Plutarch on Cato the Elder highlights:

> He also used to lend money in what is surely the most disreputable form of speculation, that is the underwriting of ships

Insuring and financing voyages by sea were considered high finance. Each voyage was a risky, multi-million dollar venture we would say in our words, supported by a sophisticated financial apparatus. Before there were private equity and hedge funds, there was maritime insurance or as the British centuries later preferred to name it marine insurance under the Marine Insurance Act 1906. Indeed, it is widely held belief by insurance professionals that marine insurance—hull and cargo specifically—is the oldest form of insurance. Some date early forms of those to Phoenician traders.

The history of business has been driven by the need to concentrate capital. That also means a concentration of risk. For instance, a contemporary idea is very clear in crypto-trading platforms such as FTX that was acting as custodian of customers' funds, namely a concentration of funds, and therefore, a concentration of risk that ended up in a fatal collapse (see Chapters 5 and 7). Specifically, the history of insurance has been driven by the concurrent need to transfer and diffuse those concentrated risks or better to distribute insurable risks and distinguish them from real forms of hazards and uncertainties (see Chapter 4).

Maritime insurance was essential to the survival of Rome, which had the largest population in the Western world until the eighteenth-century London. Specifically, a peculiar financial product emerged as a way to insure voyages. Instead of paying a fee to insure cargo, merchants took out loans. These loans had very high interest rates and carried special terms: if the borrower could not pay back the loan, then the creditor was able to seize the ship; in addition, if the ship sank, then the borrower did not have to pay back the creditor. The practice dates back to the Ancient Babylon of 1800 BC. It is known as 'bottomry'. The owner of a ship borrows money on the 'bottom' of the ship, so that if the borrower does not pay back interest given a safe voyage, then he would forfeit the ship. To better illustrate how this policy worked, I put together a table on the three outcomes of a voyage:

Voyage is successful	*Voyage is safe, but the borrower cannot pay back the loan with interest*	*Voyage is not safe*
The borrower repays the loan with interest	The creditor repossesses the ship	The loan is void. Everyone loses, except maybe the pirates

In the book 'Chances are...: Adventures in Probability' (2007), Ellen and Michael Kaplan discuss how innovative bottomry was. It is an arrangement easy to describe but difficult to characterise. It is not a pure loan, because the lender accepts part of the risk; not a partnership, because the money to be repaid is specified; not pure insurance, because it does not specifically secure the risk to the merchant's goods. It is perhaps best considered as a futures contract: the insurer has bought an option on the venture's final value. Historians record that merchants and creditors thought of high interest rates explicitly as compensation for taking risk. Romans copied the practice of bottomry from the Greeks, and they also equated high interest rates with paying for risk. However, as I will show soon, Roman law capped interest rates, and it sanctioned higher interest rates explicitly for maritime voyages because the price is for the peril and it is, therefore, considered as a possible form of speculation.

This short historical account immediately shows how important it has always been for human beings to curtail or mitigate risk-taking activities, but the concept of risk distribution has a much higher degree of sophistication that surely cannot be found in the intentions of those primordial forms of insurance. Additionally, after the Roman Empire and at the beginning of Middle Ages, the charging of interest on money lent was subject to many doctrinal and theological disputes especially during the first years of Christianity due to usury concerns that were considered as serious forms of sin—as I will show later in this chapter. For instance, sea loans were considered usurious by Pope Gregory IX in 1236, so merchants by that time employed a variety of artful disguises to mimic their function. They devised contracts that came close to true insurance contracts, in that the transfer of risk was the primary object, such as a fictitious loan to the underwriter to be 'repaid' to the merchant only if the vessel or goods did not arrive safely. An alternative method was the sharing of risk via *commenda* contract (see Sect. 2.3), in which a sedentary merchant entered into partnership with a travelling merchant, providing funds in exchange for a share of the profit on the voyage, and thus exposing himself to both sea risk and commercial risk. Both sea loans and *commenda* contracts were imperfect substitutes for true insurance contracts, in which the primary object was to spread risk and distribute risk among many people (see Chapter 6 on the failure of Lehman Brothers in 2008, and the CDSs practices of AIG).

Bottomry loans made creditors emerge as a class of financial intermediaries. Not every lender operated on a large scale. Surviving records of maritime loans indicate that a ship in Rome was typically insured by more than one lender. Modern scholarship broadly agrees that the shipping industry depended on these bottomry loans. These loans were so common that Romans developed a standard boilerplate that parties could copy for each voyage. Shipwrecks aside, merchants and their financial backers were concerned as much if not more about everyday concerns. They worried about being paid in counterfeit currency; about captains pretending that their ship sank to avoid repaying bottomry loans; and about shippers stealing cargo or lying about prices. To manage this, lenders relied on a system of inspections, information sharing, and receipts designed to allow the insurers and financiers to detect and avoid fraud. This also shows the importance of information sharing in finance and more broadly in capital markets, something that this book will have time to explore in several chapters.

In ancient Rome, credit not only circulated due to bottomry loans. Credit circulated as did coins and both were recognised as forms of money in contemporary commentaries. This credit took the form of formal loans as well as 'shop credit'. Loans were made for several purposes either to finance consumption, for production, or trade. Interest was charged on capital and payments across Roman territories could be made by bankers' draft (Temin 2004). Professional lenders recorded their loans in a *calendarium*, a ledger of loans, which may have included details of the loans' terms. The *calendarium* was so called because interest would often be due on the *calends*, the first day, of each month. As in modern times, lending was regulated to prevent abuse that could cause unrest.

Many loans were made to finance trade and they were numerous enough for commentators to speak of a market rate of interest. A legal maximum rate of one percent per month was instituted. However, the historian Livy wrote of mechanisms by which lenders avoided this limit, such as lending to *peregrini* (foreigners), who were not subject to the limit. Indeed, the one percent limit was only applicable among Roman citizens, who could enjoy the rights and remedies of the *ius civile* (i.e. the applicable law of Roman citizens). By one means or another, lenders could charge interest as high as seventy-five percent per year, and at least a subset of borrowers would nonetheless resort to utilise their services. Lenders included professional bankers,[2] sometimes set up as partnerships. Bankers usually met with their clients in the *fora* or public buildings of their home city. Not all of these many bankers were wealthy though and not all lent their own money. Rather, the conventional model was for the 'banker' to broker transactions between lenders and borrowers. In fact, one of the most famous Pompeian 'banker', Lucius Caecilius Jucundus confirms such intuition. Lucius was born around the end of Augustus' reign (15 AD), and unfortunately was one of the victims of the volcano's eruption[3] in Pompeii in 79 AD. His house was situated on the east side of Via *del Vesuvio*. The most important discovery was found in a cabinet in one of the rooms at the back of the peristyle. Here, there were one-hundred-and-fifty-four waxed tablets comprising receipts for the sale of land, animals, and slaves and for the payment of colonial taxes. Financial activities that had been recorded were similar to the Tablets of Murcine that were discovered in the Inn of the *Sulpicii*. Lucius Caecilius Jucundus was not properly a banker in the modern meaning of the word—he was mainly an auctioneer profiting on both sides of the transaction, charging the seller a commission and then lending money to the buyer at a healthy rate of interest. In other words, a speculator.

So prolific were the lending activities of the rich that the wealth of the most prosperous men in Rome was usually described in terms of either land or loan portfolios, rather than in terms of cash. To sustain such financial evolution a first attempt was made to create what today we define as the corporation or the company. A remarkable financial innovation whose modern expression will be made possible only in 1602 with the first chartered company sponsored by the Dutch Government and known as the Dutch East India Company or *Vereenigde Oostindische Compagnie* (the VOC), and that I will further illustrate in Chapter 3.

The Romans recognised the notion of a corporation or at least something similar to it. It is not by chance that the word corporation derives from the Latin word *corpus* for body, representing the body of people authorised to act as an individual. Specifically, the Roman Republic relied on private contractors to perform a variety of tasks. Contracts to build aqueducts, manufacture arms, construct temples, collect taxes—even feed the geese on the capital—were granted to firms called *publicani*. These originated as loose associations among contractors who would pool their resources to bid on contracts. Over time, the *publicani* evolved into permanent companies with numerous investors, only a handful of whom served as managers. Larger *publicani* employed thousands of workers and slaves spread across Rome's provinces. Fragmented evidence indicates that some of these received corporate status (*habere corpus*) which included a grant of limited liability for investors. Those legal bodies were independent and the members' ownership was divided into *partes*, or shares. There were two main types of shares: smaller shares called *particulae*, and larger shareholdings known as *socii* or shareholders.

Particulae shares were unregistered, this could resemble the modern over-the-counter market (Chancellor, 1999). Although there is no record of a buying-and-selling activity of those *partes*, shares, or whether the value of those shares was fluctuating, a fragment of Cicero might induce us to think about—once again—stock market behaviours when Roman consul Vatinius was accused of corruption he was asked: 'Did you extort shares, which were at their dearest at the time ... ?' Cicero referred to *partes carissimas* (most expensive shares) and claimed that buying shares in public companies was seen as a gamble which honest men avoided. Shares in the *publicani* attracted politicians and capitalists. Indeed, the *publicani* were well connected and, at times, extremely influential. Collusion with government officials was a lucrative way of business. If there was public indignation, it was balanced by investment enthusiasm. Polybius reported:

> There is scarcely a soul, one might say, who does not have some interest in these contracts and the profits which are derived from them. (Polybius 1979, p. 316)

As early as record exit, the *publicani* were tainted by scandal. During the Second Punic War, the Republic agreed to insure the ship-borne cargoes of *publicani* willing to supply the legions on credit. Later it came to light that old, rotting ships had been loaded with worthless goods and then scuttled at sea. It was evidently a fraudulent insurance claim. The perpetrators organised a mob to disrupt a public enquiry. Eventually, only the intervention by the Senate brought them to justice. Tax collecting also was one of the *publicani*'s more controversial enterprise. Rome assessed a number of taxes, including taxes on pastures, grain, and even the freeing of slaves. The *publicani* collected a number of these from Rome's provinces. Essentially, they would buy future tax revenue from the State and then pocket whatever they could collect. Rome's local governors oversaw the tax collections in each province. Some were corrupt, and the process became one of the governor and *publicani* together seizing whatever they could. Even when governors were honest, provincials understood they would be paying more than the percentages prescribed by law. Few governors would willingly antagonise their own financiers—*publicani* could work political mischief back in Rome. This is directly reported by the Roman historian Livy who commented:

> Where there was *publicanus*, there was no effective public law and no freedom for the subjects. (Livy 1912, XIV, 18, 4)

If *publicani* might be seen as possible speculators at least for their innate vocation of taking risks and making profits, the location where speculators mostly enjoyed spending their time was the *Forum Romanum*. In the play *Curculio* or The Forgery, the Latin playwright Plautus offers perhaps one of the most comprehensive and insightful descriptions of the *Forum Romanum* ever written. In his summary, Plautus gives the reader the sense that one could find just about every sort of person in the *Forum*—from criminals and hustlers to politicians and prostitutes, moneylenders, and wealthy men. The *Forum Romanum* literally translated as the 'Roman Market' or *Forum Magnum* (the Big Market), was the key political, ritual, and civic centre and much more: it probably represented one of the first stages where speculators could be identified in two main groups according to Plautus. On the one hand, the 'mere puffers', and on the second hand a very peculiar group of people described as follows:

> (…) impudent, talkative, and malevolent fellows, who boldly, without reason, utter calumnies about another, and who, themselves, have sufficient that might with truth be said against them. There, at the old shops, are these who lend and those who borrow at interest. Behind the Temple of Castor there are those to whom unguardedly you may be lending to your cost (…). (Plautus 1912, Act IV, scene I)

The *Forum* was located in a valley separating Capitoline and Palatine Hills where it developed from the earliest times and remained in use after the city's eventual decline. During the Iron Age populations had used the marshy valley separating the Palatine and Capitoline hills as a necropolis, but the burgeoning settlement of archaic Rome had need of communal space and the valley was repurposed from a necropolis to a usable space. This required several transformations, both of human activity and the natural environment. Burial activity had to be transferred elsewhere; for this reason the main necropolis site shifted to the far side of the Esquiline Hill. Beyond the death there was the life of the *Forum*. The place where the originals of the bulls and bears of later stock markets can be identified (Chancellor, 1999), although such interpretation is far too modern to be applicable to Romans at that time.

As it can be seen, this book is starting to illustrate and will continue to educate the reader about one common understanding that seems undeniable and unfortunately so truthful: the disgrace of the speculator has never been unseen in human history. Yet at the same time the possible regulation activities and supervision to counteract speculative activities have not always been successful (see also Chapters 5 and 7). For instance, a clear example of such remark can be found during the age of Emperor Diocletian, who—in 300 A.D.—tried to punish speculators for withholding goods from the public to receive higher prices as demand grew. Diocletian issued a law that stated anyone who tried to sell goods at a higher price than he set himself would be sentenced to death. Suppliers refused to bring their goods to a market that did not supply fair prices, and the result was famine and deaths of many. The law was eventually repealed (Neiderhoffer 1997). Nonetheless, under emperors, the political landscape in Rome shifted, and the *publicani* were suppressed, but the speculation in property, commodities, and currencies continued. New forms of corporations emerged. Charitable corporations were established to serve Rome's growing indigent population. The emerging Catholic Church employed the corporate form as a vehicle for joint ownership of real estate and other proprieties. Indeed, during the Middle Ages, cities, guilds, monasteries, and universities were all chartered as corporations, typically by sovereigns, local nobility, or religious authorities. All served largely public or religious functions. For centuries, Europe witnessed nothing that resembled Rome's *publicani*. This changed around 1600 when new business forms emerged to challenge the might of Spain and Portugal: it was the Dutch East India Company (see Chapter 3).

2.3 The City of God, and the Temple of Jerusalem

In Medieval Europe, the Christian culture was against financial speculation, although some exceptions apply, especially if we speak of holy warriors. One of the Fathers of the Church and perhaps the most significant Christian thinker after St. Paul., St. Augustine (also called Saint Augustine of Hippo) was openly against *appetitus divitarum infinitus*—the unlimited lust for gain—as one of the three principal sins alongside sex and power. In the City of God, there is no place for the speculator.

St. Augustine wrote the City of God, the first *magnum opus* of Christian philosophy that covers among other topics, civil and natural theology, the history of creation, eschatology, and martyrdom. Completed by the year 426 CE, the City of God took Augustine at least a decade to write. The book is in a broad meaning a response to the trauma of the Visigoth attack on Rome in 410 CE. Up to that point the Roman Empire had dominated Mediterranean civilisation—as we have seen in the previous section—for nearly a thousand years.

When Alaric sacked and plundered Rome, its citizens were shocked and devastated. The city's walls had not been breached in eight-hundred years. The attack was symbolic of a crumbling empire. Many Romans interpreted the sack as punishment for abandoning the traditional gods and goddesses in favour of the new state religion, Christianity. Within this historical background St. Augustine wrote the City of God in part to rebut this notion. He wanted to show that the Christian God is a source of solace and strength. St. Augustine highlights how Christianity actually did offer protection, since many refugees from the attack used Christian basilicas as safe havens from the invaders. He argues that Rome is a city of men. It is earthly and like other cities destined to eventually pass away. By contrast, the City of God is stable, eternal, and the source of ultimate consolation. It is the only city that will eventually come to triumph. For this reason, St. Augustin censured the pagans, who attributed the calamities of the world, and especially the sack of Rome by the Goths, to the Christian religion, and its prohibition of the worship of the gods.

Even more direct will be another Father of the Church centuries later, St. Thomas Aquinas—an Italian Dominican friar and priest—that in his *Summa Theologica* or Summary of Theology often referred simply as the *Summa* considered money as a non-durable good, which by definition should be destroyed when exchanged or consumed, and thus should not be used to generate even more money. The *Summa* was written between

1266 and 1273, and it was conceived by St. Aquinas as an instructional guide for teachers and novices and a compendium of all the approved teachings of the Catholic Church. It synthesises an astonishing range of scholarship, covering hundreds of topics and containing more than a million and half words—and was still unfinished at the time of St. Aquina's death.

In the *Summa*, money is used to acquire goods or obtain services, then it is not fair to ask for more money than is worth the service or good itself. St. Aquinas makes a distinction between the true price for a good or service, and the illegitimate price for the use of such good or service. The price of the use of money is what Aquinas calls usury because when one charges for the use of a good, one charges for more than the fair price of the good. It necessarily follows that according to Aquinas it is evil to sell goods at prices which are higher than their just price; yet he still allows merchants to make profits from their merchandise—which means that they have increased the original price of the goods they are selling. Essentially it seems that Aquinas thinks that profit is not usury. This thinking is influenced by Aristotle. For these reasons, St. Aquinas sees the just or fair price of a good as the price which corresponds to the true value of said object. But if the object provides the consumer with a lot of utility, he could pay a price higher than the fair price; similarly, if the seller does not want to sell the object, then the buyer could pay more than the fair price in case of emergency. In other words, St. Aquinas is putting conditions under which one may charge at a different price than the fair price. For example, more can be charged because of transport costs or modifications to the object of selling. But the most important and valid reason to set a higher price is when the seller sells and makes profit to support his own family or to help the poor. For these reasons, profit is allowed, if profit is not an end in itself but a compensation for the work of the merchant.

On the other hand, usury is condemned in an absolute way. People who take loans are people who really need the money, such as poor people who have to take care of themselves and their families. To do so they ask a lender, but this lender does not need the money. Lenders have more resources than necessary to cover their needs and this allows them to loan money. In these circumstances, lending with interest implies two sins for lenders: first, they take advantage of the needy, and second, they want more than they need (sins of vanity and greed). The practice of usury is wrong and detrimental to society. St. Aquinas, therefore, outlawed usury in order to defend the poor from exploitation of unscrupulous lenders. However, even with the strong condemnation of usury, St. Aquinas and the Catholic Church did not manage to stop usury and the charging of interest (Persky 2007) becoming the fundamental pillar of today's capitalist world. And the speculation on interest is something evidenced by the crusaders, the Medici family, but also and especially in contemporary terms by the vivid image of the Global Financial Crisis of 2007, and the following sub-prime mortgage crisis of Wall Street (see Chapter 6) or the traditional mismanagement of interest rate risk in the case of Silicon Valley Bank (see Chapter 7). Such sentiment of greediness and profit making is in part a natural feature of human beings, and something that is deeply rooted in our genetic code of risk and uncertainty, and anxiety, as I further explain in Chapter 4.

The Church Fathers accomplished much more than solely condemning speculation or the bearing of interest, they established the intellectual and doctrinal foundations of Christianity to stand firm forever, and in so doing they could not surely imagine that some of their teachings would have been considered the pillars of a future Order of holy warriors, and inspired their legitimacy as a congregation set up as the Knights of the Temple of Solomon in Jerusalem[4] or also known by the public as the Knights Templar featured prominently in Dan Brown's bestseller 'The *Da Vinci* Code'.

Templars were originally knights deputed to protect pilgrims travelling to Jerusalem, but they soon became the most powerful military order of the Crusades (Jones 2017). Jerusalem had been captured by the first crusade in 1099 and pilgrims began to stream in, travelling thousands of miles across Europe. Like the monks, with pilgrims and would-be crusaders desperate for cash to fund their expeditions, the Templars began offering loans. They also offered to store funds, valuables, and documents, some of which could be used as collateral against loans. In the case of a customer's death, the Templars would be the executors of their estate. Templars would issue receipts outlining what customers had deposited allowing them to withdraw funds from any other branch, so long as there was enough money on hand to cover their needs. With headquarters at either end of the Mediterranean, and enormous complexes in Paris and London, this gave rise to the world's first international banking system.

On London's busy Fleet Street, opposite to Chancery Lane, is a stone arch through which anyone may step, and travel back in time. A quiet courtyard houses a strange, circular chapel and a statue of two knights sharing a single horse. The chapel is Temple Church, consecrated in 1185 as the London home of the Knights Templar. King John stored his crown jewels in the London Temple, such as its reputation. Indeed, Temple Church is not only an important architectural, historical, and religious site. It is London's first bank.

As I said, pilgrims needed to somehow fund months of food and transport and accommodation, yet avoid carrying huge sums of cash around, because that would have made them a target for robbers. A pilgrim could leave his cash at Temple Church in London, and withdraw it in Jerusalem. Instead of carrying money, he would carry a letter of credit. It might be possible to claim that the Knights Templar were the equivalent of the 'Western Union' of the crusades, and they gave rise to the financial innovation of the letter of credit, namely a promise to pay the bearer of the letter upon request (Jones 2017). The Knights Templar did much more than transferring money across long distances. They provided a range of recognisably modern financial services. Indeed, Crusades gave the Templars a stage to project their might, but the true source of power lay within a revolutionary new financial system: the Templar bank. Much of their fortunes also derive from an active role in society that was played by their Grand Masters. For instance, as soon as Templars were set up in 1190–1120, Hughes de Payens the first Grand Master did not hang around waiting to get killed in Jerusalem. He went back to Europe and toured the royal courts attracting high-level investment. He persuaded Henry I, son of William the Conqueror, to raise treasure from his barons which was then funnelled back to fund this new organisation he had set up. It was like raising venture capital.

Templars were committed to a life of frugality and abstinence; crusading was a costly enterprise. The Templar network of preceptories across Europe helped alleviate some of these financial burdens. Many new recruits, such as Hugh of Bourbouton, handed over all their worldly possessions upon entering the order—including land, livestock, property, and even tenants. These preceptories generated more income from commerce, building links in local communities and securing donations, big and small, from mortals seeking to save their souls. People left them in their wills a donkey or a little plot of land, tiny donations that when you added them up were massive and funded military operations. Also aristocrats made their donations such as Alfonso I, the King of Aragon, left them a third of his kingdom in his will, and Queens and Kings gave them huge landed estates.

However, it was Pope Innocent II's 1139 bull, or decree, *Omne datum optimum*, that kick-started the brothers' remarkable rise from donated rags to vast riches. The decree established various privileges, it exempted Templars from paying a tenth of their produce in tithes, but also allowed them to collect tithes of their own. Their preceptories earned similar concessions from local lords across Europe, allowing them to levy tolls and customs on fairs and markets. Their reputation spread across Europe. With the Crusades draining capital from across Europe, before long, the Templars emerged as the continent's most prolific money lenders. Louis VII himself borrowed copious amounts to finance his two-year crusade, demanding so much that he almost bankrupted the Order. They soon revised their lending policies, requiring debtors to pledge security against their loans, which could take many forms. The Templars kept extensive records of all financial transactions, with the most prolific customers, such as the Queen Mother Blanche of Castille receiving detailed accounts three times a year, at Candlemas, Ascension, and All Saints. Many royals and nobles used to borrow from the Templars. When King John's excommunication was lifted in 1213, he borrowed nine marks of gold from the Templars for an offering of absolution.

However, the Templar financial network stretched far beyond just royalty. During the papal schism, Pope Alexander III himself relied heavily on Templar loans and administrative services to stay afloat. When Pope Innocent III rolled out proportional taxes in 1198, requiring the clergy to help fund the Crusades, he tasked the Templars with collecting funds and transporting them safely to the Holy Land. Because charging interest was against canon law, the Templars instead billed for administrative fees and expenses, or manipulated the currency exchange. Eventually, they dropped the act, flat out charging England's Edward I for 'administration, expenses, and interest'. It seems that not even the Third Lateran Council's decree of 1179 applied to them when it excommunicated usurers and refused the unrepentant burial in consecrated ground (Munro 2003).

Unfortunately for the Templars, by the fourteenth century, they had grown too wealthy for their own good. The fall of Acre in 1291 was one of the defining battles of the medieval world. As the Mamluks smashed down the city's walls, Christendom's one-hundred-and-ninety-five-year experiment with crusading crashed into the sea. The Templars defended Acre as long as they could. But the result was never in question. The city fell, the Holy Land would not come under Christian rule again until Britain and her imperial allies took it in 1917. As late as 1853, the Royal

Navy commemorated it with a ship—the HMS St. Jean d'Acre. They were barely any survivors, but a man named Jacques de Molay was almost certainly one. Before long, the Templars elected him their Grand Master.

Eager to relieve himself of his crushing debt to the Order, and to get his hands on their vast riches, Philip IV would make the ultimate run on the Templar banking system—coercing the Pope into ordering the seizure of all Templar assets. In fact, Philip IV, who was fighting against England, owed money to the Templars, and they refused to forgive his debts. So on the site of what is now the Temple stop on the Paris Metro, Philip launched a raid on the Paris Temple—the first of a series of attacks across Europe.

On the fourteenth of September 1307, Philip IV of France began his campaign to quash the Templars when he sent sealed orders to his offices across the kingdom, with instructions that they not be opened until the night of October twelve. His plan was to arrest every Templar in France. On Friday the thirteenth of October 1307—King Philip's men kicked in the doors of the Templars' commanderies all over France, and arrested all but a handful who evaded capture. It is still popularly believed that these arrests are why Friday the thirteenth is unlucky. Philip charged the Templars with offences designated to scandalise and horrify the public: denying Christ, spitting three times on the crucifix, idol worship, blasphemy, and obscenity. It is believed that Philip had invented most of the charges as he needed to get people heated up in order to drown out the papacy's inevitable outrage at such a blatant and unprovoked attack on the Church. Indeed, Templars were seen in Europe as heroic fighters who distinguished themselves in the Crusades. Pope Boniface VIII had praised them as 'fearless warriors of Christ' just a decade before Philip's move against them. But Boniface was no longer in the picture, having died in 1303, barely a month after Philip's agents had terrorised him, and held him hostage. The new pope was Clement V, a former French bishop far more acquiescent to Philip. However, Templars would not be the first group Philip had targeted. In 1292 he had arrested the Lombards, wealthy Italian merchants, seized their property, and forced them to buy French nationality from him if they wished to stay in France. In 1306, he ordered the arrest of some one-hundred-thousand French Jews. Needing yet another source of plunder, Philip turned his attention to the Templars, some five-thousands of whom lived in France.

When Pope Clement V heard of the arrests, he had no room for manoeuvre. So rather than confront Philip (as Gregory VII or Boniface

VIII would have), he opted to salve his wounded pride by trying to take charge of the matter. He issued the bull or decree *Pastoralis praeeminentiae* ordering Europe's kings to arrest all Templars in the name of the Pope. None of this was lost to the Italian poet Dante in his *Divina Commedia*, who railed against Clement's toadying to Philip, his lust for power, nepotism, and simony. He accused Clement of being a lawless shepherd, of turning his office into a cloaca del *sangue e de la puzza* (sewer of blood and stink), and he saved a place for him in *Malebolge*, the eight circle of Hell. Dante also accused King Philip of undermining Christendom. A Tuscan chronicler even declared that the abolition of the Templars was one of the leading causes of the Black Death.

Templars were tortured and forced to confess any sin the Inquisition could imagine. The order was disbanded by the Pope. The London Temple was rented out to lawyers and all Templars' lands and riches were confiscated and assigned to Queens and Kings and nobles. And the last grandmaster of the Templars, Jacques de Molay, was brought to the centre of Paris and publicly burned to death. The Templars were eventually disbanded in March 1312.

Centuries later, an Italian palaeographer would discover one reason de Molay may have been surprised by the cardinals' ruling. Digging through the Vatican Secret Archives in 2001, Dr. Barbara Frale shielded light on the trail of that time. Despite the majority of registries, reports, and archives disappeared, the Vatican keeps an authentic copy of the Chinon Parchment by which Frale is claiming that in 1308, Pope Clement V absolved the last Grand Master Jacques de Molay and the rest of the leadership of the Knights Templar from charges brought against them by the Medieval Inquisition. The existence of this document has long been assumed. In the bull or decree *Faciens misericordiam*, promulgated in August 1308, Clement V explained that the Templar leaders were supposed to be brought to *Poitiers* in order to be questioned by the Pope himself, but since some of them were so unwell at that time, three cardinals were sent out to perform the necessary inquiries at *Chinon*. The commissioned envoys were instructed to create an official record of their investigations and, according to the bull, upon returning they presented the Pope with the confessions and testimonies.

If those historical sources confirm a new truth, it remains still a mystery on the reasons that brought so many templars and commanders to death by burning at stake. When sources are scarce, then legend grows, and so the name and history of those holy warriors started to become immortal.

There is no doubt that the Templars were bankers and moneylenders, they were speculating with interest and with donations, and they were accumulating riches in this World possibly in open contrast with the teachings of St. Augustin and St. Aquinas. Indeed, Templars were so wealthy that it was hard to truly accept that they could only believe in the existence of a City of God. The vivid image of their last Grand Master to burn at stake is also a first warning that money and credit is the source of all evil, and when borrowers cannot repay their debt, then creditors might suffer sometime an imminent fate or by contrast debtors might be 'persuaded' to pay such as in the gunboat episodes in sovereign debt concerning Venezuela in 1902. For two centuries, the Templars waged the bloody wars for Christian Jerusalem that Europe's people demanded. But when the defeated crusaders came home, early 1300s, Europe was preparing for Dante, Giotto, Marco Polo, Petrarch, Boccaccio, Chaucer, and a world of new discoveries. There was no room for knights bent on recapturing an oriental desert 3,000 miles away.

2.4 A Pound of Flesh at the Root of International Finance

Franciscans and Dominicans began a campaign against usury in the early thirteenth century. They persuaded secular rulers to ban usury during the later Middle Ages. Hence, apart from the Templars, the payment of interest on loan agreements was not openly admitted, and the Middle Ages had been familiar with Aristotle's ideas, as I have previously highlighted. An interesting conception related to such Scholastic argument also stated that being usury calculated on the passing of time and the duration of the loan, it constituted the sinful theft of 'Time', which shall belong to God alone. Also Dante is placing usurers 'the last class of sinners that are punished in the burning sands', in the lower depths, the Seventh Circle of Hell of his Divine Comedy.

However, usury did not apply to licit forms of capital investment (Munro 2003). The difference between licit rents and profits and sinful usury was based upon ownership. If a person was owning or investing in land, or similar forms of real property, then the lease of such property to others entitled the owner or landlord to receive a rental income, even though the return was predetermined. Similarly, anyone who invested money in a standard partnership contract or a *commenda* agreement for a single venture was still entitled to receive a share of profits, or dividends, proportionally to the amount of equity capital that was invested in such effort as well as to retain ownership. Indeed, even St. Aquinas argued that non-fungible is a commodity with individual characteristics that is not consumed by its use. For this reason, a Christian could earn a licit rental income from the use of such property while renting ownership and then regaining possession, but usury was absolutely prohibited. The same ban applied to non-Christians, a prohibition of usury is found both in the Pentateuch and as *riba* in the *Quran*—the Holy Book of Muslims. Jewish too were not supposed to lend at interest, but in the Old Testament book of Deuteronomy is said:

> Unto a stranger thou mayest lend upon usury; but unto thy brother thou shalt not upon usury.

Hence, Jews could lend at interest to a Christian but not to another Jew. At first sight, it seems that charging interest to a Gentile (or non-Jew) or paying interest to a Gentile (or non-Jew) was permitted. However, a closer look at Jewish law can give rise to doubts. It is very likely that Jews were not taking advantage of Christians by charging interests as some would like to claim. In fact, both the *Torah* (Hebrew Bible) and *Talmud* encourage lending money without interest. The *Halakha*[5] (from Hebrew meaning 'the way') that prescribes interest-free loans applies to loans made to other Jews, however not exclusively. Conversely, it necessarily follows that under *Halakhah*, an interest rate loan could be constructed also within the Jewish community. Specifically, the obligation to support the poor, and the prohibition to charge interest on a loan given to them are expressly listed in the *Torah* in three different places. Those verses prohibit against *ribbis* (which roughly means 'increase' or interest) three times.

In Exodus, it states:

> When you lend money to my people, to the poor person [who is] with you, you shall not behave toward him as a lender; you shall not impose interest upon him. (Exodus 22:24)

In Leviticus, it states:

> You shall not take from him interest or increase, and you shall fear your God, and let your brother live with you. You shall not give him your money with interest, nor shall you give your food with increase. (Leviticus 25:36–37)

Further on in Deuteronomy, the *Torah* says:

> You shall not give interest to your brother, [whether it be] interest on money, interest on food or interest on any [other] item for which interest is [normally] taken. You may [however] give interest to a gentile, but to your brother, you shall not give interest, in order that the Lord, your God, shall bless you in every one of your endeavours on the land to which you are coming to possess. (Deuteronomy 23:20–21)

Probably it is from this latter passage of the Deuteronomy that the common conception of Jews taking advantage of Christians is derived from the possibility of charging interest is directly connected to the qualification of the borrower as Gentile (or non-Jew) as opposed to Brother (namely, a Jew). Yet this is a limited and superficial interpretation, as I will further explain below when I will examine the *Heter Iska* that is an indirect form of charging interest within the Jewish community too.

The word *ribbis* means—as I have said—to add on or increase, as in, adding on interest when a loan is repaid. There are no actual reasons given in the *Torah* for the prohibition of *ribbis* besides for the reward of having one's land blessed if they adhere to the law. A complete prohibition on taking interest, regardless of the borrower's socioeconomic status, is unique to the law of the *Torah*. In various laws in the Ancient East, one can find restrictions on interest in relation to widows or orphans. There were also restrictions on interest rates in Eastern law, as in modern legal methods, which distinguish between interest at the permitted rate (interest) and unusual interest (usury). Nonetheless, the prohibition of *ribbis* is known as a *chok* or law for which has no natural reason.[6] Some rabbis have attempted an explanation for *ribbis* as being the ultimate commandment of 'loving your neighbour as yourself' (Leviticus 19:18). Others have explained that thousands of years ago, the main source of livelihood was farming. Farmers would borrow money to live from and pay it back when the crops were harvested. Charging your neighbour interest would be seen as taking advantage of them.

However, in traditional Jewish law, there are two categories of laws that people must adhere to, Biblical law and Rabbinic law. Biblical laws are laws that are clearly stated in the verses of the *Torah*. The punishment for transgression of those laws is traditionally more severe. Rabbinic laws are laws that were enacted by the rabbis over the years to safeguard people from transgressing *Torah* prohibitions.

The most common occurrence of Biblical *ribbis* is the prohibition of *ribbis ketzutzah* (pre-arranged *ribbis*) where the arrangements for payment were made at the time the loan was extended. This applies regardless of when the payments are made. Even if the principal was already paid and the interest is due only a long time after it is still considered *ribbis*. If the borrower was holding onto the lender's money for safekeeping and after a while the lender allowed the borrower to use the money in exchange for interest payments, this is also called *ribbis ketzutzah*. In light of this, if an interest-free loan was given and later extended in exchange for interest payments this is also a biblical transgression of *ribbis* and the interest must not be paid or if already paid it must be paid back. In other words, *ribbis* applies no matter how much interest was charged. Even if the interest was equal to the standard rate of inflation it is still prohibited.

By contrast, rabbinically prohibited *ribbis* were transactions that include elements of interest (*avak ribbis*), including floating-rate or non-guaranteed returns (*ribbis she'aina ketzutza*), business arrangements that contain elements of interest (*ribbis derech mekach u'memkar*) or resemble interest (*mechzei k'ribbis*). For instance, to provide the reader with a rabbinical prohibition of *ribbis*, think of a borrower who borrows money from a lender at a zero rate of interest. During the lifetime of the loan it is rabbinically prohibited for the borrower to give a gift to the lender because it may be seen as an added payment on top of a loan repayment. Even though there is no actual monetary interest being paid the *ribbis* still forbids it.

As opposed to the traditional punishments for violating certain biblical prohibitions such as murder, blasphemy, and adultery was death, the penalty for *ribbis* and all other monetary transgressions is a monetary one. In certain *Torah* prohibitions, the penalty is the return of the original money and a fine in addition. The laws of *ribbis*, though, are that if it was already paid or collected, it must be returned. If, however, the *ribbis* charged was deemed to be only a rabbinical prohibition of interest, the obligation to pay back the interest is only a moral one (Orlian 2011). Besides for this practical punishment to repay the interest, there are many spiritual punishments attached to breaking the laws of *ribbis*. The *Shulchan Aruch* (Code of Jewish Law) quotes the *Talmud* that according to Rava,[7] a person who charges *ribbis* is considered to have denied the miracles of the great Jewish exodus from Egypt. Similarly another great sage, Rav Yosi, claimed that whoever charges interest is considered to deny the existence of God. Finally, Rav Shimon ben Elazar said that whoever charges *ribbis* will see his property dwindle and vanish.

One story from the times of the prophets also illustrates the severity of *ribbis*. It happened in one instance that God showed the prophet, Ezekiel, an occurrence of *techiyas hameisim*[8] in order to give us a glimpse of the future. When Ezekiel saw the dead return to life in his prophecy, he noticed one person who did not return to life. When he asked for an explanation, he was told that this man lent for *ribbis*, which served to disqualify him from returning to life at *techiyas hameisim*. It is clear from these teachings that the laws of *ribbis* are very serious. They are also quite nuanced. It is often not clear who has to keep the laws, and what they entail.

However, as I have anticipated before, it is important to highlight that there are alternatives to *ribbis*. The first one is to lend money interest-free. Jewish law treats this as the highest form of charity and relief. Indeed, most rabbis agree that where a lender is in position to extend a free loan to a borrower, then that is what they should do. However, in the event where the lender is not able to extend a free loan, a *Heter Iska* may be used.

A *Heter Iska* is a profit-sharing agreement where one person (usually a silent partner) puts up funds and a managing partner conducts the business in exchange for a 50/50split of the profits and losses. The managing partner must also be compensated for his time and effort running the business venture. This compensation is usually in the form of a higher percentage of the profits. Each *Heter Iska* partnership agrees on its own what the compensation will be. However, in the event of a loss, the managing partner would only be liable for 50% of the losses. Otherwise, this would be considered *ribbis*. The rabbis still generally agree that the spiritual reward for extending a free loan would be preferable to a *Heter Iska* but where that is not possible then the *Heter Iska* may be used. It is, therefore, possible to have a form of interest rate between members of Jewish communities.

In addition to *Heter Iska* there were also a number of methods of evading the anti-usury laws. One of the simplest methods was for a person to lend something to another and buy it back from them at a reduced price. The lender could make a profit from the difference between the reduced price and the actual worth of the loaned thing. Nowadays, the *Heter Iska* is still in common use, especially in Israel, and when Jewish would like to enter into such agreement of partnership, then a competent rabbinic authority must be consulted to draw up such a document between parties. But the institution of free loans has nevertheless always flourished in Jewish communities. In every major Jewish community, and in most smaller ones, there has always been a free loan society to provide interest-free loans to those who qualify. This way, everyone in the community can collaborate in a great *mitzvah*, which in the long run benefits all.

For these reasons, it might be possible that even in the sixteenth century in Venice, Jews were using *Heter Iska* as a possible alternative to the prohibition of *ribbis* among themselves. However, when I have also asked for confirmation of this fact to the Warburg family, who are supposed to be some of the direct descendants of Venetian Jews of *Banco Rosso* in Italy, they were unable to certify with evidences the usage of a *Heter Iska*, although they informed me that they were aware of the existence of this practice, and its possible use.

Probably due to the lack of evidences, and the more common situation in which Jews were charging interest to Christians at that time, intolerance of Jews became a fact of sixteenth-century life even in Venice, the most powerful and liberal city-state in Europe. By law the Jews were forced to live in the old walled foundry or '*Ghetto*' area of the city. After sundown the gate was locked and guarded by Christians. In the daytime any man leaving the ghetto had to wear a red hat to mark him as a Jew. The Jews were forbidden to own property. So it might be plausible that they might have been proactive in practising usury, the lending of money at interest. This practice was against Canon law and Christian teachings, as I have previously explained. The sophisticated Venetians merchants would turn a blind eye to it, but for the religious fanatics, who 'hated' the Jews, it was another matter.

This other side of the coin is magnificently crystallised in Shakespeare's play 'The Merchant of Venice'. The play is exactly telling such a story by depicting moneylenders as belonging to an ethnic minority. Written between 1596 and 1599 and based on the Italian tale '*Il Pecorone*' of the fourteenth century written by Giovanni Fiorentino, which was published in Milan in 1558, it is placed in Venice. Antonio, an anti-Semitic merchant, takes a loan from the Jew Shylock to help his friend, Bassanio, to court Portia. Antonio cannot repay the loan, and without mercy, Shylock demands a 'pound of his flesh'. The heiress Portia, disguised as a man, defends Antonio in court, and ultimately bests

Shylock with hair-splitting logic: his oath entitles him to a pound of Antonio's flesh, she notes, but not his blood, making any attempt at collecting the fee without killing Antonio, a Christian, impossible. When Shylock realises he has been had, it is too late: he is charged with conspiring against a Venetian citizen, and therefore, his fortune is seized. The only way he can keep half his estate is by converting to Christianity.

Shylock also highlights in the play how risky is to lend money to a merchant whose ships might be scattered at sea. This is the reason why interest on money lent should be seen as a compensation or the price of risk (D'Alvia 2020). The passage is clear when Shylock is commenting on the creditworthiness of Antonio by saying that Antonio is a 'good man', and confirming that lending practices are based on the level of trustworthiness of the borrower. In light of this, the interest is the price of risk. Nonetheless, each one of us today knows how a possible misprice of risk can easily turn into a global financial crisis (see Chapter 6). The play is also symbolising in a figurative manner the power of money and moneylender activities in a period when credit markets are at their beginning. Furthermore, it would like to raise the issue of ethnic minorities that can be damaged by hostile debtors belonging to ethnic majorities. It is based on true historical events at least regarding the moneylenders' existence, and the intolerance of that time for ethnic minorities especially Jews.

2.5 *Monti di Pietà*: A Mountain of Piety

In Venice, Jews were supposedly performing usury in front of the building once known as the *Banco Rosso* (the Red Bench), sitting behind tables on their benches, the *banchi*. *Banco Rosso* was located in a ghetto distant from the city centre. Venetian merchants were used to come to this ghetto if they wanted to borrow money, but Jews lent to people from all ranks of society: nobles, clergy, burghers, and peasants. Kings rarely borrowed from Jews, they 'preferred' to tax them. Records of articles left with Jews as pledges indicate the nature of loans. Of nineteen articles traced in loan documents by the scholar Gerard Nahon, eight were articles of clothing, five were animals, four were household linens, two were jewellery, and one was a cooking vessel. Lenders probably did not advance more than fifty or seventy-five percent of the value of the pledge, to compensate for depreciation, monetary changes, etc. There were a variety of other risks to take into account. There was an especially high risk that a Jewish lender would unwittingly accept a stolen item as a pledge. He would not be indemnified if the article was subsequently claimed by its rightful owner. This is also a possible interpretation that lending was a risky activity, and interest might have been a legitimate and fair type of compensation—as I said—for the risk taken by the moneylender (see Sect. 2.3 above). Furthermore, since 1208 there were churchmen who understood the necessity of allowing Christians to lend to Christians. In light of this, Pope Innocent III wrote in 1208 that:

> if the ban provided by the [Third] Lateran Council against such [Christian usurers] were to be promulgated against all transgressors, one would have to close the churches altogether, because of their multitude.

Indeed, Reinhold Mueller (1997) highlights how at least in the records of fifteenth-century Venetian bank deposit accounts there is no mention of interest to be repaid, but probably this was many times paid in secret and its book or historical value was not recorded. In the end, it is fair to admit that Christians too might have indulged in the 'sin of usury' at least from a theological prospective as also Pope Innocent III admitted.

The *Bull Inter Multiplices*, a religious decree issued in 1515 during the Fifth Lateran Council, called for alternative forms of lending to the poor to free them from supposedly predatory lenders. It also permitted the levying of some interest charges to sustain and benefit lenders. In fact, some Christian thinkers regarded even Jewish money lending to Christians as something that should be prohibited. In the late fifteenth century, a number of outstanding Italian ecclesiastics such as preachers Benardino da Feltre and Girolamo Savonarola made the campaign against usury a key element of their preaching. It was indirectly a campaign against the toleration of a Jewish presence, but also called for the creation of alternative to usurious lenders. The *Bull Inter Multiplices* sought a replacement for pawnbrokers.[9] What the Church increasingly encouraged were charitable alternatives to private lenders, and they found what they wanted in the so-called *Monti di Pietà*,[10] namely charitable organisations which, by extending loans to needy Christians at nominal interest rates, would make Jewish money lending obsolete. *Monti di Pietà* literally translates from Italian into 'mount of piety' or less literally 'the accumulation of piety'. The *Monti di Pietà* as the would be called in plural, were municipally chartered, charitable pawnshops aimed at ameliorating the condition of the poor. These sprouted up all over Italy in the Renaissance, but most notably in urban areas, in which they took up residence in prominent buildings near the city centre. Some were already in existence by the end of the fifteenth century, the first having been formed in Perugia in 1462.

Monti di Pietà were funded with donations, sometimes collected by the Church, and from state aid. Even Lorenzo de Medici of the famous banking family, who was not enthusiastic about the idea of competition, offered a token amount of money to establish a *Monti di Pietà* in Florence. However, records from the *Monti di Pietà* suggest substantial support came from the middle classes and ordinary people, though donors included governments and guilds as well. Some funding also came in the form of deposits left with *Monti di Pietà*, but which could be withdrawn on demand by depositors. This was an early instance of deposit banking but the circumstances of these deposits, which paid little to no interest, were sometimes peculiar. In Florence and Rome, some deposits were the result of legal cases where guilty defendants were required to leave money with the *Monti di Pietà* as part of their penalty. This was an example of state support for the *Monti di Pietà* which often fell short of direct financial subsidies. With the funds it raised, the *Monti di Pietà* funded loans secured by the possessions of its poor clients. A typical loan could be up to eighteen months in term and interest charged was low, usually five percent and rarely above ten percent. A borrower might expect to pay one and half denari per lira per month, this would amount to a seven-point-five percent interest rate in the system of Italian pre-decimal coinage where there were two-hundred-and-forty denari per lira. To avoid losses, the list of eligible collateral was limited and assessors attempted to ascertain that the property truly belonged to the borrower. As a further safeguard, loan amounts and the frequency of new loans per borrower were limited and the most favoured collateral were items with sentimental value.

Regarding its organisation structure, a typical *Monti di Pietà* had paid staff overseen by patrician volunteers. The latter were often appointed by the local government for a certain term of office. The staff recorded transactions on ledgers and the *Monti di Pietà* employed accountants when this task exceeded the capabilities and expertise of its overseers. The *Monti di Pietà* employed advanced accounting for the time, including the use of double-entry bookkeeping. To ensure their lawfulness, staff, and overseers may in some cases have been required to seek a guarantor to cover any indemnity should they be found guilty of wrongful behaviour, such as embezzling funds from the organisation. This new form of charitable pawnbroker became most numerous in central and northern Italy but also spread to the south. By the time the *Bull Inter*

Multiplices was issued, there were already over one-hundred-and-twenty in operation. Within a century of establishment of the first in Perugia, there were over two-hundred in Italy and six-hundred by the end of the seventeenth century. They would spread all over the rest of Europe and even to Latin America. The *Bull Inter Multiplices* enabled early *Monti di Pietà* to engage in activities more similar to that of a modern bank. Many began to accept deposits from a wide array of customers, including the Church, the state, the wealthy, and commoners. They arguably interacted with a broader segment of society than any other financial organisation in their day and for that reason look surprisingly modern. This breadth makes the *Monti di Pietà* a valuable historical resource for those studying Renaissance Italy especially because so many of their records survive. They became institutional lenders in time between the individual moneylender, operating at the edge of the law and social acceptance and the mainstream services of a modern bank. There are differences, however, not all the *Monti di Pietà* accepted deposits as many refused to accept the prospect of sudden withdrawals. In any case, even those that did accept deposits did not necessarily pay interest on them. This was not among their primary functions. They were also still medieval organisations in their intent, established without seeking profit but rather as a respectable alternative to less appreciated lenders. The *Monti di Pietà* had a radically different source of political and religious support than modern banks. Nonetheless, they are some of the earliest banking organisations developed and some survived to today, including Banca Monte dei Paschi di Siena, founded in 1472 in Siena (Italy), and still in business as the oldest bank in the world in operation.

Besides being a possible progenitor of banks, *Monti di Pietà* played a growing role against Jews and Judaism. The statutes of these pious foundations often included crude anti-Jewish language. For example, the preamble of the statutes of the Faenza *Monti di Pietà* defined the purpose of the new foundation as aiming at the 'destruction of perfidious voraciousness of the accursed usury, most specifically that of the Jews'. Jewish money lending was regarded by Church authorities as an activity that gave Jews a way to oppress the Christian population and undermined its beliefs. A credo that unfortunately became a constant in centuries to come by raising also doubts on the sources of wealth of prominent Jewish families, and the role they played in banking such as the House of Rothschild (see Chapter 5), and even more vehemently aggressive was the attack against

Judaism centuries later when Jews were deported to infamous concentration camps, and Jewish art was considered degenerate by Nazism, as I will further illustrate at the end of this chapter.

2.6 The Medici Family and the Bill of Exchange

Due to this formal prohibition to charge interest as a form of usury, Christian merchants in Italy came up with another original financial innovation since the thirteenth century: the bill or letter of exchange. This provided a method of evading the usury ban (Munro 2003). It secretly disguised the interest rate with an exchange rate that was raised in favour of the lender. A new form of speculation was born and then perfectionated during the years to come especially by the Italian Medici bills of exchange or *cambium per literas* that was a new way of financing trade (Ferguson 2019).

In the Middle Ages, before the advent of trading cities like Bruges, Antwerp and Amsterdam, trade in Europe relied on a system of fairs that followed the same circuit each year. Merchants came together in these fairs. Payments could be made in coins or in bills of exchange. Bills could also be drawn to carry over any debt into the next fair. Italian merchants developed the bills of exchange as an alternative to making payments in coins, including exchanging money in one currency for money in another. Dealing in bills also reduced the risk of loss or theft because no actual transfer of coins occurred. In other words, bills were promises to pay a specified sum at a certain time and place. Because the money would not be paid for some period of time, the bill of exchange was also a credit instrument.

If a merchant owed money at the conclusion of a fair, he might sell a bill payable by himself at the time and location of the next fair; to carry that debt into the future. However, usually a bill was used to finance inventories while they were in transit or in the process of being sold.

The mechanism worked as follows: if a Venice merchant planned to attend a Champagne fair in France, he would eventually receive payments in France but first required funds in Italy to purchase the inventory he planned to sell in Champagne. To purchase such inventory from a seller in Venice, the merchant would draw up a bill of exchange ordering a drawee, his representative in Champagne where the merchant would later make his profit, to pay a payee at a later date. The payee would be the local Champagne correspondent of the Venice based seller of inventories acquired by the merchant. By accepting the bill as a means of payment, the seller would essentially be offering financing to the merchant. Specifically, the bill of exchange was an informal letter of payment concerning a financial transaction between two principals in one city and their two agents in a second foreign city.

As illustrated by Professor Geva (2011), the bill of exchange was a short-term loan, but also a remittance contract that transferred funds, and effected payments between distant cities without movement of precious metals. Merchants would not only give bills in payment but would accept the bills of others routinely in their trade. Since they could be sold to third persons, bills would essentially circulate as money themselves. So, if a merchant in Florence had just sold some product in Bruges and received a bill payable in Bruges in return, he might sell that bill back home in Florene to a merchant needing cash in Bruges to purchase inventories there. Merchants and moneychangers would serve as intermediaries in this sort of trade, buying and selling bills paid in different cities as they would different currencies. By buying a bill before it was due, these new merchants were essentially lending money as much as changing money. The merchant-banker would purchase the bill at a discount from its full amount because payment was due at a future date; the purchasing merchant's account would then be debited when the bill became due. In doing so, the merchant-banker was effectively taking a risk that could distinguish its activity from simple lending. Those efforts to disguise these transactions as something else than lending lost importance as time went on and the practical penalties for lending at interest (i.e. usury) evaporated.

As I said, after the seller received his payment, the bill of exchange continued to function as a credit instrument until its maturity, independent of the original transaction. This was the essence of the Medici business as merchants-bankers, and it was also a source of making profits and speculation (Ferguson 2019). However, any financial innovation does not come without risks. The bill of exchange itself involved the risks of repudiation or non-payment. It was not a bond nor a notarised contract, the bill was an informal letter. Hence, to enforce payment, when a bill was dishonoured, was difficult.

The Medici were not only a family of Florence bankers whose riches powered the Renaissance, but they were amongst the most renowned art patrons in history. The modern idea of art and our belief that artworks deserve to be taken seriously not as mere decorations or religious icons but unique displays of imagination and intellect began in Italy in the Renaissance. The city that was most self-conscious about this new idea of art in the fifteenth century was Florence. Filippo Lippi's Annunciation, Sandro Botticelli's Venus and Mars, and Pollaiuolo brothers' Saint Sebastian are just some of the artists who worked in fifteenth-century Florence. All of them had close ties with one family: the Medici. The Annunciation panel by Lippi actually comes from the Medici palace, and Antonio del Pollaiuolo painted decorations for this domestic temple of the arts. Botticelli was a Medici protege, who portrayed himself among the men of this famous lineage in his Adoration of the Magi in the Uffizi.

The Adoration of the Magi by Botticelli is very significant. The work—a tempera on wood—depicts the biblical story of the three Wise Men and others coming to worship Christ at the Nativity. Botticelli painted a few depictions of Magi adoring Christ, but this 1478–1482 painting is his most famous version because it reveals important information about the religious nature of the topic, Florentine society, and Botticelli himself. The painting has surely a religious meaning because it depicts one of the most important scenes from the Bible. The Holy Family—consisting of Christ, Mary, and Joseph—is the central focus, and they are placed above all the other figures in the scene. The star that led the Magi to Bethlehem can be seen at the top of the painting, shining directly on Christ. The three Magi (the kneeling man in black to the left of Christ, the kneeling man in red directly below Mary, and the kneeling man in white/gold next to him) and their attendants (the other figures in the scene) have brought their gifts to offer to the Holy Family. This suggests that the Holy Family (and specifically Christ) deserves worship and reverence. In addition to the religious aspects of the painting, the Adoration of the Magi portrays some important figures from Florentine society. Several members from the powerful Medici family are featured. The Medici chose to have themselves portrayed not working at the bank, but in the robes of the Magi. They commissioned paintings not of the marketplace, but of mythology. To this end, Hans Holbein's Portrait of a merchant surrounded by the instruments of his trade has no equivalent in the art associated with the Medici family.

The Medici—as I said—were also the architects of modern economy. They were the greatest bankers of their age, and the Medici Bank pioneered crucial aspects of modern finance. The Medici were members of the *Arte de Cambio* (the Moneychangers' Guild), and they were foreign exchange dealers, who enacted a 'transfiguration of finance' as pointed out by Ferguson (2019). It seems that the modern banking system developed in parallel with the most important artistic flowering in the history of the Western world.

The Medici started to be known as *banchieri* or bankers similar to Jews of Venice that did their business literally seated at benches behind tables in the street. The Medici family became involved in Florentine banking in the latter 1300s, and since then the Medici could operate on a fractional reserve principle by creating fiduciary money to the extent that transferable deposits were not entirely covered by cash in vault. Indeed, the prominent Italian family of bankers were early adopters of fractional reserve banking, a practice that Medici Bank customers were unaware of. The double-entry bookkeeping was the 'technology' used to enable the Medici Bank's fractional reserve banking practices. The double-entry scheme involves a ledger that records both debits and credits and is still used in the modern financial world today. At that time, the Franciscan Friar Luca Pacioli wrote a book about double-entry accounting with help from the well-known Renaissance artist Leonardo da Vinci. Although Pacioli and da Vinci did not claim to invent the new system, their research led to the wider and more structured use of double-entry bookkeeping that is still used today. While Luca Pacioli's system was a disruptive force in the financial world allowing the Medici Bank to fractionalise reserve with ease, Satoshi Nakamoto's triple-entry bookkeeping system, introduced with Bitcoin, has also disrupted today's financial system (see Chapter 5).

Soon after the method was popularised, Giovanni de Medici implemented the concept into his family's bank. It allowed the House of Medici to operate with less than ten percent of deposits and extend its lending practices far and wide until liquidity completely dried up. The Medici Bank was brought to the forefront of the European economy by Giovanni di Bicci de' Medici, who died in 1429. In 1393 Giovanni de' Medici, took ownership of the Roman branch, a bank owned by one of his Florentine cousins. He moved the headquarters of his bank to Florence in 1397, the official founding date for the Medici Bank. In the first five years of operation, the Medici Bank grew rapidly, and before the financial institution's demise, it established branches all over Western Europe. Similar to bankers in the early twentieth century like J.P. Morgan, Jacob Schiff, Paul Warburg, and George F. Baker, members of the House of Medici were extremely powerful. The Medici Bank was known to be one of the largest business enterprises during the Renaissance but ultimately failed after close to one-hundred years of operation.

The Medici set up a system of subsidiaries of the bank, any subsidiary was independent. Such structure protected the parent bank from the bankruptcy of individual subsidiaries caused by local economic difficulties. Soon the Medici Bank became the chief bank for the Roman Catholic curia, and it had subsidiaries in the major cities of Italy, as well as in London, Lyon, Geneva, Bruges, and Avignon. The Medici Bank was organised as a partnership, with the Medici family as the largest investor in the parent company. The parent company was the largest investor in the branch partnerships and functioned like a modern holding company. Partnerships were preferred to companies whose modern ancestor will not originate until the beginning of the seventeenth century. Yet partnerships were not only a Medici business and long existed before their time. For example, the largest Sienese partnership was the *Gran Tavola* (the big table or bank) of the Bonsignori that had been established in the first quarter of the thirteenth century. At that time Siena (a small city-town) in opened countryside-Tuscany was probably for seventy-five years, the main banking centre in Europe, with Piacenza as a close rival (Chandler 1963). Eventually, the *Gran Tavola* failed in 1298, and its place was taken over by Florence. Between 1300 and 1345, three main Florentine banks dominated the scene: Bardi, Peruzzi, and Acciaiuoli. The Peruzzi was the second largest of the 'big three', it had fifteen branches scattered all over Western Europe and the Levant, from London to Cyprus. The Italian chronicler, Giovanni Villani (1276–1348) was a partner of the Peruzzi, and called them 'the pillars of Christian trade'. However, as the records show all three banks collapsed shortly before the Black Death (1348). These bank runs were mainly connected to over-extension of credit and excessive loans to sovereigns especially to Edward III, King of England, and to Robert the Angevin King of Naples. Villani reports that when the Peruzzi company failed in 1343, Edward III of England owed them 'the value of a realm'. Loans to nobles and Kings were always threatening the solvency of medieval companies, but it is possible to claim that was difficult to avoid doing business with courts. After the collapse of those three major banks, the Pope was looking for a banking firm that offered him the same facilities for the transfer of papal revenues or subsidies. The Alberti, a Florentine firm took advantage of the circumstances and succeeded in capturing the papal business. However, the Alberti company soon split into several rival firms because of family quarrels. The place of the Alberti was taken by the Medici, the Pazzi, the Rucellai, and the Strozzi. Eventually, the Medici succeeded in overshadowing their competitors but they never attained the size of the Bardi or the Peruzzi, the giants of the fourteenth century.

2.7 A Mountain of Debt, and the Bond Revolution

Securities markets took centuries to develop, although the idea of *publicani* in ancient Rome (see Sect. 2.1) can be considered to some extent as the first direct evidence of the fact that shares' value fluctuates, and speculation is about taking advantage of that moment, namely to buy at low prices and resell at higher valuations. As opposed to equity, the idea of debt dates back to the ancient world with certainty. For example, in ancient Mesopotamian clay tablets recording interest-bearing loans (Ferguson 2019). However, tradable bonds were a more recent innovation, spearheaded by the Italian city-states of the late medieval and early Renaissance periods. In fact, the reader might wonder how Ancient Rome could finance its public debt. The short answer is it did not. When the state needed extra money, it usually simply debased the coinage. The result was the inflation the Roman Empire was known for. Government bonds are an example of something the Romans did not have that medieval civilisations had. Venice was the first city-state to issue government bonds to its citizens in the same way governments today issue sovereign bonds. Before the Venetian *prestiti* (Italian for loans) and even after, kings, queens, emperors, and others borrowed money to fight wars or feed their royal megalomania (the episode of King Philip IV of France and the Knights Templar that I have illustrated before is a self-evident example). When the rulers were unable to pay their debt, they defaulted, often bankrupting their creditors. Venice was different, at least at first glance.

In the latter half of the Middle Ages, Venice was the preeminent European naval power in the Eastern Mediterranean, and it was the medieval equivalent of Athens, a democracy for the elites. The Republic of Venice controlled an empire spanning the eastern coast of the Adriatic, Crete, and Cyprus. Some of these territories were captured as early as during the Crusades, which coincided with the expansion of Venetian power. Venice was interested in keeping its hegemony of trade between Europe and the East. At the peak of its power and wealth, it had thirty-six-thousand sailors operating three-thousand-and-three-hundred ships, dominating Mediterranean commerce. This dominant position was expensive to maintain, especially for a single city. Financing frequent wars made the city a centre of financial innovation, both fiscal and commercial. Indeed, defending their empire meant wars with other Italian city-states, such as Florence and Genoa, and wars meant borrowing money.

The financial revolution that occurred in Italy in the Middle Ages, much like that of Britain in the late seventeenth century, was born of necessity.

A voluntary loan in 1164 was among the first instances of long-term state borrowing in the form of a syndicated loan by a European country. The loan of one-thousand-one-hundred-and-fifty silver marks was secured by eleven years' worth of revenues from the markets in *Rialto.* There was a problem with borrowing because Venice had to compete with higher yielding investment opportunities, and sovereign debt was new to the scene. To avoid high-interest charges, the government in Venice opted to require its taxpayers to subscribe to loans. Such subscriptions were constructed to be applicable and compulsory on wealthy citizens in proportion to their wealth, or better the level of taxes that they paid. The first of these forced loans was raised in 1167 and was used to finance a war against the Byzantine Empire. For its part, the *Consilium Sapientium* (Great Council of Venice) that governed the city-state pledged not to borrow for another two years. The next of these loans did not come until 1171. By the mid-thirteenth century, there were several different loans outstanding simultaneously, of varying terms, together comprising the Venetian state debt. The complexity brought the government to conduct audits to find out just how indebted it was. The decision was made in 1262 to consolidate the public debt into a new fund; the outcome of this fiscal restructuring was what was later called the *Monte Vecchio* (from Italian 'Old Mountain' but more appropriately translated as 'Old Fund'). The *Monte Vecchio* was essentially a single series of perpetual obligations with no specific maturity date, called *prestiti* (from Italian 'loans') of which new issues were occasionally made. In eighteenth-century Britain, the consol[11] was an equivalent instrument.

With *prestiti* no physical bonds were issued, but all bonds were registered through the Loan Officer, the *Ufficiale dei Prestiti.* This move institutionalised the *prestiti* as long-term loans rather than short-term borrowings. The *prestiti* paid a nominal interest rate of five percent on the outstanding capital, two instalments of two-point-five percent paid per annum (in March and September) for over one-hundred years. Periodic principal repayments were made when funds became available but over the centuries the general trend was upward.

However, there were protections for bondholders. The Great Council of Venice decreed that the government would reserve merely the first three-thousand lire (almost five-hundred ducats) a month in tax revenue for itself. Beyond that, revenue went to pay interest on the *Monte Vecchio*, and only once interest was paid could the government claim the residual.

The *prestiti* became a popular form of investment for Venetian nobles. They were used as endowments for charities, and were used as dowries for daughters upon their marriage. Since the elites of Venice owned *prestiti* and were part of the government, this reduced the likelihood the city would default on its debts (though the government did forgo interest payments in 1379–1381, 1463–1479, and 1480). Owning *prestiti* was a privilege. Foreigners, who trusted the Venetian government more than their own, could only obtain *prestiti* through an act of the Council of Venice.

The claims on these bonds could be sold and transferred to others who then had all the rights of the original purchaser. In other words, investors traded *prestiti* in a secondary market. This was important given that many holders were unwilling investors and, therefore, they could monetise on their assets. Two centuries later, the *Monte Vecchio* was complemented by a newer series of bonds, called the *Monti* (literally translated from Italian as the 'Mountains' or as I said better referred to as the 'Funds'). New issues of forced loan were important to fund Venice's wars against Genoa in the fourteenth century. The wars brought the stock of debt under the *Monte Vecchio* from one-hundred-and-fifty-four-thousand ducats when it was established to over five-hundred-thousand ducats after the conclusion in 1299 of one of the many wars with Genoa. The debt pile grew to over one million ducats by 1314 though three decades of peace allowed some repayments to be made on the bonds, bringing the 'Old Mountain' of debt back down to 423,000 ducats by 1343.

Sidney Homer, in his 'History of Interest Rates', provides historical data on the prices of *prestiti*, and the reader can see how the price of the bonds and their yield fluctuate in response to the fortunes of Venice. The worst decline of *prestiti* was in the fourteenth century during the War of Chioggia between 1738 and 1381 with Genoa. By that time Venice suspended interest payments, made the *prestiti* no longer immune from tax levies, and expanded the debt six to nine times its level in 1344. In the 1400s, interest rates were variable and were reduced to 4%. Expensive wars continued to be waged against the Ottomans in the 1460s and 1470s further encumbering the public finances. Some interest payments due in the 1470s were not received until the subsequent century. In a new debt restructuring, the *Monte Nuovo* (from Italian the 'New Mountain' or 'New Fund') was created in 1482 to finance a war against the Duchy of Ferrara. Under this series of new *prestiti* the interest rate was restored to 5%, and the interest payment was secured by new taxes. However, prices for the new bonds fell much like they did for the old ones. They lost value during and after continued wars against the Ottomans at sea and against the French on land in Italy. The Battle of Agnadello in 1509 against the French army took the prices on the *Monte Nuovo* bonds down to 40% of face value. The next series of *prestiti* was uncreatively named *Monte Nuovissimo* (from Italian the 'Very New Mountain or 'Very New Fund') created in 1509 when the bonds of *Monte Nuovo* became as depressed as those of the *Monte Vecchio*. This was not enough though; when these series were trading at massive discounts to face value, they were supplemented by still a newer series. The *Monte Sussidio* (from Italian the 'Subsidy Mountain' or 'Subsidy Fund') created in 1526 replaced the *Monte Nuovissimo*. As it can be seen, new forced loans often depressed prices for old ones as investors had to liquidate to fund their new subscriptions. This was a weakness in the system of forced loans. The possibility to ignore market forces by forcing subscriptions was likely to degrade the fiscal credibility of the bond issuer. Those forced to participate in the loans questioned why it was that they had to pay face value for the bonds while secondary market purchasers could purchase the same *prestiti* at depressed prices: speculation was the answer. The scheme went on, and the *Monte Vecchio* was not completely redeemed until the late sixteenth century.

Venice's rival Genoa city-state had a need for innovative borrowing too. In fact, Genoa was often at war with Venice, as I said. Genoa was a financial centre of Northern Italy too. Genoa was stuck with the limited natural resources available in Liguria region. However, the winds and currents made the city an excellent location for a port. The sea became the source of much of Genoa's employment and wealth. As just one example, shipbuilding created demand for an array of crafts, creating employment for craftsmen specialised in making sails, anchors, nails, and ropes. Whatever the role of shipbuilding the most relevant dimension to Genoa's economy for financial development was trade, which generated much of the city's wealth. By the fourteenth century, Genoa was trading in spices with Egypt and in cloth with England and Genoese merchants and financiers found themselves in Spain and other destinations far from their Mediterranean home, like London, Bruges, and Antwerp. Trade offered high returns and captured a lot of investment, much of it raised through a *commenda* (a partnership between investors and merchants, the former provided money, the latter did the travelling and conducted business). Investors pooling capital for voyages would receive shares called *loca*, transferrable interests in a voyage, and these changed hands while ships were underway, creating something of a stock market. However, as I said also in relation to Ancient Rome in Sect. 2.1 of this chapter, voyages could be dangerous and the threat of storms and pirates constituted the primary threat to profits. Besides travelling in armed convoys or taking other preventative measures, there were forms of insurance. Among them were 'sea loans' which combined a credit and insurance instrument. Sea loans to a merchant, who might use the money to outfit a ship or purchase supplies or inventories, did not have to be repaid if the ship was lost. Marine insurance—as I have illustrated in Sect. 2.1—is one of the oldest forms of insurance and so, as a centre for maritime trade, it is not surprising that Genoa became an early insurance centre in the Mediterranean. Even there though, only a quarter of voyages were insured. Besides the sea loan, which required the merchant to take a loan he might not have needed, insurance also took the form of a more conventional insurance policy. Involved in insurance policies would have been notaries and their records show that insurance contracts could be quite specific. They specified the type of ship and its cargos, who the captain was, and what route would be taken. Also listed would have been the underwriters. However, at this time, there was not a dedicated insurance industry, even if there was an insurance market. Most insurance underwriters were merchants themselves. There usually were several involved in a particular transaction as insurance policies were underwritten by syndicates so that an underwriter's individual exposure might be manageable.

Besides representing fractional shares in voyages, *loca* would represent pieces of the public debt. Genoa used several forced loans as a means to raise money, often wars. The wealthy would often take up the contributions required of those who could not afford to meet their share of the loan and this meant that the loans still had to be appealing on their merits. The city also raised money on a voluntary basis. To service this debt, new taxes called *gabelle* were instituted. These were taxes on specific goods like salt, wheat, or wine. The government would sell rights to future tax collections by issuing *compera* and outsourcing the collection of taxes to private individuals. The *compera* were divided into *loca*, also known as *luoghi* (literally translated from Italian as 'spaces' more appropriately 'shares'). Holders of *luoghi* were entitled to receive all of these tax revenues and not only a specified constant rate. Interest rates paid on fifteenth-century *luoghi* ranged from four percent to ten percent. Specifically, after the wars with Venice, Genoa consolidated its public debt. The debt burden was then divided into shares—as I said *luoghi*—which were freely tradable by their owners. Because of the fact that people trusted that the powerful Genoese state would honour its debts, people were also able to use the *luoghi* as collateral for their own borrowing. Merchants, bankers, and the wealthy would speculate in these bonds. They were also used by wealthy property-owners to leave wealth to widows or heirs. *Luoghi* could only be seized in few scenarios and these did not include seizure to satisfy personal debts. Their use in inheritances was enhanced by their divisibility; as such, they could allow an estate to be divided more evenly than discrete real estate properties would allow and were useful in funding dowries and annuities. Such a link between the public debt and inheritances, specifically the creation of an instrument by which to support widows and orphans, was found almost everywhere in Europe where governments borrowed.

Later, in 1407, Genoa's Bank of Saint George was hired to consolidate the public debt which was against rising after further wars with Venice. The Bank, perhaps one of the earliest examples of a European investment bank, was an institution at the core of Genoa's system of public finance. This was a bank located in the city's customs house, the Palazzo San Giorgio. Established in 1407, the *Casa di San Giorgio* gradually consolidated the state debt over the next fifty years or so. It was a corporate entity managing the public debt and representing the state's creditors. Genoa's government would turn to the bank when raising fresh money by a loan. As the state struggled to pay its debts, the *Casa di San Giorgio* also received control of lands. The political scientist Niccolo Machiavelli wrote that the *Casa di San Giorgio* controlled most of the lands and cities of the Genoese Empire, which included Corsica and lands in Italy, Cyprus, and Crimea. To consolidate the public debt the *Casa di San Giorgio* placed new *luoghi* on behalf of the state with investors who bought them voluntarily. These *luoghi* were similar to *prestiti* in Venice in some respects; like *prestiti*, they were perpetual obligations. There was also a market for what was called '*paghe*' which were interest payments on the *luoghi*. Interest was often paid irregularly so a market formed where people could expend with their *paghe* when they wanted rather than when the bonds finally made their interest payment. The *Casa di San Giorgio* managed a payment system by recording transfers of *paghe* in ledgers; the *paghe* were used as a type of bank money. Finally, the *Casa di San Giorgio* administrated most of the *gabelle* instituted to pay interest on the debt, outsourcing the collection to subcontractors called *gabellotti*. The *gabellotti* could make their payment of taxes collected, at least partially, in *paghe* trading in the market, usually at discount. Consequently, by withdrawing *paghe* from circulation, interest payments were defeased against taxes revenues without actually paying them in full in cash.

From this short historical *excursus*, it is clear that the value of those securities (namely, the *prestiti* or *luoghi*) could easily fluctuate between periods of war and peace, but even more: *prestiti* and *luoghi* are financial innovations, and it is often when the public finances are in the most dire shape that creative thinking is most needed.

2.8 A City of Gold

As the Italians were improving their banking system, the Spanish were lagging behind as they were cursed with an abundance of precious metal. In Spain between the 1520s and 1530s, Spaniards when led in expeditions by the conquistador Francisco Pizarro ruled over what was the Inca Empire, then formally dissolved in 1572, and ironically failed to find a city of gold, but what they found in the 1540s instead was almost as great: *Cerro Rico* (the 'Rich Hill'), a mountain of silver in what is now Bolivia.

The City of Gold (*El Dorado*), as opposed to St. Augustine's the City of God, was a mythical city said to be rich with gold, first reported in Europe in the sixteenth and seventeenth centuries. The rumoured location of *El Dorado* is disputed by different sources, but most commonly said to have been in South America. In some accounts, *El Dorado* is a man (indeed, *El Dorado* literally translates as 'the golden one'), in others a lake, a valley, or a city. By 1835, the myth of El Dorado was already three centuries old, but its origin and whether a real city of gold existed is still disputed. The thought of a legendary city of gold sitting undiscovered in the Central American jungle just sounds too good to be true, but it definitively sounded impressive to Spanish explorers and conquistadors of the sixteenth century. *Cerro Rico* and Potosi the mining city that it spawned, produced almost sixty percent of the World's silver output, and the mines started a significant net flow of gold and silver from the New World to Spain during the sixteenth and seventeenth century.

For Pizarro and his men, silver was more than shiny decorative metal. It could be made into money: a unit of account, a store of value, in other words a portable power (Ferguson 2019). Still today mining is deeply embedded in Bolivia's national identity. Potosi's fame came not only from its wealth, but also its notoriety for appalling working conditions. At the peak of production in the 1590s almost two-hundred-thousand kilogrammes of silver were mined each year, not counting thousands more that escaped official records. Potosi's silver flooded the global market; the wealth it generated stimulating demand for, and the production of, linen and fine cloths from the Netherlands and France, as well as silk and porcelain from China and cotton cloths from India. It enabled Spain to conduct costly European wars and to overcome the Ottomans. *Valer un potosi*, 'to be worth a potosi' is still a Spanish expression meaning to be worth a fortune.

On the other hand, Potosi has an extraordinary negative and depressing record in claiming human lives: it almost costed eight million slaves, who died in Potosi alone (Lane 2021). Conditions were so harsh that from the late sixteenth century a system of forced labour (*la mita*) had to be introduced in order to conscript men aged between eighteen and fifty from the highland provinces for seventeen weeks a year. Mortality was so high because of constant exposure to the mercury fumes generated by the patio process of refinement. Printed illustrations of work in the mines promoted the image of Potosi as 'the mouth of hell' and fuelled the black legend that saw the Spanish as cruel and greedy.

It might be intuitive that the flood of precious metals from Potosi would massively enrich the Spanish Empire. Pizarro was after silver not by chance. He knew that metals were synonyms of power: a 'mountain of money'. Indeed, this time the speculation did not come from moneylending activities or financial innovations, but simply through a simple discovery.

What Pizarro and his men probably did not fully understand was that the value of precious metal is not absolute. Money is worth only what someone is willing to give you for it because money is based on trust. An increase in the supply of money might enrich the government that has the monopoly of the production of money, as it did with Spain for a time, but ultimately, it ended up helping to drive a sustained period of inflation across multiple European countries that became known as the Price Revolution and left the Spanish Empire worse off than it started. Monetary expansion is many times likely to make prices of goods and services higher. This is in brief what happened over one-hundred-and-fifty years in Europe, at the time of the Price Revolution when the high rate of inflation consumed Europeans and European countries from the late fifteenth century to mid-seventeenth century.

2.9 Conclusions

This chapter is the first direct account that speculators might have had a bad reputation because several forms of profit are sometimes necessarily connected to unlawful activities or at least to immoral ones. Usury is a case in point. However, the innate instinct of human beings to make profit and surge from financial instability has also been an important trigger in relation to financial innovation and it is not necessarily negative per se. For instance, the bill of exchange and the *commenda* as well as bottomry in Ancient Rome and the primordial sovereign bonds of Venetian *prestiti* and Genovese *luoghi* in Italy have been fundamental financial instruments serving economic purposes. Without bottomry Rome could not develop in *Caput Mundi* (literally translated from Latin the 'Head of the World') or without Venetian *prestiti* and Genovese *luoghi*, Italian city-states could not soar from ruined public finances. Indeed, the Venetian and Genovese story directly shows us that it is when public finances are in the most dire shape that creative thinking is most needed. At the same time, equity and debt could easily fluctuate in value and this could provide room for direct speculation, namely buying at low prices and selling high by taking advantage of market conditions.

For these reasons, financial innovations have both a 'bright' and a 'dark' side. On the bright side, creativity becomes a vital reading key of financial markets and economic interactions. Nonetheless, the Global Financial Crisis of 2007–2010 in the United States (see Chapter 6) has spurred renewed widespread debates on the 'dark' sides of financial innovation. The traditional innovation-growth view claims that financial innovations help innovate the quality and variety of banking services (Merton 1992; Berger, 2003), facilitate risk sharing (Allen and Gale 1991, 1994), complete the market (Duffie and Rahi 1995; Elul 1995; Grinblatt and Longstaff 2000), and ultimately improve allocative efficiency (Ross 1976; Houston et al. 2010). The innovation-fragility view, on the other hand, focuses on the 'dark' side. Specifically, it identified financial innovations as the root cause of the Global Financial Crisis and led to an unprecedented credit expansion that helped feed the boom and subsequent bust in housing prices (Brunnermeier and Pedersen 2009) by helping banks develop structured products to exploit investors' misunderstandings of financial markets (Henderson and Pearson 2011). Such policy and academic debate is a never-ending matter. However, as Chapter 4 will further illustrate, without creativity there would be no financial innovations and without financial innovations there would be no possible solution to uncertainty. Simultaneously uncertainty-aversion policies would consistently reduce profit. Hence, financial innovations play a pivotal role in societal progress especially when they are aligned to moral objectives and sustainable growth as this book would like to argue. In other words, this chapter has illustrated that risk-taking activities are not an easy task, and a misprice of financial risk might also sometimes produce negative consequences such as financial crisis (see Chapters 5 and 6). In light of this, Chapter 3 continues to further explore financial innovations and to introduce milestones of human progress such as the corporation, the limited liability, and the rise of stock exchanges.

Relevant Historical Events in Financial Innovation and Speculation

Date	*Financial Innovation and/or Speculation*
1800 BC	Marine insurance so-called 'bottomry' in Ancient Babylon, later adopted by Ancient Greeks and Ancient Romans
146 BC	*Publicani* in Ancient Rome represents one of the primordial forms of corporations
46 BC	The *Forum Romanum* is completed and it becomes a place where 'speculators' gather
426 CE	The Father of the Church, St. Augustine completed writing the City of God where usury is condemned, but an alternative contract provided for the sharing of risk via *commenda*
1185	Temple Church is consecrated as the London home of the Knights Templar, and the first bank in modern terms
1262	Venice to consolidate the public debt and promote a fiscal restructuring it issued the *Monte Vecchio* (from Italian 'Old Mountain' but more appropriately translated as 'Old Fund'). The *Monte Vecchio* was essentially a single series of perpetual obligations with no specific maturity date, called *prestiti* (from Italian 'loans') of which new issues were occasionally made. In eighteenth-century Britain, the consol

(continued)

(continued)

Relevant Historical Events in Financial Innovation and Speculation

Date	*Financial Innovation and/or Speculation*
1273	The Father of the Church, St. Thomas Aquinas—an Italian Dominican friar and priest—wrote the *Summa Theologica* or Summary of Theology. Usury is condemned, but an alternative contract is provided for the sharing of risk via *commenda*
c. 1200 – c. 1300	The Bill of Exchange attained wide use during the thirteenth century among Medici of Florence and the Lombards of Northern Italy, who carried on considerable foreign commerce
1407	Genoa consolidated its public debt by issuing '*luoghi*' which were primordial examples of sovereign bonds. Luoghi were similar to Venetian *prestiti*
1515	The *Bull Inter Multiplices*, a religious decree issued during the Fifth Lateran Council called for alternative forms of lending to the poor to free them from supposedly predatory lenders (the so-called *Monti di Pieta*)

Notes

1. The Republic is one of the main historical stages into which the history of Rome is conventionally divided. Specifically, the origins of Rome are seen in the Monarchy period in the eighth century B.C. to 509 B.C. This period is followed by that of the Republic from 509 B.C. to 27 B.C. which is further divided into the early Republic and later Republic until its last development during the phase of the Empire from 27 B.C. to 565 A.D. This macro-division can be regarded as a common understanding of Roman history according to Jolowicz (1972), Mousourakis (2007), and Grosso (1965). However, such conventional division shall never be read into a static segmentation, but as an evolutionary process that is dynamic in nature and evolves continuously.
2. In Rome bankers were also called *argentarii*. *Argentarii* were private persons, who carried on business on their own responsibility, and were not in the service of the republic but the shops or *tabernae* which they occupied and in which they transacted their business about the forum, were state property. Their chief business was that of changing money; the exchange of foreign coin for the Roman coin was called *permutatio* (in which case a small agio (*collybus*) was paid to them). In later times when

the Romans became acquainted with the Greek custom of using bills of exchange, the Roman *argentarii* received sums of money which had to be paid at Athens, and then drew a bill payable at Athens by some banker in that city. Other times, *argentarii* were used to keep sums of money for other persons, such money might be deposited by the owner merely to save himself the trouble of keeping it and making payments, and in this case, it was called *depositum* (deposit); the *argentarius* then paid no interest, and the money were called *vacua pecunia*. Or the money was deposited on condition the *argentarius* paying interest; in this case the money was called *creditum* (credit) and the *argentarius* might of course employ the money himself in any lucrative manner. *Argentarius* thus did almost the same sort of business as a modern banker.

3. Pompeii was a flourishing resort city south of ancient Rome that was nestled along the coast of Italy in the shadow of Mount Vesuvius, an active volcano. Its most famous eruption took place in the year 79 AD, when it buried the city of Pompeii under a thick carpet of volcanic ash. Two-thousand people died, and the city was abandoned for almost as many years. When a group of explorers rediscovered the site in 1748, they were surprised to find that beneath a thick layer of dust and debris, Pompeii was mostly intact. The building, artefacts, and skeletons left behind in the entombed city have given to posterity a great deal about everyday life in the ancient world.
4. The crowning achievement of King Solomon's reign was the erection of the magnificent Temple in the capital city of ancient Israel—Jerusalem. His father, King David, had wanted to build the great Temple a generation earlier, as a permanent resting place of the Ark of the Covenant which contained the Ten Commandments. A divine edict, however, had forbidden him from doing so: 'You will not build a house for My name', God said to David 'for you are a man of battles and have shed blood' (I Chronicles 28:3). The Bible's description of Solomon's Temple (also called The First Temple) suggests that the inside ceiling was 180 feet long, 90 feet wide, and 50 feet high. The highest point on the Temple that King Solomon built was actually 120 cubits tall (about 20 stories or about 207 feet). When the Temple was completed, Solomon inaugurated it with prayer and sacrifice, and even invited non-Jews to come and pray there. He urged God to pay particular heed to their

prayers: 'Thus all the peoples of the earth will know Your name and revere You, as does Your people Israel; and they will recognise that Your name is attached to his House that I have built' (I Kings 8:43). Sacrifice was the predominant mode of divine service in the Temple until it was destroyed by the Babylonians some four-hundred years later in 586 BCE. Seventy years later, after the story of Purim, a number of Jews returned to Israel—led by the prophets Ezra and Nehemiah—and the Second Temple was built on the same site. Sacrifices to God were once again resumed. The Second Temple, however, met the same fate as the first and was destroyed by the Romans in 70 CE, following the failure of the Great Revolt. To this day, traditional Jews pray three times a day for the Temple's restoration.

5. In Judaism indicates the totality of laws and ordinances that have evolved since biblical times to regulate religious observances and the daily life and conduct of Jewish people.
6. There are two categories of commandments in the Torah, *Mishpat*, and *Chok*. *Mishpat* is laws or judgements which are logical. Examples of *Mishpat* are the prohibition of stealing, murder or kidnap. *Chok* are decrees that are not understood. Other examples of *Chok* besides for *ribbis* are the dietary laws of *Kosher*, keeping the *Sabbath* and prohibition of *shatnez* or weaving together wool and linen.
7. He lived between 280 and 322 CE. He was a famous rabbi and frequent contributor to the Talmud.
8. Revival of the dead. Judaism, like Christianity, believes in a messiah who will return and restore all of the Jewish people to Israel and rebuild Solomon's Great Temple. Anyone who is dead at the time of this redemption will be revived and returned to Israel as well.
9. For ordinary people, one of the most frequented late medieval financial institutions was the local pawnshop. Here pawnbrokers would make loans secured by specific possessions of the borrower. It was one of the venues in which Jewish lenders would do business with a Christian customer base. Even during the strictest application of usury rules, pawnbrokers operated legally. In Italy, they had to pay a sizable fee for a license to conduct operations. While open even to the poor, pawnbrokers provided an expensive source of funds, offending many religious opponents of the lenders. One

Italian pawnbroker, the *Banca della Vacca*, disclosed in a tax declaration that it earned 879 lire on 3,000 lire it lent, almost a 30% return.

10. Historically, the word *mons* was used during the Middle Ages to designate funds collected for a specific purpose, *pietatis* being added to identify them as non-speculative. The original object of the *monti* was to provide loans at a relatively low rate of interest (4–15%) to small artisans and dealers and to the poor in general, on the pledge of various goods. The interest was used to defray administrative expenses and salaries of employees.
11. The consol was British government security without a maturity date. The name is a contraction for Consolidated Annuities, a form of British government stock that originated in 1751. The first issue of consols carried an interest rate of 3% (reduced to 2.75 percent in 1888 and to 2.5 percent in 1902). Between the years 1926 and 1932, 4% consols were issued. Although consols formed the larger part of Britain's funded debt before World War I, in 1961 they accounted for less than 3% of the total national debt because of the vast expansion of other forms of government debt during the two world wars. The 4% consols became redeemable on three months' notice after 1 February 1957; the 2.5% consols are in practice irredeemable by the government, and their price tends to vary with the bank rate (the interest rate charged by the Bank of England for loans of reserve funds to commercial banks and other financial intermediaries).

Bibliography

Aquinas T, *Summa Theologica* (Ave Maria Press 2000)

Allen F, Gale D, 'Arbitrage, short sales and financial innovation' (1991) 59 Econometrica 1041–1068

Allen F, Gale D, *Financial Innovation and Risk Sharing* (MIT Press 1994)

Benes Carrie E, *A Companion to Medieval Genoa* (Brill 2008)

Berger A, 'The economic effects of technological progress: Evidence from the banking industry' (2003) 35 Journal of Money, Credit and Banking 141–176

Brumnermeier M, 'Deciphering the liquidity and credit crunch 2007—2008' (2009) 23 Journal of Economic Prospective 77–100

Calomiris C, 'Financial innovation, regulation, and reform' (2009) 29 Cato Journal 65–91
Chancellor E, *Devil Take the Hindmost: A History of Financial Speculation* (Douglas & McIntyre Ltd 1999)
Chandler A D, *The Rise and Decline of the Medici Bank* (Harvard Studies in Business History 1963)
Church, A, 'The rise and fall of leading international financial centres: Factors and application' (2018) 7 (2) Michigan Business & Entrepreneurial Law Review 283–340
Cicero, *Ad. Familias XII*, 10.2 (cited by Tenney Frank, Economic History of Rome, 1927, 282)
D'Alvia D, (2018) 'From public law to private law: The remarkable story of bona fides' in *The future of Commercial Contract in Scholarship and Law Reform: European and Comparative Prospective* (M. Heidemann, and J. Lee, eds.) Springer, 343–368.
D'Alvia D, 'Risk, uncertainty, and the market: A rethinking of Islamic and Western Finance' (2020) 16 (4) International Journal of Law in Context 339–352
Dennis P. Kehoe, *Investement, Profit and Tenancy: the jurists and the Roman agrarian economy* (University of Michigan Press 1997)
De Roover R, 'The Medici Bank Financial and Commercial Operations' (1946) 6 (2) The Journal of Economic History 153–172
Doosselaere VQ, *Commercial Agreements and Social Dynamics in Medieval Genoa* (Cambridge University Press 2009)
Duffie D, Rahi R, 'Financial market innovation and security design: An introduction' (1995) 65 Journal of Economic Theory 1–42
Elul R, 'Welfare effects of financial innovation in incomplete markets economies with several consumption goods' (1995) 65 Journal of Economic Theory 43–78
Ferguson N, *The Ascent of Money: A Financial History of the World* (Penguin 2019)
Gatto A, 'Historical Roots of Microcredit and Usury: The Role of Monti di Pieta in Italy and in the Kingdom of Naples in XV–XX Centuries' (2018) 30 (5) Journal of International Development 911–914
Geva B, *The Payment Order of Antiquity and the Middle Ages: A legal history* (Hart Publishing 2011)
Goetzmann W, Geert R, *The origins of value: The financial innovations that created modern capital markets* (Oxford University Press 2005)
Grinblatt M, Longstaff F A, 'Financial innovation and the role of derivative securities: An empirical analysis of the Treasury STRIPS program' (2000) 55 Journal of Finance 1415–1436
Grosso G, *Lezioni di Storia del Diritto Romano* (Giappichelli 1965)

Henderson B, Pearson N, 'The dark side of financial innovation: A case study of the pricing of a retail financial product' (2011) 100 Journal of Financial Economics 227–247

Homer S, *A History of Interest Rates* (4th edn Wiley 2005)

Houston J, et al., 'Creditor rights, information sharing, and bank risk taking' (2010) 96 Journal of Financial Economics 485–512

Jacobi L, *The Architecture of banking in Renaissance Italy: Constructing the spaces of money* (Cambridge University Press 2019)

Johnston D, *Roman Law in Context* (CUP 1999)

Jolowicz H F, *Historical introduction to the study of Roman law* (CUP 1972)

Jones D, *The Templars: The Rise and Fall of God's holy Warriors* (Head of Zeus 2017)

Jowett B, *The Politics of Aristotle: Translated into English* (ed. Jowett B) (Oxford 1995)

Kaplan M, Kaplan E, *Chances are...: Adventures in Probability* (Penguin Books 2007)

Khoe D P, *Investment, Profit, and Tenancy: The Jurists and the Roman Agrarian Economy* (University of Michigan Press 1997)

Kindleberger C, *A Financial History of Western Europe* (George Allen & Unwin 1984)

Lane K, Potosi: *The Silver City that Changed the World* (University of California Press 2021)

Livius T, *The History of Rome* (trans. Rev. Canon Roberts, JM Dent and Sons 1912)

Markus K Brunnermeier, Lasse Heje Pedersen, 'Market liquidity and funding liquidity' (2009) 22 (6) The Review of Financial Studies, 2201–2238.

Menning C B, 'The Montes Monte: The early supports of Florence Monte di Pieta' (1992) 23 (4) Sixteenth Century Journal 661–676

Menning C B, *Charity and State in Late Renaissance Italy: The Monte di Pieta of Florence* (Cornell University Press 1993)

Merton R C, 'Financial Innovation and Economic Performance' (1992) 4 Journal of Applied Corporate Finance 12–22

Miner J, 'Profit and Patrimony: Property, markets, and public debt in late Medieval Genoa' (2020) 94 (1) History Review 73–94

Mosselaar J S, *A Concise Financial History of Europe* (Robeco 2018)

Mosselaar J S, 'Low volatility in historical prospective: Fund investing since 1774' (21 September 2016) Pure Play Asset Management—Robeco.com, Robeco

Mousourakis G, *A legal History of Rome* (Routledge 2007)

Muller R, *Money and Banking in Medieval and Renaissance Venice: II: The Venetian Money Market, Banks, Panics, and the Public Debt*, 1200–1500 (Baltimore 1997)

Munro J H, 'The Medieval origins of the financial revolution: Usury, rentes, and negotiability' (2003) 25 (3) The International History Review 505–562

Neal Larry, *A Concise History of International Finance: From Babylon to Bernanke* (Cambridge University Press 2015)

Neiderhoffer, V, *The Education of a Speculator* (Wiley 1997)

Orlian M, *Laws of Interest* (Business Halacha Institute 17 June 2011)

Persky J, 'Retrospectives: From usury to interest' (2007) 21 (1) Journal of Economic Prospectives 227–236

Petronious G, *Satyricon* (trans. Peter G Walsh, OUP 1997)

Plautus T M, *Curculio, or The Forgery* (Henry Thomas Riley Edition 1912)

Polybius, *Rise of the Roman Empire* (trans. Ian Scott-Kilvert 1979)

Ross S, 'Options and efficiency' (1976) Quarterly Journal of Economics 1, 431–449

Temin P, 'Financial Intermediation in the Early Roman Empire' (2004) 64 (3) The Journal of Economic History 705–733

CHAPTER 3

The Speculator and Financial Innovations: A New Portrait

3.1 Introduction

This chapter provides further historical evidence of the importance of financial innovations, and how financial innovations shaped the modern world. It is undeniable that the company is one of the catalysts of economic progress through the concept of limited liability and mutual assistance. In fact, historically guilds in Europe started to spread as associations of craftsmen and merchants formed to promote the economic interests of their members as well as to provide protection and mutual aid. These were a primordial form of associationism that will be further expanded into more sophisticated forms of associations such as the Dutch East India Company or *Verenigde Oostindische Compagnie* (abbreviated as VOC). This is mentioned as a primordial example of public company with the incorporation of the principle of limited liability to further foster the promotion of business ventures. By that time, the Amsterdam Stock Exchange was also set up as a key financial innovation in order to allow shareholders to trade their shares in a secondary market, and Mr. Adriaan van Ketwich was setting up in Amsterdam the first mutual fund. Specifically, this chapter is dedicated to analyse the evolution of stock exchanges or market venues. In Chapter 2, I have already illustrated the role played by moneylenders in Europe, who filled an important gap left by the larger banks. Moneylenders traded debts with each other; a lender looking to

D. D'Alvia, *The Speculator of Financial Markets*, Palgrave Macmillan Studies in Banking and Financial Institutions,
https://doi.org/10.1007/978-3-031-47901-4_3

unload a high-risk, high-interest loan could exchange it for a different loan with another lender. These lenders also bought government debt issues. As the natural evolution of their business continued, the lenders began to sell debt issues to individual investors. Venetians were the leaders in the field and the first to start trading securities from other governments as well as to issue new debt instruments to consolidate the government debt (i.e. *prestiti*). Equivalent debt instruments in Genoa were referred to as *luoghi*. The natural evolution of trading shares and bonds was the opening of physical places to allow negotiations to happen or exchanges.

The first exchange in London was officially formed in 1801 following the opening of coffeehouses in the 1700s in Exchange Alley close to what today is Bank Tube Station. In 1792, on the other side of the Atlantic, two dozen stockbrokers signed in New York a famous pact agreeing to trade directly with each other, bypassing any middlemen, under a Buttonwood tree on Wall Street. This agreement known as the Buttonwood Agreement is thought of as setting the foundation for what would become the New York Stock Exchange (NYSE). The NYSE was not the first stock exchange in the United States, however. Philadelphia Stock Exchange located in Pennsylvania was the first to be set up two years before in 1790, originally known as the Board of Brokers, but NYSE quickly became the most powerful on Wall Street. Always in New York, the American Stock Exchange got its start in the 1800s and was known as the 'Curb Exchange' until 1921 because it met as a market at the curb-stone on Broad Street near Exchange Place. This was an informal market venue where strict rules were not applicable and such informality could also provide for anonymity as well as discretion in determining prices and securities' values offering room for speculation as well as for active companies' growth. It was not until 1953 that such market venue officially became known as the American Stock Exchange. However, the popularity of the NYSE was always greater. Its location was key because it was in the heart of all the business and trade coming to and going from the United States, as well as the domestic base for most banks and large corporations: Wall Street. By setting listing requirements and demanding fees, the New York Stock Exchange became a very wealthy institution. The NYSE faced very little serious competition for the next two centuries. Its international prestige rose in tandem with the burgeoning American economy, and it was soon the most important stock exchange in the world. On the international scene, London emerged as the major exchange for Europe, but many companies that were listed internationally were also listed in New

York. Many other countries including Germany, France, the Netherlands, Switzerland, South Africa, Hong Kong, Japan, Australia, and Canada developed their own stock exchanges, but these were largely seen as proving grounds for domestic companies to inhabit until they were ready to make the leap to the London Stock Exchange and from there to the big leagues of the NYSE. This trend is still seen today with the important financial innovation of Special Purpose Acquisition Companies or SPACs that between 2020 and 2023 took New York exchanges by storm. Specifically, I will examine SPACs in the last section of this chapter as an alternative acquisition model and possibly as a new possible alternative to traditional initial public offerings. The chapter further examines the financial history of the United States both during the American Civil War with the issuance of Cotton Bonds as well as the emergence of Alfred Winslow Jones, the man who firstly set up the hedge fund structure as a new way for profit.

3.2 Guilds and Chartered Corporations

In Chapter 2, Sect. 2.2, I have said that under emperors, the political landscape in Ancient Rome shifted, and the *publicani* as a form of partnership were suppressed. Chartered corporations emerged as a new corporate form especially during the fourteenth and fifteenth centuries in Europe. Guilds were chartered primarily to enforce a monopoly in certain businesses or geographic regions. In exchange for a grant of monopoly, a guild would make ongoing fee payments to its chartering authority. In fact, the word guild derives from the Saxon word 'gildan' which means 'to pay' since members paid for belonging to the fraternity. Guilds were craft or trade societies, and did not favour the free association of capital, instead channelling it up the hierarchy of masters. The apprentice system developed craftsmen, who traded on their own accounts. Craft guilds were made up of craftsmen and artisans in the same occupation, such as hatters, carpenters, bakers, blacksmiths, etc. Each industry would have its own guild of artisans and craftsmen. Many craft guilds came about because growing population in cities and towns led to increases in specialisation and division of labour (Richardson 2010). This increased worker productivity by the creation of human capital. However, guilds also created indirect barriers to entry by not allowing non-guild members to work in the occupation. This is because guilds often had a great deal of influence over local governments. Guild leaders or Master Craftsmen frequently served as local government officials. This enabled guilds to have legislation passed in their favour. Guilds were also heavily involved in helping their members, improving their community and philanthropy. In fact, today in London there are more than one-hundred liveries[1] (the equivalent of ancient guilds) and though trading conditions changed, since their inception, their work is as pertinent as it always has been. They share the same ethos: to support trade, education, charity, and fellowship, working in the best interests of the communities in which they operate. The charitable dimension of their work is substantial. Charity and relief were and are key principles of livery companies. For instance, each livery company and guild will have a charitable trust or trusts, with each trust governed by its own trust deed, which sets out how funds may be used. Charitable giving by the livery is in excess of sixty-seven million pounds (GBP) a year, in addition to which significant sums are also expended by organisations such as the City Bridge Trust, the City of London's principal charitable foundation. A relatively small number of livery companies give a significant proportion of the sixty-seven million pounds (GBP), having built up their charitable trust funds with endowments and bequests over several centuries. Much of their giving is however already designated for fulfilling their historic objectives, such as the advancement of education or the provision of alms houses. Donations by many of the modern companies, formed from 1926 onwards, are on the whole more modest. In the past guilds helped member families in need, and performed functions such as paying for burials and dowries for poorer families. Even when the Black Death caused the population of Europe to plummet during the fourteenth century, guilds became extended families for plague survivors.

Conventionally and historically a Master Craftsman would have apprentices, who would learn the secrets of their trade. The apprentices would be in early adolescence, about fourteen years of age, and would complete an apprenticeship of between five and nine years. They received no pay but were given food and lodgings. In fact, some families paid the Master Craftsman for their son to serve an apprenticeship with them. Maintaining a good reputation as a man as well as a Master Craftsman meant there was work. Living with the Master Craftsman, the apprentice was taught to respect the Master's wife, his daughter, and his maid. He would be dressed appropriately at the meal table and be prompt. He would treat all the Master's clients courteously for that would bring in the work. If he did not keep to this professional and personal standard he was sent back to his own family, unqualified. After completing their apprenticeship the qualified craftsman would then become a journeyman, travelling from job to job, Master to Master, following the work and honing his skills. To become a Master himself a journeyman had to produce a 'masterpiece' which would be judged by established Masters in the guild. If successful he could then open up a workshop of his own with his own apprentices working to the high standard set by the guild not only in the work produced but also as a citizen, ensuring that they did not bring the guild into disrepute. The guilds held their own professional courts to investigate complaints in order to maintain their high standing in the community. Some also claim that it is at the time of guilds or in London named livery companies that Freemasonry has been alleged to originate. This is just one possible interpretation or theory that does not have a direct evidence apart from possible similarities between the current structure of Blue Lodge Degrees in Freemasonry and the stages of development of the apprentice under the supervision of a Master Craftsman, as I have illustrated. Specifically, the peak period for the formation of guilds and livery companies in England was the fourteenth century when many received charters or ordinances. At that time Europe was going through religious turmoil. It was a time of pilgrimages and the Crusades of the Middle Ages (see Chapter 2). The English monarchs from Henry VIII to William III were changing between Catholicism and Protestantism. A period known as the Reformation which began in 1517 and culminated in the Act of Settlement in 1701, stating that the Monarch had to be a Protestant. England during this period was very religious to the point that employers, members of the guilds, insisted their employees attended church. The reputation of the guilds became such that honourable and established Freemen of the town or city wanted to be associated with them and so these honourable men were accepted as social or 'speculative' members, hence the phrase 'Free and Accepted or Speculative'.

This brief *excursus* on guilds is showing that corporations started to exist to mainly serve a public purpose, and to achieve such objective they were granted certain privileges. The government or state would charter corporations that it deemed worthy. The building of highways, canals, and railroads was a public need as well as charity and relief among members of the society, and numerous corporations were chartered for these purposes. Nonetheless, such a process could be marked by political intrigue and arbitrary decisions about which business the government selected to favour. The subsequent solution to such an issue was to allow the incorporation by registration of companies. However, such evolution had to wait some centuries until the English Industrial Revolution in the 1830s and 1840s.

Chartered companies were provided with some monopoly—for instance—over trade with some region or an exclusive right to build a certain canal. However, over time, transferability of shares and limited liability became more important. For instance, in England, regulated companies could sponsor voyages which were the company's own ventures, participants enjoyed limited liability. Regulated companies that sponsored equity-finance voyages came to be called joint-stock companies. In the seventeenth century the Dutch financial market was more developed than the English, and the English borrowed institutions and practices from it at the end of the century. Two early joint-stock companies were Holland's and England's respective East India Companies, which were chartered to challenge Portugal's dominance of the spice islands. Initially, neither company had fixed capital. Each voyage would have its own equity subscription. This proved impractical, and soon capital from one voyage was rolled over to finance subsequent voyages. In light of this, companies evolved to become much like today's business corporation. The separation of investors and management became one of the great strengths, and at the same time great weaknesses of limited liability joint-stock companies. The joint-stock companies cultivated influence at the highest levels of government. The Queen and nobility had significant investments in the English East India Company, and they looked out for the company's interests in the halls of government. Alike guilds in the Middle Ages, the new joint-stock companies continued the practice of making ongoing payments to the government, and they multiplied and grew during the seventeenth century. The financial bubble and collapse in 1720 led to restrictions on these companies, and they did not grow much if at all in the eighteenth century. However, it is important to highlight that joint-stock companies pooled resources and facilitated equity investments by informed participants. In other words, they played a part in credit intermediation. Their shares could be used as collateral for bank loans. This began in the Netherlands in the early seventeenth century, using shares from the Dutch East India Company and spread to England. By the time of the South Sea Bubble in 1720 (see Chapter 5), it was common for borrowers to pledge stocks as securities for bank loans. After the English government straightened out its finances and introduced consols, government bonds became good collateral, but the practice of using shares to secure credit intermediation began with shares of private joint-stock companies.

3.3 Securities Markets, the VOC, and the First Mutual Fund

From 1568 to 1648, the Dutch fought the Eighty Years War to cast off their Spanish rulers. The main causes of the war were Philip II's political and religious policies in the Spanish Low Countries (the Netherlands), particularly high taxation and persecution of Protestants. Eventually the Eighty Years' War broke Spain's power in the Low Countries, and divided the region into what became the Netherlands in the north and the countries of Belgium and Luxembourg in the south. This launched a period that has come to be known as the Dutch Golden Age.

The formation of the Dutch East India Company was greatly influenced by activities in other European shipping and financial centres. In England, there were several trading companies chartered by King Henry VIII and Queen Elizabeth I in the sixteenth century. There was, for example, the 'Spanish Company'—established in 1530—which had a monopoly on English trade with Spain and Portugal. The 'Eastland Company' was formed in 1579 for trading with the Baltic and Scandinavia, and the list goes on. Among them the most famous of these firms was the British East India Company, which was set up in 1600. These companies were established as monopolies in order to empower them over suppliers in the lands they traded in.

The Dutch were not keen on being left behind. They founded on 20 March 1602, the Dutch East India Company (the 'Company' or *Verenigde Oostindische Compagnie* abbreviated as VOC) that became a symbol of the economic independence of the Dutch Republic. At that time the Netherlands became the world's foremost maritime and economic power with the establishment of largely peaceful relations with its Catholic neighbours. The construction of a massive fleet of trading ships and burgeoning trade with the East and the Baltic states gave rise to a very wealthy aristocracy and merchant class. With the flood of Protestant immigrants from Belgium and France occurring through the seventeenth century, the small port city of Amsterdam grew into one of Europe's most important commercial centres. The Netherlands flourished like no other nation in Europe with developments in technology and science combined with the rise of religious tolerance and a new middle class. A major expression of the age's prosperity and social outlook is apparent in the visual arts. With the development of oil painting, Rembrandt van Rijn became the master of the medium. With wealthy patrons replacing the patronage of the Church, such artists as Rembrandt, the Delft master Johannes Vermeer, Frans Hals, and the landscape painter Jacob van Ruisdael enjoyed both wealth and celebrity. New trade guilds, along with middle-class households, could now afford the often self-aggrandizing adornments on their walls. Works such as the 'Girl with the Pearl Earring' would take the observer to realms of exploration.

The Dutch sailed all over the world, but even more: they formed the first stock exchange by carrying out the first initial public offering in the world (Ferguson 2019). Indeed, the Dutch East India Company was a chartered corporation sponsored by the States General of the Dutch Republic. It was formed as a joint-stock company with shares that were readily tradable. Unlike other countries' trading companies, the Company was formed from the combination of six existing trading companies. In fact, rather than having many companies competing with each other, the Dutch East India Company was given a twenty-one-year monopoly on trade with the East Indies.

According to the Charter of the Company any citizen of the Netherlands could buy shares in the Company without a minimum investing amount. This was a remarkable innovation because each semi-autonomous province in the Netherlands was responsible for raising capital for the Company. Each region had a certain proportion of the Company's capital and it was responsible for its raising. For instance, Amsterdam was assigned the largest share, at half the capital. Zeeland, in the southwest of the country, was tasked with raising a quarter, and so on. The offering period ran from April through August 1602. During these five months, investors could subscribe the shares in any of six different cities. In all, the Company raised almost six-point-five million guilders in the offering. In the case of the Dutch East India Company, the capital raised in the IPO was to be paid in four instalments with the final one not due until 1606. Operating capital was also provided by virtue of debt, and the first fleet did not set sail until December 1603. The shares sold began trading on the secondary market before the firm had even commenced any meaningful operations.

As it can be seen, the Dutch East India Company had some peculiar features uncommon in other trading companies. Firstly, shares were redeemable, but only after ten years had elapsed from when the firm was founded. This optionality was stipulated in the charter. As a result, unlike the six independent trading companies in the Netherlands, the Dutch East India Company did not liquidate after each voyage but had a fixed capital. This means that investors who would prefer to liquidate their holdings could not just wait until the end of the next voyage. This helped the creation of a secondary market for the shares. However, shareholders were rewarded well for their investment. The Company paid an average dividend of over sixteen percent per year from 1602 to 1650.

The creation of a secondary market for shares of the VOC coincided with the creation of the Amsterdam Stock Exchange, arguably the oldest in the world. The process of trading shares was still cumbersome. In fact, buyers and sellers had to go to the Company's headquarters and have the transaction approved by two directors, who reflected the change in ownership in the Company's books. The shares were not bearer securities, but had a central record of ownership held by the firm. However, the actual trading did not occur in the Company's headquarters but near the *Nieuwe Brug*, a bridge which crossed the *Damrak*, a canal in central Amsterdam where commodities traders were already doing business at the *Hendrick de Keyser* Exchange, after the building's architect. Indeed, this was first of all a commodities exchange, where merchants in beer, salt, grain, timber, and many other goods came to do their business. However, since 1611, when the building opened, right at the back was the place where shares were bought and sold and share transactions were negotiated.

This building no longer exists. After two centuries of subsidence problems, Amsterdam decided to tear it down in the nineteenth century. The *Hendrick de Keyser* had a large open courtyard, just like the exchange buildings of Antwerp, London, and Rotterdam, which all predated the Amsterdam exchange. As I said, since 1611 share trading was done at the *Hendrick de Keyser* building. No one—the VOC or anyone else—had designated this place for the share trade. It was just that Amsterdam merchants owned much of the capital in the Amsterdam chamber, and they were not deterred by the idea of trading shares. After all, they were doing deals on commodities and bills of exchange day in and day out. They were used to negotiating to strike a deal. Their presence on the bridge and in the chapel attracted others who wanted to trade VOC shares: the chances of finding a buyer or seller of shares were simply greatest in these locations. Share trade was running over the clock. Indeed, when the *Hendrick de Keyser* Exchange closed, speculators moved to Dam Square. In the late afternoon, they returned to the exchange building, and then gathered at night in coffeehouses and inns in *Kalverstraat*. The VOC did not interfere at all with the exchange building and its rules and regulations, nor with the trade in VOC shares. It did not found the stock exchange. It held an IPO in 1602 because it needed capital and laid down the procedure for transferring ownership of a share. The company laid the foundations for the stock exchange, but it was the shareholders, the speculators who really developed the market. And for their trade, they used open spaces in the city, cafes, and inns, and an exchange building that was mainly used for commodities trade. A secondary market of shares was quite unprecedented at that time. For example, shares in the British East India Company, founded two years earlier, were not transferable. The liquidity afforded by stock exchanges enabled companies to more easily raise equity capital and lock up that capital for longer: a crucial feature for contemporary companies.

Financial innovation in Amsterdam took many other forms. For example, Amsterdam was also home to a large bond market as foreign nations continued to float their sovereign bond offerings, and in 1774, a merchant and broker Adriaan van Ketwich took advantage of this situation by creating an investment fund with pre-identified investment objectives. His creation outlined in the research of William N Goetzmann and Geert Rouwenhorst from Yale University is reputed to be the world's first mutual fund. The fund was called '*Eendraft Maakt Magt*' which translated from Dutch means 'unity makes strength' and its prospectus, or '*Negotiatie*' survives to this day.

Van Ketwich was the owner of one of the many brokerage offices in Amsterdam. His clients suffered massive losses due to investments in the English East India Company. The entrepreneur Van Ketwich thought of an idea which was way ahead of its time. He created a diversified fund of bonds that would reduce the investment risk for small investors. Investment strategies, portfolio creation—especially conservative portfolios—is not a modern invention if one reads the investment strategy outlined in '*Negotiatie*'. According to this document, the fund was fairly limited in its scope, was intended to have a fixed life, and was to pay out its returns to investors rather than reinvesting them, suggesting that its investors anticipated a fairly passive approach with little trading. This may have been in vogue following the financial disasters of the previous few years brought on by excessive speculation.

Specifically, the fund would consist of several share classes and would invest in ten different categories of securities, fifty in total, which were all listed in the prospectus. The categories included government bonds from Russia, Sweden, and Denmark, as well as bonds securitising Danish and Spanish toll revenues, but the fund focused mainly on Caribbean plantation loans, the predecessors of mortgage-backed securities. Dutch government bonds were not included, as their perceived low risk was felt not to require diversification. Equity investments were deemed to be too risky and were excluded from the investment universe. The fund was thus essentially an international bond fund because foreign bonds paid higher yields than could be found in 'safer' countries like Britain or the Netherlands. The investments were equally weighted to ensure the benefits of diversification (see Chapter 2). Despite the higher yielding investments, the fund—as I said—targeted a rather conservative return of four percent annually to be paid out in dividends to its investors rather than reinvested, and it would be terminated after twenty-five years. This was the most novel feature of the mutual fund, namely how it passed on returns to investors.

While the fund paid a four percent dividend, the securities it owned paid out more than that, generally between four percent and six percent. This 'excess spread' was used rather creatively. The prospectus laid out how any return over four percent would be used to redeem the fund's shares at a twenty percent premium. The shares to be redeemed were chosen by lottery. For example, if the one million guilder portfolio earned five-point-two percent one year, forty-thousands guilders would be used to pay the four percent dividend while the remaining twelve-thousands guilders in returns would be used to redeem twenty randomly selected shares at six-hundred guilders a piece. Randomly selecting shares for redemption at a premium seems to introduce an element of luck into investors' performance. However, this likely served a purpose besides merely satisfying a gambling urge (see Chapter 4). As closed-end fund, an investor looking to exit his investment needed to find someone willing to buy his shares. However, by steadily redeeming shares, the fund was able to provide some liquidity to its investors and also served to limit the life of the fund. Further, redeeming shares using income generated from the fund's investments meant that dividends to the remaining investors could be increased. Dividends that would have gone to redeemed shares were redirected to remaining investors, but not equally. Rather, dividends were assigned to the adjacent shares by number. As such, if share

n. 50 was redeemed, its four percent dividend would be redirected to shares n. 49 and n. 51. This feature seems to have needlessly complicated the fund's functioning. However, incorporating seemingly gambling-like features like this into securities was quite common in the eighteenth century.

As with all mutual fund tough, investors had to pay up for the benefits provided by the fund's managers. However, it is interesting to note just how modest the management fees were on this antiquated, yet innovative, investment fund. Van Ketwich collected a fee of one-hundred guilders from each share class for managing the fund. Since each share class consisted of a hundred shares of five-hundred guilders a piece, the fee amounted to a zero-point-twenty percent a year. This is hardly out of line with the less expensive mutual funds available nowadays. Regardless though, it provided Van Ketwich with an income of two-thousands guilders annually for his services as a fund manager. This was still a hefty income in mid-to-late eighteenth-century Holland.

Van Ketwich launched also more funds such as the *Voordelig en Voorsigtig* (namely, 'profitable and prudent') and *Concordia Res Parvae Crescunt* (namely, 'where there is harmony, small things will grow'). Unfortunately due to wars with England and France at the end of the eighteenth century, the Dutch economy suffered badly and London took over from Amsterdam to become the global financial centre. The funds did not do well but one of the funds continued for another one-hundred years before it was liquidated—a record longest running mutual fund that it still holds. While the funds may have failed to achieve the investment objectives for the investors, the fact that Van Ketwich could think of a diversified investment two-hundred-and-fifty years back is unbelievable but true. The philosophy behind '*Negotiatie*' spread and became popular across Europe and later evolved into an investment trust, eventually giving birth to closed-ended funds.

3.4 Modern Finance in London, and the Rise of the Exchange Alley

The same year in which de la Vega published his 'Confusion of Confusions' that I mentioned in Chapter 1 of this book, financial techniques and talent started to be spread from Amsterdam to London through the 'Glorious Revolution', in which Dutch-born William of Orange ascended to England's throne. William sought to modernise England's finances. The kingdom's first government bonds were issued in 1693, and the Bank of England was set up the following year. Soon thereafter, English joint-stock companies began going public, and its first informal stock exchange was formed, Exchange Alley.

It was the seventeenth century that saw the emergence of modern finance, and banking in particular. Long before New York became the financial capital of North America, let alone the world, London already had the institutions befitting a city of finance and commerce. The Royal Exchange had been founded by a merchant and an advisor to the monarch, Sir Thomas Gresham—one of the most powerful men in Tudor finance—in 1571. Lloyd's insurance market would be founded in a coffeehouse a century later.

In the early 1700s, on the eve of the infamous South Sea Bubble (see Chapter 5), London also had an active stock market. It was one that operated without a grand venue to house trading under one roof. Stock-jobbers, as they were called, traded shares in several joint-stock companies in a handful of London alleyways and coffeehouses. These companies included such well-known shipping and trade firms as the South Sea Company itself and the East India Company but also banks and insurance companies.

The trading took place outside the Royal Exchange, in which commodities were traded. Stockjobbers, who acted as dealers for stocks, were judged to be too rude for the Royal Exchange. They did not stray far. For over a century, the alleyways just outside the Royal Exchange acted as London's first stock exchange.

Exchange Alley or known at the time as 'Change Alley', used to house manufacturers and sellers of equipment used by the shipping industry. By the late seventeenth century it was home to a number of coffeehouses where stock prices were posted and traders bought and sold their shares. Two of the more famous were Jonathan's Coffee-House and Garraway's Coffee-House. In a puritanical period, coffeehouses proliferated as an alternative to alehouses and taverns. The coffeehouses of Exchange Alley were where London's stockbrokers and dealers did business.

Exchange Alley connected Cornhill and Lombard Street. It was close to the Bank of England on Threadneedle Street and the Royal Exchange between Threadneedle and Cornhill. These three major roadways radiated out, as they still do, from just outside the Lord Mayor's residence where the London Underground's Bank Station sits today.

Perhaps the most important local establishment was the post office on Lombard Street. The General Post Office that some of the coffeehouses on Exchange Alley even offered a private courier service to their share-trading patrons. The reason for this was how essential the post office was to the flow of information. When news outside London came into the city, it often came through the General Post Office first. Early access to information is priceless to traders or better speculators. In light of this, the post office became, like the Bank of England and the Royal Exchange, another crucial institution in London's financial heart. The rise of London as a financial centre in this period may even owe a small amount of credit to the decision by King Charles I to allow the public to use the Royal Mail, which before 1635 was used as the monarch's private postal service. Given the proximity to the principal post office in central London, the use of Exchange Alley as an unofficial stock exchange seems logical. Imagine you were a trader or speculator in 1720 and you were looking to invest and profit on news of a shipwreck affecting an East India Company vessel. The news would first come through the post office; if you were trading at the Royal Exchange, the news would take longer to get to you than if you were standing on Exchange Alley. The location was ideal.

Earlier, I made reference to the stockjobbers. They were not simply stockbrokers. They were dealers who held securities in inventory and supplied them to brokers. They also acted as market makers, providing liquidity by taking up the other side of trades for those looking to transact. Until 1986, the job of the stockbroker and the stockjobber (as a market-maker and dealer) had always been kept separate in Britain. The idea was that a broker should not be able to sell a stock to a client in which they themselves had a position. To do so would be in conflict of interest. As a result, stockbrokers sold to clients by buying from stockjobbers who held the inventory.

Specifically, stockjobbers derived their name from 'jobbing' referred to frequent changes in employment. So as an itinerant worker who changed employers often might be called a 'jobber', so would a trader frequently adjusting the employment of his capital instead of his labour. The stockjobbers were trading both in shares of private companies, and more importantly, in the bonds issued by the British state, the Bank of England, the South Sea Company and the East India Company, the largest borrowers in London's markets. In the early 1700s, once the famous South Sea Bubble burst (see Chapter 5), stockjobbers were making large sums of money and achieving nearly unreachable social status for commoners.

The stockjobbers had their own share of dubious practices and public dislike. One *exposes* written about the stockjobbers was 'Every Man his Own Broker' by Thomas Mortimer, the first published in 1761. Written for those investors looking to protect themselves from the unscrupulous speculation of the stockjobbers:

> (...) the iniquitous art of the stock-jobbing has sprung, like a great many other abuses, out of the best of blessings, Liberty (...) (Mortimer 1761)

As it can be seen, Mortimer refers to stock-jobbing as an 'iniquitous art' for the various abuses that could inflict on public investors, namely retail investors of public society. Mortimer refers also to an older warning in 1713, an anthology of essays published in London titled 'The Young Man's Counsellor' that warned of the evils of stockjobbers in a section on the 'deceits used in particular trades and professions'. The eighteenth-century dealers and speculators were thought by many to belong to a deceitful profession. They were listed alongside quack doctors and astrologers.

Both Mortimer and Lefevre in their book 'Reminiscences of a Stock Operator' detail how company insiders spread 'a flood of bull rumours' about a firm called Tropical Trading in order to bring about a short squeeze, a situation where those having sold borrowed stock are forced to repurchase it a higher price to return it to their creditor. A short squeeze favours those who want the stock to go higher. Fake news was just a part of the trader's or better speculator's toolkit. Mortimer frequently points out the stockjobbers' proclivity for spreading false news:

> If a magistrate of a renowned city, whose government is in alliance or at peace with us, sends over a letter to his correspondent at London, in which he assures him, that on such a day, and at such a place, the French gained a considerable advantage over the allied army (...) those who want the stock to fall, take the utmost pains to propagate the intelligence, and to enlarge on the authority, credit, and veracity of the latter-writer. (Mortimer 1761)

It seems that in eighteenth-century London and turn-of-the-century New York, financial speculation was regarded as a form of refined gambling (see Chapter 4). Lefevre's book likened old 'bucket shops' to casinos and depicted the common speculator as little more than a gambler, placing bets based on hope with little to no sound logic behind predictions for the movement of stocks. Mortimer likewise explained the appeal of stock-jobbing as a quicker path to riches than trade or industry, like gambling but with higher stakes than any card game with fewer rules:

> The sucker has always tried to get something for nothing, and the appeal in all booms is always frankly to the gambling instinct aroused by cupidity and spurred by a pervasive prosperity. (Lefevre 1923)

It is worth noting that Lefevre compared stock-jobbing to gambling; the former was ever worse than the second. Indeed, in a game of cards some players can be more skilful but still no player has an advantage in information, whereas the markets were rife with insider trading. The foreign magistrate in the earlier quote from Mortimer not only spreads inside information about a military setback to his brokers but also goes on to trade for himself on the news.

I have earlier mentioned Jonathan's Coffee-House in Change Alley. Jonathan's burnt down in 1778 following the South Sea Company Bubble (see Chapter 5), and the stockjobbers clubbed together to build 'New Jonathan's' nearby in Sweeting's Alley. It was this building that was transformed into the Stock Exchange. The building had an entrance fee, and traders could enter the stock room and trade securities. However, this was not an exclusive location for trading, as the selling and buying of shares occurred in the Rotunda of the Bank of England too. Likewise the possibility of speculation and fraud did not end, and as a deterrent it was suggested that users of the stock room would pay an increased fee. This was not a popular decision, and therefore an annual fee was charged turning the Exchange into a subscription room. The subscription room was created in 1801, and this was the first regulated exchange in London, and a new venue was planned at Capel Court, next to the popular Mendoza's Boxing Room. William Hammond laid the first foundation stone for the new building on 18 May 1801. 'The Stock Exchange' was incised on the entrance.

Today a blue ceramic plaque still commemorates the Jonathan's Coffee House as the principal meeting place of stockbrokers between 1680 and 1778. As I have stated, it was Jonathan's that eventually became the London Stock Exchange, and still the members' bar in the London Stock

Exchange is called Jonathan's, whose current premises are situated in Paternoster Square close to St. Paul's Cathedral in the City of London.

Such historical accounts of the operations of the financial markets in the days before financial regulation paint an unflattering portrait. This is a testament to how much markets have cleansed themselves in the past hundred years.

3.5 From the Tontine Coffee-House to the New York Stock Exchange

Those who know a bit about New York's financial past have almost certainly heard of the Buttonwood Agreement. In 1792, two dozen stockbrokers signed a famous pact agreeing to trade directly with each other, bypassing any middlemen, under a Buttonwood tree on Wall Street. This agreement is thought of as setting the foundation for what would become the New York Stock Exchange. Connecting this agreement signed in 1792 to today's stock exchange on the corner of Wall and Broad is a story involving an antique insurance product and a coffee shop by the same name.

Needing a place to do business outside the rain, Wall Street's earliest brokers settled on a coffee shop. No existing one would suffice, and a new one, called the Tontine Coffee-House would be created for the purpose of being New York's first post-Buttonwood exchange. The start-up capital for the place was provided for by an archaic annuity-like scheme called a tontine.[2]

The tontine that financed the construction of the coffeehouse in New York had a total of 203 shares sold. Each was two-hundred dollars (USD) in value proving a start-up capital of over forty-thousand dollars (USD). This is over one million dollars (USD) in today's money. Once built in 1793–1794, the Tontine Coffee-House was no ordinary coffee shop. It became a hub for traders in the fast-growing city around it. It may have been no Royal Exchange but in time it would evolve into one of the most influential exchanges in the World. The Tontine Coffee-House stood on the corner of Wall Street and Water Street. Paintings and engravings of the three-story building show it on the northwest corner of the intersection, where 82 Wall Street stands today just one block past the former Deutsche Bank's New York offices at 60 Wall Street (today relocated in One Columbus Circle). A 1797 painting by Francis Guy with the coffee shop located on the far left, shows the masts of ships close by. Water street really was by the water; landfills have since expanded the profile of Manhattan by one block in that direction.

Today the coffeehouse is no more there. In 1817, trading moved up the street when the New York Stock & Exchange Board was formed and rented space at 40 Wall Street. The old Tontine Coffee-House would go on to become a tavern, a hotel, and then a newspaper publishing office before being demolished in the middle of the century. The New York Stock Exchange, as it was renamed in the 1860s moved once more in 1865, and then again to its present location in 1903. The tontine was wound down in 1870 when the number of beneficiaries was reduced to seven, all of whom were children when the tontine was set up over 75 years earlier. By comparison, the NASDAQ is a youngster, having been established in 1971.

It is important to highlight that the Tontine Coffee-House was a 'members only' association and third parties were precluded to engage in trading. For this reason, many non-member brokers started to trade and speculate out in the sun along the curb of Wall Street.

In the mid-1800s, brokers would meet on the Broad Street sidewalk to trade shares, often those of most speculative companies, outside the institutionalised structure provided by formal stock exchanges. The so-called Curb market (the Curb) where anyone could show up and trade whatever shares were available, whether they were listed on other exchanges or not. This informal and outdoor arrangement was not unheard of. The oldest venue for trading shares in London was set in Exchange Alley, as I have already illustrated (Picture 3.1).

In New York, the shares traded on the curb market were those of most speculative companies, often dealing in booming and risky industries like oil and gas. It was the place where company shares could increase in value exponentially from ten cents to ten dollars in the course of a few weeks or even days. Orders were communicated by yelling or signalling out a window, and anyone with lungs could trade. Financial journalist Edwin C. Hill claimed in 1920 'some of those whirling dervishes down the street could borrow a million on their moral credit; for others the jail beckons'. The New York Curb Market evaded regulation and served as unofficial market where New York Stock Exchange brokerages could participate in more speculative transactions. The Curb rejected the institutional trappings that signified an organised securities market because anyone could simply walk up to the market and trade with any other trader. The Curb was not just seen as unorganised, informal, and semi-illegitimate market.

Picture 3.1 Wall Street Brokers (Sect. 3.5 From the Tontine Coffee-House to the New York Stock Exchange) Wall Street brokers gesturing to signal trades on the Curb Market in the mid-1920s. The Curb Market was for stocks not listed on the New York Stock Exchange (*Note* It is written this picture is of public domain https://upload.wikimedia.org/wikipedia/commons/5/54/Curb_market.jpg [WIKIPEDIA])

It kept itself that way to preserve its relationship with the NYSE. The NYSE used the Curb as an unofficial 'seasoning market', or place to test out new issuances. Although the relationship was never formalised, the Curb was widely accepted by the NYSE as a preliminary market for newly issued or speculative securities, and was what is now known as a small-cap market. Much of this was the work of Mendels Jr., who became known as the 'father of the curb'. The best stocks, including Coca Cola, General Motors, Shell, Standard Oil, Goldwin Pictures, and Philip Morris, started on the Curb and quickly moved to the NYSE. Indirectly by keeping risky securities to the Curb, the NYSE managed to preserve its reputation while still making a market for these more speculative stocks.

By the early 1900s, the New York Curb Market had become a heave for frauds, and Mendels sought to clean up the market by purging it of trading in fraudulent companies' shares. The time was ripe for some self-regulation as scrutiny of securities trading practices rose after the Panic of 1907. Perhaps the most significant step in the formalisation of the Curb was its relocation into a new building between Greenwich Street and Trinity Place in 1921. Moving indoors was probably the final step in formalising the market. Though renamed several times, the Curb was rebranded as the American Stock Exchange (AMEX) in 1953, the name it would go by until merging with the NYSE in 2008.

Trading shares—as always—was also entailing possible speculative practices. For instance, Professor Geisst in his book 'Wall Street: A History' (1998) reports a very interesting case of 'stock cornering' on the early years of the New York Stock Exchange. In the United States, one of the most important economic sectors with growing opportunities following the War of 1812 was transportation. Companies building roadways and canals were a possible source of profitable investments, but it was not until 1840 that the United States claimed 3,000 miles of rail, and more than twice the amount of track in Europe. The first steam locomotive produced in the United States made the transportation industry grow exponentially. Yet speculative finance and politics proved to have strong ties too. When the Harlem Railroad (one of the early railroads in New York, and the world's first street railway) was built by the New York and Harlem Railroad company (incorporated in 1831) and listed on the New York Stock Exchange, Senator Kimble opposed its expansion through additional stock issues. At that time, investors were used to buy railroad stocks because they represented the expansion of the country, and the last evolution in technology. Railway companies were the equivalent of today's high growth companies in the FinTech industry or electric vehicles' markets. Kimble acquired enough shares of the New York and Harlem Railroad company to be able to manipulate its price. He did not actually own the stock, but he was selling it short (see Chapter 5), expecting the price eventually to drop rather than raising. To be able to ensure a price drop, Kimble facilitated the passing of a law bill calling for the enlargement of the railroad, causing the stock to fall on the exchange and investors to have their shareholdings diluted. In fact, when the price fell, the short sales were covered and profits made. It was a speculation on the price of the stock and—at the same time—it was a form of controlling the supply of the stock available for trading (i.e. cornering).[3]

According to Professor Geisst, the same sort of speculation occurred in the 1830s when the stocks of the Second Bank of the United States were cornered, and although at that time stock prices were not regularly reported, the press published news articles on many high growth companies coming to market. Unfortunately it was not uncommon to receive 'fake news' or flattering articles, which soon became the preferable technique to manipulate stock prices. To this end, the publication of unflattering news on a particular stock could help speculators to corner shares cheaply as the price fell, and then to sell them later at a higher price.

Another type of deal that was in vogue during the early years of the New York Stock Exchange was the forward trading, namely deals to be done on a 'time-delivery' basis. The trader could buy stocks at prearranged prices and then have the delivery of the consideration in cash delayed for one or two months. Speculators were hoping to buy low and sell high, making an instant profit. However, such transactions were not formal and they were not legally binding, meaning that a trader could dishonour his part of the contract and avoid payment. However, because traders were businessmen and gentlemen, they were assumed to honour their contracts. Traders on the exchange were divided into two groups: bulls and bears. Bulls anticipated rising prices; bears were short sellers. For these reasons, volatility was a constant in the early years of Wall Street, but much more progress would have come soon especially through foreign investors.

3.6 American Civil War and Cotton Bonds

In the mid-nineteenth century, while the United States was experiencing an era of growth, a fundamental economic difference existed between the country's northern and southern regions. In the North, manufacturing and industry was well established, and agriculture was mostly limited to small-scale farms, while the South's economy was based on a system of large-scale farming that depended on the labour of black enslaved people to grow certain crops, especially cotton and tobacco.

Growing abolitionist sentiment in the North after the 1830s and the northern opposition to slavery's extension into the new Western territories led many southerners to fear that the existence of slavery in America—and thus the backbone of their economy—was in danger. In 1854, Senator Stephen Douglas of Illinois proposed a bill to organise the Territory of Nebraska, a vast area of land that would become Kansas,

Nebraska, Montana, and Dakotas. The US Congress passed the Kansas–Nebraska Act. The controversial bill raised the possibility that slavery could be extended into territories where it had once been banned. Its passage intensified the bitter debate over slavery in the United States, which would later explode in the Civil War. The discovery of gold in California in 1849, and California's subsequent request to become a state, sparked a fierce battle in Congress. As California had banned slavery, its admission to the Union would upset the fragile balance between slave and free states. By the end of 1850, Senator Henry Clay had persuaded the Congress to accept the Compromise of 1850.[4] By its terms, California entered the Union as a free state, while the territories of Utah, New Mexico, Nevada, and Arizona (all acquired in the Mexican–American War) were left to decide for themselves whether to permit slavery within their borders. Douglas hoped this idea of 'popular sovereignty' would resolve the mounting debate over the future of slavery in the United States and enable the country to expand westward with few obstacles. But the Compromise of 1850 galvanised the abolitionist movement and fuelled mounting debate over whether the institution of slavery should be allowed to expand along with the nation. Pro- and anti-slavery forces struggled violently in 'Bleeding Kansas',[5] while opposition to the act in the North led to the formation of the Republican Party, a new political entity based on the principle of opposing slavery's extension into the Western territories. After the Supreme Court's ruling in the Dred Scott case (1857) confirmed the legality of slavery in the territories, the abolitionist John Brown's raid at Harper's Ferry in 1859 convinced more and more southerners that their northern neighbours were bent on the destruction of the 'peculiar institution' that sustained them. Abraham Lincoln's election in November 1860 was the final straw, and within three months seven southern states—South Carolina, Mississippi, Florida, Alabama, Georgia, Louisiana, and Texas—had seceded from the United States. Even as Lincoln took office in March 1861, Confederate forces threatened the federal-held Fort Sumter in Charleston, South Carolina. On 12 April, Confederate artillery fired the first shots of the Civil War.

The American Civil War had a lasting effect on the American economy and on American finance. However, one of the most curious financial innovations of the war period was introduced in Europe: the cotton bond, also known as the Erlanger loan. It was a novel bond offering for a sovereign issuer, an issuance of bonds convertible into a commodity.

The fiscal condition of the secessionist Confederacy was never good. An aversion to high taxes deprived the breakaway state of much-needed revenue. However, even if taxes were kept at high rates, it hardly would have helped matters. Cotton, the commodity that drove the local economy, was stuck in the Southern interior and unable to be exported overseas amidst a blockade of its ports by the Union navy. Thus, the breakaway government in Richmond resorted to flooding the economy with locally issued bonds. One of these was raised in 1861 to the tune of fifteen million dollars (USD); and another the following year ran up one-hundred million dollars (USD) in debt. Alongside the liberal issuance of bonds was a persistent over-emission of currency. While new printing of paper money was a feature of wartime finance in both the North and the South, it was far more pronounced in the South. Regular issuance of Confederate dollars helped finance their armies. The money's steady devaluation and wartime shortages triggered inflation and a widening disparity between the value of the paper dollars and gold coins. In early 1863, on the eve of the Erlanger loan, it took five dollars (USD) in paper dollars to purchase one dollar (USD) by face value in gold coins. That premium would only grow far larger with time.

It was in these unconventional circumstances that a foreign loan was arranged for the Confederacy in 1863. The two men most immediately responsible for effectuating the loan were John Slidell, a former Louisiana Senator and then a Confederate diplomat in Paris, Frédéric Émile d'Erlanger. A year and half earlier, Slidell had been one of the diplomats at the centre of the Trent Affair,[6] when he was captured by the Union navy while aboard a British vessel, an act that tested British restraint and American reversal. Slidell was eventually released and made it to Europe in early 1862. At the time, d'Erlanger was a well-connected German banker who proposed floating a bond offering to Slidell while the latter was in Paris. As it happens, d'Erlanger went on to marry Slidell's daughter, Marguerite Mathilde Slidell, the following year. In the winter of 1862–1863, many in Europe believed the prospects for Confederate victory to be good. With the possibility of a successful offering high, Slidell and d'Erlanger secured Confederate authorisation for a three million pounds (GBP) million loan in January 1863. From there, it took little time to arrange the offering and a prospectus was published on March 19th. D'Erlanger's firm Emile Erlanger & Company was to manage the offering.

The bond offering for the belligerent nation was, as would be anticipated, hardly borrower-friendly. Investors were to be paid a seven percent coupon in pounds sterling and the Confederacy was to amortise the bond over its twenty-year term in forty equal semi-annual payments. Further, it was not to receive the net proceeds from issuance all at once but over the course of the year since investors' subscriptions were payable in instalments over seven months. However, these were the terms set out by Emilie Erlanger & Company for what was to be the Confederacy's only foreign loan. That said, European investors were already familiar with Confederate paper as some domestic bonds were also traded across the ocean in Europe.

Perhaps the most interesting feature of the bonds was not any of those terms already described, since they were standard for speculative bond issues in the nineteenth century, but rather the convertible aspect of the bonds. The Erlanger loan, as the issue was called, was redeemable in cotton within six months after the conclusion of the war at a rate of eight bales, each roughly five-hundred pounds (GBP), per one-hundred pounds (GBP) in face value of the notes. This equated to a conversion price of just six pence per pound of cotton, an extraordinary discount when prices in Liverpool, Britain's cotton textile centre, were as high as twenty-four pence at the time.

In terms of the American dollar this was twelve cents per pound of cotton. The novel feature allowed the South to monetise cotton stuck on its side of the Atlantic, cotton which could not be safely exported in large quantities amidst a Union blockade, but which could serve as collateral for a loan. In Europe, where prices for the commodity surged amidst the scarce supply, the feature added value to investors. This convertibility even caused the Erlanger loan to be known simply as the 'Cotton Loan' in Britain.

Emile Erlanger & Company stood to make a fortune from the cotton bonds' issuance. The bank purchased the issue at seventy-seven percent of face value and, along with its syndication partners, sold it at ninety percent to investors across Europe. The bond was syndicated in London, Liverpool, Paris, Amsterdam, and Frankfurt. The hefty spread was not the only source of the bank's profit on the offering for it also collected a five percent commission for each note sold and a further 1% for handling the sinking fund which required at two-point-five percent of the loan amount be set aside twice a year to gradually retire the debt. In all, Erlanger would make over five-hundred-thousand pounds (GBP) off the three million pounds (GBP) transaction. Erlanger itself was to syndicate the bonds destined for the markets in Paris and Frankfurt. Sales in London and Amsterdam were handled by the firm JH Schroder & Co. and in Liverpool were doled out by Fraser, Trenholm and Co. The former firm was the ancestor to today's asset management company Schroders while the latter bank, though based in Liverpool was run by George Trenholm, the Confederacy's future Secretary of the Treasury. Fraser, Trenholm and Co.'s inclusion may have been an act of reciprocity since it was George Trenholm who helped arrange John Slidell's troubled secret transport to Europe in 1861.

In the end, the offering was a success. The issuance was more than five times oversubscribed with orders of sixteen million pounds (GBP) against the three million pounds (GBP) size. Prices for the bonds traded a premium over the first few days on the secondary market. So popular was the cotton loan that even several British Members of Parliament were said to have invested, a potential conflict of interest as the decision to intervene on the side of the Confederacy was an open question in British foreign affairs. Remarkably, one alleged investor was none other than the future Prime Minister William Gladstone, then the Chancellor of the Exchequer under the government of Lord Palmerston.

Over the subsequent two years, prices for the bonds in Europe tracked the course of the war in America. Records of prices from the more developed sovereign debt markets in Europe, specifically that of London and Amsterdam, show the ups and downs of victory and defeat. Almost immediately, the bonds struggled. Prices fell below ninety percent of face value in their first month on the market but purchases by Confederate agents in Europe, like Erlanger, supported prices as did occasional military victories by the South. Nonetheless, the notes fell again below the offering price of ninety percent in May 1863. This came about despite frantic buying by the bonds' issuer. By mid-May, it is said that over half of the issued bonds had been repurchased by the Confederate government through its agents. It may seem strange that the rebellious republic would be so concerned with the prices for its debt in Europe, especially while the economic and military situation at home was so dire. Would not that money be better spent on weapons or economic necessities?

However, the structure of the cotton bonds' sale necessitated such a move. Recall that investor subscriptions were payable in instalments. In theory, if prices collapsed before the first couple of payments were made, investors may have been inclined to accept their losses and abandon the bonds. This would have deprived the Confederacy of the full proceeds. As a result, the price needed to be supported so that subscribers would not abandon the bonds and stop paying their instalments. Only once they had paid for much of the issuance could the Confederate government back away and let the market take its course. Thereafter, it could always resell the bonds it acquired, albeit likely at a loss.

This is exactly what occurred. The Confederacy set aside roughly one-point-five million pounds (GBP), half the issuance amount, to be used to repurchase bonds, and most of this was later resold at prices as low as forty percent of face value, recouping some money. The combined effect of Erlanger's fees and losses sustained in the repurchases of notes meant that in the end, perhaps as little as just over one-point-four million pounds (GBP), or six-point-eight million pounds (GBP), was raised from sales of the cotton bonds. Repurchases did support the price long enough to prevent abandonment though and the bonds' value was still hovering around the issuance price of ninety percent through the spring of 1863. From there, market prices fell with Southern defeats and rose with the occasional Southern victory or increased prospects for foreign intervention or an armistice. Prices plummeted in July following the twin Confederate defeats at Vicksburg and Gettysburg; they fell to around sixty-four pounds (GBP) per one-hundred pounds (GBP) of face value that summer. However, prices recovered all the way back to eighty-four percent of face value in 1864 on hopes for General McClellan's victory in the Presidential elections that year. That said, McClellan lost but not before another Southern defeat, the fall of Atlanta in September 1864, caused prices to plummet once again. Still, the bonds' prices in Europe held up better than the falling value of Confederate paper money in America. Whereas they started 1863 at a five-to-one rate against gold, the paper bills were now at fifteen-to-one against the equivalent face value of gold coins. In the face of unstable domestic coinage and limited access to hard-currency, the cotton-backed Erlanger bonds served as money the Confederacy could use in external trade. Confederate purchasing agents in Europe used the cotton bonds repurchased by the government as currency in trade, exchanging them for arms and ships produced in Britain. Some of these ships in Britain were put to use in blockade running and not long before its eventual defeat, the Confederate States had been planning a new fifteen million pounds (GBP) loan. However, with its credit damaged in Europe, the Confederacy could no longer monetise its cotton holdings at home by issuing cotton-backed bonds abroad. Instead to finance the war, the South increasingly came to rely on smuggling exports of cotton around the Union navy vessels patrolling off the shore of its port cities. With prospects for victory evaporating and new issuance of money abounding, the Confederate dollar had fallen to sixty-to-one against gold by early 1865. Even then, just a few months before the South's surrender, their cotton bonds were still trading hands at prices as high as fifty-seven percent of face value.

After the Confederate general Robert E. Lee surrendered to the Union Army's Ulysses S. Grant at Appomattox in April 1865, the end had come for the cotton bonds. Prices fell below ten pounds (GBP); though they continued to trade on hopes of a partial redemption. It was not to be. However, with respect to their foreign bonds at least, the Confederacy was a compliant borrower. Until their surrender they had made every principal and interest payment on the cotton bonds even though they had already defaulted on other domestic debt issues. Those payments were all bondholders would ever see from the cotton loan. Investors' bonds were never redeemed in money or cotton reserved for them in America, the latter of which was confiscated by the Union government after the war.

3.7 Art and the Second War World

There has always been interest in alternative investments for those willing to dabble in less liquid and professionalised asset classes. Among these alternative investments are collectables, from stamps to cars. It is art however, and paintings in particular, that got the most regular attention thanks to the price records broken so frequently at auction.

Though not seen as an asset class until the mid-to-late twentieth century, there has been a trade in art for perhaps as long as there has been art itself. Like in all markets, this trade was also correlated to broader economic trends. During the Renaissance, for example, art was frequently traded at markets and fairs, particularly cities with growing mercantile classes. It was in these increasingly prosperous urban centres that art found interested consumers in the largest numbers. Annual fairs gave way to fixed auction houses. Perhaps the first art auction house, the *Stockholms Auktionsverk*, opened in 1674 in Sweden. Sotheby's and Christie's were later established in Britain in the mid-1700s. A formal, if far from efficient, market in art has been around for centuries, even though art 'investing' had not yet existed.

That would change in the twentieth century but first, before art could be an investment, it had to be considered a store of value and not merely a consumption good. During the Gilded Age, America's *nouveaux riche* spent millions of dollars bringing fine art across the Atlantic from Europe. This was still 'art for consumption' but did help globalise the market for art. Because profitability and international recognition are valuable aspects of any asset, this was no doubt important.

Almost a century later, surging values of impressionist paintings thanks to demand from a new nouveaux riche class in Japan continued the globalisation of the art trade but by then the idea that art was investment was becoming more widely accepted. That said, there was a transitional phase between the 'art for consumption' of the Gilded Age and the 'art for investing' of today.

In the mid-twentieth century, artwork was finally put to the test as a store of value. During the Second World War, the characteristics of art were discovered to be of particular value when dangers lurked everywhere else for those seeking to preserve wealth. During its four-year-long occupation, France, in particular, saw its art market inflate as people sought new ways to protect their wealth.

For much of the nineteenth century, the art market in France cantered on large public institutions, namely the *Académie des Beaux-Arts* and the *Salon*. The *Académie* was where budding artists would train with the hope of being featured at the *Salon*, one of the world's premier art exhibitions. In that era, receiving valuable commissions and fame was contingent on recognition at the *Salon* and market values of art corresponded to that recognition. However, this system became less centralised and more informal in the late nineteenth century as artists increasingly sought to work outside of the *Salon* system and dealers found market niches being unserved, particularly in more avant-garde artistic movements. By the start of the twentieth century, at the tail of the *Belle Époque*, Paris had the most important art market by volume being traded. Data collected from the *Gazette de l'Hôtel Drouot*, the weekly publication of one of Paris' largest art auction houses reveals the performance of art prices during the first half of the twentieth century. It reveals that activity evaporated during the First World War, when many fled Paris which was just thirty kilometres from the Western front at its closest. That depression did not last long though, art market volume boomed immediately after the war ended, perhaps on pent up demand. Over two thousand paintings, drawings, and watercolours were sold in the first half of 1922 at the *Drouot* auction house alone. This brisk pace of sales slowed over the next two decades. Both volume and sales in art auctions fell in the 1930s during the economic slump. During this period, much like during the First World War, art galleries and auction houses closed up shop.

The industry's direction changed drastically when Germany invaded France in the spring of 1940. Transactions surged during the occupation of France. In 1942 and 1943, *Drouot* was once again seeing auctions in which a thousand pieces changed hands. In 1942, a single landscape painting by Paul Cézanne sold for five million francs. This did not turn out immediately to be the start of a long-run trend. Following the liberation of France, sales actually plummeted, at odds with the experience of the First World War. By both volume and value, artworks sold at *Drouot* fell back to pre-war levels by 1945. By contrast, the immediate post-war period a generation earlier saw surging demand. However, something about the Second World War was different. For one, during the earlier war, neither Paris nor the vast majority of France was occupied and that wartime experience did not involve the same degree of economic restriction, such as through capital controls and other wartime measures. Perhaps the disorders and fear of the occupation period revealed some useful characteristics of art as a store of value.

Before elaborating on that though, it is worth noting that the art market did not operate in the vacuum during the war. It was very much shaped by the ideological nature of the conflict. For example, just before the war started in 1939, art regarded as 'degenerate' by the Nazis had been sold abroad and was banned from reimport into Germany. Indeed, Nazi leaders sought to control Germany not only politically, but also culturally. The regime restricted the type of art that could be produced, displayed, and sold. In September 1933, the Nazis created the *Reich* Chamber of Culture. The Chamber oversaw the production of art, music, film, theatre, radio, and writing in Germany. The Nazis sought to shape and control every aspect of German society. They believed that art played a critical role in defining a society's values. Additionally, the Nazis believed art could influence a nation's development. Several top leaders became involved in official efforts on art. They sought to identify and attack 'dangerous' artworks as they struggled to define what 'truly German' art looked like. In 1937, Nazi Propaganda Minister Joseph Goebbels also made plans to show the public the forms of art that the regime deemed unacceptable. He organised the confiscation and exhibition of so-called 'degenerate' art. The Nazis linked modern art with democracy and pacifism. Reception to modern art in Germany had varied under past governments. When Kaiser Wilhelm II ruled (1888–1918), the country had a conservative social climate. Avant-garde art was not widely appreciated. After World War I, Germany was ruled by a democratic government known as the Weimar Republic (1918–1933). The country saw a more liberal cultural atmosphere. Styles of modern art like Expressionism were more warmly received. Nazi leaders asserted that *avant-garde* art reflected the supposed disorder, decadence, and pacifism of Germany's post-war democracy. They claimed that the ambiguity of modern art contained Jewish and Communist influences that could endanger public security and order. Modern art conspired in their view to weaken German society with 'cultural Bolshevism'. According to Nazi ideology, only criminal minds could be capable of creating such so-called 'harmful art' or 'degenerate'. The term suggests that the artists' mental, physical, and moral capabilities must be in decay. At the time, 'degenerate' was widely used to describe criminality, immorality, and physical and mental disabilities.

The regime attempted to clarify what 'truly German art' looked like in summer 1937. The first annual Great German Art Exhibition opened in Munich at that time. Hitler reviewed selected artworks the month before it opened. He furiously ordered the removal of many examples of German *avant-garde* art. Goebbels witnessed this outburst and began making hasty plans for a separate exhibition. He intended to define and mock the types of art that the regime considered 'degenerate'. Hitler approved the plan. The Nazis began confiscating thousands of artworks from German museums. The 'Degenerate Art' exhibition was thrown together in less than three weeks. Minor were not allowed inside because of the art's supposedly harmful and corruptive nature. The exhibition's organisers arranged more than six-hundred artworks in internationally unflattering ways. They crowded sculptures and graphic works together. Many works were even left unframed. Slogans painted on the walls mocked artworks as 'crazy at any price' and 'how sick minds viewed nature'. The walls also displayed quotes form Hitler and Goebbels. Their words provided the public with the official Nazi Party views on the purpose of art.

The Nazis began hastily confiscating more than 20,000 works of modern art in 1937. At that time, they made no plans for what would happen to the art. A year later, the Nazis passed a law legalising the sale of confiscated art. They planned a large international art auction in Switzerland in June 1939 and they profited from the sale of confiscated works by famous artists like Pablo Picasso, Vincent van Gogh, Henri Matisse. The 1939 auction at the Fischer Galleries in Lucerne attracted worldwide attention but most of the works were sold individually by four collectors, one of whom was Hildebrand Gurlitt. From 1943 Hildebrand Gurlitt was one of the privileged few given a commission to purchase works for the *Fuhrer-museum*. And it is clear that he also took the opportunity to expand his own collection.

In fact, Hildebrand Gurlitt's son, Corenelius is the one who will be in February 2012 at the centre of a scandal when in his Munich flat, German customs authorities seized 1,280 paintings, drawings and prints by artists including Picasso, Monet, Chagall, Otto Dix, and Paul Klee (the so-called Munich Art Hoard). The father, Hildebrand Gurlitt in the pre-war was an advocate of the modern art that Hitler condemned as 'degenerate'. Yet Gurlitt's anti-Nazi beliefs could not overcome the lure of the money and prestige he was to earn as Hitler's chief art buyer in occupied Paris. It is obvious that Gurlitt became successful, but it is clear that his success relied largely on the exploitation of other Jewish dealers and collectors to acquire pictures and profit. Membership of the *Reich* Chamber of Fine Arts became compulsory for dealers and from 1935 Jews were systematically excluded, forcing them to liquidate their collections and allowing dealers like Gurlitt benefit from lower-than-market prices as well as the increasing lack of competition. This was a form of looting and art theft that was centred on exploitation and hardship of dealers who had a pressure to sell. In fact, Gurlitt took advantage of vulnerable position of Jewish collectors forced to sell work to finance punitive Nazi fines or the cost of emigration. One such example is the Adolph von Menzel drawings bought from the Cohen family in the mid-1930s, most likely to finance a flight to the United States. He paid between 120 and 200 *Reichsmarks* per drawing which was a fraction of what they were worth at the time. The artists Gurlitt favoured were also suffering due to the virulent campaign against 'degenerate' art. Max Beckmann was accused of being a 'cultural Bolshevik' and dismissed from his teaching post, as was Otto Dix. Despite declaring his allegiance to Hitler and the Nazis, Heckel was also deemed 'degenerate'.

The Nazis assured hesitant foreign art dealers that profits would not fund Germany's ability to wage war. They promised that all funds would go to German museums, but as the reader might imagine, they did not keep this pledge. The regime funnelled some of its foreign profits into armaments production. In 1939, the Nazis burned more than 5,000 paintings that they could not profit from in the yard of Berlin's main firehouse.

Roughly one-third of the most valuable confiscated artworks were ultimately sold to enrich the Nazi regime. Much of this art found its way also to France. Even a couple of years later, ownership of 'degenerate art' was not controlled in occupied France as it was in Germany. As a result, France found itself awash in new supply and the occupation period also brought new buyers from Germany looking to acquire some of the artefacts of their vanquished rival's achievements. Even Nazi leadership like Hitler and Goring used the depressed franc as an opportunity to pick up French art on the cheap. From the Diary of Joseph Goebbels, we read:

> Paintings from the degenerate art action will now be offered on the international art market. In so doing we hope at least to make some money from this garbage.

Whatever its style, paintings turned out to have some valuable financial characteristics. For one, art was being used to store and move wealth in occupied France. Others used purchased art as a way to hide wealth accumulated in black market activities which constituted perhaps ten to thirty percent of French GDP during the occupation. This activity was far different from the purchasing of art for conspicuous consumption alone; indeed, it was very much the opposite. In this case, it was discretion that was sought. The desire to keep a low profile meant the prices of small canvases outperformed larger ones.

Certainly, an advantage of owning art in times of war is that it can be easily moved; valuable paintings can store a lot of value in a physically small item. It can be trafficked across borders even when capital controls otherwise limit the flows of money. Thanks to its secrecy, art can be both a 'discrete' and 'discreet' investment. In auctions, names of buyers and sellers are usually unknown and in a private transaction, not even the price or whether a sale even occurred at all is known. By contrast, in the modern financial system, most other means of transacting leave some trace. To this day, art has continued to be used as a store of value by those in more state-directed economies that are nonetheless connected to the global economy. For instance, in Saudi Arabia many, including Saudi royalty, used art as a means of moving capital out of the country. For example, in 2017, the Crown Prince of Saudi Arabia (Mohammed bin Salman) transferred hundreds of millions of dollars of his nation's wealth to a Russian oligarch via a painting of Jesus, Leonardo da Vinci's *Salvator Mundi*. As it can be seen, art along with cryptocurrencies and gemstones are alternative investments that can be used to skirt capital controls. This undeniably creates new regulatory issues (see Chapter 6).

3.8 The Rise of Hedge Funds

In the decades after the 'roaring twenties' and the crash of 1929 (see Chapter 5), American financiers gained a reputation for conservatism now rarely attributed to Wall Street. Investors, though still in search of good returns, seemed to appreciate the sound and tested and grew suspicious of the new and untried. New regulations introduced in the 1930s and 1940s threw the government's support firmly behind this trend. Nonetheless, innovative approaches to investing were also sprouting up and one of them was the concept of the hedge fund. Among the investors of this new form of investment management was Alfred Winslow Jones, said to be the founder of the first hedge fund.

Alfred Winslow Jones was born in Australia in 1900 but from the age of four on, grew up in Schenectady, New York after his father's General Electric job brought the family back to the United States after some years in Australia. He graduated from Harvard in 1923 but the innovative future investor never attended business school and had alternative career aspirations, far from Wall Street. Instead of a banking or investment job in New York, Jones worked in the American Foreign Service in Berlin during the 1930s. While in Europe, he travelled through Spain with his wife and reported on the civil war then underway there on behalf of a Quaker relief organisation. Indeed, the activities of the investor of hedge funds in Germany and Spain may have been motivated by Communist sympathies. Jones even attended courses at the Marxist Workers School in Berlin and is said to have involved himself in the work of a secret anti-Nazi group called 'the Leninist Organisation'. Back in the United States, Jones obtained a Ph.D. in sociology from Columbia University in 1941 and became director of the university's Institute for Applied Social Analysis. Among his first projects was a book published in 1941 'Life, Liberty, and Property' which reported on public attitudes towards large corporations.

From 1941 to 1946, Jones was a writer for Fortune magazine and continued to contribute even after his employment there ended. One of the articles Jones wrote for Fortune revealed the link between his academic work in sociology and his foray into finance. The article, published in the March 1949 issue of the magazine was titled 'Fashions in Forecasting' and converted technical analysis, methods of predicting markets using current and historical prices and trading volume data. It was his research for the piece that convinced him he could succeed in investing and helped connect Jones with the investment community. From the article it is clear his knowledge of sociology helped Jones recognise that technical investment strategies were based on the 'undoubted fact of momentum in psychological trends'. Market rises and falls could be predicted by measuring optimism and pessimism at social level. This much was known but how to consistently profit from these trends remained a mystery. Jones also observed that once certain strategies become popular and well known, their effectiveness wears off. As the sociologists would say, markets exhibit 'reflexivity'.

While writing 'Fashions in Forecasting', Jones must have been laying the groundwork for his new firm, A. W. Jones & Co., which he established the same year the Fortune article was published. The partnership was founded with one-hundred-thousand dollars (USD) in assets under management of which forty-thousand dollars (USD) was Jones' own money. Despite whatever attention and contacts his Fortune article produced, the balance came from four of Jones' existing friends, one of whom he met doing relief work during the Spanish Civil War just over a decade earlier.

A. W. Jones & Co. was structured to avoid regulation under the Investment Company Act of 1940 by having no more than ninety-nine investors. Rather than distribute widely and accept any willing investor, this approach also avoided the need for publicity and advertising which matched well with Jones' preference for a low profile. It also allowed Jones to keep more of his management fees as profit.

The differences between this new fund and those offered by traditional asset managers went further, extending to investor liquidity. To reduce the likelihood of investors redeeming during market swings and forcing the closing out of positions, redemptions (and new investments), could only be made at the end of each fiscal year. Further, unlike most investment funds of the day, what Jones created was essentially a long-short hedge fund, or as Jones called it a 'hedged' fund. This investment strategy balanced long positions, or bets that a security would rise in price, with short positions, those that bet another security would fall. The idea was that such an approach would reduce exposure to market swings but also allowed the fund to take on more leverage, which it did. Internally, the fund was also unusually entrepreneurial. There were no centralised investment committees as more traditional firms had employees who managed money relatively independently. The amounts they worked with would be increased if their performance justified it. Jones and his deputy, Donald Woodward, would reject trades only when they did not fit with the fund's overall exposures, for example, when one manager was increasing a short position in a particular stock that was already widely shorted by other employees. This structure put more employees in the shoes of a fund manager, because that is precisely what they were. Rather than be fired for underperformance, an employee would just be given less money to manage. Just like the firm overall, an employee had to justify new investor inflow by investing it well. If a manager truly believed strategy would turn out well in the end, then he would happily stick around until proven right with at least slightly reduced fear of losing his position. That said, leaving was always tempting. As the heralds of a new industry, there was increasing success to be found outside and alumni of A. W. Jones & Co. launched funds of their own, as did some of the brokers who gained valuable knowledge processing the firm's trades.

A. W. Jones & Co. delivered its investors strong returns, beating the market and the best performing mutual funds of the day, like Fidelity's Trend Fund, then managed by acclaimed investor Gerald Tsai. Jones achieved a cumulative return of over one-thousand percent in the ten years ending with 1968, by which point the firm managed one-hundred million dollars. Since inception, it had delivered a five-thousand percent return by 1968. For Jones losing years were rare; the first did not come until 1962, thirteen years into the fund's history and the firm was able to make gain even in down years for the market. Of these strong profits, Jones and his team got to keep a large share. The firm charged investors a fee of twenty percent of any gains. Jones likened this fee to the practice of ancient Phoenician sea captains keeping a fifth of journey profits for themselves. According to Carol Loomis, who covered Jones' career for Fortune in the 1960s, his performance was more attributable to good stock picking than accurately timing the market. In reality, he was frequently 'too long' when the market fell and 'too short' when it rose, losing out in both cases. A competitor once called Jones a 'financial hippie'. His background and interests might justify such an assertion but so too would his work on Wall Street. Jones' innovative firm was counterculture in a financial sector still shocked from the crash of 1929 and wary of the unfamiliar.

3.9 The Special Purpose Acquisition Company (SPAC) and the SPAC Mafia

Special Purpose Acquisition Companies (SPACs) have come a long way from obscure legal innovation of the 1980s-era in the United States to a celebrity status symbol in 2020–2021 in New York. From Wall Street bankers to celebrities and stars, investors from Silicon Valley, respected businessmen, famous showbiz stars, and finally ordinary people: these are all among the cast of characters that have promoted or bought into the SPAC fever that has swept the United States in 2020.

The SPAC craze has been shaking the United States mainly for its simplicity: investors decide to buy shares at a fixed price in a company that initially has no assets. In this way an SPAC, also known as a 'blank check company', is created as an empty shell with a lot of money to spend on a corporate shopping spree. It is a bit like a lottery ticket—the initial stake is small, but in terms of potential gains, the sky's the limit. At the same time, every SPAC is finite: if it does not find a target within a pre-set time frame (usually about a year or two), the SPAC is liquidated, and the investors get their money back, increased by a modest profit from investing in short-term US government securities (and reduced by certain expenses, commissions, and fees). The asymmetrical relationship between the risk and the potential of profit leaves the impression that it is impossible to lose. SPACs are risk-free investments until the moment of the business combination. Once the SPAC finds a suitable target company, it merges with it. Then, the business runs the same operational, financial, or reputational risks as any other company.

By the end of 2020, more than two-hundred-and-forty SPACs were listed in the United States (on NASADQ or NYSE), raising a record eighty-three billion dollars (USD). The momentum carried over into 2021 with one-hundred-and-fifteen-point-six billion dollars (USD) raised via more than four-hundred SPACs in 2021, mainly on Wall Street, where SPACs make up two-thirds of all IPOs. In other words, the importance and legitimacy of SPACs is becoming a compelling reality today, and it is imposing a new economic order through which for instance, start-ups and tech companies can finally compete with well renowned companies, such as Airbnb or Facebook, to access public markets.

Many have identified sponsors of SPACs and their qualified investors (mainly hedge funds) as the main speculators of SPACs. In other words, those were the only actors that according to the press would have benefited from an SPAC transaction. Indeed, once the SPAC issues units composed of common shares and warrants, SPAC managers or sponsors usually acquire twenty-five percent of the capital raised for a nominal value (often twenty-five-thousand dollars (USD) that equals to 0.0035 or 0.00435 dollars (USD) per share as well as a reserved offer of founders shares for a symbolic par value per share such as 0.0001 dollars (USD)). At merger time, the SPAC shares maintain their ten dollars (USD) nominal value. However, the real value drops due to dilution when the merger occurs. For all shareholders, dilution arises from paying the sponsor's fee in shares (called the 'promote', often about twenty percent of the equity). In other words, SPAC sponsors receive a promote which typically grants them equity in the SPAC equal to twenty-five percent of the capital raised or twenty percent of the fully diluted SPAC shares. This is what has been defined as the sponsor compensation or sometimes in a critical way as the SPAC bonanza. Indeed, for example Michael Klein had more than sixty million dollars (USD) from a twenty-five-thousand dollars (USD) investment in his founders' shares in June 2020 (the merger between Churchill Capital Corp. IV and Clarivate Analytics PLC). It means that the initial investment of twenty-five-thousand dollars (USD) coverts into a slice of equity of the new merged entity when the SPAC finalises a business combination. The main reason to justify the promote has been its construction as compensation for the management's efforts in finding the target company and executing the merger. However, it is undoubtful that the promote might constitute a speculative practice in case of low value creation for public investors.

Usually, all warrants in a SPAC are tradable and detachable until the moment of the business combination to make this appealable to investors, and especially, as some would like to claim to hedge funds. Indeed, a couple dozen obscure hedge funds like Polar Asset Management and Davidson Kempner, known by insiders as the 'SPAC Mafia' have been the driving force of the SPAC boom. Some ninety-seven percent of these hedge funds redeem or sell their IPO shares before target mergers are consummated making returns around twenty percent. It seems there is only one loser in this equation. As always it is the retail investor, the

Robinhood novice, the good-intentions fund company like Fidelity. They all bring their pickaxes to the SPAC gold rush, failing to understand that the opportunities were mined long before they got there—by the sponsors who see an easy score, the entrepreneurs who get 'fat exits' when their companies are acquired, and the 'SPAC Mafia' hedge funds that lubricate it all. However, to better understand SPACs, it is important to contextualise their financial history in the United States of America.

SPACs are born as blank check companies firstly listed on the Penny Stock Market (PSM) in the 1980s in the United States, performing mostly notorious 'pump-and-dump' schemes. While movies like 'Wall Street' and 'Barbarians at the Gate' evoke cultural images of the 1980s-era leveraged buyouts, 'Boiler Room' and 'Wolf of Wall Street' evince what was happening off-exchange with blank check penny stock schemes and outright scams. For instance, in 1988, Mary L. Shapiro, Commissioner of the United States Securities and Exchange Commission defined the PSM and its investment vehicles as a dangerous tool in the following terms:

> (…) Many penny stocks represent legitimate investment opportunities, and the market for these stocks is an honest one. However, experience has shown that many other penny stocks are used in a fraudulent schemes which involve 'shell' companies with no operating history, few employees, few assets, no legitimate prospects for business success, and markets that are manipulated to the benefit of the promoters of the companies and/or the market professionals involved.

The SEC Commissioner Shapiro illustrated a negative image of the Penny Stock Market as a primary example of market venue where illegal activities of blank check companies might flourish. This includes pre-arranged trading, nominee accounts, and securities fraud. Furthermore, the North America Securities Administrators Association strongly argued a year later, in 1989, that the blank check companies were a per se fraudulent investment tool:

> (…) blank check blind pool offerings are inherently defective because of failure to disclose material facts concerning the offering and issuer, and such offerings have been subject of pervasive, recurrent abusive and fraudulent practices in the sale of securities (…) the Association declares that the sales of blank check blind pool securities *per se* constitute fraudulent business practices.

It is clear that by the end of the 1980s, the Penny Stock Market was dominated by fraud and manipulation of asset prices, which had a negative influence on trading practices in penny stock offerings, because the primary capital market was basically not regulated, and broker firms were usually unscrupulous, as I said. Blank check companies were listed on the PSM, which was non-exchange venue. Hence, it did not impose pre-trade transparency or basic listing requirements on the issuers of securities. This made the market a fertile playground for the cash-shell companies' game.

The main purpose of a blank check company was to be listed on the PSM to raise funds, through an IPO, and complete a business combination with an unidentified target company. In particular, at the IPO stage, the management of the blank check companies did not sell their securities directly to retail investors, but condescending brokerage firms. Subsequently, the brokers misled the investors about a possible imminent acquisition or just circulated official statements, according to which the blank check company had merged with an important operating company with profitable turnovers. This circumstance contributed to exaggerate the price of the issued securities and attracted new retail investors. At that point the managers of the blank check company and the brokers sold their securities and caused a collapse of the market in relation to the price of equity and to the value of the firm with high returns for their investment portfolios. In other words, they committed fraud against investors who did not possess enough information to assess their financial risk, and who just trusted the information provided by the broker firms. In the 1980s, there were neither legal instruments nor a sophisticated legal framework to protect investors from the frauds that were often perpetrated by blank check companies.

Thus, the US Congress enacted the Securities Enforcement Remedies and Penny Stock Reform Act (PSRA) on the 20 July 1990. The PSRA 1990 (US) was passed to protect investors, and definitively regulate the PSM. The PSRA 1990 (US) read for the first time a definition of penny stocks under Sect. 3 (a) of Securities Exchange Act 1934 (US) (SEA 1934), which was further implemented by virtue of Rule 3a51-1 of the SEC. specifically, a company would be entitled to issue equity securities (penny stock) if—*inter alia*—they had an authorised share capital value not exceeding five million dollars (USD), and the company had no less than three-year financial history with a minimum set income of seven-hundred-and-fifty-thousand dollars (USD). Thus, the scope of the PSRA 1990 (US) was to define the content of penny stocks, the legal nature of the companies operating on the PSM, and to fix a minimum cap in relation to the authorised share capital. Additionally, the PSRA 1990 (US) amended, *inter alia*, Sect. 7 of the Securities Act 1933 (US) entitling the SEC to enact different rules in order to impose restrictions and disclosure duties to the blank check companies.

The SEC adopted the famous Rule 419 by which blank check companies that were issuing penny stocks as defined in Rule 3a51-1 of the SEC, were, *inter alia*, compelled to fulfil three main obligations:

i. first, all of the securities and proceeds raised during the initial public offering should have been deposited in an escrow account or held on trust, and the interests or dividends earned on the deposit funds could not be distributed until an acquisition was completed;
ii. the acquisition should have been carried out within a very short period (i.e. eighteen months), and the funds held on trust should have been released—in the measure of at least 80%—in the case of completion of a business combination, otherwise the funds should have been returned in full to investors;
iii. shareholders should have expressed their consent to the proposed acquisition, providing that those who dissented had the right to rescind from their shareholders position and receive funds, interests or dividends of a pro rata aggregate amount of the securities held on trust (i.e. conversion right).

As a result, in the late 1990s, the blank check companies slowly disappeared due to the onerous conditions imposed by the SEC in Rule 419 and on the basis that cash-shell companies without any form of financial data were definitively forbidden from listing on the PSM. However, this was not the end but rather the beginning of SPACs.

Following the PSRA 1990 (US), and the sharp fall of blank check offerings; a new phoenix arose from the ashes with the name of Special Purpose Acquisition Company.

SPACs were exempted from the application of Rule 419 because they started to issue securities through IPOs, which did not fit into the definition of penny stocks, and—since 2003—they started to be listed on capital markets, which required less strict requirements such as the Over-the-Counter Bulletin Board (OTC Bulletin Board) and the American Stock Exchange (AMEX). Hence, they were subject to common provisions, which generally governed the initial public offering in the United States. However, SPACs voluntarily complied with the conditions set forth in Rule 419 in order to prioritise the confidence of investors. For instance, SPACs were used to deposit the securities and proceeds of the IPO in an escrow account until the acquisition was completed and to use at least 80% of funds held on trust to finance the acquisition, and they provided public investors with a conversion right (namely, the right to convert securities into cash if the shareholders voted against the proposed acquisition). This was an example of 'self-imposed' SPAC restrictions. This approach is credited to Mr. David Nussbaum (chairman of the GKN Securities). This evolution of a modern conception of SPACs that are run by well-known managers and that they tend to secure investment through a trust is known as SPAC 2.0.

Hence, the voluntary compliance with Rule 419 and the implementation of new features made SPACs an attractive investment tool. This historical event also contributed to the development of a modern conception of SPACs, which were different from blank check companies based on fraudulent practices. This circumstance created a new SPAC identity in relation to their corporate structure that would have been adopted with slight modifications by other US capital markets regulations. In fact, in 2008 the NASDAQ and NYSE issued a proposal to allow the listing of SPACs on their exchanges. Until then, SPACs were not listed on those regulated capital markets, but only on the OTC Bulletin Board and the AMEX (namely, capital markets with less strict and generic listing requirements). In the end, the SEC approved the proposals and the SPACs started then to be listed on the NASDAQ (Rule IM-5101–2 of the NASDAQ listing rules) and the NYSE (Rule 102.6 of the Listing Company Manual). Finally, the NYSE American (formerly known as AMEX) and more recently as NYSE MKT adopted in November 2010 similar listing rules in relation to SPACs. The NYSE AMEX underlines that the exchange does not contemplate the possibility of listing a cash-shell company unless specific conditions set out in the NYSE MKT Company Guide are fulfilled under Sect. 119 of the 'Listing of companies whose business plan is to complete one or more acquisitions'. In particular, a listing company must also comply with the corporate governance requirement of part 8 of the NYSE MKT Company Guide.

The US capital markets have evolved since the blank check companies' phenomenon in the 1980s. The main regulated markets such as NYSE, NASDAQ, and NYSE MKT have adopted strict and specific listing requirements in order to list SPACs. Furthermore, the market rules clearly indicate that an SPAC must fulfil specific conditions before its listing. However, those conditions are only minimum mandatory requirements which do not prevent any exchange to exercise its unlimited discretion in order to delist the SPAC even when all the listing requirements are met, because the SPAC might constitute a threat against the public interest and the protection of investors' interests. This serves as a continuous reminder of the possible financial risks that were generated by blank check offerings, although modern SPACs have implemented more corporate safeguards for investors that distinguish them from their ancestors.

3.10 Conclusions

This chapter has shown how financial innovations are perfected during years and decades. From the time of stockjobbers operating in London's Exchange Alley to the setting up of the New York Stock Exchange, speculators were often seen as villains. The prosperity of a few could attract the envy of many, but at the same time the rise of modern stock exchanges is representing a fundamental moment of human progress and economic development by which liquidity is increased, and companies can expand their shareholding capital and being more popular once listed on the market. As many times in financial history, the first stock exchange in Amsterdam originated from a pragmatic necessity. At that time, as I have illustrated, shareholders of the VOC did not want to be paid in spices also because spices were difficult to store and to resell. Their need for liquidity 'in cash' brought them to sell share certificates to other investors by giving rise to a secondary market of equity instruments. It seems that at first glance financial innovations have positive purposes and they rarely emerge in negative terms. The same has been seen—for instance—in Chapter 2, where Temple Church in London has provided a solution to pilgrims in Jerusalem. In the same light, the New York Curb Market was created as an informal market, and it was accepted by the NYSE as an unofficial 'seasoning market' or place to test out new issuances. The same dynamic between informal and formal or official markets can be traced to the origin of the London Stock Exchange, and also in Paris with the distinction that I will further illustrate in Chapter 5 between the official and formal stock exchange called *Parquet* and the informal one referred to as the *Coulisse*. Membership was free; anyone could become a *coulissier* and hold their own inventory of securities, as opposed to brokers alone as the *Parquet* had.

However, this chapter has also provided direct evidences as to how financial innovations or alternative investments can be used for immoral or distorted objectives (see also Chapters 5 and 6) such as financing a war in the case of the Cotton Bonds of the American Civil War or the 'degenerate' art of the Nazism era. From London to New York, this chapter has evidenced that an early trading of information is key in financial markets to take advantage of markets' opportunities, but such opportunistic behaviour is one of the reasons why financial markets were registering and still register a lack of confidence and efficiency. The economic effects of the financial crisis are experienced, on the side of investors, in terms of confidence due to information asymmetry and agency cost issues, whereas on the side of managers and financial intermediaries, they are seen in terms of moral hazard concerns. Establishing a legal and economic order is a necessity. However, financial regulation is not the only answer, because the most important means to mitigate or prevent future crisis centres on the correct pricing of financial risk, as I will further explain in the next chapter. To this end, during centuries, economics has gained an enhanced role in financial markets, and law has lost its appeal in regulating markets, also because many times the issuing of new rules can produce unintended consequences of legitimisation of risky financial products as well as a limitation of the evolution of financial innovations especially in the case of digital financial innovations (see Chapters 4, 5, and 7).

Relevant Historical Events in Financial Innovation and Speculation

Date	*Financial Innovation and/or Speculation*
c.1001–1100 / 1501–1600	Guilds started to be spread as associations of craftsmen and merchants formed to promote the economic interests of their members as well as to provide protection and mutual aid
1602	Set up in Amsterdam of the Dutch East India Company or *Verenigde Oostindische Compagnie* (abbreviated as VOC), which is the first public company to trade shares on a stock exchange (the so-called *Hendrick de Keyser* building)
1693	United Kingdom's first government bonds were issued
1694	Setup of the first Central Bank of the United Kingdom or so-called Bank of England

(continued)

(continued)

Relevant Historical Events in Financial Innovation and Speculation	
Date	*Financial Innovation and/or Speculation*
Early 1700s	In London, Exchange Alley or known at the time as 'Change Alley' was home to a number of coffeehouses where stock prices were posted and traders bought and sold their shares. Two of the more famous in London were Jonathan's Coffee-House and Garraway's Coffee-House
1774	The merchant and broker Adriaan van Ketwich set up in Amsterdam the world's first mutual fund. The fund was called '*Eendraft Maakt Magt*' which translated from Dutch means 'unity makes strength' and its prospectus, or '*Negotiatie*' survives to this day
1792	Two dozen stockbrokers signed in New York a famous pact agreeing to trade directly with each other, bypassing any middlemen, under a Buttonwood tree on Wall Street. This agreement known as the Buttonwood Agreement is thought of as setting the foundation for what would become the New York Stock Exchange
1801	The London Stock Exchange is set up and share trading no more occurs in coffeehouses
1817	The New York Stock & Exchange Board was formed and rented space at 40 Wall Street. The old Tontine Coffee-House would go on to become a tavern, a hotel, and then a newspaper publishing office before being demolished in the middle of the century
Mid-1800s	Brokers in New York would meet on Broad Street sidewalk to trade shares, often those of most speculative companies, outside the institutionalised structure provided by formal stock exchanges. The so-called Curb market (the Curb) where anyone could show up and trade whatever shares were available, whether they were listed on other exchanges or not
1860	The New York Stock & Exchange Board is renamed the New York Stock Exchange
1863	The Confederate Congress secretly authorised the Paris-based bankers at Erlanger et Cie—which rivalled Rothschild for European royalty connections—to underwrite $15 million of Confederate bonds, denominated in British Pounds or French Francs
1939	Art regarded as 'degenerate' by the Nazis had been sold abroad and was banned from reimport into Germany. Nazi leaders sought to control Germany not only politically but also culturally. The regime restricted the type of art that could be produced, displayed, and sold
1949	Alfred Winslow Jones set up A. W. Jones & Co. and he created the first hedge fund structure. Jones referred to his fund as being 'hedged', a term commonly used on Wall Street to describe the management of investment risk due to changes in the financial markets
1980	Blank check companies are firstly listed on the Penny Stock Market in the United States

(continued)

(continued)

Relevant Historical Events in Financial Innovation and Speculation

Date	*Financial Innovation and/or Speculation*
1990	The blank check companies slowly disappeared due to the onerous conditions imposed by the SEC in Rule 419 and on the basis that cash-shell companies without any form of financial data were definitively forbidden from listing on the PSM. However, this was not the end but rather the beginning of Special Purpose Acquisition Companies (SPACs)
1971	The NASDAQ is established in New York as the second major Stock Exchange

Notes

1. When some guilds introduced their own distinctive clothing and regalia—or livery (possibly based on various monks' habits)—to distinguish their members from those in other guilds, they soon became known as livery companies. In fact, the term 'livery' used to mean the allowance of food and clothing to retainers and officers of great households, colleges, or crafts and the wealthier merchants' guilds but gradually came to be restricted to the wearing of distinctive clothing as a symbol of privilege and protection. For example, a particular privilege in being a liveryman was the right to the use of the Company's Pall or coffin cloth, some examples of which still survive. However, with time the use of distinctive clothing became the privilege of liverymen only, and this privilege survives today in the ceremony of admission to the Company at which a Freeman (the name to identify a new member of a livery company and to be necessarily distinguished from a freemason) is 'cloathed' as of the livery.
2. Tontines have history that goes back long before the Tontine Coffee-House. The scheme named after a seventeenth-century banker from Naples, Lorenzo de Tonti, combined retirement planning with a lottery. The financial product worked as follows: investors bought shares in the tontine, akin to paying up front for an annuity. The pool of capital was then invested, and investors received dividends on their shares until their deaths. Once the number of survivors shrinks to a small group, the investment would wound

down. With a tontine, the distribution that does not go to deceased investors is used to increase the benefits of the surviving ones. This is the lottery part of the scheme.
3. A 'corner' occurs when all of the available shares of a company have been purchased or are otherwise controlled by a speculator or group of speculators acting in concert (known as syndicate). This forces all would-be buyers to deal with the individual or syndicate that organised the corner. A corner is the anti-short sale, in that its purpose is to extract as much money as possible from short sellers.
4. The Compromise of 1850 was made up of five bills that attempted to resolve disputes over slavery in new territories added to the United States in the wake of the Mexican–American War (1846–1848). It admitted California as a free state, left Utah and New Mexico to decide for themselves whether to be a slave state or a free state, defined a new Texas–New Mexico boundary, and made it easier for slaveowners to recover runways under the Fugitive Slave Act of 1850.
5. Bleeding Kansas describes the period of repeated outbreaks of violent guerrilla warfare between pro-slavery and anti-slavery forces following the creation of the new territory of Kansas in 1854. In all, some 55 people were killed between 1855–1859. The struggle intensified the ongoing debate over the future of slavery.
6. On 8 November 1861 Charles Wilkes a US Navy Officer captured two Confederate envoys aboard the British mail ship, the Trent. Great Britain accused the United States of violating British neutrality, and the incident created a diplomatic crisis between the United States and Great Britain during the Civil War. Jefferson Davis, President of the Confederate States of America, had dispatched these envoys—James Mason, former Chairman of the US Senate Foreign Relations Committee and John Slidell, a prominent New Orleans lawyer—to secure British and French recognition of the Confederate States as a sovereign nation. Great Britain and France had recognised the Confederacy as a belligerent power, but not a sovereign government, in early 1861.

Bibliography

Bowen A, 'The recent evolution of the UK banking industry and some implications for financial stability' (1999) Bank for International Settlements

Brown WO, Burdekin R, 'Turning points in the US Civil War: A British prospective' (2000) 60 (1) The Journal of Economic History 216–231

Centre for Policy Studies, *Big Bang 20 Years On: New Challenges Facing the Financial Services Sector* (City of London Corporation 2006)

Chancellor E, *Devil Take the Hindmost: A History of Financial Speculation* (Douglas & McIntyre Ltd 1999)

Church, A, 'The rise and fall of leading international financial centres: factors and application' (2018) 7 (2) Michigan Business & Entrepreneurial Law Review 283–340

D'Alvia D, *Mergers, Acquisitions, and International Financial Regulation: Analysing Special Purpose Acquisition Companies* (Routledge 2021)

D'Alvia D, 'From Darkness to Light: A Comparative Study of Special Purpose Acquisition Companies in the European Union, the UK, and the US' (2022) 24 Cambridge Yearbook of European Legal Studies 201–238

De La Vega J, *Confusion de Confusiones [1688]: Portions Descriptive of the Amsterdam Stock Exchange* (Martino Fine Books 2013)

Edwin Lefevre, *Reminiscences of a Stock Operator* (Albatross Publisher 2017)

Ferguson N, *The Ascent of Money: A Financial History of the World* (Penguin 2019)

Geert Rouwenhorst K, *The Origins of Mutual Funds* (12 December 2004) Yale ICF Working Paper No. 04–48

Geisst C R, *Wall Street: A History* (OUP 1998)

Gentry J F, 'A Confederate success in Europe: the Erlanger Loan' (1970) 36 (2) The Journal of Southern History 157–188

Goetzmann W, Geert R, *The Origins of Value: The Financial Innovations that Created Modern Capital Markets* (Oxford University Press 2005)

Kindleberger C, *A Financial History of Western Europe* (George Allen & Unwin 1984)

Lefevre E, *Reminiscences of a Stock Operator* (Albatross Publishers 2017)

Lester R, 'An aspect of Confederate finance during the American Civil War: the Erlanger Loan and the plan of 1864' (1974) 16 (2) Business History 130–144

Mortimer T, *Every Man His Own Broker: Or, a Guide to the Stock Exchange. In Which the Nature of the Several Funds, Vulgarly Called the Stocks, is Clearly Explained. Also, an Historical Account of the Origin* (Gale ECCO 2010)

Mosselaar J S, *A Concise Financial History of Europe* (Robeco 2018)

Mosselaar J S, 'Low volatility in historical prospective: fund investing since 1774' (21 September 2016) Pure Play Asset Management – Robeco.com, Robeco

Neal Larry, *A Concise History of International Finance: From Babylon to Bernanke* (Cambridge University Press 2015)

Oosterlinck K, 'Art as a wartime investment: conspicuous consumption and discretion' (2017) 127 (607) The Economic Journal 2665–2701
Persky J, 'Retrospectives: from usury to interest' (2007) 21 (1) Journal of Economic Prospectives 227–236
Richardson G, 'Medieval Guilds' in *Encyclopaedia of Economic and Business History* (2010)
Taylor B, 'The Confederate cotton zombie bonds' (2019) Global Financial Data
Thomas Mortimer, *Every Man His Own Broker: Or, a Guide to Exchange-Alley* (Cambridge University Press 2010)

CHAPTER 4

Uncertainty: The Necessary Unknowable Road to Speculation

4.1 Introduction

This chapter is devoted to further exploring the figure of the speculator from both an epistemological and an ontological point of view. Markets are full of risks. This should never worry us though, as risks can and should also be understood as profitable opportunities, especially where we can mitigate against them. But markets are also just as full of uncertainties; unknowns which cannot be quantified as risks, cannot be mitigated against, and which may offer heightened profit opportunities, but which can also spell disaster. Recalling Frank Knight's core 1921 message, but this time around with application to financial (investment) instruments, the chapter provides a fascinating contemporary overview of risk, uncertainty, and profit. Are financial innovations themselves investrisk management tools in our search for constant profit, thus, minimising the dangers of renewed market collapse in heightened uncertainty? This chapter tackles this question and more. It focuses on the subjective feature of the speculators who are theorised as modern risk-takers: their desire for profit and their 'fear of missing out' represent a key element in any financial market. Beliefs, opinions, and desires are all linked and deeply connected to the *dramatis personae* of the speculator rather than markets' inefficiency. In other words, a risk-taker is able to calculate the probabilities of profit, but cannot control the necessarily unknowable feature of

D. D'Alvia, *The Speculator of Financial Markets*, Palgrave Macmillan Studies in Banking and Financial Institutions,
https://doi.org/10.1007/978-3-031-47901-4_4

markets: uncertainty. To this end, the speculator is seen as a brave man who absorbs the negative externalities produced by uncertainty and in his risk-taking activity is following a unique and extraordinary intuition for profit. This is how wealth and progress are produced in our Western financial markets, namely by taking risks, sometimes even unreasonable ones.

4.2 Ways of Gambling: From Chance to Skills

John 19:23–24 reads:

> When the soldiers crucified Jesus, they took his clothes, dividing them into four shares, one for each of them, with the undergarment remaining. This garment was seamless, woven in one piece from the top to bottom. "Let's not tear it" they said to one another. "Let's decide by lot who will get it"

The immediate question by reading this passage is what was the purpose of soldiers keeping the blood-soaked clothes of Jesus? Did they keep those clothes in the form of trophies to keep count of those whom they crucified? Does the Roman Catholic Church have an official teaching on this incident?

To briefly answer this question the possessions of an executed prisoner were a standard perk for soldiers of the time. It may not seem like much of a perk to us, but clothing was a significant expense at the time (as it is in many parts of the world today). Blood-soaked would not have been a problem, especially if they were valuable and could be cleaned.

However, in Psalm 22:18 found in the biblical Book of Psalms, and used in Christian and Jewish worship, it is written:

> For dogs have surrounded Me; the congregation of the wicked has enclosed Me. They divide My garments among them, and for My clothing they cast lots (Psalm 22:18)

It was a prophecy that was being fulfilled even in the act of Jesus's death. Besides that, the Roman soldiers probably were just making a game out of an everyday situation for them. They were unfortunately gambling while Christ suffered on the cross.

Gambling has always been a widespread activity in Ancient and Modern societies. The Roman Emperor Marcus Aurelius was accompanied by his personal croupier. George Washington hosted games in his war tent in 1778, Alexander Fordyce, the short seller of the East India Company was depicted as a 'Macaroni Gambler' (see Chapter 6), and the earliest known form of gambling was a kind of dice game played with what was known as an astragalus bone found in vast archaeological contexts around the Mediterranean. The bone derives from the hind leg of sheep and goats and has been recorded in both secular and spiritual spheres. In the modern world the astragalus is perhaps better known as the knuckle bone or as the game with the same name. Because of its characteristic and cubic shape it is furthermore often considered the forerunner of modern dice. Indeed, craps, an American invention, derives from various dice games brought into Europe via Crusaders. Those games were generally referred to as 'hazard', from *al zahr*, the Arabic word for dice.

Gambling is one of the oldest activities in the world. The history of gambling has been traced back to Ancient Greece, Ancient China, and Ancient Egypt. These are key civilisations that have been explored extensively by archaeologists. The presence of gambling artefacts in each of them shows that the act was quite widespread, and gambling could have been a global affair that might even explain the gesture of Pontius Pilate's soldiers, who casted lots for Christ's robe, as I said at the incipit of this chapter.

Egyptian tomb paintings picture games played with astragali dating from 3500 BC. The story of the development of gambling in Egypt is believed to be religious. *Senet* is a gambling game closely related to backgammon that was invented to solve a dispute among Egyptian Gods.[1] It is an easy concept that is similar to evidence found in other civilisations. They include Sumerian *Seneta* of Mesopotamia, *Thaayyam* in Ancient India, and *Pachisi* of Arab origin. Beyond legend, the greatest evidence to show the presence of gambling in ancient Egypt is the papyri that are believed to have dated from 3000 to 4000 BC. They contained laws that were made to stop the spread of gambling in this region. The presence of such laws simply means that the activity was so rampant that it required to be controlled. The consequences of gambling, according to these texts were quite dire. They involved being sent to quarries to provide forced free labour. This punishment was among the worst at the time, and it is comparable to life imprisonment of modern times.

Card games developed in Asia from ancient form of fortune-telling. Chinese card games were a popular pastime among the general public, either as a medium for conversation or for gambling, and they developed as early as the ninth century. Cards were often decorated with human forms. *Da Lao Er* (literally means 'big old two', but also has a vulgar meaning), is still one of the most popular Chinese card games. This two–four player game is played both casually and competitively in gambling settings. A unique aspect of this game is that two is the largest card of the game. The goal of the game is to play cards from the hand via combinations, such as pairs, triples, flushes, or straights. Other players can counter with the same combination but of a higher value. A player wins once they clear their hand. However, those games with cards did not become popular in Europe until the invention of printing. As games spread throughout Europe, the human forms of Kings and Queens which we are more familiar with began to appear in cards.

The most addictive form of gambling seems to be the pure games of chance played at the casinos. The first casinos or gambling houses appeared in Italy in the seventeenth century. The *Ridotto*[2] was established in Venice in 1638 to provide a controlled gambling environment, and casinos started to appear throughout continental Europe in the nineteenth century. Games like *Roulette* and *Vingt-et-un* arrived in the United States with early settlers from France. Indeed, poker's closest European predecessor was *Poque*, which caught on in France in the seventeenth century. *Poque* and its German equivalent, *pochen*, were both based on the sixteenth-century Spanish game *primero*, which featured three cards dealt to each player and bluffing (or betting high on poor cards) as a key part of the game. French colonists brought *Poque* to their settlements in North America, including New Orleans and the surrounding area, which became part of the United States thanks to the Louisiana Purchase of 1803. English-speaking settlers in the region anglicised *Poque* to poker and adopted features of the modern game, including five cards for each player and (by 1834) a 52-card deck. From there, poker spread up the Mississippi River and throughout the country, thanks in part to its popularity among crews of riverboats transporting goods via that great waterway. Soldiers in both the North and South played poker during the Civil War (see Chapter 3), and it became a staple of Wild West saloons in frontier settlements in the 1870s and 1880s. In 1871 the game was introduced to Europe after Queen Victoria heard the US minister to Great Britain explaining the game to members of her court and asked him for the rules. More general acceptance of poker in Europe occurred several decades later, largely thanks to the influence of American soldiers during

World War I. Today millions of players in the United States and worldwide regularly play poker, confident of their ability to outwit their opponents.

One of the biggest debates among gamblers is whether or not winning a particular game is dependent on skill or chance. In fact, it is vital to distinguish between games of chance and games in which skill makes a difference. With one group of games the outcome is determined by fate; with the other by choice. The odds—the probability of winning—are what is needed to bet in a game of chance. In a game of skill the player needs more information to predict who will win or lose as well as a bit of luck. There are cardplayers that are real professionals, but no one makes a successful profession out of shooting craps.

To further clarify, a game of skill is determined by a player's mental dexterity, rather than sheer luck. In a skilled game, a player wins based on his capabilities. Skilled players usually know how to implement strategies to their gameplay to win. Usually the more experienced a player is, the better their chances of winning a game of skill. This means that a game of skill requires constant practice. On the other hand, a game of chance is determined by a randomiser (or random number generator). A random number generator is any hardware or software that can produce a sequence of random numbers. Most web casino games like playing cards, online slots or roulette use software algorithms to generate random data and are all considered games of chance. Although chanced-based games are largely dependent on luck, a few games like poker also involve some level of skill to succeed. Games of chance are generally easier to play because they require little technical knowledge, and as I have illustrated chance-based games (e.g. the dice game) have existed long before skill-based games. However, it seems that the rise of crypto finance in modern days might be assimilated to gambling. Crypto trading and crypto markets are not like traditional finance, and they do not serve a common good for societies. Crypto trading is gambling where crypto traders bring money—fiat currency—into a casino or online game and convert the winnings or losses back into money (see Chapter 7).

4.3 From Numbers to the Mastery of Risk

One might be tempted to assume that the lapse of time between the invention of the astragalus and the invention of the laws of probability was a historical accident. As I have illustrated in Chapter 2 up to the time of Renaissance, people perceived the future as a matter of luck and most of their decisions were driven by instinct. If the conditions of life are linked to nature, not much is left to human control.

When Christianity spread across the Western world, the future became a matter of moral behaviour and faith, and the future no longer appeared inscrutable. St. Augustine saw faith as a spur to inquiry rather than putting an end to questions. His writings are full of questions and earnest pleas to God to enlighten his mind and grant him greater understanding. Rather than avoiding the pagan's challenging question: 'What was your Creator God doing for all that infinite time before he got around to making the world?' St. Augustine gave a serious consideration to this question in Book XI of his Confessions, where he was striving to get deeper insight into the first verse of the Bible:

> In the beginning, God created heaven and earth

St. Augustine reflected very deeply about the nature of time itself. As noted by the physics Nobel laureate Steven Weinberg, Book XI of Augustine's Confessions contains a famous discussion of the nature of time, and it seems to have become a tradition to quote from his chapter in writing about quantum cosmology. Indeed, for St. Augustine time is a measure of change. As such, it presupposes the existence of things that change—which, of course, must be created things. Consequently, he said 'there can be no time without creation'. Time is thus an aspect of the created world and is itself a creation of God. And this led St. Augustine to the most remarkable insight, which is that it is meaningless to speak about times before creation. For if time is passing, then something created is already in existence, namely changing things and time itself, meaning that all times must be times after creation.

Modern physics arrived at essentially the same insight in the twentieth century. Whereas St. Augustine began with the notion that time is something created, modern physics starts with the notion that time—or space–time—is something physical. Einstein's theory of General Relativity (his theory of gravity) argues that space–time is a dynamic entity: it can bend and have ripples in it. If space–time is an aspect or part of the physical universe, it follows that the beginning of the physical universe must have been the beginning of space and time itself. This means that one cannot meaningfully speak of time before the beginning of the physical universe. However, when St. Augustine wrote his thinking, time was still not susceptible to any sort of mathematical expectation, and even more time was considered as a creation of God, and it would have not been appropriate for human beings to consider their selves in possess of time.

Things started to change when through Crusades (see Chapter 2), Westerners collided with an Arab empire that had been stretched as far eastward as India. The Arabs, through their invasion of India, had become familiar with the Hindu numbering system. The Hindu–Arabic notation, with its place value and zero, gradually replaced the *abacus*,[3] though it was still widely used in Europe as late as the seventeenth century. The new numbering system would transform mathematics and measurement in astronomy, navigation, and commerce. Although still the Hindu–Arabic numbering system was not enough to induce Europeans to explore ways of replacing randomness with systematic probability, the invention of the zero or *sunya* as the Indians called it, and *cifr* as it became in Arabic, already made the whole structure of the numbering system immediately visible and clear. Indeed, the concept of cipher which means empty and refers to the empty column of the abacus, highlights that zero has nothing to do with counting. As the English philosopher Alfred North Whitehead put it, no one goes out to buy zero fish. Zero unleashes something more profound than a method of counting and it allows people to use only ten digits from zero to nine to perform every conceivable calculation. Something that with Roman numerals was not possible. The zero reminds humanity that the future might be predictable and maybe even controllable and subject to measurement via calculation to some degree.

The story of numbers in the West begins in 1202 when a book titled *Liber Abaci* or Book of the Abacus or Book of Calculation appeared in Italy. The author was Leonardo of Pisa or Leonardo Pisano, and he dedicated the book to Michael Scotus, who was the astrologer to Holy Roman Emperor Frederick II. Leonardo Pisano was known as Fibonacci, and he was the one responsible for introducing to Europe the Hindu–Arabic numeration system that we use today. The first edition of *Liber Abaci* was a dense work suited more to scholars than the average man. Many consider Fibonacci's book the greatest arithmetic text of the Middle Ages, for he was the first mathematician to demonstrate the superiority of the Hindu–Arabic numeral system versus the Roman system exemplified by Boethius. He did this by providing numerous examples of how to solve problems related to every major contemporary field of business. Fibonacci was an advocate for systemic change. Knowing the superiority of the new system of calculation for business, he devoted several chapters of his book to showing calculations of profit, interest, and currency conversions. This effort was done to encourage everyone (especially merchants) to abandon Roman numerals and use the superior Indian system of numbers.

Holy Roman Emperor Frederick II[4] had a special interest in mathematics and impressed after reading *Liber Abaci*, the emperor invited Leonardo to his *palazzo* in Pisa. One of the emperor's court mathematicians, Johannes of Palermo, proposed three mathematical problems for Fibonacci to solve. Emperor Frederick II was so impressed that he granted Leonardo an annuity which enabled him to devote himself to his studies. If this is true, that could explain how Fibonacci was able financially to devote more time to writing a revised version of the *Liber Abaci*. Indeed, soon after the meeting, the mathematician dedicated his major work to the emperor, perhaps in appreciation for sponsorship. Specifically, Fibonacci was able with Hindu–Arabic numeral system to introduce his most famous sequence of numbers: 1, 1, 2, 3, 5, 8, 13, 21, 34, 55, 89, 144, and on to infinity. Every number in the sequence is generated by adding together the two previous numbers. They are the simplest example of a recursive sequence where each number is generated by an equation in the previous numbers in the sequence. The mathematical equation that describes it looks like this:

$$\mathrm{X}n + 2 = \mathrm{X}n + 1 + \mathrm{X}n$$

Basically, each integer is the sum of the preceding two numbers, as I said. Hidden inside the sequence is another important number in mathematics: the golden ratio (1.6180339887498948482). If one divides a number in the Fibonacci sequence by the previous number in the sequence (for example, 5/3) then this fraction gets closer and closer to the golden ratio as you take larger and larger Fibonacci numbers. This is regarded by many artists as the perfect proportion for a canvas, and some they think that the golden ratio also appears in the arts, because it is more aesthetically pleasing than other proportions. The Parthenon in Athens, the Great Pyramid in Giza, and Da Vinci's Mona Lisa or Vitruvian Man all incorporate rectangles whose dimensions are based on the golden ratio. For example, Leonardo Da Vinci illustrates the proportion of the male body with an anatomical scale that signifies the exactitudes of the manner a body can fit into a series of shapes. In further notes the Italian polymath, his scrupulous and obsessive studies of human anatomy lean further on these ancient mathematical ideas. Here, mathematics no longer represents numbers, but like logic that would come largely from Greek study, these mathematical formulations become philosophical representations as well as tried-and-tested ideas that occur both physically and naturally all throughout the world.

There are still mysteries about these numbers. For example, are there infinitely many Fibonacci numbers that are also prime numbers? Like 2, 3, 5, and 13. We do not possess a definitive answer to this.

Fibonacci explained that these numbers are at the heart of how things grow in the natural world. The golden ratio, also identified as the 'Divine Ratio', it can be witnessed in flowers, the human face, the gorgeous geometry of the flowering artichoke, and the ratio of male and female honeybees present in their family tree (i.e. how many female and males are present in the ancestry of one particular bee). Nature uses what it has grown so far to make the next move. If one takes squares whose dimensions correspond to the Fibonacci numbers, then it is possible to arrange them in an expanding rectangle, which explains how they help grow things and why they give rise to spirals. Fibonacci explains also that these numbers keep track of the population growth of rabbits. If a pair of rabbits take a month to mature before it can give birth to a new pair of rabbits, how many pairs of rabbits will there be each month? The answer is in the Fibonacci sequence, but while some would argue that the prevalence of Fibonacci numbers in nature are exaggerated, they appear often enough to prove that they reflect some naturally occurring patterns. Think of the array of seeds in the centre of a sunflower. It is possible to notice the golden spiral pattern. If one counts these spirals, the total will be a Fibonacci number. The same is true in pine cones, pineapples, and cauliflower that also reflect the Fibonacci sequence in this manner. The same Fibonacci sequence is to be found in trunks. One trunk grows until it produces a branch, resulting in two growth points. The main trunk then produces another branch, resulting in three growth points. Then the trunk and the first branch produce two more growth points, bringing the total to five. This pattern continues following the Fibonacci numbers. Same if one counts the number of petals on a flower, it is often the case that the total is a number in the Fibonacci sequence. For example, lilies and irises have three petals, buttercups and wild roses have five, delphiniums have eight petals, and so on. Other examples in nature are in storm systems such as hurricanes and tornadoes, which often follow the Fibonacci sequence (for instance, the hurricane spiralling on the weather radar), and also the human body follows the same pattern.

Human beings have one nose, two eyes, three segments to each limb, and five fingers on each hand.

The spiral of Fibonacci numbers was also imagined and visualised by Salvador Dali when he first met with Sigmund Freud on 19 July 1938 at Freud's home in London, where Freud had arrived just a few weeks earlier as a refugee from Nazi-occupied Vienna. The young Salvador Dali imagined Freud's cranium as a snail with his brain in the form of a spiral to be extracted with a needle. By the time of their meeting, both Freud and Dali had gained widespread recognition. Freud, by then 81, was widely regarded as an intellectual giant. Dali was only thirty-four years old, but had already established himself as a key figure in the surrealist movement. Dali had been trying to meet Freud for a long time because like many of the surrealists, he revered psychoanalysis for the radical new light it shed on the life of the mind. As a student in Madrid, Dali had immersed himself in Freud's writings on the unconscious, sexuality, and dreams. Dali yearned to meet Freud. He had already travelled to Vienna several times but failed to make an introduction. Instead, he wrote in his autobiography, he spent his time having 'long and exhaustive imaginary conversations' with his hero. Freud and Dali had a mutual friend in the Austrian author Stefan Zweig, who in 1938 was also living in exile in London, and arranged the meeting.

Scientists have pondered the question about why do so many natural patterns reflect the Fibonacci sequence and in some cases, the correlation may just be a coincidence. In other situations, the ratio exists because that particular growth pattern evolved as the most effective.

Fibonacci extensions are ratio-derived extensions that are commonly used also in financial markets. For example, by traders to determine support and resistance levels that may form in the future and that can be used to identify potential take profit targets. It might appear as a peculiar coincidence that a speculator might exploit the chart by using the Fibonacci sequence. It is most practical to compute Fibonacci extensions when stocks are at new highs or lows, and when there are no clear support and resistance levels on the chart, the new high or below the new low. Hence, the golden ratio has a strong psychological importance in herd behaviour. Traders are more likely to take profits or cover losses at certain price points, which happen to be marked by the golden ratio. Retracement levels alert traders of a potential trend reversal, resistance area, or support area. Retracements are based on the prior move. A bounce is expected to retrace a portion of the prior decline, while a correction is expected to retrace a portion of the prior advance. Once a pullback starts, chartists can identify specific Fibonacci retracement levels for monitoring. As the correction approaches these retracements, chartists should become more alert for a potential 'bullish' reversal.

Despite Emperor Frederick's patronage of Fibonacci's book and the book's widespread distribution across Europe, the introduction of the Hindu–Arabic numbering system provoked intense and bitter resistance up to the early 1500s. Part of the resistance also stemmed from a solid ground of fraud. It was easier to commit fraud with the new numbers than with the old Roman numerical system. Turning a 0 into a 6 or a 9 was easier, and 1 could be converted into 4 or 6, 7, or 9 (this is why Europeans write 7 with a dash in the middle). For instance, in Italy, in Florence it was issued an edict in 1229 prohibiting bankers from using the 'infidel' symbols. The invention of printing was the catalyst to overcome opposition to the full use of the new numbers. However, the final adoption of the new calculation system in Europe would have been brought about by the Renaissance and the Protestant Reformation. The mastery of risk would have come at a hard price for the Roman Catholic Church to weaken its dominance.

4.4 The Renaissance Period: Towards the Law of Probability

Perhaps Donatello's landmark work—and one of the greatest sculptural works of the early Renaissance—was his bronze statue of David. The work signals the return of the nude sculpture in the round figure, and because it was the first such work like this in over a thousand years, it is one of the most important works in the history of Western art. The work was commissioned by Cosimo de'Medici for the *Palazzo Medici*, but it is not known when during the mid-fifteenth century Donatello cast it. David is shown at a triumphal moment within the biblical storyline of his battle with the Philistine, Goliath.

According to the account, after David struck Goliath with the stone from his slingshot, he cut off his head with Goliath's sword, here Donatello shows David standing in a contemplative pose with one foot atop his enemy's severed head. David wears nothing but boots and a shepherd's hat with laurel leaves on top of it, which may allude to his victory or to his role as a poet and musician. Before Donatello's work, David was typically depicted as a king, given his status in the Old Testament. In light of this, Donatello's work is a remarkable change. Not only he is shown in the nude, but he is also a youth. In the Middle Ages, nudity was not used in art except in certain moral contexts, such as the depiction of Adam and Eve, or the sending of souls off to hell. In the classical world, nudity was often used in a different, majestic context, such as with figures who were gods, heroes, or athletes. Here Donatello seems to be calling to mind the type of heroic nudity of antiquity, since David is depicted at a triumphal point in the biblical narrative of his victory over Goliath.

In any case, Donatello's David is a classic work of Renaissance sculpture, given its Judaeo-Christian subject matter modelled on a classical sculptural type. It was revolutionary for its day because it wanted also to represent human beings as no more subservient to divinity—a message that appears over and over again in the art of the Renaissance. Think of Brunelleschi's great dome in Florence and the cathedral, it proclaims that religion has literally been brought down to earth. Also very symbolic will be the painting of Piero della Francesca, who painted the picture of the Virgin (The *Brera Madonna*). The painting was executed between 1472 and 1474. The work represents a *sacra conversazione* with the Virgin enthroned and the sleeping Child in the middle, surrounded by a host of angels and saints (Picture 4.1).

On the right low corner, kneeling and wearing his armour, the Duke, patron of arts and *condottiero* Federico da Montefeltro. The background consists of the apse of a church in Renaissance classical style. The child wears a necklace of deep red coral beads, a colour which alludes to blood, a symbol of life and death, but also to the redemption brought by Christ. Coral was also used for teething and was often worn by babies. The saints at the left of the Madonna are generally identified as John the Baptist, Bernardino of Siena, and Jerome; on the right would be Francis, Peter Martyr, and Andrew. In the last figure, the Italian historian Ricci has identified a portrait of Luca Pacioli, the Franciscan monk and mathematician born in Sansepolcro like Piero della Francesca. Pacioli wrote in 1494 the '*Summa de artithmetica, geometria, proportioni et proportionalita*': an important work on mathematics, arithmetic, algebra, geometry, foreign exchange calculations, and double-entry bookkeeping. Luca Pacioli was a teacher of mathematics, not a mathematician, but his work represents a further step into the legitimisation of Hindu–Arabic numerical system, and—for this—he directly acknowledges his debt to Fibonacci's *Liber Abaci* written nearly three-hundred years earlier (see Sect. 4.3).

Picture 4.1 Piero della Francesca, 'Brera Madonna' executed 1472–1474 (*Source* It is written that this painting is public domain https://it.wikipedia.org/wiki/Pala_di_Brera#/media/File:Piero_della_Francesca_046.jpg [WIKIPEDIA])

The *Brera Madonna* provides another clear evidence of the reformed world of the Renaissance where men and women are free-standing human beings, who might even question God. In fact, the Renaissance was also a time of discovery not by chance. For instance, the son of a wool merchant, Christopher Columbus, was born in Genoa, Italy, in 1451, and his passion for adventure and exploration led him to become the first who stumbled upon the Americas, and whose journeys marked the beginning of centuries of transatlantic colonisation. He made four trips across the Atlantic Ocean from Spain: in 1492, 1493, 1498, and 1502. He was determined to find a direct water route west from Europe to Asia, but he never did. Instead, he stumbled upon the Americas. Though he did not really 'discover' the so-called New World, his journeys marked the beginning of exploration of North and South America. Indeed, during the fifteenth and sixteenth centuries, leaders of several European nations sponsored expeditions abroad in the hope that explorers would find great wealth and vast undiscovered lands. By the end of the fifteenth century, Spain's *Reconquista*—the expulsion of Jews and Muslims out of the Kingdom after centuries of war—was complete, and the nation turned its attention to exploration and conquest in other areas of the world (see Chapter 2 when I illustrated the City of Gold that *conquistadores* found). Those discoveries paved the ground for the sixteenth century and the Protestant Reformation that was an important religious, political, intellectual, and cultural upheaval that splintered Catholic Europe, setting in place the structures and beliefs that would define the continent in the modern era.

In northern and central Europe, reformers like Martin Luther, John Calvin, and Henry VIII challenged papal authority and questioned the Catholic Church's ability to define Christian practice. They argued for a religious and political redistribution of power into the hands of Bible— and pamphlet-reading pastors. The disruption triggered wars, persecutions, and the so-called Counter-Reformation, the Catholic Church's delayed but forceful response to the Protestants.

The Protestant Reformation usually dates in 1517 with the publication of Martin Luther's 95 Theses. Its ending can be placed anywhere from the 1555 Peace of Augsburg, which allowed for the coexistence of Catholicism and Lutheranism in Germany to the 1648 Treaty of Westphalia, which ended the Thirty Years' War. The key ideas of the Reformation—a call to purify the Church and a belief that the Bible, not tradition, should be the sole source of spiritual authority—were not themselves novel. However, Luther and the other reformers became the first to skilfully use the power of the printing press to give their ideas to a wide audience. I shall say that the Reformation meant more than just a change in humanity's relationship with God. By eliminating the confessional, it warned people that they would have to walk on their own and would have to take responsibility for the consequences of their directions. Human beings could not remain passive in the face of an unknown future. They had no choice than to make decision over a far wider range of circumstances. For these reasons, the 1500s and 1600s were a time of geographical exploration, confrontation with new lands and new societies, and experimentation in art, poetic forms, science, architecture, and mathematics.

Speaking of advances in the knowledge of the secret mysteries of nature and science, Girolamo Cardano and Galileo Galilei are essential historical thinkers. Cardano was a sixteenth-century physician, who lived an impoverished life. Through his poverty, he used the little money he had in dice games and soon became addicted to gambling. Throughout his addiction to gambling, Cardano tried to find a job that he deserved. Many employers rejected him, not for his addiction, but for the fact of his illegitimate birth. However, he did not give up hope. Cardano kept researching probability and chance. His gambling addiction led him to discover one of the fundamental laws of the theory of probability. He was possibly the first to realise that there is in fact a theory of chance.

One of the first works ever written on the theory of probability is Cardano's *Liber de Ludo Aleae* (Book on Games of Chance). It was the first thorough treatment of sample spaces and probability. Cardano's book is mainly written about dice games and how the die could fall during a dicing game. There are few scenarios that deal with playing cards. His book showed the different number of ways that a specified number of dice may fall in a certain dice game. Cardano worked to formulate the probability of an event as a ratio of favourable to total causes (or outcomes). In his book, Cardano began by giving explanations of terminology and ideas before he delved into his research. He created the mathematical terms 'circuit' and 'equality'. However, it is also fair to say that modern mathematicians and researchers do not always appreciate Cardano's book. Cardano used, in his book, the standard method and the reasoning on the mean method. Specifically, the standard method is what we use today in statistics. It takes favourable cases and divides them by the circuit. This is the method that is taught in many introductory statistics classes. For example, if one is casting a single die, the probability of one throwing an odd number is 1/2. This is understood by dividing the possible odd number outcomes by the number of total outcomes. By doing this, one would get 3/6, which simplifies to 1/2. On the other hand, the reasoning method is displayed alongside the standard method in *Liber de Ludo Aleae*. Cardano reasoned in his book that in six throws, theoretically each of the faces should have appeared once. When a die is thrown, each of its six faces should, in the long run, appear equally often. However, many of the results that Cardano tried to provide with the reasoning method are erroneous.

Along with the two methods he also writes about morals and ethics and who, when, and with whom one should gamble. He begins with the condition of play. For example, money must be spent in moderation. Cardano makes it very clear that one must in no circumstance gamble alone. This could create suspicions that the gambler is developing an addiction. In his view, women should not be permitted to gamble at any time because at that time in history, it would have not been 'lady-like' in the least. One's opponent should be on the same proficiency level as the player to save the humiliation of losing. There were many reasons as to why Cardano believed that a man should gamble. In fact, the book could be viewed as a gambling manual. Several commentators on the book have concluded that it is a mishmash of several, sometimes contradictory, results and statements written over an approximate 40-year period. Nonetheless, the book is essential to establish a link between probability and randomness, which is what games of chance are about.

The importance of probabilities becomes more explicit with Galileo Galilei, who referred to this by using the word '*probabilità*' that means 'probability' in Italian, and he did so in respect to theories of his time that believed that the Earth was at the centre of the Universe. He defined such theories as 'improbable'. According to Galileo, the Sun is at the centre of the universe and the Earth constantly revolving around it on its axis. This is not a simple statement, but an affirmation that would cost Galileo Galilei a strong opposition by the Roman Catholic Church. Galileo was famous, and he won the patronage of leading Italian powers like the Medici and Barberini for discoveries he had made with the astronomical telescope he had built. But when his observations led him to prove the Copernican theory of the solar system, in which the Sun and not the Earth is the centre, and which the Church regarded as heresy, Galileo was summoned to Rome by the Inquisition. Forced to recant.

Specifically, Galileo adopted the Copernican astronomy theory presented in a book published in 1543 by the Polish scientist Nicolaus Copernicus in opposition to the prevailing theory, advanced by the second-century astronomer Ptolemy, that the Sun and the rest of the cosmos orbited the Earth. The contest between the two models was purely on theoretic and theological grounds until Galileo made the first observations of the four largest moons of Jupiter, exploding the Ptolemaic notion that all heavenly bodies must orbit the Earth.

In 1616, the Copernican view was declared heretical because it refused a strict biblical interpretation of the Creation that:

> God fixed the Earth upon its foundation, not to be moved forever

Galileo obtained the permission of Pope Urban VIII, a Barberini and a friend, to continue research into both the Ptolemaic and the Copernican views of the world, provided that his findings drew no definitive conclusions and acknowledged divine omnipotence. But when, in 1632, Galileo published his findings in 'Dialogue Concerning the Two Chief World Systems' (*Dialogo Sopra i Due Massimi Sistemi del Mondo*) the work was a compelling endorsement of the Copernican system.

Summoned to Rome for trial by the Inquisition one year later, Galileo defended himself by saying that scientific research and the Christian faith were not mutually exclusive and that study of the natural world would promote understanding and interpretation of the scriptures. But his views were judged 'false and erroneous'. Ageing, ailing, and threatened with torture by the Inquisition, Galileo recanted on 30 April 1633. Because of his advanced years, he was permitted house arrest in Siena for eight years before his death in 1642 at the age of 77. Legend says that when Galileo rose from kneeling before his inquisitors, he murmured: '*e pur, si muove*' (from Italian, 'even so, it does move').

The renunciation of his own scientific findings as 'abjured, cursed and detested' caused him great personal anguish but saved him from being burned at the stake. It took more than three-hundred years for the Roman Catholic Church to admit that Galileo was right and to clear his name of heresy. Thanks to Pope John Paul II, who rectified one of the Church's most infamous wrongs after thirteen-year investigation into the Church's condemnation of Galileo Galilei in 1633.

The dispute between the Church and Galileo has long stood as one of history's great emblems of conflict between reasons and dogma, science and faith. The Vatican's formal acknowledgement of an error, moreover, is a rarity in an institution built over centuries on the belief that the Church is the final arbiter in matters of faith. Whatever the course of events could have been at that time, the history of Galileo Galilei reminds us of the importance of the primordial idea and word of 'probability' that carries a meaning close to approbation. In other words, how much can we accept of what we know? In Galileo's context, the probability was how much human beings could approve of what they were told. The more recent view of probability as a science and subject of statistics did not emerge until mathematicians had developed a theoretical understanding of the frequencies of past events. Cardano might have been the first to introduce this statistical side of the theory of probability, but the contemporary meaning of the word during his lifetime still does not have any connection with measurement. However, since Cardano and Galileo Galilei the seed of doubt was planted, and the Renaissance directly confirms that without numbers there are no odds and no probabilities, and without probabilities the future can only be a matter of God.

4.5 Making Probability Mathematical

Ideas about probability and risk were emerging at a rapid pace as interest in the subject spread through France and on to Switzerland, Germany, and England. France had an explosion of mathematical innovation during the seventeenth and eighteenth centuries that went far beyond Cardano's dice-tossing experiments. Advances in calculus provided the foundation for many practical applications of probability, from insurance and investment to far-distant subjects such as medicine, conduct of war, and weather forecasting.

Italian writers of the fifteenth and sixteenth centuries, notably Pacioli (1494), Tartaglia (1556), and Cardano (1545) had discussed the problem of division of a stake between two players whose game was interrupted before its close.

However, when the problem was proposed to Blaise Pascal and Pierre de Fermat in 1654, by the *Chevalier de Mere*, a gambler who is said to have had unusual ability 'even for the mathematics', a modern conception of probability theory was established for the first time. The correspondence between Pascal and Fermat was fundamental in the development of modern concepts of probability, specifically expectation value. Until the invention of 'expected value' people lacked a simple way to quantify the value of an uncertain future event.

A gamble's value obviously depends on how much one can win. But Pascal and Fermat further concluded that a gamble's value also should be weighted by the likelihood of a win. Thus, the expected value is computed as a potential event's magnitude multiplied by its probability, thus in the case of a single gamble:

$$\mathrm{E(x)} = \mathrm{x} * \mathrm{p}$$

This formula is now so common that it is taken for granted, but the expected value is deep in its implications for choice. The equation represents the expected value of a random variable x, whose value is subject to randomness or uncertainty, and which is denoted as E (x). The formula states that the expected value of x is equal to the product of x and the probability of x occurring, denoted as p. In other words, the probability of x taking a certain value represents the likelihood of that value occurring. For instance, suppose we have a random variable x that represents the outcomes of rolling a fair six-sided dice. The possible outcomes of x are 1, 2, 3, 4, 5, and 6, each with an equal probability of 1/6. To calculate the expected value of x using the formula above, we need to multiply each possible outcome of x by its probability and add up the results:

$$\mathrm{E}(x) - (1 + 2 + 3 + 4 + 5 + 6)/6 = 3.5$$

Therefore, the expected value of rolling a fair six-sided dice is 3.5, which is the sum of all possible outcomes of the dice, divided by the total number of outcomes.

This open view of all possible outcomes implies optimal choice—to maximise expected value, simply head for the highest hill. Thus, the expected value is both elegant in its computation and deep in its implications for choice. Even today, the expected value forms the backbone of dominant theories of choice in fields including economics and psychology. Recent replacements have tweaked the key ingredients of expected value—adding a curve to the magnitude component (in the case of expected utility) or flattering the probability component (in the case of prospect theory). Beyond its longevity, the expected value represents an innovation of the seventeenth century by which human beings may faithfully trust on their capabilities and skills. Expected value can be used to predict diverse choices ranging from what to buy, to which investment to make, to whom to trust.

Thus, the expected value is beautiful in its simplicity and utility—and almost true. Like any scientific theory, expected value is not only quantifiable, but also falsifiable. As it turns out, people do not always maximise their expected values. Sometimes they let potential losses overshadow gains or disregard probability (as highlighted by prospect theory). These quirks of choice suggest that while expected value may prescribe how people should choose, it does not always describe what people do choose. In fact, as I will explain in the next section the measurability of risk in objective terms shall be read in conjunction with a subjective nature of risk based on intuition, desires, and belief.

Pascal applied his thinking on expected value also and especially to the wagering or betting on the existence of God, and he did a calculation of sorts in making this bet. Pascal argues that we are incapable of knowing whether God exists or not, yet we must 'wager' one way or the other. The so-called 'Pascal's Wager' provides a pragmatic rationale for theistic belief. Its most popular version says that it is rationally mandatory to choose a way of life that seeks to cultivate belief in God because this is the option of maximum expected utility. If you bet on the existence of God and it turns out that God exists, then you get an infinite reward. Otherwise, if you bet against the existence of God when he exists, then you get either a negative infinite or finite utility value. You are only finitely rewarded for either betting on or against God when he does not exist. Given that your subjective probability for God's existence is some positive real number, your expected utility for betting on God will be infinite, making it much greater than your expected utility for betting against God, which will be at most equal to some positive finite number. Thus assuming that such a decision matrix is right, the principle of expected utility maximisation requires you to bet on God's existence.

As it can be seen, Pascal's wager goes a step further into epistemology of certainty or uncertainty of our knowledge, namely an argument for believing, or for at least taking steps to believe in God. Pascal aims to show that we ought to believe in God, rather than that God exists. He seeks to provide prudential reasons rather than evidential reasons for believing in God.

This thinking translated in modern probability theory implies that in any decision problem, the way the world is, and what an agent does, together determine an outcome for the agent. Utilities are assigned to such outcomes, numbers that represent the degree to which the agent values them. It is typical to present these numbers in a decision table, with the columns corresponding to the various relevant states of the world, and the rows corresponding to the various possible actions that the agent can perform.

In decisions under uncertainty, nothing more is given—in particular, the agent does not assign subjective probabilities to the states of the world. Still rationality dictates a unique decision nonetheless. By contrast in decision under risk, the agent assigns subjective probabilities to the various states of the world. According to decision theory, rationality requires you to perform the action of maximum expected utility (if there is one).

4.6 The Nature of Human Beings

Mark Spitznagel is a famous hedge fund manager specialising in tail risk black swan type funds. He built his fund, Universa Investments LP, working with Nassim Taleb, and has produced quite spectacular results since its founding in the late 2000s. He is a strong advocate for the importance of the geometric average, and he has dedicated important speculations on Daniel Bernoulli's paper on expected returns and the measurement of risk that was presented in 1738 at the Papers of the Imperial Academy of Sciences in St. Petersburg.

Daniel Bernoulli, a Swiss mathematician, was thirty-eight years old when he presented the paper, who made significant contributions to many fields of mathematics including probability theory, statistics, and physics. He is best known for his work on fluid dynamics, including Bernoulli's principle, which describes the relationship between the pressure and velocity of a fluid. One of Bernoulli's lesser-known contributions is—in fact—his work on the geometric mean. In other words, a mathematical concept that relates to probability and statistics. Most finance articles that quote Bernoulli do so to talk about personalised investor risk tolerance and risk aversion. Indeed, economists latched on to this paper in creating modern-day economic utility theory.

Nonetheless, the paper is not about utility *sic et simpliciter*. It is about expected value. Up until this point in history, people used the arithmetic average as the expected future outcome for a risky proposition. In this way—as I have explained in the previous section—the arithmetic average became known as the expected value. Therefore, Bernoulli developed the concept of utility to get the reader to abandon the traditional view of expected value (arithmetic average). He then used utility as an intermediate step to derive the proper equation for managing risk. In doing so, he created a new method to measure risk that does not use utility.

Bernoulli starts the paper by confirming that traditional risk evaluation comes from expected values, calculated from arithmetic average. Then he points out that this average ignores the specific financial circumstances of the participant. Simply put, someone with little wealth will value a gamble differently than someone with greater wealth. Therefore, the original rule for determining expected values must not be correct. An item is valued by its usefulness (utility), therefore, the expected value must also reflect the usefulness it yields.

Bernoulli noticed a disconnect between using the arithmetic average as the expected value and how people act in the real world. Instead of calling people flawed because they clearly do not follow logic, he chose to call the theory flawed instead. The arithmetic average was entrenched as the foundation of the decision-making at the time. So Bernoulli chose to use the concept of utility (which he called '*emolumentum*' in Latin) to divorce people of this belief that the arithmetic is 'expected'. What matters is not price, but growth, and growth is utility.

After dividing into some extreme examples of how the arithmetic average clearly does not work, he returns from the side discussion, stating one should focus on what is typical for most people. He says that most people find usefulness from money in inverse proportion to their current wealth. As in: usefulness = new money/wealth. Bernoulli is claiming that human beings derive usefulness from growth, not absolute price. This is his foundational point. Nearly everybody will derive the usefulness of a risky proposition from the growth it provides them.

Now that the hypothesis is clear—usefulness comes from growth, not absolute gains—he begins to derive a formula for measuring growth. He maps the current world's beliefs of expectation risk measurement into his chart method. The equation of Bernoulli is meant to find the value of the risky proposition. It is supposed to convey the risk worth in actual real dollars, not an imaginary utility value. The geometric average or geometric mean represents the value of the risky proposition. Bernoulli only used utility to convince people that they were valuing risk incorrectly, and then to derive the final solution that does value risk correctly. The solution Bernoulli found is the power of the geometric average. The geometric mean is a type of average that is calculated by taking the nth root of the product of n numbers. For example, if you want to find a geometric mean of the numbers 2, 4, and 8, you would multiply them together ($2 \times 4 \times 8 = 64$), and then take the cube root (since there are three numbers) to get the geometric mean, which is 4. Alternatively, if we have two numbers, a and b, then the geometric mean of those numbers would be the square root of the product of a and b: $\sqrt{a \times b}$.

Bernoulli's geometric mean is a modification of the traditional geometric mean. It is used to calculate the expected value of a random variable when the possible outcomes are not equally likely. Suppose we have a set of possible outcomes, with probabilities, p1, p2, ..., pn. Then, the c as:

$$(p1^\wedge(1/p1) * p2^\wedge(1/p2) * \ldots * pn^\wedge(1/pn)^\wedge(1/p1 + p2 + \ldots + pn))$$

where the exponents 1/p1, 1/p2, ..., 1/pn are known as the 'weights' of the corresponding probabilities. Bernoulli's geometric mean is useful in situations where the probabilities of different outcomes are not equally likely, but it is still necessary to calculate an expected value that takes into account the relative importance of each outcome.

Bernoulli three-hundred years ago may have been the first person to prove that the concept of utility is experienced intuitively. It conveys the sense of usefulness, desirability, or satisfaction. Risk involves two different and yet inseparable elements: the objective facts and a subjective view about the desirability of what is to be gained, or lost, by the decision. In other words, people ascribe different values to risk. In doing so, Bernoulli is also introducing for the first time the centrality of the figure of the risk-taker with his/her subjective beliefs that cannot be measured. This is the subjective connotation of risk that cannot be anticipated.

Finally, Bernoulli may have been the first to appreciate the benefits of diversification in an economic context:

> Another rule which may prove useful can be derived from our theory. This is the rule that it is advisable to divide goods which are exposed to some danger into several portions rather than to risk them all together.

The idea of diversification conveys the introduction of a variety to a set of objectives. In finance, diversification is perhaps the most important investment principle by which a risk-averse investor will want to diversify. It is roughly understood as the mitigation of overall portfolio risk by investing in a wide variety of assets. It is undeniable that Bernoulli's paper has inspired or influenced the seminal work of Harry Markowitz (1952), who will establish the first mathematical foundations of portfolio theory in the Journal of Finance. This was the moment of the birth of modern financial economics, and as Markowitz himself points out in his historical review of portfolio theory, Bernoulli is also not the first to appreciate the benefits of diversification. For example, in the Merchant of Venice, Act I, Scene I, William Shakespeare has Antonio say:

> … I thank my fortune for it,
> My ventures are not in one bottom trusted,
> Nor to one place; nor is my whole estate
> Upon the fortune of this present year …

Antonio rests easily at the beginning of the play because he is diversified across ships, places, and time. 'Don't put all your eggs in one basket' is a familiar adage highlighted in many textbooks of microeconomics and finance. Diversification in finance is equivalent to the reduction of overall risk (but not generally its elimination), and it reminds us that an economic agent who chooses to diversify is understood to prefer variety over similarity. In a world without uncertainty, the diversification principle simply reflects the desire for variety, but in a world where uncertainty is dominating the scene, it reflects the desire to hedge against uncertainty. In fact, I shall argue that uncertainty rather than risk has always had the power to influence the objective manifestations and expressions of the world, so that human beings cannot anticipate uncertainty. Against common wisdom, uncertainty rather than risk is where the analysis should focus on, and the next sections are dedicated to introduce the concept of uncertainty by starting from human calamities that have deeply affected our everyday life.

4.7 Pandemics: From the Black Death to Covid-19

The Black Death is known as being:

> the huge plague epidemic that ravaged Europe, Asia Minor, the Middle East and North Africa in the years 1346 – 1353 (Benedictow, 2004)

Believed to have originated in the Tibetan-Qinghai Plateau in Central Asia, the bubonic plague—*Yersina pestis*—a bacterium carried on fleas that lived on rats travelled along trade routes both on land and then eventually over water which led the plague to Europe. It seems that the trade routes of the Mediterranean have increased the speed of the spread and introduced the Black Death to the ports along the coasts. In fact, the highly commercialised world of the Mediterranean by that time ensured the plague's swift transfer on merchant ships to Italy.

The Black Death was a pandemic that affected people of all nationalities and ages. The symptoms of this pandemic included pain in their bodies, the vomiting of blood, and ultimately the death (Nohl, 1969). The young, old male, female, rich, and poor were impacted by its ruthless invasion. Between 1345 and 1350 half of the population in Europe had succumbed to the plague. This huge number of deaths was accompanied by general economic devastation. With a third of the workforce dead, the crops could not be harvested and communities fell apart. For instance, one in ten villages in England and in Tuscany, and other regions in Europe were lost and never re-founded. Houses fell into the ground and were covered by grass and earth, leaving only the church behind. Historians have argued that the labour shortage allowed peasants that survived the pandemic to demand better pay or to seek employment elsewhere. Despite government resistance, feudal system itself was ultimately eroded. The broader trend of the post-Black Death fourteenth and fifteenth centuries was a concentration of resources—capital, skills, and infrastructure—into the hands of a small number of large companies. In Aberdeen in Scotland, John of Fordun, a Scottish chronicler recorded that:

> This sickness befell people everywhere, but especially the middling and lower classes, rarely the great. It generated such horror that children did not dare to visit their dying parents, nor parents their children, but fled for fear of contagion as if from leprosy or a serpent

The idea that the Black Death was nature being victorious over man, threatened the idea that man is powerful and able to take decisions. Until Fibonacci, Pacioli, Galileo Galilei, Pascal and Fermat, and Bernoulli—as I have illustrated in the previous sections—the centrality of the man was lost, and it was hard to conceive risk management tools and the importance of subjective beliefs and desirability in human beings. Indeed, the discourse on risk becomes much more complex if its subjective dimension is taken into account, and it is constructed as a value that varies according to the context.

Human beings have always been obsessed with counteracting risks and particularly in imagining or in trying to build a risk-free world. Despite a risk-free world that might be made theoretically possible by implementing highly restrictive policies, still those would often be likely to achieve unreasonable objectives. For instance, imagine a case of zero automobile fatalities; this might be possible, and any risk could be eradicated by outlawing motor vehicles. The same is true for drowning, which could be eradicated by outlawing swimming and bathing. These examples already tell us something about the irrationality of such restrictive and hard policies. It means that we cannot totally eradicate risk or live in a risk-free world, otherwise the same science of probability and statistics would have never proved useful for measuring risk. By contrast, our level of accuracy in measuring risk is necessarily and intrinsically limited due to our limited intuition and our tendency to commit mistakes.

Following the Black Death, we have realised that life is short and full of risks. It was an historic disruption of everyday life, the likes of which we have not seen in most of our lifetimes. Hence, the very compelling question of today can be summarised in the following: could we witness very long-term effects from the present contagion of Covid-19?

Covid-19 is not as deadly as the bubonic plague, and our tools to deal with pandemics today are far better stacked than when the pestilence reached the harbour of Messina on the north-eastern coast of Sicily in late 1347. However, our thinking to deal with pandemics is still highly influenced by our incapacity to deal with uncertainty. For instance, since the outbreak of Covid-19 governments around the world have been trying to handle the pandemic. Governments have frequently offered their citizens the possibility of a zero-Covid world. This is as irrational as speaking of zero automobile fatalities or zero-drowning world. Risk can be curtailed or measured, but it cannot be wholly eradicated. In other words, we must deal with uncertainty in our societies. And yet New Zealand, Australia, and especially China have embraced zero-Covid policies. Those countries have imposed the most onerous lockdown since Covid's inception in 2020, and they have imposed sharp restrictions on international travel, business closures, and so on. Nonetheless, once the restrictions were lifted and after the celebration of a zero-Covid world, the same virus came back in the form of Delta variant in 2021. Since the inception of the Delta variant, many have indeed started to wonder whether this pandemic is permanent. This is because the Delta variant is more than twice as infectious as the virus humanity has been fighting since 2020. This variant seems to be able to evade even the best defences, which are the mRNA vaccines produced by Pfizer and Moderna, and vaccinated people with breakthrough infections can further spread the virus. Breakthrough cases caused anxiety for many as Covid transmission rose again in the United States in the summer of 2021. Fully vaccinated people could contract Covid-19 but this did not mean that vaccines were not working because no vaccine is 100% effective, and health authorities around the world were expecting breakthrough cases. Indeed, the real function of mRNA vaccines is to prevent severe illness and death, even from the Delta variant. Vaccines—to this end—are a form of measuring risk and reducing contagion risk as well as a form of protection against severe illness from the Delta variant, but they cannot wholly eradicate the virus itself or prevent transmission.

Furthermore, it is hard to know what the post-Covid period has in store. It is not by chance that China's economy—for instance—underperformed in July 2021, with widespread flooding and an outbreak of the coronavirus Delta variant strongly challenging the country's growth. And not surprisingly the answer to this phenomenon has once again been strict travel restrictions and policies in response to the largest outbreak that began in mid-July 2021 in the city of Nanjing and has since led to hundreds of new infections across multiple cities. The same happened in Australia, which decided to reimpose lockdowns threatening the country with the prospect of a double-dip recession. The same negative effects of the Delta variant have been experienced in Israel, which in mid-summer 2021 was one of the first countries in the world to experience an alarming fourth wave of infections despite 70% of its population having been jabbed by early April 2021.

By the end of November 2021, a new strain of Covid-19 virus nicknamed the Omicron variant first identified in South Africa has again posed new challenges to national economies. Omicron has ranked as the predominant strain in the United States for over a year between 2022 and 2023. By December of 2022, Omicron was causing daily case numbers in the United States to skyrocket to over a million. In 2022, it spawned a number of subvariants, including BA.5, BQ.1, and BQ.11. By January 2023, a new Omicron subvariant called XBB.1.5 was causing the most infections in the United States.

As it can be seen, the story is infinite and despite vaccines playing an essential role, Covid is likely to be here to stay like many other hazards or risks in our lives. It will almost certainly become endemic, continuing to spread and to flare up at different times and in different places for many years. Indeed, although the respiratory disease has had a catastrophic impact on commodity and asset prices, a recovery may not close the chapter. The coronavirus can leave a durable imprint. Indeed, variants can evade infection-induced immunity, and immunity from infection is not as strong as immunity from vaccination. Masking remains one of the ways of controlling contagion risk and infections, although with a modest effect on viral transmission. However, masks are another form of managing risk and mitigating Covid infections.

It is unrealistic to imagine a risk-free world, although this will always be a desired objective pursued by human beings. Risk—as I have said—is everywhere and anywhere and represents the 'human-humanity' of progress. Without risk and tools to measure it, society could never be able to progress and evolve in any sector, from financial markets to science. Even the strictest policy in the world cannot totally eradicate risk. Risk can be measured and curtailed, but it cannot be eradicated. Stricter policies do not equal better policies. For instance, imposing further lockdowns in a pandemic is not necessarily the best answer or the final answer to eradicating infection risk. Nonetheless, mask-wearing in public places becomes essential to try to manage infection risk especially if the contagion risk is high. Even booster programmes after eight months from a second shot can still help to reduce risk. This shows that human beings are destined to co-habit with anxiety and risk, and especially with uncertainty.

4.8 From the Secret of Felicity to the Chicago School of Economics

Under conditions of uncertainty, both rationality and measurement are essential to decision-making. Daniel Bernoulli—as I said—introduced utility as the unit for measuring preferences, but every advance in decision-making theory were new discoveries rather than extensions of Bernoulli's original formulation. Utility theory was rediscovered in the eighteenth century by Jeremy Bentham, a popular English philosopher. He advocates that if the consequences of an action are good, then the act is moral, and if the consequences are bad, the act is immoral. Central to his argument was a belief that it is human nature to desire that which is pleasurable, and to avoid that which is painful. As a self-proclaimed atheist, he wanted to place morality on a firm, secular foundation. At the beginning of his 'Introduction to the Principles of Morals and Legislation', Bentham wrote:

> Natura has placed mankind under the governance of two sovereign masters, pain and pleasure. It is for them alone to point out what we ought to do, as well as to determine what we shall do

It is because of this emphasis on pleasure that his theory is known as hedonic utilitarianism. However, this does not mean human beings can do whatever they like. Importantly, for Bentham, it is not just one's own happiness or pleasure that matters. He notes that ethics is the art of directing men's actions to the production of the greatest possible quantity of happiness. The moral agent will perform action that maximises happiness or pleasure for everyone involved, but how can happiness be measured?

Bentham defended an objective form of morality that could be measured in a scientific way. As an empiricist, he came up with a way to 'weigh' or quantify pleasure and pains as the consequences of an action. He called this set of metaphorical scales the 'hedonic' or 'felicific calculus' allowing a rational moral agent to think through, and then act on, the right—moral—thing to do. The 'hedonic calculus' is used to measure how much pain or pleasure an action will cause. It takes into consideration how near or far away the consequences will be, how intense it will be and how long it will last, if it will lead on to further pleasure or pains, and how certain this consequence will result from the action under consideration.

The moral decision-maker is meant to act as an 'impartial observer' or 'disinterested bystander' to be as objective as they can be and choose the action that will produce the greatest amount of good. There are some applications of utilitarianism. For example, a politician in charge of making decisions that effects a large group of people should act in a way that maximises happiness and minimises pain and suffering. In this way, the hedonic calculus supports a welfare system that reduces unfair outcomes by redistributing wealth and resources. Bentham's theory relies on accurately predicting outcomes, and as such holds the moral agent accountable for moral luck. One might intend to do a good deed, but if an unpredictable result occurs, leading to a negative outcome, then they are still to be held morally responsible.

As it can be seen, Bentham is talking about life in general, but economists of the nineteenth century fastened onto utility as a tool for discovering how prices result from interactive decisions by buyers and sellers. This led directly to the law of supply and demand. The focus of mainstream economists of the nineteenth century was whether one opportunity was superior to another. The possibility of a loss was not a consideration. Consequently the distractions of uncertainty were not contemplated. By contrast, those economists spent their time to analyse the psychological and subjective factors that motivate people to pay for goods. The idea that someone might not have money to buy bread was unthinkable.

Alfred Marshall, a preeminent economist of the Victorian age marked 'no one should have an occupation which tends to make him anything less than a gentlemen'. William Stanley Jevons was one of the prime contributors to this body of thought, and he launched the 'Marginal Revolution' of 1871–1874 that gave birth to Neoclassical economics. Jevons was born in Liverpool on 1 September 1835, the ninth child of a family of prosperous iron merchants. However, the death of his mother in 1845 and the collapse of the family firm in 1848 circumscribed Jevon's opportunities. His early education was acquired at home, at Liverpool Mechanics Institute, and finally at a preparatory school in London. As a Unitarian (a non-conformist Protestant sect), Jevons was legally barred from taking the traditional educational route through Oxford and Cambridge. So, in 1852, Jevons entered University College London (UCL), a Benthamite institution that accepted non-conformists to study chemistry, mathematics, and logic. It was here that he came under the influence of the logician Augustus De Morgan. However, financial circumstances forced him to withdraw in his second year and accept a post as Assayer at the new Royal Mint in Sydney, Australia. After his father's death in 1855, Jevons returned to London in 1859 and earned his BA at UCL in 1860. His MA in Logic, Philosophy, and Political Economy was acquired in 1862. Eventually, in 1866 he launched—as I said—the 'Marginal Revolution'. He outlines the principle of diminishing marginal utility and shows how it governs individual choice via the equi-marginal principle. Jevons shows how this principle serves as a foundation for a new and comprehensive theory of value. By combining two 'laws' of exchange—that every exchange must be mutually beneficial and that every portion must be exchanged at the same rate—Jevons states that a higgledy-piggledy exchange process will work its way necessarily to the market equilibrium because utility varies with the quantity of a commodity already in one's possession. The ability to express everything in quantity terms could solve the issue of value. Once again Jevons brushed off the problem of uncertainty by announcing that probabilities learned from past experience and observation can be applied, and utility is no more connected to subjective value. Francis Edgeworth, a contemporary of Jevons, went as far as to propose the development of a 'hedonimeter'. This was a rush towards measurement.

However, the optimism of the Victorians was snuffed out by the destruction of human life on the battlefields of the First World War, the uneasy peace that followed, and the Russian Revolution. When Sigmund Freud declared that irrationality is the natural condition of humanity, he became a celebrity overnight. Up to this point, the classical economists had defined economics as a riskless system that always produced optimal results. Such convictions died hard even in the face of economic problems that emerged in the wake of the war.

In 1921, the University of Chicago economist Frank Knight wrote 'Risk, Uncertainty and Profit' opening the doors to economic decisions under uncertainty conditions. John Maynard Keynes echoed Knight's and rejected Jevon's faith in the universal applicability of measurement. The law of probabilities with well-ordered preferences was no more sufficient to direct the decisions of the economic agent. Researchers sought for ways of conducting a systematic analysis of the unexpected. What do you do when a decision leads to a result that was not even contemplated in the original set of probabilities? Knight and Keynes confront such question in a serious fashion, and they define risk as it has come to be understood today.

Knight was an American economist, who is considered the main founder of the Chicago School of Economics. He was educated at the University of Tennessee and at Cornell University where he obtained his Ph.D. in 1916. He then taught at the University of Iowa, and the University of Chicago becoming an emeritus professor in 1952. Among his more notable economics students were future Nobel laureates Milton Friedman, George Stigler, and James Buchanan. Knight's book 'Risk, Uncertainty, and Profit' published in 1921 is one of the most important contributions to economics. In it, he makes an important distinction between insurable and uninsurable risks.

According to Knight, profit—earned by the entrepreneur who makes decisions in an uncertain environment—is the entrepreneur's reward for bearing uninsurable risk. As Knight saw it, an ever-changing world brings new opportunities for businesses to make profits, but also means that the economic agent has imperfect knowledge of future events. Therefore, according to Knight, risk applies to situations where the risk-taker does not know the outcome of a given situation, but can accurately measure the odds. Uncertainty, on the other hand, applies to situations where the agent cannot know all the information he needs in order to set accurate odds in the first place. In other words, 'true uncertainty' as Knight called it, is 'not susceptible to measurement'. An airline might forecast that the risk of an accident involving one of its planes is exactly one per 20 million take-offs. But the economic outlook for airlines 30 years from now involves so many unknown factors as to be incalculable. Some economists have argued that this distinction is overblown. In the real business world, all events are so complex that forecasting is always a matter of grappling with 'true uncertainty', not risk; past data used to forecast risk may not reflect current conditions, anyway. In this view 'risk' would be best applied to a highly controlled environment, like a pure game of chance in a casino, and 'uncertainty' would apply to nearly everything else. Even so, Knight's distinction about risk and uncertainty may still help to analyse the behaviour of financial firms and other investors. Investment banks and commercial banks that in recent years regarded their own apparently precise risk assessments as trustworthy may have thought they were operating in conditions of Knightian risk, where they could judge the odds of future outcomes. Once the banks recognised those assessments as inadequate, however, they understood they were operating in conditions of Knightian uncertainty—and may have held back from making trades or providing capital, further slowing the economy as a result. Knightian uncertainty can also explain the behaviour of investors in times of financial panic. When investors realise that their assumptions about risk are no longer valid and that conditions of Knightian uncertainty apply, markets can witness 'destructive flights to quality' in which participants rid their portfolios of everything but the safest of investments, such as US Treasury bonds.

Keynes was from the opposite end of the intellectual and social spectrum from Knight. He was born in 1883 to an affluent, well-known British family, one of whose ancestors had landed with William the Conqueror. Among Keynes's close friends were prime ministers, financiers, philosophers Bertrand Russell and Ludwig Fry, and Virginia Woolf.

Keynes was educated at Eton and Cambridge, where he studied economics, mathematics, and philosophy under leading scholars. He was an active player in the stock market where his own fortunes fluctuated and like many contemporaries, he failed to predict the Great Crash of 1929. He designed Britain's war financing during the Second World War, negotiated a large loan by the United States to Britain immediately after the war, and wrote much of the Bretton Woods Agreements that established the post-war international monetary system.

Keynes rejects the term 'event' as used by his predecessors in probability theory because it implies that forecasts must depend on mathematical frequencies of past occurrences (from latin '*e venio*', namely 'it derives from'). He preferred the term 'proposition' which reflects degrees of belief about the probability of future events. Probability for Keynes is a subjective concept rather than objective knowledge of a past circumstance.

In light of this, financial speculation (from Latin '*speculum*'—'mirror') as opposed to investment is based on a subjective belief in order to become profitable. At least Keynes in his famous book 'The General Theory of Employment, Interest and Money' can confirm this understanding by pointing out the difference between knowable in principle and necessarily unknowable. What is knowable in principle refers to our conception of risk, but the necessarily unknowable refers to this new subjective feature of capital markets. On this point, Keynes compared the financial markets to a beauty contest. Here the judges instead of focusing their attention on the winner, therefore, on the most beautiful girl, try to second-guess the opinion of other judges. In the same fashion, in capital markets the speculator tends to focus its efforts not on objective reality of financial assets that are sold or offered on the market, but on the information that other speculators will trade on in the near future. Hence, the evaluation of financial assets is not only based on an assessment of past performance of assets but on the uncertainty of the decision that will be taken by other speculators. To state it plainly, the objective discourse on risk does not apply alone in capital markets, because there will be always a subjective component in the final decision of the speculator. Indeed, this trade on information before somebody else trades on the same information is vital to unwind positions early and it is also essential to set the price of the financial asset. In this game, the value of information for a speculator depends on the uncertain behaviour of another speculator (necessarily unknowable). In addition, because the markets will always present a lack of perfect information (i.e. information asymmetry) the value of the financial assets based on new information as well as erroneous information might lead to mispriced assets. Hence, even a speculator in good faith can affect the value of the financial assets in a negative way. This is why I shall argue that supervision of financial markets is required, but cannot definitively solve the issue (see Chapter 6).

As it can be seen, Keynes's view of economics ultimately revolves around uncertainty. Uncertainty as to how much a family will save or spend, uncertainty as to what portion of its accumulated savings a family will spend in the future, and uncertainty as to how much profit any given outlay on capital goods will produce. As Frank Knight noted fifteen years before Keynes published 'The General Theory', the economic environment is constantly changing, and all economic data are specific to their own time period. To this end, it is very significant to examine today what Keynes wrote in 1937 in response to criticisms of 'The General Theory':

> By "uncertain" knowledge (...) I do not mean merely to distinguish what is known for certain from what is only probable. The game of roulette is not subject, in this sense, to uncertainty (...) the sense in which I am using the term is that in which the prospect of a European was is uncertain, or the price of copper and the rate of interest twenty years hence, or the obsolescence of a new invention. (...) About these matters, there is no scientific basis on which to form any calculable probability whatever. We simply do not know!

In other words, it can be said that uncertainty has made human beings free. All previous thinkers from Pascal to Jevons thought about the laws of probability because human beings did not have control on the next throw of the dice, or where the next error in measurement will occur. This was a story of the inevitable where everything works according to the laws of probability. It might seem a well-ordered world, but it is not realistic. Human beings are characterised by their inherent fragility and as I define 'human-humanity'. Therefore, Keynes's economic prescriptions reveal that as an economic agent makes decisions he does change the world. Whether the change turns out to be for better or for worse is up to him. The spin of the roulette wheel has nothing to do with it.

Notwithstanding, the new ideas portrayed by Knight and Keynes, rational behaviour and measurement in risk management still persisted throughout the turmoil of the Great Depression in 1929 (see this chapter), and the Second World War. Theories on these matters began to move along divergent paths, one pursued by the followers of Keynes ('we simply do not know') and the other by the followers of Jevons ('pleasure, pain, labour, utility, value, wealth, money, etc., all notions admitting of quantity').

4.9 Game Theory Between Rationality and Passion

During the quarter-century that followed the publication of Keynes's 'General Theory', an important advance in the understanding of risk and uncertainty appeared through the theory of games of strategy. In 1921, Emile Borel, a French mathematician, published several papers on the theory of games. He used poker as an example and addressed the problem of bluffing and second-guessing the opponent in a game of imperfect information. Borel envisioned game theory as being used in economic and military applications, and his ultimate goal was to determine whether a 'best' strategy for a given game exists and to find that strategy. Despite his efforts, Borel did not develop his ideas very far. For that reason, most historians give credit for developing and popularising game theory to John Von Neumann, who published in 1928 the first paper on game theory, sever years after Borel.

Von Neumann was born in Budapest, Hungary, in 1903, and distinguished himself from his peers in childhood for having a photographic memory, being able to memorise and recite back a page out of a phone book in a few minutes. By 1929, Von Neumann was known as a young mathematical genius and his fame had spread worldwide in the academic community. In 1929, he was offered a job at Princeton. Upon marrying his fiancée, Mariette, Neumann moved to the United States. In 1935, Mariette gave birth to Neumann's daughter, Marina. Two years later, Mariette left Neumann for Kuper, a physicist. Within a year of his divorce, Neumann began an affair with Klara Dan, his childhood sweetheart, who was willing to leave her husband for him.

Neumann was described as a practical joker and always the life of the party. He loved games, which probably contributed in great part to his work on game theory. An occasional heavy drinker, he was an aggressive and reckless driver. According to William Poundstone's 'Prisoner's Dilemma':

> An intersection in Princeton was nicknamed 'Von Neumann Corner' for all the auto accidents he had there. (Poundstone, 1993, 25)

His colleagues found it 'disconcerting' that upon entering an office where a pretty secretary worked, Von Neumann habitually would 'bend way way over, more or less trying to look up her dress' (Poundstone, 1993, 26). Despite his personality quirks, no one could dispute Von Neumann was brilliant. Beginning in 1927, he applied new mathematical methods to quantum theory. His work was instrumental in subsequent philosophical interpretations of the theory. For Von Neumann the inspiration for game theory was poker (see Sect. 4.2 of this chapter), a game he played occasionally and not terribly well. He realised that poker was not guided by probability theory alone, as an unfortunate player who would use only probability theory would find out. Von Neumann wanted to formalise the idea of 'bluffing', a strategy that is meant to deceive the other player and hide information from them. In his 1928 article 'Theory of Parlor Games', Von Neumann first approached the discussion of game theory and proved the famous minimax theorem, which provides a mathematical solution for two-player zero-sum games, where one player's gain is equal to the other player's loss.

From the outset, Von Neuman knew that game theory would prove invaluable to economists. He teamed up with Oskar Morgenstern, an Austrian economist at Princeton, to develop his theory. Their book, 'Theory of Games and Economic Behaviour', revolutionised the field of economics. Although the work was intended for economists, its applications to psychology, sociology, politics, warfare, recreational games, and many other fields soon became apparent. Von Neumann and Morgenstern claimed that the winnings that will accrue to an individual who maximises his utility will depend upon how much he can get if he behaves rationally. He may get more if others make mistakes (behave irrationally). Von Neumann appreciated game theory's applications to economics, he was most interested in applying his methods to politics and warfare. He used his methods to model the Cold War interaction between the US and the USSR, viewing them as two players in a zero-sum game. From the very beginning of World War II, Von Neumann was confident of the Allies' victory. He sketched out a mathematical model of the conflict from which he deduced that the Allies would win, applying some of the methods of game theory to his predictions. In 1943, Von Neumann was invited to work on the Manhattan Project. Von Neumann did crucial calculations on the implosion design of the atomic bomb, allowing for a more efficient, and more deadly weapon. Von Neumann's mathematical models were also used to plan out the path the bombers carrying the bombs would take to minimise their chances of being shot down. The mathematician helped select the location in Japan to bomb. Among the potential targets he examined were Kyoto, Yokohama, and Kokura.

Mathematician John Nash further expanded the work of Von Neumann and Morgenstern by giving the concept of Nash equilibrium. It refers to a set of strategies that each player has. This strategy does not allow any member to change their plan of action after knowing other player's plans. It means that a player should stick to their chosen strategy even after knowing the other player's strategy or plan. After this equilibrium is applied, the player cannot change his strategy. As the player knows the opponent's strategy here, he will not change course, as there is no incentive or prize to change. All members of the game are satisfied with their plan of action; hence an equilibrium is achieved. For example, when a tie is achieved in the game and the scores of both parties are the same, equilibrium seems to have occurred. Shapley value is another concept used in game theory. It is a solution to a game and involves distributing gains or rewards equally among players of a team or group. This concept works in cases where the contribution of players is unequal but they are working cooperatively to achieve the rewards or gains. Equal contributors get equal pay or gains, and people who do not contribute at all, do not receive gains. For example, a company wants to market their product. They use Facebook marketing, email marketing, and Instagram marketing to advertise their product. All these marketing options are players and the incentive they receive for their work is their reward. They are all part of the same party as they are selling the same product through different mediums. As it can be seen, Von Neumann's original work has evolved in various fields, including political science, computer science, marketing, etc. Some of the notable advancements in game theory also include Artificial Intelligence (AI). Indeed, the development of AI systems is based on multi-agent environments, and game-theoretic approaches that help AI agents reason and strategies in interactions with other agents. Game theory provides a framework for decision-making, negotiation, and coordination in AI systems, enabling AI agents to achieve optimal or satisfactory outcomes (see Chapter 6).

I shall argue that much of the enthusiasm for rationality, for measurement, and for the use of mathematics in forecasting in game theory emerged from the optimism of the victories of the Second World War. The aim of the Bretton Woods Agreements was to recapture the stability of the nineteenth-century gold standard. The International Monetary Fund and the World Bank were set up to nourish economic progress among disadvantaged people around the world. The United Nations would keep peace among nations. It is like if the Victorian concept of rational behaviour regained its former popularity. Rational people make choices on the basis of information rather than emotion. Once they have analysed all the available information, they make decisions. They tend to maximise their utility, but they are also risk-averse in the Bernoullian sense that the utility of additional wealth is inversely related to the amount already possessed. In other words, game theory brings a new meaning to uncertainty. In fact, previous theories accepted uncertainty as a fact of life and did not identify its source. Game theory says that the true source of uncertainty lies in the intentions of others. Every decision that is made is the result of negotiations in which economic agents try to reduce uncertainty by trading off what other agents are likely to desire in return. Unlike poker or chess, no one can expect to be a winner in these games. Choosing the alternative that an economic agent thinks will bring him to the highest payoff tends to be also the riskiest decision, because it may provoke a strong defence from players who stand to lose. It necessarily follows that the parties will settle for compromise alternatives, which may require to make the best of a bad bargain: think of parent–child, President–Congress, boss–employee, husband–wife, soloist–accompanist, etc.

Such a concept of rationality so well defined was soon then transformed into rules for governing risk and maximising utility to influence the world of investing and managing wealth. The achievements that followed brought Nobel Prizes to gifted scholars and the definitions of risk and the practical applications that emerged from these achievements revolutionised investment management, the structure of markets, and the instruments used by investors. For example, a similar approach to game theory in investment is called portfolio diversification as theorised by Nobel laureate Markowitz in 1952. This is because diversification is the best weapon for investors to act against variance of return. Diversification is indirectly reducing volatility and uncertainty. Although Markowitz never mentions game theory in his paper 'Portfolio Selection' in the Journal of Finance, there is a close resemblance between diversification and games of strategy. However, criticisms against this theory are still alive and they point out whether investors are rational enough in their decision-making to follow the prescription that Markowitz set out for them. If intuition is preferred to measurement in investing, then the whole exercise could turn out to be a waste of time. In other words, the classical model of rationality—the model on which game theory and most of Markowitz's concepts are based—specifies how people should make decisions in the face of risk and what the world would be like if people did in fact behave as specified. Departures from this model occur more frequently than most of human beings admit. In fact, rational decisions are rare as distinguished behavioural psychologists Daniel Ellsberg and Richard Thaler admit. We tend to misbehave. Specifically Richard Thaler launched a new field of study called 'behavioural finance or behavioural economics'. Behavioural finance analyses how investors struggle to find their way through the give and take between risk and return, one moment engaging in calculation and the next yielding to emotional impulses. The result of rational and not-so-rational is a capital market that itself fails to perform consistently in the way that the theoretical models predict that it will perform (see Chapter 6, and the March Madness of 2023).

4.10 God Is Dead

As the previous sections clearly show, our lives are often affected by unexpected or uncertain events, from natural disasters such as hurricanes and tornadoes to pandemics. Some represent external shocks, such as pandemics or natural events, and others are simply internal failures of the system, such as financial crises that will be further analysed in this chapters, Chapters 5 and 6 of this book. For instance, the collapse of Lehman Brothers in 2008, the failure of the crypto exchange FTX in late 2022, and the bank runs of Silicon Valley Bank, Signature Bank, and First Republic Bank in March 2023. In other words, risk is everywhere and anywhere—as I said—especially in financial markets that are intrinsically permeated by risk-taking activities in seek for profit maximisation (see Chapters 2 and 3). However, any investment decision is necessarily occurring under conditions of uncertainty. In fact, human beings cannot predict and anticipate uncertainty, and they can only be subject to its results. Additionally, the decision-makers are rarely rational individuals—as I have shown—and any investment decision is very often taken under complex conditions. Nonetheless, the same activity of investing and/or speculating represents one of the most important features of the 'human-humanity' of mankind. Indeed, sometimes a risk-taking approach can also be seen as the only alternative to nihilism.

In line with Nietzsche's most famous statement declared in 1882 'God is Dead'. The sentence pronounced by the German philosopher that echoed down in the twentieth century does not mean that atheism is true. Nietzsche means that because the belief in the Christian God has become unbelievable everything that was built upon this faith is destined to collapse. Indeed, in the aftermath of the Enlightenment, science, mathematics, and philosophy arose across Europe to displace Christianity as the guiding authority on truth about life and the universe—as I have shown in the previous sections. For centuries, Christianity's teachings about reality were entirely dominant. However, the scientific revolution and the separation of Church and State across Europe undermined the authoritative figure of the Church. Atheism became not only acceptable among citizens, but also popular. Without a divine power underpinning existential situations and moral outlooks, our paths into the future became rather uncertain. Nietzsche questions in 'The Gay Science' or 'La Gaya Scienza':

> God is dead. God remains dead. And we have killed him. How shall we comfort ourselves, the murderers of all murderers? What was holiest and mightiest of all that the world has yet owned has bled to death under our knives: who will wipe this blood off us? What water is there for us to clean ourselves? What festivals of atonement, what sacred games shall we have to invent? Is not the greatness of this deed too great for us? Must we ourselves not become gods simply to appear worthy of it? (Book III, aphorism 125)

In other words, if God's authority is no longer unquestionable, how on earth should we live our lives? The appropriate response to the age of Enlightenment leading to the death of God, Nietzsche argues, should not be a jeering celebration, nor a shrug of indifference, but a period of deep disorientation and mourning. God was not just an innocuous source of faith and worship, God was the indubitable authority that lent power and legitimacy to Judeo-Christian moral values. While Judeo-Christian moral values are not Nietzsche's preference (he argues in the 'Genealogy of Morality', for instance, that Christianity is characterised by an ascetic ideal, the twisted, harmful condemnation of desires we cannot help but have, like those for food and sex) he sees their sudden removal as dangerous.

In fact, the Judeo-Christian moral system is at least a mechanism for value creation, Nietzsche says. And this mechanism is deeply embedded within Western culture with many of its values like pity, altruism, and compassion regarded as natural. Hence, to overcome nihilism, human beings need to start a revaluation of values as Nietzsche puts it. Therefore, risk-taking is a positive activity and a value creation process. Removing the comfort of God, Judeo-Christian morals, and an afterlife, and having nothing to really replace them with—moving from certainty about what life is for, to uncertainty about what life is for—could lead to an all-pervading numbness or anguish about our lives not mattering in a seemingly pointless universe. If there is no longer an absolute, incontestable authority telling us how to live our lives, then how should we go about living? How can we evolve our values to avoid slipping into meaninglessness and nihilism? We necessarily have to become risk-takers.

In other words, the revolutionary idea that I try to convey here and in the previous sections is that the ontology of risk can be described in terms of 'open human control' by using the words of the English sociologist Anthony Giddens. Essentially, human beings are agents in charge of decision-making who aim to transform reality by risk-taking and risk selection activities. Risk-taking is a prominent idea in Western economics, and human beings in Western countries tend to conceptualise risk as a synonym for progress (D'Alvia, 2020). Someone who takes no risk cannot evolve, so it can be said that the ontology of risk in the West contains an authentic human quality.

For these reasons, the West has allowed risk selection activities and sees risk as a tool for determining the progress of society, so it acknowledges its subjective aspect that relates directly to the fragility of human beings and to their desires, hopes, and speculative visions of profit. This vision has brought to finance the essential concepts and methods of portfolio selection, diversification, the capital asset pricing model, and the prospect theory in behavioural economics. In philosophical and mathematical terms those economic methods and statistics are related to the laws of probability, and they have paved the way for the activities of risk-taking, transfer, and pooling (i.e. banking, investment, insurance, etc.) that constitute per se a source of legitimate profit in Western countries. In other words, risk management has become the new means of identifying risk, in ontological terms, and specifically from a financial point of view. Only in this way can progress be an outcome of the human activities that are evidence of relativity and subjectivity, leading to—sometimes—the negative outcomes experienced during financial crises, market failures (see this chapter), or generally in the establishment of risk societies where any human activity is the result of risk distribution (Beck, 1992).

4.11 Uncertainty, Possibility, and Anxiety

Uncertainty is an important feature of the economic system where competition also plays an important role, and in addition uncertainty is considered as the main catalyst of profit (Knight, 1921). This is the position of neo-classical economics, as opposed to traditional economics, according to which uncertainty was reduced or eliminated through belief systems where the unknowable became knowable by means of symbols, which were also in charge of reducing human anxiety. The 'invisible hand' of Adam Smith, who is a classic economist, is self-explanatory in this regard.

Specifically, the association of uncertainty with anxiety is very important to provide a vivid image of the existential status of human beings, and also to study the intimate essence of uncertainty in philosophical and ontological terms. Indeed, many of the central themes and concepts of existentialism—freedom, choice, responsibility, bad faith, anxiety, despair, and absurdity—are fundamental in studying uncertainty, and also to justify the freedom of choice of the economic agent. Existentialism originated in the writing of Soren Kierkegaard in ground-breaking works such as Either-Or (1843), Fear and Trembling (1843), and The Concept of Anxiety (1844). Existentialism is undoubtedly rooted in Kierkegaard's idiosyncratic Christianity as it is in the 'God is dead' proto-existentialism of Arthur Schopenhauer and Friedrich Nietzsche (see Sect. 4.10). The radical view of Kierkegaard on faith, religious commitment, and the individual, and his rejection of a conformist, passive, rationalist, dispassionate, inauthentic approach towards the religious life and the infinite, make him a true existentialist with his concept of anxiety.

Kierkegaard recognises that anxiety, angst, anguish, or dread is central to the human condition as it is lived and is suffered by every human being. To understand the true nature of anxiety is therefore to understand a great deal about being human. Firstly, although it is certainly related to fear in various ways, anxiety must be clearly distinguished from fear. In the book 'The Concept of Anxiety', Kierkegaard argues that fear is a person's concern about what threatens him from outside—from a myriad threat to life, limb, livelihood, and happiness over which he has limited control. Anxiety, on the other hand, is a person's concern about what, so to speak, threatens him from inside, from within his own consciousness. An anxious person is concerned about what he might choose to do given his freedom to choose. He is troubled by his own freedom and spontaneity; by the awareness that there is nothing whatsoever preventing him from choosing to perform a foolish, destructive, or disreputable act at any moment, other than his choice not to perform it. Hence, says Kierkegaard 'anxiety is the dizziness of freedom' (Kierkegaard 2015, 61). To be anxious is to be bewildered by one's own freedom; to be worried and disturbed by the realisation that one always has many options in any situation and must continually choose one option or another. Hence, the importance of the meaning of diversification theories and game theories in economics is based on human choices.

This dizziness of freedom is most clearly manifested in the sensation of vertigo. Kierkegaard takes the example of a man standing on the edge of a tall building or cliff. The man fears he might fall over the edge, that the safety rail or the ground might give way, that someone might push him off, and so on. Greater than his fear of falling, however, is his anxiety that he is free to jump if he decides to—that his not jumping is an ongoing choice which he might abandon at any moment in favour of jumping. He experiences this anxiety, the treat of his own freedom, as vertigo, an overwhelming giddiness. The drop obsesses him, the void seems to beckon him down; but in reality it is his own freedom that beckons to him—the very fact that he can always choose to go down the quick way. Vertigo is dread of this alarming and persistent possibility, and all our alarming possibilities produce in us a psychological state akin to vertigo. That is to say, what a person overlooking a sheer drop dreads is not the possible inadequacy of the physical guard rail, but that he ultimately lacks a psychological guard rail to prevent him from choosing to climb over and plunge to his death. If it appears on the face of it that his dread is of the void itself, this is because his vivid awareness of the void immediately forces him to confront his own possibilities, his own dreadful existential freedom. The void is the occasion of his dread, but not its source.

Interestingly, if the man fancies he has a fixed psychological guard rail that prevents him from choosing to jump, then he is deluding himself—in existentialist jargon he is resorting to bad faith—because whatever psychological barrier he possesses is merely a flimsy construct consisting of nothing more than the choice not to jump, a choice he is free to replace at any moment with a self-destructive decision. His anxiety is precisely his awareness of the ease with which he can spontaneously overturn the self-determinations that he wishes would permanently fix, define, preserve, and protect him.

The example of the anxious person on the tall building or cliff has become famous in existentialist circles, not least because it has been reformulated by various existentialist philosophers who came after Kierkegaard, most notably Jean-Paul Sartre, who was heavily influenced by Kierkegaard. Sartre calls the anxiety we experience whenever we consider dangerous experiments in freedom 'the vertigo of possibility', saying that 'consciousness is frightened by its own spontaneity' (Sartre, 1991, 100).

4.12 From Risk-Aversion to Uncertainty-Aversion Paradigms

As I said in the previous sections, investment decisions or speculation necessarily occur in today's financial markets under a complex environment. For this reason, the next step is to introduce the environment in which the economic agent faces risks today.

This paves the way for a new phenomenology of contemporary financial markets that can be defined as a complex system dominated by risk and uncertainty and especially by competition in terms of financial innovations and adaptability. As in physics the concept of the disorganisation of the universe is measured as entropy, and in the same way entropy measures the uncertainty of a system, so free markets always look disorganised, but uncertainty produces competition that is the equilibrium feature of the system itself. To continue the analogy with physics, I could say that the complexity of the systems was introduced by thermodynamics, which for the first time took into account a dissipative structure that highlights how a movement towards greater complexity can be created spontaneously under the impulse of energies that are sufficiently powerful to push a system away from the areas of Boltzmann's equilibrium thermodynamics.

This means that in the contemporary phenomenology of financial markets there is no central planner, and competition serves the role of decentralised planning. If this image is imposed onto the broader economy, we come to the concept of the entrepreneur, or if you prefer the speculator, who faces risks and adapts his actions to answer in terms of financial innovations. The entrepreneur-speculator becomes the manager of the plan and by taking on responsibilities and engaging in uncertain activities contributes to the money creation process. In other words, it can be said that the entrepreneur-speculator explains the function of absorbing uncertainty from the system. In the end, disorder can be neutralised through information. Indeed, in economics, risk and uncertainty are also defined as information economics or informed economics.

Knight and other thinkers have provided the reader with a theoretical background which distinguishes between risk and uncertainty and provides a dogmatic justification for the sharp devaluation of financial assets, but they have not been able to guide policymakers in preventing future crisis (see Chapters 5 and 7). This is because financial risk is not only composed of its objective dimension in terms of ontological realism, but it is also especially influenced by a subjective element that leads to a more complex dialogue on its essence and that seems at first glance ungovernable. Therefore, the impossibility of measuring opinions and judgements has rendered the discourse on financial risk much more complex. Hence, disaster myopia becomes the definition of this unperceivable essence of financial risk in its subjective dimension. If the subjectivity of financial risk is, therefore, intelligible but not knowable due to its necessarily unknowable nature, the future, at least in the phenomenology of contemporary financial markets, is no longer perceived as an opportunity, but as something that is feared and must be controlled. Since the collapse of Lehman Brothers in 2008 (see Chapter 6), the start of the 2007–2010 global economic crisis, and the 'March madness' in 2023 (see Chapter 7), uncertainty-aversion has dominated the markets, but the management and correct pricing of risk in its objective dimension is still vital for governing markets. Therefore, the figure of the risk-taker, namely the investor in financial markets, has shifted to the figure of the speculator, who through his second-guessing influences the choices of other speculators and can contribute to a potential mispricing of the negotiated financial assets.

As a result, the figure of the risk-taker who sees the future as an opportunity has shifted to an uncertainty-aversion paradigm by means of what can be defined as the contemporary phenomenology of financial markets, where their subjectivity has superseded and overwhelmed the objective realism of their own ontology. Nonetheless, justification for the idea of uncertainty-aversion is controversial because according to Knight's theory, profit is connected to uncertainty, and complex systems such as financial markets cannot exist without uncertainty. Without uncertainty, there is no profit or in other words money creation processes based on profit are strictly dependent on uncertainty. Indeed, any money creation process, rather than being undermined by uncertainty, is underpinned by it. Therefore, a new economy characterised by uncertainty-aversion such as is being proposed today by financial regulators and governments can be translated, in the worst possible scenario, into a considerable diminution, or indeed full elimination, of profit.

This is the paradox of modern economies. On the one hand, regulators and supervisors blame uncertainty due to the indeterminacies of the decisions of the speculator and its mysterious character that prevents us from measuring it, but on the other hand the elimination or diminution of uncertainty inside free markets can irreversibly contribute to the diminishing of progress and innovation. Without uncertainty there is no competition and without competition there is no adaptability of the system. It seems that the contemporary phenomenology of financial markets would benefit from finding a spontaneous order by allowing the functioning of a free market structure beyond financial regulation concerns, as I will further explain in Chapter 7.

4.13 Conclusions

This chapter has illustrated a possible historical account of risk and uncertainty by illustrating the influences of a group of thinkers, who tried to provide a definition for risk and uncertainty both in economic and philosophical terms. However, the most challenging aspect of theorising financial markets as financial systems is explaining the structures of those systems. As I said, four main structures can be identified in the markets, namely risk, uncertainty, competition, and financial innovation.

Risk is an immanent feature of the world. In financial markets, risk can be explained through the constant interrelation that shapes the structure of financial markets between savers (i.e. lenders) and users (i.e. borrowers). The financial market is where the different interests of lenders and borrowers are matched. Specifically, lenders aim to be risk-averse, whereas borrowers are essentially risk-takers, and they are more aggressive because they aim for profit. For this reason, it is important to underline that risk is a measurable entity, and the ontological discourse on risk represents what is knowable in principle or a priori by virtue of the laws of probabilities. It is knowledge of objective facts that derive from the observation of a previous experience. On the other hand, in economic terms, complexity is associated with uncertainty. Something complex cannot be controlled, and therefore cannot be predicted. Essentially, the same need to reduce complexity is expressed in modern economies by anxiety to reduce economic uncertainty (for instance, a proactive approach by regulation or by enforcement that is promoted through the financial regulator when a major disruption of the market occurs). Indeed, reducing uncertainty makes things more predictable, and from an epistemological point of view the knowledge of uncertainty is based on the conception of a 'controllable' future. Nonetheless, the opinions and beliefs of investors about circumstances that might arise and affect future events have revealed a subjective element of financial risk that is relative and conditioned to personal instincts. It is the necessarily unknowable feature of financial risk, as Keynes argued, due to the tendencies of erroneous perceptions of instincts. It is the reason why financial markets are a beauty contest where the second-guessing observation of inventors can turn them back into speculators, who trade information ahead of market movements.

As opposed to classical economics, I have illustrated that market actors are not rational, and markets are fundamentally destined to fail as argued by Hyman Minsky, who was an economist at Washington University in St. Louis. Minsky proposed a theory he labelled the financial instability hypothesis, which holds that the economy creates its own bubbles and crashes. The gist of his theory is that stable economies sow the seeds of their own destruction because stability, seeming safe, encourages people to take risks. That risk-taking creates financial instability that eventually results in panic and crisis. Unfortunately, during his lifetime, neither Minsky nor his hypothesis was taken seriously. He died in 1996, before the dotcom bubble and the Great Recession, both of which gave credence to his ideas. His theory is now accepted as a primary explanation for the boom-and-bust cycles in the economy. The financial instability hypothesis is rooted in swings between excessive risk-taking and panic that follow when the risk-taking overheats and the economy collapses. Specifically, Minsky hypothesised three stages of lending he dubbed hedge, speculative, and Ponzi. During the hedge stage, lenders and borrowers are cautious because of the losses they incurred in the prior recession. Borrowers are wary of leverage, and lenders make loans in modest amounts with stringent credit requirements. During this stage, the amount of debt in the system is reasonable. In the following speculative stage, market participants become more confident of a recovery. Borrowers take on greater amounts of debt, and the economy begins to boom. Lenders grant credit based on ever-lower standards, assuming that asset prices will continue to rise. During this stage, borrowers can cover the interest on the loans, but become less able to repay the principal. By the final Ponzi stage, lenders and borrowers have forgotten the lessons of the prior crisis. Everyone is sure that asset prices will continue to rise, and debt is granted with repayments based on that assumption. The economy becomes over-leveraged; debt and risk-taking have created a financial house of cards. Finally, a 'Minsky Moment'—as the Paul McCulley of PIMCO dubbed it—occurs. Market insiders take profits, everyone panics, and a crash ensues before the cycle starts over. Paradoxically, Minsky's hypothesis teaches us that the time of greatest investment risk is when everything seems good, but stability itself is destabilising because, during times of economic stability, healthy investments lead to speculative euphoria.

For these reasons, as this chapter has claimed, it is important to take into account the role of uncertainty from an ontological point of view. Reducing complexity does not only mean reducing profit; uncertainty tends to underpin rather than undermine money creation processes. To reduce uncertainty means to reduce competition—that is the one feature or structure that makes each financial system adaptable. Indeed, competition has two sides: on the one hand, it represents the 'dark side' of modern economies in relation to financial crisis or business collapse (for instance, if enterprises are not adaptable and innovative enough they are pushed out of the market, or alternatively too much innovation can generate new financial risks that might be unsustainable); on the other hand, competition creates innovation that makes the system adapt to a new environment (i.e. creative-construction). Indeed, if in a complex system—such as complex financial systems—the investor second-guesses the opinions of other investors, it means that the interpretation of information is relative, but could also lead to inefficiencies in the economic process because knowledge is fragmented. Despite such limitations, entrepreneurs can effectively take advantage of such inefficiencies and turn them back into opportunities. To this end, in financial markets, risk opportunities are identified as the lost chances of profit. This is because uncertainty is deeply connected to profit, and at the same time the inefficiencies created by speculation represent an opportunity for the entrepreneur who can turn profit into an uncertainty absorption tool. Therefore, complexity is a process rather than a 'feature' of markets, and competition lead to a free market's complexity to identify the risk opportunity and innovate the system through a legit form of profit. As opposed to such creative function of uncertainty, financial crises represent clear evidences of the negative outcomes that uncertainty can generate when is not managed in a responsible manner. For these reasons, financial crises are the subject matter of the next chapter that is going to outline the underestimation of financial risk, and the possible negative aspects of speculation.

Notes

1. It is believed that the God of the sky, Nut, married Geba, the God of the earth, against the will of Ra, who was the supreme God. Ra opposed this union because they were siblings. He asked Shu, the God of air, to destroy this union. However, as expected, the culprits resisted and decided to fight for their love. As a result, there were disasters on the land that led to the separation of the world into continents. The couple was finally separated, and Geba was left to be the God of the earth, and Nut became the God of the sky. Ra further punished Geba by casting a spelt that would keep her from conceiving for 360 days. Then, Teuta of Illyria, the God of love, knowledge, and wisdom intervened by coming up with *Senet*, a gambling game. He convinced, Khonsu, the God of the moon, to make bets as one seventy-second of the lunar year. This story is attributed to be the origin of the current calendar. The moon God won five days, which are free from the spell of Ra thus the calendar has 365 days. The five days were gifted to Nut, and this is how she was able to give birth to other gods like Horus, Isis, and others. Hence, *Senet*, a gambling game, solved this problem.
2. The *Ridotto* (a retreat or private room) was a wing in the *Palazzo Dandolo* in Venice, which was converted at the behest of the city leaders into a government-owned gambling house in 1638. It was the site of Europe's first public, legal, mercantile casino but players were supposed to wear three-cornered hats and masks in order to participate. A reform proposed in 1774 was passed with an overwhelming majority and the casino was closed.

3. The word abacus is probably derived through its Greek form *abakos* from a Semitic word such as the Hebrew *ibeq* ('to wipe the dust'). Abacus is a calculating device, probably of Babylonian origin, that was long important in commerce. It is the ancestor of the modern calculating machine and computer.
4. The emperor was called *Stuper Mundi* ('Wonder of the World') by his contemporaries because he was highly educated and inquisitive man who encouraged learning and scholarship of every kind.

Bibliography

Baxandall M, *Painting and experience in fifteenth-Century Italy: A Primer in the Social History of Pictorial Style* (Oxford University Press 1988).

Beck U, *Risk Society: Towards a New Modernity* (SAGE Publications 1992).

Benedictow O J, *The Black Death 1346–1353: The Complete History* (The Boydell Press 2004)

Bernstein P L, *Against the Gods: The Remarkable Story of Risk* (John Wiley & Sons 1996)

Corby B, 'On risk and uncertainty in modern society' (1994) 19 (72) The Geneva Papers on Risk and Insurance, 235

Daniele D'Alvia, Risk, uncertainty and the market: A rethinking of Islamic and Western finance (2020) 16 (4) International Journal of Law in Context, 339–352.

De Roover R, 'The Medici Bank financial and commercial operations' (1946) 6 (2) The Journal of Economic History, 153–172

Eadington W R, *Roll the Bones: The History of Gambling* (Gotham 2006)

Fiorani F, *Shadow Drawing: how science taught Leonardo how to paint* (Picador Paper 2022)

Fisher I, *Nature of Capital, and Income* (Palgrave Macmillan 1906)

Greenblatt S, *The Swerve: How the World Became Modern* (WW Norton & Co In. 2012)

Giddens A, *Modernity and Self-Identity* (Stanford University Press 1991)

Hardy C O, *Risk and Risk Bearing* (Risk Books 1923)

Kent D V, *Cosimo De' Medici and the Florentine Renaissance: The Patron's Oeuvre* (Yale University Press 2000)

Kettell B, *Introduction to Islamic Banking and Finance* (Wiley 2011)

Kierkegaard S, *The Concept of Anxiety—A Simple Psychologically Oriented Deliberation in View of the Dogmatic Problem of Hereditary Sin* (Liveright reprint 2015)

Knight F, *Risk, Uncertainty, and Profit* (first published 1921, Martino Publishing 2014)

Krimsky S, Golding D (eds), *Social Theories of Risk* (Praeger Publishers 1992)

Lianos I, Kokkoris I, *The Reform of EC Competition Law* (Wolters Kluwer 2010)

Llewellyn D T, 'Re-engineering the regulator' (1996) 1 (3) The Financial Regulator, 21

Luhmann N, *Risk: A Sociological Theory* (Transaction Publishers 2008)

Luhmann N, *Introduction to Systems Theory* (Polity Press 2013)

Markowitz H, 'Portfolio selection' (1952) 7 (1) The Journal of Finance, 77

Maturana H R, Varela F, *Autopoiesis and Cognition: The Realisation of the Living* (Reidel 1980)

Mitchell M, Pulvino T, 'Arbitrage and the speed of capital' (2012) 104 (3) Journal of Financial Economics, 469

Moloney N, 'EU financial market regulation after the global financial crisis: "More Europe" or more risks?' (2010) 47 (5) Common Market Law Review, 1317

Monti G, *EU Competition Law* (CUP 2007)

Nohl J, *The Black Death A Chronicle of the Plague* (Harper & Row 1969)

Pidgeon N, Kasperson R E, Slovic P (eds), *The Social Amplification of Risk* (CUP 2003)

Poundstone W, *Prisoner's Dilemma: John Von Neumann, Game Theory, and the Puzzle of the Bomb* (Anchor Books 1993)

Sartre J P, *The Transcendence of the Ego: An Existentialist Theory of Consciousness* (Hill & Wang Inc. 1991)

Snyder F, 'Soft law and governance: Aspects of the European Union experience' in Luo Haocai (eds) *The European Union Experience* (Peking University Press 2009)

Tabari N M, 'Islamic finance and the modern world: The legal principles governing Islamic finance in international trade' (2010) 31 (8) Company Lawyer, 249

Taleb N N, *The Black Swan: The Impact of Highly Improbable* (Penguin 2008)

Tennekoon R, *The Law and Regulation of International Finance* (LexisNexis 1991)

Weisskopf W A, 'Reflections on uncertainty in economics' (1984) 9 (33) The Geneva Papers on Risk and Insurance, 335

Visser H, *Islamic Finance: Principles and Practice* (2nd ed., Edward Elgar Publishing 2014)

Voegelin E, *Order and History* (Louisiana State University Press 1956)

Von Neumann J, Morgenstern O, *Theory of Games and Economic Behaviour (Princeton Classic Editions): 60th Anniversary Commemorative Edition* (Princeton University Press 2007)

CHAPTER 5

Economic Bubbles, Schemes, and Market Failures

5.1 Introduction

In the previous chapters, I have critically analysed whether or not speculators have played a role in financial markets. Specifically, I have argued that financial innovations are catalysts of economic progress, and they represent a necessary answer to uncertainty (Chapter 4) due to the creativity instinct of the entrepreneur that is capable of absorbing uncertainty. Risk and uncertainty are two fundamental features or structures of financial systems, but unreasonable risk-taking activities might be the trigger of negative economic outcomes sometimes giving rise to credit bubbles and financial crises. To this end, this chapter focused on exploring whether speculators have played a role in financial crises and economic bubbles. There are two main views on economic bubbles: the ontological vision and the epistemological explanation. From an epistemological point of view, economic bubbles can occur, but one cannot predict when they happen, and we can only limit the damage caused by the bubble and try to prevent an economic crisis happening. On the other hand, in the ontological view, economic bubbles do not exist and, therefore, damage limitation can occur only after a crisis has appeared. In both cases, regulatory disasters cannot be totally avoided. Indeed, in an epistemological conception a financial regulator might be blamed for over-regulation, whereas according to an ontological view it might be too late to act.

D. D'Alvia, *The Speculator of Financial Markets*, Palgrave Macmillan Studies in Banking and Financial Institutions,
https://doi.org/10.1007/978-3-031-47901-4_5

In Chapter 4, I—therefore—call for a re-interpretation of uncertainty as a market structure, as a feature of financial systems and a necessary element that cannot be avoided, prevented, or calculated in advance. This chapter indirectly examines the role that financial regulators play or do not play in avoiding crises, and what role the speculator had or has had in past and present economic bubbles. Specifically, the chapter examines this tension and conflict by analysing specific economic bubbles from the Tulip mania during the Dutch golden age and its dramatic collapse in 1637, the Mississippi Bubble (1719–1720), the South Sea Bubble in England (1720), the bull market of the Roaring Twenties (1924–1929), the collapse of Herstatt Bank in 1974, the Dotcom Bubble (1990s), and contemporary bubbles with a specific focus on crypto assets and crypto exchanges, namely QuadrigaCX (2019) and FTX (2022). Among many financial crises and schemes, I have selected those because best reflect the role played by speculators, but also highlight the role of the law and legislative responses to market failures.

5.2 Tulip Mania

In the seventeenth century, one of the first recorded speculative bubbles held Holland firmly in its grip and it involved one of the most unlikely of assets, not stocks or bonds or real estate, but tulip bulbs. Even more than the time and place, it is the asset involved that makes the tale of 'tulip mania' so uniquely preposterous. Though all bubbles have some common characteristics, the flower boom of the 1630s is about as peculiar as these financial follies get. This is because the events were driven by the very biology of the flowers themselves as much as the economic characteristics of the society they entranced. Despite these peculiarities and all the historical uncertainties surrounding tulip mania, the episode has become the archetypical boom and bust, perhaps precisely because of how strange the events appear in hindsight.

By the early 1600s, the Netherlands was the richest country in the world (see Chapter 3). Developed financial markets are said to have facilitated the growing prosperity of the Dutch, whose reputation for creditworthiness no doubt helped secure further riches. The autonomous cities and provinces in the country housed a sizable and growing mercantile class which competed for wealth by trafficking goods between seas of Europe and oceans of the world. The Netherlands was uniquely well connected to the rest of the globe by trade, a fact obscured by its peripheral location in Continental Europe. These connections helped bring the tulip to Holland. Part of the flower's value resulted from its relative rarity in Europe in which it was an introduced species.

Tulips originally came from the mountain ranges of central Asia, just north of the Himalayas. They were said to have been introduced to Europe by Ogier de Busbecq, the Holy Roman Emperor's ambassador to Ottoman Turkey. He sent many bulbs back to Europe in the 1550s. The flower's eastern origin is subtly exposed in its name. The word 'tulip' is derived from the Persian word for turban, which the flower resembled. Following its introduction, botanists and horticulturists replanted the bulbs elsewhere and acclimatised the plants for the cold damp climates of Northern Europe. In Europe, tulips typically bloom for a week in April or May before becoming dormant during the summer months. It was then, from June to September, that bulbs could be uprooted and traded among cultivars and consumers. Both the former and the latter were particularly impressed with tulips that exhibited combinations of colours. These flowers were unique because tulip petals are typically only of a single colour; indeed, it was the brilliance of this colour that made the plans so sought after. However, tulip fanciers occasionally noticed specimens with more striking designs; these were diseased flowers produced by plants infected by tulip breaking virus. Varieties of distinct tulips were often given extravagant names. As an example, there was the *Viceroy*, with purple and white stripes. There was also the *Childer*, which was reddish orange. Others were named after particular cultivars, famous Dutch persons, or historical figures. Whether diseased or not, tulips typically reproduce both by seeds and by buds that sprout from the bulb. However, because tulip breaking virus does not infect the seeds of a plant, they could not be relied upon to give rise to a tulip of similar pattern. Because cultivars specifically sought diseased tulips, they had to rely on the buds alone to replicate the flowers. This slowed the process of multiplying the special varieties.

Tulips proved to be popular among the wealthy and the middle classes of the Netherlands. The market for tulip bulbs was driven by this growing demand for the flowers and the limited pace with which horticulturalists were able to reproduce the plants. The market turned botanists, previously academics mostly interested in sharing specimens for experimental purposes, into entrepreneurs being paid large sums for their bulbs. Prices paid depended on the exact specimen and the weight of a particular bulb;

larger bulbs developed more outgrowths and could produce more buds and thus supplied more future bulbs.

However, there was a major limitation in the tulip market. Because the bulbs could only be uprooted and replanted in the summer months, the time period in which a trade in the physical bulbs could take place was limited to a fraction of the year. In reality, it was more limited still because buyers, wanting to protect themselves from fraud, often demanded to see the flowers given off by a particular bulb before committing to a purchase. This meant that trades usually took place immediately after the flowers bloomed and thus limited activity in the 'spot' market to June.

The temporal limitation did not prevent a year-round trade in tulips though. In 1630s in Holland there was an active forward market for bulbs. Outside of the summer, when the market in physical bulbs blossomed, traders made agreements to buy and sell tulip bulbs when the following summer arrived. This was convenient; a buyer could secure a bulb without expending cash immediately, payment would take place upon delivery.

However, because payment would not actually occur until the future, this allowed speculators to make bold bets while paying little to nothing upon entering a commitment. In the futures markets of today, the risk inherent in this is solved by revaluing contracts daily and requiring a payment to be posted to make good on any interim price movements. This way, a buyer is not discovered to be unable to honour his commitment when the delivery date arrives. Having said that, such sensible practices did not exist four-hundred years ago.

For reasons that are not entirely known, the prices for tulip bulbs took off in the mid-1630s. The rise in prices attracted speculators looking for quick riches. Many supposedly expected the wealthy everywhere would come to Amsterdam to buy bulbs, raising future demand. Whether this was based on any sound reasoning or was just a justification for gambling is not clear. What is certain was that this was a craze of the previously unheard-of proportions. Many bought bulbs on credit and it is recorded in the lore of the mania that some bulbs traded ten times in a day, a claim probably more fantastical than factual. Nonetheless, so great was the craze that much satire was inspired by the events, including a painting by Jan Breughel the Younger showing the trafficking, trading, and ultimately the abandonment of the tulips by a group of speculators that are assimilated to monkeys (Picture 5.1).

Picture 5.1 Tulip Mania (Sect. 5.2 Tulip Mania) Jan Breughel the Younger—Satire on Tulip Mania c. 1640 (*Source* It is written that this painting is public domain. https://en.wikipedia.org/wiki/Tulip_mania#/media/File:Jan_Brueghel_the_Younger,_Satire_on_Tulip_Mania,_c._1640.jpg [WIKIPEDIA])

Before the bust though, prices rose to extravagant levels. A single sought-after bulb would easily sell for over a thousand guilders in the mid-1630s; some went for closer to five-thousand guilders each. For comparison, the annual wages of a skilled worker then might have been around 250 guilders and may have been perhaps twice that much for a very educated professional such as a lawyer. Perhaps more remarkably still, note that the entire island of Manhattan was bought from a Native American tribe for sixty guilders by the Dutch a decade earlier. The rarest bulbs were so valuable that, to ease transactions, properties, and other assets were traded directly for bulbs, bypassing the need for liquidating property into chests of coins or bullion with which to buy tulips.

After a phenomenal amount of enthusiasm, things began to change, once again for relatively unknown reasons. The mania reached its peak in 1635–1636 and it turned in 1637 when prices began to fall. Surviving records of bulb prices are few but they suggest values may have fallen by ninety percent or more. Ruined speculators petitioned to have any forward agreements they made cancelled before they were forced to pay up come summer. However, the government was disinterested in intervening and the courts resolved not to get involved either, interpreting the speculation as a form of gambling beyond the law (see Chapter 4). Because gambling debts were not to be legally enforced, the courts left transaction parties to sort out disputes among themselves. With that, the tulip mania came to an end.

5.3 The Battle of Waterloo: War and Finance

Nathan Mayer[1] Rothschild[2] was born in Frankfurt at the house of the Hinterpfann on 16 September 1777. In the intervening fifty-nine years, Nathan Mayer Rothschild led his brothers to the pinnacle of the financial world.

Nathan almost burst out of Frankfurt, the first of his brothers to found a branch of the family firm, to settle in England in 1798, initially as a textile merchant in Manchester and subsequently as a London bill broker nonpareil. Nathan was a larger than life figure on the London exchanges, giving himself totally to his business, permitting no half measures. His brusqueness and off-handedness were legendary, and his tactics were examined and re-examined time and time again. No one knew quite how he became so supreme in his world, but all recognised the fact. His marriage to Hannah, daughter of Levi Barent Cohen, gave him a position in society and a range of business contacts which might have taken him years to achieve alone. Building on this foundation and wedding it to the Rothschild network, Nathan was credited by his brothers with securing for them the best opportunities to achieve their position in the world of finance. Among those opportunities, the most important was the part played by Nathan and his brothers in helping the British government to finance military operations against Napoleon. Nathan's London House dealt in bullion and foreign exchange, and his remarkable success in these fields earned him a contract from the British government to supply the Duke of Wellington's army in Spain and France with gold and silver coins to pay the troops in 1814 and 1815, leading up to the Battle of Waterloo. Nathan himself is said to have described it as 'The best business I ever did'.

Two-hundred years might have passed since Napoleon was defeated at Waterloo on 18 June 1815 but some things in war and finance do not change, such as the absolute importance of being ahead of the game.

The Battle of Waterloo banished the spectre of Napoleon's domination of Europe. No one was more delighted than the denizens of the London Stock Exchange, Nathan Rothschild especially, as Gilts soared on the good news. Indeed, it seems that Nathan cleaned up on the gilt market thanks to his rapid, reliable, and finely honed communications system that brought him news of Wellington's victory ahead of anyone else in Westminster and the City of London.

For the preceding two decades of war since the French Revolution, bond prices had been buffeted by news from battlefields. A victory by Britain or its allies sent prices north since it reduced the risks of defeat, default, and more government borrowing. A defeat sent prices south for opposite reasons. These conditions provided plenty of opportunity for market manipulation through the manufacture of battlefield news given that information travelled at the speed of horses and sailing ships.

The most notorious scam occurred in February 1814. Napoleon was in trouble and his fall seemed likely. Speculators built up huge positions in gilts expecting prices to rise. The plan was to trade 'within the account', meaning that they only had to put up a modest amount of margin. But then came news of French successes that left them facing large losses. Two days before the end of the account, an officer dressed in the uniform of *aide-de-camp* to the British commander in France appeared in Dover in the middle of the night claiming to have just crossed the Channel with urgent news. Napoleon had been killed by Cossacks and the French monarchy restored. He sent word to the Dover Port Admiral evidently hoping that he would inform the government via the Admiralty's system of semaphore relay stations resulting in an official announcement. But it was too foggy for the semaphore system to operate.

The next day around noon, an open carriage containing three men dressed as French Royalist officers crying '*Vive Le Roi*' drove around the City of London. Again, the story was that Napoleon was dead and the French monarchy restored. They then supposedly set off for Downing Street to tell the prime minister. The appearance of the 'royalists' and their news was a tonic for gilt prices that rose twenty percent. But they slumped again when the London Stock Exchange messengers to Whitehall returned without confirmation. The authorities were unamused by the pantomime hoax. The London Stock Exchange quickly identified sales by seven individuals that 'stank to high Heaven'. Sensationally their number included Lord Cochrane MP, a naval hero. They were found guilty of fraud and jailed for a year. Eventually, Cochrane went abroad and commanded the Chilean and Brazilian navies in their wars of independence, enjoying markedly greater success than in gilt manipulation.

Nathan Rothschild—as I said—was surely aware of the value of early and accurate information as any other speculator. Rapid and reliable communications were crucial for his complex and risky payments and arbitrage operations. He set up a private courier system with shipping agents in Dover, Calais, and Ostend with fast light vessels ready to sail at any time. There were relays of horses to speed messages from the Channel to London. And a farm on the coast at Hythe for courier pigeons. As night descended at Waterloo on June 18 a Rothschild agent dashed to Dunkirk. Conveyed by a Rothschild ship and Rothschild steeds, Nathan received news of the victory on the night of Monday 19th (just twenty-four hours afterwards). The Duke of Wellington's official messenger did not arrive until Wednesday evening. In the meantime, Nathan called on the prime minister but was refused entry by a butler, because the prime minister was resting. His duty done, he proceeded to the London Stock Exchange where he was in sole possession of the momentous news. It is not known how much Rothschild made from Waterloo but it must have been a great deal. The collective assets of the five Rothschild brothers in spring 1815 came to £500,000 (at a time when the average wage was about £50 per year); in July 1816 it was £1 million. The Duke of Wellington observed that Waterloo was 'A damn close-run thing – the nearest run thing you ever saw in your life'. Maybe on the battlefield, but not on the London Stock Exchange.

Thirty years after the dust had settled on the fields of Waterloo, what is now Belgium, a poisonous anti-Semitic pamphlet signed 'Satan', circulated in Europe and it went nineteenth-century viral, claiming the Rothschild family had accrued its vast wealth on the back of Wellington's triumph. 'Satan' told that:

> Nathan Rothschild, the founder of the London branch of the bank, was a spectator on the battlefield that day in June 1815, as night fell, he observed the total defeat of the French army. This was what he was waiting for. A relay of fast horses rushed him to the Belgian coast, but there he found to his fury that a storm had confined all ships to port. Undaunted – "Does greed admit anything is impossible?" asked Satan – he paid a king's ransom to a fisherman to ferry him through wind and waves to England. Reaching London 24 hours before official word of Wellington's victory, Rothschild

> exploited his knowledge to make a killing on the Stock Exchange. "In a single coup" [the pamphlet charged] "he gained 20 million francs".

Although this type of speculation was widespread throughout anti-Semitic circles in the late nineteenth and twentieth centuries it was notably strong in the United States, where radicals of every stripe seemed obsessed by financial conspiracies. The Rothschilds combined Jewishness, banking, and international ties. They were an attractive target. They still do, just not via pamphlet. Today, the conspiracy theories about the Rothschilds—and other groups from freemasons to Jewish—are spread in online forums, self-published books, and religious radio programmes where seemingly normal and harmless people spin complicated, illogical theories that viewers seeking to confirm their own views can easily find.

'Satan' was, in reality, a left-wing controversialist called Georges Dairnvaell, who made no attempt to hide his loathing for Jews, and the Rothschilds in particular. Though they had been little known in 1815, by 1846 the Rothschilds had become the Rockefellers of their age. Nathan himself had died in 1836 and so could not rebut the claims. The first modern attempt to challenge the myth was made in the 1980s by a Rothschild—Baron Victor, a retired scientist and public servant who wrote a book about his ancestor Nathan. It was Victor who identified the powerful role played by the Satan pamphlet, and he debunked many of the dafter allegations. But he also discovered in the Rothschild archives an important document. This was a letter written to Nathan Rothschild by a bank employee in Paris about a month after Waterloo, and it included the statement:

> I am informed by Commissary White you have done well by the early information which you had of the victory gained at Waterloo.

It seemed, that the legend had some foundation in fact, but the first person to bring authentic news of the victory at Waterloo to London was not Nathan Rothschild; rather it was a man who had learnt of it in the Belgian city of Ghent and made a dash to England. This shadowy figure identified as 'Mr. C of Dover' was telling his story freely in the City from the morning of Wednesday 21 June at least twelve hours before the official news arrived. It was published in at least three newspapers that afternoon. A news report written that Wednesday evening referred to Nathan Rothschild receiving a letter from Ghent reporting a victory and passing his news to the government—though this was noted alongside reports of two other, similar letters. So while it is confirmed that Rothschild had early news, he was not the only one. Surely in the thin market of the period, it could not have been enough time to accumulate holdings sufficient to earn him the millions that Dairnvaell wrote of. Nor did he manipulate the market to double his gains, for, contrary to legend, there was no slump in prices that Wednesday. Nathan may have done well from his purchases when share prices rose sharply following the confirmation of the victory, but his gains were dwarfed by those of numerous rival investors who, without any advantage of early information, had bought government securities earlier, more cheaply and in quantity.

5.4 The Great Sovereign Bond Bust

One of the most pronounced bubbles in nineteenth-century finance was a boom in emerging market debt that hazardously swelled during the 1820s. During that decade, sovereign bonds were issued by several newly independent countries following Latin America's successful revolt against Spanish colonial rule. These new-born borrowers found a strong market for their first bonds across the sea in London as investors there looked for new sources of investment returns in the face of declining interest rates. Eventually, the sovereign bond boom turned into a sovereign bond bust. By the end of that decade, nearly every single new emerging market issuer had defaulted.

In London in the early 1820s, the financial markets were distinguished by compressing returns on lower-risk assets. This was most evident in the steady erosion of bond yields. For instance, the consols, the perpetual obligations issued by the British government were earning just three-point-five percent in 1823, down from five percent eight years earlier. In fact, yields had been as high as six percent just before the turn of the century. Though these levels do not seem all that high when compared to those of a century earlier or those seen in late twentieth century, they were remarkable at the time. These were the highest yields on British state bonds in at least several decades and they would not be matched until a century later. The previously high returns were driven in part by the inflation and fiscal deficits that accompanied the French Revolutionary Wars and those fought against Napoleon immediately thereafter. The military spending of the era caused British state indebtedness to rise as high as two-hundred-and-thirty percent of GDP by the late 1810s. This situation reversed after Napoleon's defeat at Waterloo brought peace to Europe. Thereafter, the supply of consols dwindled as deficits were eliminated and the government began to pay down its massive debt. The British Treasury was regularly setting aside money that went into a sinking fund that periodically bought bonds to extinguish the state's liability. Because the Bank of England was also buying consols, the decade after the end of the wars saw a dwindling supply of bonds available to private investors. The reduced issuance and central bank purchases caused interest rates to slide lower. The Bank of England cut rates by one percent in 1822. Once again, this may not sound like a terrific move but it was the first cut in the bank's discount rate in slightly over a century. Returns on other assets were also falling. Dividend yields contracted as stock prices rose. Those circumstances were setting the stage for the boom and bust to come.

Another outcome of the Napoleonic Wars, one that played out far from London, was the independence of most of Spain's American colonies. When France invaded Spain in 1807 and installed Napoleon's brother Joseph Bonaparte as King, governance of the colonies fell into the hands of local rulers who increasingly favoured separation from Spain. The resulting wars of independence led to the creation of several new countries that would fight among each other for control of resources over the succeeding century. To finance their civilian administrations and their armies, these countries relied on debt financing. The two biggest borrowers were Mexico and Gran Colombia; the latter country then included modern-day Ecuador, Colombia, and Venezuela. Gran Colombia was among the first to be welcomed to the London sovereign bond markets. The country floated a two million (GBP) issue paying six percent interest in 1822. Because of the higher interest rates and steep discounts to face value, the cost of borrowing for these Latin American sovereigns was high. However, this only attracted more yield-starved investors and other nations followed Gran Colombia's entry into the London bond markets. Mexico sold three-point-two millions of five percent coupon bonds in 1824. They were issued at a whopping forty-two percent discount to face value. Those were ultra-speculative bonds. A year later, Mexico issued a six percent coupon bond at eighty-nine-point-seventy-five percent of face value. Though they were smaller borrowers, Argentina, Chile, Guatemala, and Peru also found London firms to place their bonds. Investor appetite was strong despite the sharp discounts.

These discounts to face value were a characteristic of all the offerings. The average Latin American government bond was selling at a discount of twenty-five percent. In the early part of 1820s, there was little distinction made by investors between the bonds; news from Latin America was scarce and investors could generally not tell which nations' obligations were better credits. Pricing was more a factor of size, the interest rate on the bonds, and the prestige of the arranging firm than a reflection of risk.

This lack of meaningful information led to what is illustratively called the 'lemon problem' as uncreditworthy nations were able to borrow excessively because of investor ignorance. In truth, the borrowing was still small relative to the British state debt of eight-hundred million (GBP). Collectively, the Spanish American nations issued perhaps forty million (GBP) in sovereign bonds during the 1820s. Nonetheless, the years leading to the French Revolution were still fresh in everyone's memory. That history showed that fiscal meltdown can be brought on by even small debts. This was especially true for nations with weak political and economic institutions. Some issuers had no institutions at all. One 'country' selling bonds in London was Poyais (see Sect. 5.5), a fictional country in Central America. By 1826 there were over twenty bond issues in London from new Latin American countries. Most of the London offerings were designed to mimic the consols. For one, they were mostly structured as perpetual bonds, without a maturity date. They typically paid a five percent or six percent coupon; only Denmark came to market with anything less than a five percent rate on its bonds. This was designed to offer investors a sizable premium to the British consols. The bonds also occasionally came with sinking funds into which the borrowing nation would make occasional deposits to set aside money for the eventual repayment of the notes. The use of sinking funds was a British peculiarity and their presence in more than one offerings reflect London's importance in the market for sovereign debt.

After the course of just a few short years, the sovereign bond boom of the early 1820s turned to bust. It came abruptly; in April 1826, the government of Peru missed a bond payment and became the first South American sovereign government to default. By January 1828, following an Argentine default, every Spanish American government that issued sovereign bonds in London defaulted. Argentina had been seen as one of the more creditworthy countries but its default left Brazil the only South American government with performing bonds. The wave of defaults included European issuers as well. Greece missed a payment on its debt in January 1827 and they were followed by Portugal in June 1828. By this point, bond prices had been firmly in freefall for a couple of years. However, for the first time, there was also a dispersion of prices as investors began to understand the credit differences of the borrowers. Whereas all the Latin American bonds yielded close to seven percent in 1824, creditors began to take a more discerning eye to these bonds following the Peruvian default. Within two years, some bonds issued by the likes of Colombia and Peru were yielding twenty percent, while others issued by Brazil saw their yields rise more modestly, staying below ten percent. Many of the defaulted sovereigns suffered from ineffective tax systems and poor governance. Expensive military conflicts with their neighbours certainly did not help matters. However, not all borrowers defaulted. Indeed, the crisis helped secure the reputation of Nathan M. Rothschild as a prudent underwriter because they underwrote only successful bonds. Many of their clients in the 1820s included the relatively safe and prosperous nations of Austria and Prussia but the bank also arranged a bond offering for Brazil and Naples. These were only credits from South America and Southern Europe, respectively, that did not default. Clearly, prudence counted for something but it was in short supply in London among many sovereign bond investors.

The remarkable sovereign bond crisis of the 1820s shows how markets may very well have been less connected then; eventually, investors in foreign bonds usually struggled to get any good information. However, markets were nonetheless connected enough to bring together lenders and borrowers separated by an ocean and cause a crisis that shook those on both sides.

5.5 Financial Fiction and Schemes

In 1820, self-proclaimed Scottish nobleman Gregor MacGregor launched one of the most audacious and elaborate frauds of all time, tricking thousands of British citizens into investing in 'Poyais', a territory in Central America which turned out to be entirely fictional.

The Poyaisian Scheme (or Fraud) was the brainchild of the Scottish soldier Gregor MacGregor, who began his life of adventuring as an independence fighter in Venezuela and Colombia, and in 1820 he visited what is today Honduras. There, he claimed, he obtained a grant of eight million acres from George Frederick Augustus I, King of Mosquito Shore and Nation. Returning to London, MacGregor styling himself Gregor I, Cazique of the Independent State of Poyais, he set about publicising an ambitious scheme to colonise the land, setting up an office in London and selling bonds to investors. This started to unravel when echoing the Darien Scheme of the late seventeenth century, a group of around two-hundred settlers sailed to Poyais, only to discover that the land they had been promised did not exist.

Gregor was born in 1786 and was raised by his widowed mother in Edinburgh following the death of his father, who had been a captain in the East India Company. In 1805, MacGregor married a wealthy young woman named Maria Bowater, whose dowry allowed him to purchase the rank of captain prematurely for the sum of £900. As captain of the 57th Foot, MacGregor became known as a formidable pedant for uniform, insisting that his men be meticulously dressed at all times. He had a desire for status and prestige, and in 1810 he relocated to London, where he attempted to win a place in high society by falsely adopting the title of 'Sir Gregor MacGregor', claiming chieftainship of the clan, posing as a member of a Portuguese knightly order, and telling tales of military prowess to anyone who would listen.

Upon the death of Maria, however, the financial buttress that had far supported his pretence vanished. With his money and social contacts melting away, MacGregor set off for Latin America to join the revolutionary movement in Venezuela. There, he fought first under General Francisco de Miranda, and then alongside another revolutionary leader, Simon Bolivar, whose cousin Josefa became the second Mrs. MacGregor in 1812. After several years of action, during which he distinguished himself to a much greater extent than he had ever done in the British Army, MacGregor set his sights on expanding the independence movement to other regions in South and Central America.

Arriving back on British soil in 1820. MacGregor announced that he had been created the Cazique of the Principality of Poayis, an independent nation on the Bay of Honduras. In 1822, a 'Sketch of the Mosquito Shore' was published to promote the project, a book supposedly penned by Thomas Strangeways, Captain in the 1st Native Poayis Regiment and MacGregor's aide-de-camp, but undoubtedly the work of MacGregor himself. The 'Sketch' provided a great deal of information on the colony: the capital of St. Joseph had been founded by English settlers in the 1730s, huge deposits of gold and silver lay hidden beneath its fertile soil, local labour promised to be cheap, and the terrain was beautiful, being 'full of large rivers, that run some hundred miles up into a fine, healthy and fruitful country'. It was also sheltered from Spanish incursion by an impassable mountain range. Moreover, the country already had the beginnings of a civilisation: a democratic government, a bank, and an opera house awaited the Europeans there. All of this was, of course, total fiction.

MacGregor also presented a range of other documentation to the public, including a manifesto that he had drawn up for the native Poyers, promising that the only immigrants permitted would be the industrious and honest, and the official certificate issued by George Frederic Augustus to place him in charge of Poayis. These documents were all headed by an official crest surmounted by the letters 'M.G.C.' which purportedly signified membership of the Order of the Green Cross, named after the symbol on the flag of Poayis, but also bear a suspicious resemblance to MacGregor's name. In Scotland MacGregor presented the scheme as the chance to redress the disaster of the nation's only other attempt at colonialism, the failed Darien Scheme of the 1690s,[3] when as many as 2,000 Scots were lured to Panama by hope of untold riches and opportunity, but in the end lost their lives to poor management and exaggerated promises. MacGregor explained that himself was descended from one of the unfortunate would-be settlers of the Darien, although, like all of his claims, this ought to be taken with a healthy pinch of salt.

The inspiring project, the exotic nature of Poayis, the multitude of documentation available to the public, and the general mania that surrounded Latin America at the time, generated thousands of investments, with the result that MacGregor, running out of land to grant, was forced to issue bonds. These ensured backers a healthy share of the profits that were bound to come from a Poayis invigorated by European investment and immigrants. So popular was the scheme that the share price of 2 shillings and threepence per acre originally advertised was soon advanced to 2 shillings and sixpence, and then later increased again, eventually reaching 4 shillings.

From farmers attracted by the promise of cheap and fruitful land, to wealthy families who bought commissions in the new Poyaisian army for their sons, thousands of Brits were won over by the machinations of MacGregor. MacGregor arranged the first voyage of 70 emigrants from London aboard the Honduras Packet, whose crew had apparently been present at his creation as the Cazique two years earlier. He saw off the voyage, which set sail on 10 September 1822 under the Green Cross flag of Poayis. Months later a second ship, the Kennersley Castle, set off from the Port of Leith with almost 200 would-be settlers. After doing the rounds of the passenger quarters, MacGregor himself was rowed back to shore amid cheers and applause, while the ship set off on its journey across the Atlantic.

When the new arrivals set foot on the sandy shores of Poayis, they were met not with an official welcome party organised by the local government, but by the desperate settlers who had arrived a few months earlier on the Honduras Packet, and who were still living in tents on the beach. It transpired that the broad boulevards, porticoed buildings, and friendly natives promised by MacGregor had yet evaded their searches; they had not even been able to find the opera house.

The passengers of the Kennersley Castle set about building their own camp. The official leader of the expedition was General Hector Hall, who had also been deceived by MacGregor's false claims. It nevertheless fell to him to explain away the disappointment faced by the 250 men, women, and children who had packed up their lives in Britain to make the long and difficult journey to Poayis. Hall failed to provide a sufficient justification for the complete lack of civilisation, and his regular disappearances from the camp as he travelled to Cape Gracias a Dios to try to make contact with either the enigmatic Mosquito king or a rescue ship were misconstrued by the other settlers, who believed that he was part of the ploy.

Coupled with the arrival of torrential rains that brought with them insects, diseases, and landslides, the disappointment was too much for the new inhabitants of Poayis, who sunk into despair, mutiny, violence, and suicide. At last, in May 1823, a ship carrying an embassy to the Mosquito King from British Honduras discovered their rudimentary camp. To their horror, the settlers were informed that Poyais did not actually exist and were advised that their only hope of survival lay in travelling onwards with the ship to Belize. By coincidence, Hall arrived from another expedition to Cape Gracias a Dios a few days later, accompanied by King George Frederic Augustus himself, who confirmed that MacGregor had never been recognised as an authority over Mosquito land, and told the Brits that they were in fact illegally settled on his territory. All the settlers decided to take their chances in Belize rather than remain there as subjects of the Mosquito King.

Of the two-hundred-and-fifty immigrants that set off to Poyais, only fifty lived to see Britain again. Upon their return, they denied that they had been duped by MacGregor, blaming instead his associates and agents who had so passionately pitched the wonders of Poyais to them. Even before the return of the Poyaisian victims, MacGregor was already suffering financially as a result of reduced investment in the scheme. In 1823, shortly before their return, he had fled to Paris where, unbelievably, he set up another similar fraud selling share in Poyais, presenting himself with the Gallicised title of 'Cacique'. He was even imprisoned in Paris but eventually acquitted. By the time he returned to London in 1826, the initial scandal that had blown up around the Poyaisian Fraud had died down. MacGregor was able to maintain his reputation because public disapproval was focused on the speculators in South American loans rather than on his misrepresentation of Poyais. Incredibly, a pamphlet warning investors about Poyais published in 1827 makes no mention of MacGregor at all. Finally, MacGregor managed to continue selling even more land shares in Central America throughout the late 1820s and early 1830s, although on a far smaller scale than his previous scam. He was never brought to court and there was little controversy in the press, but his business was by no means a success.

5.6 The South Sea and Mississippi Schemes: 'A Real Beauty and a Panted Whore'

During the time of the South Sea Company, the media was undergoing a revolution. Hundreds of publications appeared serving every possible niche. It was in the coffeehouse of London where the merits of the stories were debated and financial deals were done (see Chapter 3). Many of the famous literary figures from that period, such as Daniel Defoe, Jonathan Swift, Richard Steele, and Alexander Pope, were involved in the South Sea Bubble, either as investors or as propagandists writing for the slew of publications that caught coffeehouse drinkers attention. Defoe was a prolific writer and an able propagandist. From the beginning of 1720 he ran a newspaper called 'The Commentator'. He is reported to have compared the South Sea Company to John Law's Mississippi Company as like 'a real Beauty and a panted Whore', while also condemning the unworthy imitators. A passion for gambling meant the public quickly got taken in by the potential for huge gains. The desire to invest in any project, no matter how extreme, or even whether it was genuine or bogus reached manic proportions in the Mississippi Company and the South Sea Company.

It is likely that most readers have heard of the Mississippi Scheme and the South Sea Bubble. They were also popularised in Mackay's 'Extraordinary Popular Delusions and the Madness of Crowds' (1841) as early instances of speculative bubbles. What is not as widely known is the fact that these schemes—essentially frauds—were backed by the French and English governments. In the early 1700s, both nations had large war debts they wanted to quickly retire. Both nations pursued a strategy of engraftment. Publicly owned government debt would be exchanged for shares in some corporation, which would then hold all the debt. The governments could then extract reduced interest rates from those corporations in exchange for generous monopoly grants. This was the theory. In practice, the French and the English governments implemented their engraftment schemes with struggling corporations with questionable prospects. The French did with the Mississippi Company, which was a struggling, mismanaged corporation with vague plans to promote emigration to the Americas and acquire a grant of monopoly over tobacco. The English did so with the South Sea Company, which was formed by the government specifically for the purpose of engraftment. It was granted certain monopolies over English trade with South America. Since Spain was in control of those regions, the company's monopolies were probably worthless. Speculative bubbles developed for both corporations' stocks. The Mississippi Company bubble burst in the Summer of 1720. Fortunes were lost, and France's semi-feudal economy was crippled. The South Sea Bubble burst soon afterwards. Its impact on the more robust English economy was not as severe, but it had repercussions across all the economies of Europe.

The brainchild of the Mississippi Bubble was an expatriate Scot, John Law. This scheme has been hailed as the most ambitious economic experiment prior to the establishment of the Soviet Union in 1917. Like Lenin's creation, the short-lived Mississippi Bubble burst in spectacular fashion. Law was born in 1671, the son of an Edinburgh goldsmith. In adulthood, he became by turn a dandy, gambler, murderer, entrepreneur, economist, central banker, and finance minister. As an economist, Law was a monetarist, an early forerunner of the late Milton Friedman. At the height of what he called his 'System', Law was the richest and most powerful man in Europe. An unknown person back then, John Law presented an idea to the Duke of Orleans that would help France get rid of debt. Law believed that France suffered from a dearth of money and that an increase in its supply would boost economic activity. Indeed, after being defeated at Waterloo, Napoleon Bonaparte was forced to give up control of France. The treaty that finally ended the long Napoleonic Wars nonetheless imposed on the defeated country responsibility for paying a large indemnity. In France, public finances were in shambles; so meeting such payments would be difficult in any era, let alone in one when sovereign bond markets were largely underdeveloped. Law's idea which would later lead the demise of the French economy had two major steps:

- Firstly, John Law convinced the Duke of Orleans to introduce fiat currency in the system. This meant establishing a state-owned bank that would take in gold and give out paper receipts: the *Banque Royale*, in effect France's central bank. The receipts could technically be redeemed for gold on demand. However, such a situation would seldom arise. John Law convinced the Duke that such a system would enable the state to make loans to entrepreneurs with money that they did not have, collect interest on such non-existent loans, and pay off the debt owed. The Duke liked the plan, and fiat currency was introduced in France.
- The second step was to create an exciting company called the Mississippi Company. The Mississippi Company incorporated all of France's overseas trading companies—one of which claimed title to half the landmass of what is now the United States, along with monopolies for tax collection, tobacco, and coinage. This company would be given a royal charter which provided them with the exclusive privileges of conducting trade with Louisiana region of the United States which was then a French colony. Because trade with the East Indies had brought riches to Europe, the public opinion was that trade with the United States would result in similar riches. Hence, there was considerable hype around the Mississippi Company, and when people were given the option to exchange their debt for shares in this company, most people grabbed the offer with both hands.

In early 1720, the Mississippi stock was fixed at nine-thousand livres with the support of the central bank. In attempting to set the price of the shares, Law lost control of the money supply. In fact, one of the benefits of the coexistence of fiat money and newly created shares was that John Law could just inflate the stock prices at will. Whenever the stock prices went down, John Law would create more fiat money. A significant portion of this newly created money would reach the shares of the Mississippi Company thereby raising its price and creating the illusion of a successful company. In reality, the company was performing badly. The Louisiana colony in the United States was nothing except a swamp, and there was no way that it would lead to riches. However, John Law used the Louisiana illusion to keep the prices of the Mississippi Company inflated. Indeed, its shares surged some 20-fold in value in the open air stock market of Paris's *Rue Quincampoix*. This early case of 'irrational exuberance' (see Chapter 7) did not come out of nowhere. Rather—as I said—it was the consequence of Law's monetary policy. Within four years, however, Law's System had exploded, the stock market bubble burst, confidence in bank notes evaporated and the French currency collapsed. In late 1720, Law was forced into exile. He died nine years later and was buried in a pauper's tomb in Venice's San Moise. The Mississippi Bubble was, therefore, an earlier version of the get rich quick schemes that we see today in crypto finance, but was also a direct evidence of how monetary policies might spoil speculation that in turn boosts inequality.

As an effort to regulate the stock market after the Mississippi Bubble, the Paris *Bourse* had its origins in a royal decree from 1724. By decree, the right to buy and sell securities was conferred on sixty brokers appointed by the Ministry of Finance, the *agents de change*. These stockbrokers would function as civil servants, closely supervised by the state. This official stock exchange would be called the *Parquet*. Trading took place mainly in government debt for just one hour a day in a room on Paris's *Rue Vivienne*. *Agents de change* traded only on a commission basis as brokers, and not for their own accounts, as the law required. Trading activity was very limited compared to exchanges in London or Amsterdam and the *Parquet* could not absorb large orders. The *Parquet* would close during the French Revolution. In 1801, it reopened and remained under government control while possessing an official monopoly. In 1805, the *agents de change* formed an exclusive guild with the government approval, the *Compagnie des Agents de Change*, or CAC. The growing size of the bond market after large state borrowings in the 1810s led to new developments to encourage investment in securities. Pricing was made transparent as *agents de change* would announce their orders in an 'open outcry' and these orders matched to establish a clearing price in a fairly transparent setting; prices were then published. Also a permanent fund was established in 1822 to guarantee the obligations of brokers who led cash or securities on behalf of other brokers or their clients. This fund would be enlarged to six million francs in 1852. In the nineteenth century, the *Parquet* generally became more regulated and professional.

Similarly to New York (see Chapter 3) also the *Parquet* was not the extent of the Paris securities market. An unofficial market was formed nearby at the *Palais Royal*. It was called the *Coulisse*. Membership was free; anyone could become a *coulissier*. The *Coulisse* welcomed dealers who held their own inventory of securities, as opposed to brokers alone as the *Parquet* had. The banks emerging in the nineteenth century favoured the *Coulisse* since they could trade freely there without an *agent de change* acting as an intermediary. At the beginning the differentiation between the *Coulisse* and the *Parquet* came to the investors and traders served and not in the types of securities traded, since government bonds were the extent of the securities market in those days. Trading on the *Coulisse* was quicker but less transparent. *Coulissiers* traded bilaterally rather than in a public 'open outcry' format and so prices were not recorded or published. However, because dealers held their own inventories of securities, trades on the *Coulisse* could be more speedily executed. There was a strict legal separation between the official Paris *Bourse* and the *Coulisse*. *Agents de change* were prohibited from operating at the *Coulisse* or entering into partnerships with the *coulissiers*. Still, the government put up with the existence of the *Coulisse* because it benefited from the liquidity it provided to state bonds, at least when markets were performing favourably. Technically, trading in the French government bonds, the *rentes* was the preserve of the official market the *Parquet*. No transfer of *rentes* could take place without an *agent* as an intermediary. Eventually the strict distinction between a regulated and unregulated market venue tended to disappear after the Second World War when the *Coulisse* merged with the *Parquet* to form a single unified Paris Bourse in 1961 and the provincial exchanges outside Paris soon disappeared too.

The year 2020 marked the three-hundred-year anniversary of England's most notorious speculative mania, and one of the first of many economic and financial crises in modern terms. The South Sea Bubble of 1720 had the same essential ingredients that make investing challenging today: geopolitical turmoil, rapid globalisation, novel financial products, innovative business modules, new communication technologies, misinformation, and an abundance of tricksters ready to prey on the unwary and gullible. In fact, South Sea Bubble or speculation mania are synonyms that ruined many British investors in 1720.

The South Sea Company was a British joint-stock company founded in 1711 by an Act of Parliament. Daniel Defoe, the author of Robinson Crusoe was a director of the company and had persuaded the British government to set up a company as a way of consolidating, controlling, and reducing the national debt and to help Britain increase its trade and profits in the South Seas (now referred to as the islands of the South Pacific Ocean) and South America. Indeed, the book Robinson Crusoe published on 25 April 1719 tells the tale of a young and impulsive Englishman who leaves his hometown, defying his parents' wishes in order to seek excitement and adventure on the high seas. The book definitively helped feed the mania of the South Sea Company as people speculated on the potential riches of the company.

In 1713 the South Sea Company was granted a trading monopoly in the Americas. At the time the South Sea Company was created, most of South America was controlled by the Spanish and the Portuguese, and so there was little prospect of the British capturing much of that trade. However, part of the plan was the *Asiento*[4] (the Spanish granted the monopoly contract or *Asiento* to the South Sea Company) which allowed for the trading of African slaves and to the Spanish and Portuguese Empires. Often overlooked amid the mania that was to follow, the actual business of the South Sea Company was to transport African slaves to work. The incumbent Spanish and Portuguese colonialists were suffering from a shortage of labour to mine gold, silver, and other commodities—slaves were a must have. However, the maritime trade involved substantial risks: the voyage could be intercepted by pirates eager to capture the precious metals, ships could be shipwrecked in storms and traders faced the prospect of losing hundreds of their slaves to disease.

Furthermore, the slave trade had proved immensely profitable and there was a huge public confidence in the scheme, as many expected slave profits to increase dramatically, especially when the War of the Spanish Succession came to an end and trade could begin in earnest.

Under the terms of the agreement the South Sea Company was contracted to import four-thousand-and eight-hundred *piezas de Indias* annually. A *pieza* was the value of a healthy male or female slave between fifteen and twenty-five years of age. Slaves between twenty-five and thirty-five and between eight and fifteen years were valued at 2/3 *peca*. Slaves outside this age range and those infirm attracted a lower value. However, the terms and conditions offered an exclusion to account for the risk that shipwrecks and mortality during the crossing would affect the supply of slaves.

As well as the South Sea Company, the French Mississippi Company—as I have illustrated—was also set up to exploit trade with the Americas.

The slave trade was seen as a key route by which the British could capture some of the power that Spain wielded over the Atlantic trade.

The South Sea Company is estimated to have transported around thirty-four-thousand African slaves during the period when it was in existence. Tragically, many of the slaves transported either died during the crossing or after they were put to work. Around fifteen percent of slaves are estimated to have died during the voyage across the Atlantic Ocean—some five-thousand men, women, and children.

The South Sea Company was offering those who bought stocks a six percent margin on dividends. However, then the War of the Spanish Succession came to an end in 1713 with the Treaty of Utrecht, the expected trade explosion did not happen. Spain only allowed Britain a limited amount of trade and even took a percentage of the profits. Spain also taxed the importation of slaves and put strict limits on the number of ships Britain could send for 'general trade', which ended up being a single ship per year. This could not generate anywhere close to the profit that the South Sea Company needed to sustain it.

However, King George himself took governorship of the company in 1718. This further inflated the stock as nothing instils confidence quite like the endorsement of the ruling monarch. This is where the bubble began to wobble, as the company was not actually making anywhere near the profits it had promised. Instead, it was trading in increasing amounts of its own stock. Those involved in the company began encouraging their friends to purchase stock to further inflate the price and keep demand high.

By 1719 the directors of the South Sea Company looked eagerly across the Channel and wished to imitate the system that John Law had established in France with the Mississippi Company. Not because they were eager to help the British economy. No, they were rubbing their hands at the potential massive wealth. Whereas John Law—as I explained—was trying to create an open credit pump that would energise the French economy, John Blunt of the South Sea Company was deliberately trying to create a closed circuit that would only support the price of South Sea shares.

In 1719, the South Sea Company directors made a proposal to the British government for it to take on the entire national debt. On 12 April 1720, the offer was accepted. As so often happens in the world of financial engineering, an innovative idea was taken to the extreme. The root of the financial innovation was a direct result of the massive debt incurred by wars between France and England culminating in the War of the Spanish Succession. Both countries were spluttering under the weight of all of that debt. Specifically, the national debt of England also included sea-man pay tickets[5] in addition to war expenses. In fact, starting in the late 1670, the bookseller Thomas Guy began purchasing sea-man pay tickets at a large discount. In 1711, these tickets became part of the short-term floating national debt and were converted into shares of the South Sea Company. Guy had effectively been picking up lottery tickets for decades, and so through luck he had effectively become a major shareholder in the company.

In 1720, the Westminster Parliament allowed the South Sea Company to take over the national debt, and the company purchased thirty-two million pounds (GBP) national debt at the cost of seven-point-five million pounds (GBP). The purchase also came with assurances that interest on the debt would be kept low. The idea was the company would use the money generated by the ever-increasing stock sales to pay the interest on the debt. Or better yet, swap the stocks for the debt interest directly. Stocks sold well and in turn generated higher and higher interest, pushing the price and demand for stocks. By August 1720 the stock price hit one-thousand (GBP). It was a self-perpetuating cycle, but as such, lacked any meaningful fundamentals. The trade had never materialised, and in turn the company was just trading itself against the debt that it had bought. Furthermore, in early 1720 England was again at war with Spain and so the company's trading monopoly was basically worthless. The company's entire income was derived from the fixed interest payments it was receiving from holding government debt.

In September 1720, some would say an inevitable disaster struck. The bubble burst. Stocks plummeted down to a paltry one-hundred-and-twenty-four pounds (GBP) by December, losing eighty percent of their value at their height. Investors were ruined, people lost thousands, there was a marked increase in suicides and there was widespread anger and discontent in the streets of London with the public demanding an explanation. Even Newton himself could not explain the mania or hysteria that had overcome the populous. Indeed, Newton once said that he could calculate the motion of heavenly bodies, but not the madness of people.

The House of Commons called for an investigation and when the sheer scale of corruption and bribery was unearthed, it became a parliamentary and financial scandal. Not everyone had succumbed to the speculation of mania. A vociferous pamphleteer by the name of Archibald Hutcheson had been extremely critical of the scheme from the beginning. He had placed the actual value of the stock at around two-hundred pounds (GBP) which subsequently turned out to be about right. The person that came to sort out the issue was Robert Walpole. He was made Chancellor of the Exchequer, and he handled the crisis. In an effort to prevent such events from happening again, the Bubble Act was passed by Parliament on 11 June 1720. This forbade the creation of joint-stock companies such as the South Sea Company without the specific permission of a royal charter. In other words, competition was eliminated. In fact, there is a common misperception that the Bubble Act was passed as a response to the bursting of the South Sea Bubble. By contrast, it was passed while the bubble was forming in an attempt to block new corporations from competing with the South Sea Company for investors' capital. For almost a hundred years following the bursting of the bubble, the Bubble Act and a general anti-corporate sentiment severely limited the formation of new English corporations.

Notwithstanding this regulatory effort, the South Sea Company persisted in trading until 1853. During the bubble nearly two-hundred 'bubble companies' had been created, and while many of them were scams, not all were nefarious. The Royal Exchange Assurance[6] and the London Assurance[7] survive to this day. Those companies were launched at the time, hoping to cash in on the speculative mania that was gripping the South Sea Company. Some of these ventures actually involved tapping investors for money for apparently worthy business ideas—improving the Green land fishery or importing walnut trees from Virginia. Most however were shady ventures looking to extract as much money from gullible investors in the shortest time possible. The cash-shell company nature of these businesses is something that we still experience in our days when between 2020 and 2022 Wall Street's new financial innovation made his debut on financial markets under the acronym of Special Purpose Acquisition Companies (SPACs). Nonetheless, I do not believe that SPACs are the direct descendants of the South Sea Company or the 'bubble companies', but rather a contemporary incarnation of the VOC at least in their 'venturing spirit', and this is why I have already illustrated SPACs as a form of financial innovation in Chapter 3 rather than a form of financial calamity.

Finally, usually with the attention focused on the South Sea Company and Mississippi Bubble one might forget that the Netherlands also had its own bubble. The Netherlands also incurred significant debts as a result of the War of the Spanish Succession. Unlike France or England it did not import and introduce the same degree of financial innovation. The price of West Indies Company shares rose dramatically in 1720 before slumping to a fraction of their peak value. In addition to multiple share offerings of West Indies Company shares, there was also an attempt to launch an insurance firm (Stad Rotterdam) to compete with the British maritime insurance companies. Within weeks of Stad Rotterdam's flotation, at least thirty other Dutch companies floated fearing that if they delayed they would miss the wave of speculative fervour. Like their counterparts in England these businesses had multiple lines of business activities, as well as maritime insurance. Accounts from the time described the sudden burst of speculation as '*Windhandel*'—trade in wind.

5.7 The Bull Market of the Roaring Twenties and the Crash of Wall Street

The 1920s were an exuberant era in the United States, and in American finance in particular. Not only was the economy performing well but the common man seemed able to participate in that prosperity to a higher degree than was previously possible. This expansion was peculiarly characterised by consumer spending; this seemed to set it apart from earlier booms. The decade ushered in the modern American economy.

In financial markets, the public invested more of their money as stock prices rose. The range of investment products offered to individual investors was growing, especially with respect to the stock market, which had previously been virtually inaccessible to ordinary people. Now they could buy stocks with borrowed money. Closed-end funds kept sprouting up and still had no trouble finding new investors during the boom. These investment trusts were set up by banks and were listed on the exchange. So easy were they to access and so sought after were they that the funds' shares often traded above their net asset value.

Goldman Sachs entered this era of plenty on an unsteady footing. Henry Goldman, whose pro-German views got in the way of his fellow partners' desires to participate in syndicating loans to Allied governments during the First World War; had departed the firm. His departure, after thirty-five years at Goldman Sachs, caused money and clients to exit the firm. The remaining partners looked outside the Goldman and Sachs families for a new chief executive, a first for the company. To manage their firm they secured Waddill Catchincs, an ambitious and experienced man but also a self-assured risk taker. The partner must have thought this was the ideal man for the times though and he was not only hired from outside the founding families but was hired from outside the firm altogether. Judged to already be on an illustrious career path, Catchings was a Harvard Law School graduate, who had experience leading reorganised companies. Catchings was initially suspicious of the investment boom underway but this caution gave way as the decade went on, although a bubble was awaiting.

The beginning of the end came in 1929 with the stock market crash and the panic that led to the Great Depression. This was not the best time to a banker, and it was an even worse time to be a trader as strategies that worked in the boom years now produced only losses. For instance, Goldman Sachs by that time was both a banking and a trading organisation, shepherded into the latter business by its chief executive Waddill Catchings. His creation, the Goldman Sachs Trading Corporation (GSTC), invested the firm's equity capital and the investments of clients in the stock market using leverage. The crash took those investments down to nearly zero, and it took years for Catchings' successor Sidney Weinberg to restore the firm's standing.

Specifically, Catchings wanted Goldman Sachs to enter the investment trust business. To do this, the firm established Goldman Sachs Trading Corporation, an investment trust, in 1928 just as the twilight of the era's prosperity drew near. As it was being drawn up, the contemplated size of the new venture grew from twenty-five million dollars (USD) to one-hundred million dollars (USD). Of this amount, Goldman Sachs retained ten percent in the form of GSTC shares. Goldman would also be paid twenty percent of GSTC's net income as a management fee. The remaining shares were sold to the public at a four percent premium and were still oversubscribed. Thereafter, they quickly doubled in value, twice the trust's book value, partly because of investor enthusiasm perhaps but also because the firm was a heavy buyer of its own shares. By acquisition of another firm, the assets of GSTC reached two-hundred-and-forty-four million dollars (USD) within three months of the initial issue. Under Catchings, Goldman Sachs attempted to wring more profits out of GSTC and that meant managing more money. However, doing this by simply issuing more GSTC shares would also dilute its stake in the trust by an equal degree. So, a new trust, Shenandoah Corporation, was formed in July 1929. This new vehicle issued both common and preferred stock;

GSTC took most of the common stock and other investors bought the preferred stock. The one-third of the capital structure comprised of preferred stock, that in some ways resemble debt financing, allowing Goldman Sachs to leverage the investments it managed.

Just twenty-five days later, Blue Ridge Corporation was established by Shenandoah Corporation and copied the Shenandoah model. Shenandoah kept most of the common stock and preferred shares were sold to the public. The effect of these nested companies, Blue Ridge within Shenandoah and Shenandoah within GSTC meant that Goldman Sachs was able to leverage its investment holdings even further. The result was that small increases in share prices could translate into larger increases in the value of Goldman Sachs's investments but large losses were also magnified. In the end, debt is an amplifier. Indeed, in the infamous stock market crash that began in October 1929, common shares in GSTC fell from a peak of three-hundred-and-twenty-six dollars (USD) to a measly one-point-seventy-five dollars (USD) down more than ninety-eight percent from its initial offering price. The shares did so poorly because investment income fell so much that the company could not make the required dividend payments on its preferred shares, which had priority over the common stock. The virtual failure of GSTC stood a chance of ruining Goldman Sachs, not only because of its own investment in GSTC, but because the damage GSTC sustained to its reputation.

Nonetheless, the first months of 1929 began very well. The Down Jones Industrial Average[8] started in 1929 at three-hundred and peaked at three-hundred-and-eighty-one on 3 September 1929. New common stock issues, which averaged five-hundred million dollars (USD) per year in the past, had summed to five-point-one billion dollars (USD) that year, with investment trusts dominating the list of issuers. In September 1929 alone, more than six-hundred million dollars (USD) in investment trust securities were issued. However, stock prices began to decline by the end of September and early October 1929, and on 18 October a big drop in stock prices began. Panic soon set in, and on 24 October, 'Black Thursday' a record 12,894,650 shares were traded. Investment companies and leading bankers attempted to stabilise the market by buying up great blocks of stock. On Monday, however, the storm broke anew, and the market went into free fall. Black Monday was followed by Black Tuesday on 29 October 1929 during which stock prices collapsed completely and over sixteen million shares were traded on the New York Stock Exchange in a single day. Billions of dollars were lost, wiping out thousands of investors, and stock tickers ran hours behind because the machinery could not handle the tremendous volume of trading. After 29 October 1929, stock prices had nowhere to go but up, so there was considerable recovery during succeeding weeks. However, prices continued to drop as the United States slumped into the Great Depression, and by 1932 stocks were worth only about twenty percent of their value in the summer of 1929.

The stock market crash of 1929 was not the sole cause of the Great Depression, but it did act to accelerate the global economic collapse which it was also a symptom. Stock prices continued to drop through 1932 when the Down Jones Industrial Average—a widely used benchmark for blue-chip stocks in the United States—closed at 41.22, its lowest value of the twentieth century, eighty-nine percent below its peak. By 1933, nearly half of America's banks had failed, and unemployment was approaching fifteen million people or thirty percent of the US workforce. The Down Jones Industrial Average would not return to its pre-1929 heights until November 1954, about twenty-five years later. African Americans were particularly hard hit, as they were the 'last hired, first fired' (Greenberg 2010). Women during the Great Depression fared slightly better, as traditionally female jobs of the era like teaching and nursing were more insulated than those dependent on fluctuating markets. Life for the average family during the Great Depression was difficult.

However, the relief and reform measures in the New Deal programmes enacted by the administration of President Franklin D. Roosevelt helped lessen the worst effects of the Great Depression; the US economy would not fully turn around until after 1939 when World War II revitalised American industry. On 4 March 1933 during the bleakest days of the Great Depression newly elected President Franklin D. Roosevelt delivered his first inaugural address before 100,000 people on Washington's Capitol Plaza. 'First of all', he said 'let me assert my firm belief that the only thing we have to fear is fear itself'. He promised that he would act swiftly to face the 'dark realities of the moment' and assured Americans that he would 'wage a war against the emergency' just as though 'we were in fact invaded by a foreign foe'. His speech gave many people confidence. The next day, Roosevelt declared a four-day bank holiday to stop people from withdrawing their money from shaky banks.

On 9 March 1933, Congress passed Roosevelt's Emergency Banking Act, which reorganised the banks and closed the ones that were insolvent.

In his first 'fireside chat'[9] three days later, the president urged Americans to put their savings back in the banks, and by the end of the month almost three-quarters of them had reopened.

Roosevelt's quest to end the Great Depression was just beginning, and would ramp up in what came to be known as 'The First 100 Days'.[10] Roosevelt kicked things off by asking Congress to take the first step towards ending Prohibition[11]—one of the more divisive issues of the 1920s—by making it legal once again for Americans to buy beer (at the end of the year, Congress ratified the 21st Amendment and ended Prohibition for good). In May, he signed the Tennessee Valley Authority Act into law, creating the Tennessee Valley Authority and enabling the federal government to build dams along the Tennessee River that controlled flooding and generated inexpensive hydroelectric power for the people in the region. June's National Industrial Recovery Act guaranteed that workers would have the right to unionise and bargain collectively for higher wages and better working conditions; it also suspended some antitrust laws and established a federally funded Public Works Administration. In addition, Roosevelt had won passage of twelve other major laws, including the Glass–Steagall Act (an important banking bill) and the Home Owners' Loan Act, in his first 100 days in office. Despite the best efforts of President Roosevelt and his cabinet, however, the Great Depression continued. Unemployment persisted, the economy remained unstable, farmers continued to struggle, and people grew angrier and more desperate. So, in the spring of 1935, Roosevelt launched a second, more aggressive series of federal programmes, sometimes called Second New Deal. In April, he created the Works Progress Administration (WPA) to provide jobs for unemployed people. WPA projects were not allowed to compete with private industry, so they focused on building things like post offices, bridges, schools, highways, and parks. The WPA also gave work to artists, writers, theatre directors, and musicians. In July 1935, the National Labor Relations Act, also known as the Wagner Act, created the National Labor Relations Board to supervise union elections and prevent businesses form treating their workers unfairly. In August, Roosevelt signed the Social Security Act of 1935, which guaranteed pensions to millions of Americans, set up a system of unemployment insurance, and stipulated that the federal government would help care for dependent children and the disabled. Still, the Great Depression dragged on. Workers grew more militant: in December 1936, for example, the United Auto Workers strike at a GM plant in Flint, Michigan lasted for forty-four days and spread to some one-hundred-and-fifty-thousand autoworkers in thirty-five cities. By 1937, to the dismay of most corporate leaders, some eight million workers had joined unions and were loudly demanding their rights. Despite difficulties and hard times, it is undeniable that from 1933 until 1941, President Roosevelt's New Deal programmes and policies did more than just adjust interest rates, tinker with farm subsidies, and create short-term make-work programmes. They created a brand-new political coalition that included white working people, African Americans, and left-wing intellectuals. More women entered the workforce as Roosevelt expanded the number of secretarial roles in government. These groups rarely shared the same interests but they did share a powerful belief that an interventionist government was good for their families, the economy, and the nation. Many of the New Deal programmes that bound them together—social security, unemployment insurance, and federal agricultural subsidies, for instance—are still with us today.

In the same fashion, the Glass–Steagall Act has been an important act of the first New Deal, and it has since then highly influenced the future of the banking industry. Specifically, the Glass–Steagall Act sets up a firewall between commercial banks, which accept deposits and issue loans, and investment banks which negotiate the sale of bonds and stocks. The Banking Act of 1933 also created the Federal Deposit Insurance Corporation (FDCI), which protected bank deposits up to twenty-five-thousand dollars (USD) at the time (now up to two-hundred-and-fifty-thousand dollars (USD) as a result of the Dodd–Frank Act of 2010). As the bill stated, it was designed:

> to provide for the safer and more effective use of the assets of banks, to regulate interbank control, to prevent the undue diversion of funds into speculative operations, and for other purposes.

Some of those 'undue diversions' and 'speculative operations' had been revealed in congressional investigations led by a firebrand prosecutor named Ferdinand Pecora. As chief counsel to the US Senate's Committee on Banking and Currency, Pecora—an Italian immigrant who rose through the ranks of Tammany Hall, despite his reputation for honesty—dug into the actions of top bank executives and found rampant reckless behaviour, corruption, and cronyism.

Part of the problem, as Pecora and his investigative team revealed, was that banks could lend money to a company and then issue stock in that same company without revealing to shareholders the bank's underlying conflict of interest. If that company then failed, the bank suffered no losses while its investors were left 'holding the bag'. Pecora exposed the deeds of people like Charles Mitchell, head of the largest bank in America, National City Bank (now Citibank), who made more than one million dollars (USD) in bonuses in 1929 but paid zero taxes. National City Bank, testimony uncovered, had taken on bundles of bad loans, packaged them as securities, and unloaded them on unsuspecting customers. Meanwhile, a top executive of Chase National Bank (a precursor of today's J. P. Morgan Chase) had gotten rich by short selling his company's shares during the 1929 stock market crash. In testimony from financier J. P. Morgan, the public learned that Morgan had issued stocks at discounted rates to a small circle of privileged clients, including former President Calvin Coolidge. Pecora's hearings captivated an increasingly disgusted American public, which began to refer to these men as 'banksters' a term coined to refer to financial leaders who had put the nation's economy at risk while pocketing profits. President Roosevelt and lawmakers harnessed this wave of anger for the financial industry to push through the Glass–Steagall Act, which Roosevelt signed into law on 16 June 1933. Under the act, bankers could take deposits and issue loans, and brokers at investment banks or better securities firms could raise capital and sell securities, but no banker at a single firm could do both. Over time, however, barriers set up by Glass–Steagall gradually melted.

Starting in the 1970s, large banks began to push back on the Glass–Steagall Act's regulations, claiming they were rendering them less competitive against foreign securities firms. The argument, embraced by Federal Reserve Chairman Alan Greenspan, who was appointed by President Ronal Reagan in 1987, was that if banks were permitted to engage in investment strategies, they could increase the return for their banking customers while avoiding risk by diversifying their businesses. Soon, several banks began crossing the line once established by the Glass–Steagall Act through loopholes in the act. For example, the act stipulated that while a Federal Reserve member bank could not deal in securities, a bank could affiliate with a company that did as long as that company was not 'engaged principally' in such activities. One of the most prominent deals that exploited this loophole was the 1998 merger of banking giant Citicorp with Travelers Insurance, which owned the now-defunct investment bank Salomon Smith Barney. One year later, President Bill Clinton signed the Financial Services Modernisation Act, commonly known as Gramm–Leach–Bliley, which effectively neutralised Glass–Steagall by repealing key components of the act. Some economists point to the repeal of the Glass–Steagall Act as a key factor leading to the housing market bubble and subsequent Great Recession, the Global Financial Crisis of 2007–2008 (see Chapter 6). Joseph E. Stiglitz, a Nobel laureate in economics wrote in a 2009 opinion piece that by bringing:

> investment and commercial banks together, the investment bank culture came out on top. There was a demand for the kind of high returns that could be obtained only through high leverage and big risk-taking.

But other economists, including former Treasury Secretary Tim Geithner argued that a boom in subprime mortgage lending, inflated scores by credit-rating agencies. and an out-of-control securitisation market were more significant factors than any dismantling of federal regulation.

5.8 From the Ponzi Scheme to Ponzi Schemes

The year 2020 marked one-hundred years after Charles Ponzi was charged for committing what some have referred to as the 'fraud of the century'. Indeed, there are not many criminals who have their work named after them. But such was the case with the Ponzi scheme, a confidence scam that fraudsters continue to commit to the present day.

A Ponzi scheme is a fraudulent investment scheme in which existing investors are paid with funds collected from new investors. Typically, the scheme unravels once the number of new investors declines, meaning insufficient funds are available to pay everyone. In terms of the history of this particular scam, it actually pre-dates Charles Ponzi, with the first known schemes of this type traced back to the latter half of the nineteenth century in both the United States and Germany. Charles Dickens even described such a scheme in his 1857 novel Little Dorrit. The central theme of Dickens' novel was imprisonment, whether it was imposed by others with iron bars or by oneself because of a closed heart or misanthropic social mores. In his graphic depiction of the Marshalsea debtors' prison Dickens drew upon his own childhood experience, when his bankrupted father, John Dickens, became a 'resident' of a jail for a few months to the eternal dismay of the whole family. As I said, Little Dorrit also contained a first-rate description of a Ponzi scheme: William Dorrit meets Mrs. Merdle at Martigny, who invites him to invest his money in her husband's London bank. Many people including the hero, Arthur Clennam have done so. To cut a long story short, Merdle's bank collapses and the owners commit suicide; Arthur himself lands at Marshalsea as a debtor. But by the end of the novel everything gets sorted out: the hero comes out of prison, thanks to mysteriously returned papers and codicils. He sorts out his emotional emptiness by marrying the heroine. But the million dollar question is: how realistic is all this? Can fortunes once lost ever be recovered due to repentance or magnanimity shown by the very people who benefited most from the dubious schemes?

Charles Ponzi was born in Lugo, Italy, in 1882. At the age of twenty-one, having already worked as a postal worker, Ponzi decided to set sail for the United States in pursuit of a better life—although somewhat infamously, he arrived on American shores with only two dollars (USD) to his name, having gambled the rest of his money away on the ship. Having arrived in the United States, Ponzi soon moved to Canada, where he became an assistant teller at the recently established Banco Zarossi in Montreal. It was there that he first witnessed in action what would later become known as the Ponzi scheme. The bank was in serious financial trouble on the back of a number of real estate loans that went sour. As such, founder Luigi 'Louis' Zarossi attempted to remain afloat by funding the interest payments using customer deposits from newly opened accounts. The bank failed, however, and Zarossi fled to Mexico with much of the bank's money.

Falling on though times shortly after the bank's failure, Ponzi then attempted to forge a cheque he made payable to himself and was duly caught and imprisoned in Canada for almost three years. Upon his release in 1911, he returned to the United States, where he became involved in a new criminal scheme of smuggling illegal Italian immigrants across the border. But again, he was caught and imprisoned for another two years.

By 1919, Ponzi was living in Boston, and in the summer of 1920, Ponzi was front-page news virtually every day in the Boston papers. But prior to 1920, few people outside Boston's Italian community had ever heard of Charles Ponzi. He told the New York Times that he had come from a well-to-do family in Parma, Italy. He also claimed to have studied at the University of Rome, but said that he was not suited to the academic life. In Boston, Charles Ponzi began devising various schemes to make money. It was here that he first discovered the international reply coupon (IRC). Created by the United States Postal Service (USPS), this coupon allowed a sender to pre-purchase postage and include it in the letter being sent. The recipient in another country could then exchange the IRC at a local post office for airmail postage stamps that could be used for sending the reply correspondence. According to Ponzi's autobiography, he first encountered the IRC in a letter he received from a business correspondent in Spain who purchased the coupon for thirty centavos. In the United States, the same IRC could be exchanged for five cents—significantly more than its value in Spain, especially with the Spanish peseta weakening against the dollar at the time.

As such, Ponzi figured out that purchasing massive quantities of coupons from weaker European economies and selling them for higher prices in the United States could net him huge sums of money. Indeed, Ponzi was claiming at the time that such a scheme could generate net profits of up to 400%. Of course, this method of arbitrage—whereby an asset is purchased in one market and sold in another market at higher price—was completely legal and remains so today. And had Ponzi simply confined himself to such an operation, he would have remained in the clear.

Instead, however, he turned his business into a scam, setting up his Securities Exchange Company in early 1920 and persuading people to invest in the business in return for an additional fifty percent in interest within ninety days. Such eye-watering returns were too enticing to pass up, and interest from investors mounted. Ponzi also lied to investors by telling them that he had amassed an elaborate network of agents throughout Europe able to purchase the coupons in bulk for him and that he could easily turn these coupons into financial gains back in the United States.

Ponzi, however, did not use this growing pile of new investor funds to purchase more IRCs but rather kept some of the money for himself and paid the rest to longer-standing investors, many of whom were so thrilled with their returns that they reinvested their earnings back into Ponzi's scheme, thus inadvertently helping to keep the scam going. Whenever he was asked to reveal the inner workings of his operation, he simply said that he needed to conceal such information from the public to prevent competitors from emerging. But as Ponzi enjoyed a meteoric rise in wealth and fame, suspicion over his dealings soon followed. He sued a financial writer for claiming that it was impossible for him to guarantee such high returns over a short period of time. And although he won the lawsuit as the writer failed to prove his allegations, Ponzi began to come under increasing scrutiny. Another unsuccessful lawsuit filed against Ponzi by a Boston furniture-maker only ensured that even more eyes became fixed on the workings of the Securities Exchange Company, including those of the Boston Post's publisher at the time, Richard Grozier, who asked reporters in July 1920 to investigate Ponzi.

One reporter, financial journalist Clarence Barron, found that Ponzi himself was not investing in his purported scheme, despite offering such exorbitant returns for his customers. Instead Ponzi, had previously told journalists that he invested his own money in real estate, stocks, and bonds, which thus begged the question: why did he prefer traditional assets that would yield him five percent maximum returns to his own scheme that claimed to offer fifty percent returns? Barron also calculated that covering the volume of investments made through Ponzi's scheme would have required around one-hundred-and-sixty million coupons to have been traded, and yet only twenty-seven-thousand coupons were in circulation. Much of Barron's findings were included in a front-page article run by the Boston Post in July 1920. And although many investors still chose to side with him, Ponzi must have realised that his scam was slowly unravelling. He hired publicist William McMasters to shore up his public image; but having realised that his client was full of lies, McMasters instead chose to denounce Ponzi in the press. 'The man is a financial idiot. He can hardly add … He sits with his feet on the desk smoking expensive cigars in a diamond holder and talking complete gibberish about postal coupons' was McMasters' assessment of Ponzi as reprinted in James Walsh's book 'You can't cheat an honest man'.

The following month, Ponzi's office was raided by regulators. An audit of his business revealed that he was in possession of a grand total of sixty-one dollars (USD) worth of postal coupons. The post also ran another front-page story about Ponzi, this time detailing his criminal activities in Montreal and his role at Banco Zarossi. Ponzi eventually surrendered to authorities and was charged with mail fraud by the federal government. He served three and half years in prison plus an additional nine years on state charges. After serving his whole sentence, he was deported to Italy upon his release and spent the remainder of his life in poverty. He died in Rio de Janeiro, Brazil, in 1949.

Despite the notoriety of Charles Ponzi, the scheme that carries his name appears to have been first perpetrated by Sarah Howe in Boston in 1879, when she created the Ladies' Deposit to help invest money for women. Sarah Howe's early life is mostly a mystery. There are no surviving photographs or sketches of her, so it is impossible to know what she looked like. She may, at one point, have been married, but by 1877 she was single and working as a fortune-teller in Boston. It was a time of boom and invention in the United States. The country was rebuilding after the Civil War (see Chapter 3), industrial development was starting to take off, and immigration and urbanisation were both increasing steadily. Money was flowing freely (to white people anyway), and men and women alike were putting that money into the nation's burgeoning banks. In 1876, Alexander Graham Bell invented the telephone, and in 1879 Thomas Edison created the lightbulb. In between those innovations, Sarah Howe opened the Ladies' Deposit Company, a bank run by women, for women. The company's mission was simple: help white women gain access to the booming world of banking. The bank only accepted deposits from so-called 'unprotected females', women who did not have husband or guardian handling their money. These women were largely overlooked by banks who saw them—and their smaller pots of money—as a waste of time. In return for their investment, Howe promised incredible results: an eight percent interest rate. Deposit $100 now, and she promised an additional $96 back by the end of the year. And to sweeten the deal, new depositors got their first three months' interest in advance. When sceptics expressed doubts that Howe could really guarantee such high returns, she offered an explanation: the Ladies' Deposit Company was no ordinary bank, but instead was a charity for women, bankrolled by Quaker philanthropists.[12]

Word of the bank spread quickly among single women—housekeepers, schoolteachers, widows. Howe, often dressed in the finest clothes, enticed ladies to join, and encouraged them to spread the news among their friends and family. This word-of-mouth marketing strategy worked. Howe's bank gathered investments from across the country in a time before easy long-distance communication. Money came in from Buffalo, Chicago, Baltimore, Pittsburgh, and Washington, all without Howe taking out a single newspaper advertisement. She opened a branch of the bank in New Bedford, Massachusetts, and had plans to add offices in Philadelphia and New York to keep up with the demand. Many of the women who deposited with the Ladies' Deposit Company reinvested their profits back in the bank, putting their faith, and entire life savings in Howe's enterprise. All told, the Ladies Deposit would gather at least two-hundred-and-fifty-thousand dollars (USD) from eight-hundred women—although historians think far more women were involved. Some estimate that Howe collected more like five-hundred-thousand dollars (USD), the equivalent of about thirteen million dollars (USD) today. It did not take long for the press to notice a woman encroaching on a man's space. And not just a woman, a single woman who had once been a fortune-teller. Reporters were particularly put off by their inability to access even the lobby of Howe's bank, turned away at the door for being men. One particularly intrepid reporter, determined to find out what Howe's secret was, returned dressed as a woman to gain entry and more information. Then, in 1880, it all came crashing down. On 25 September 1880, the Boston Daily Advertiser began a series of stories that exposed Howe's bank as a fraud. Her eight percent returns were too good to be true. Howe was operating what we know as a Ponzi scheme—forty years before Ponzi would try his hand at it. When a new depositor arrived, Howe would use their money to pay out older clients, so the whole scheme required a constant influx of new depositors to pay out the old ones. Like every other Ponzi fraudster, Howe's bank would have eventually run out of new money. The run of stories in the Boston Daily Advertiser instilled enough fear in the bank's investors that they began to withdraw their money, and eventually there was a run on Howe's bank. It took two weeks and five days from the first story published in the Advertiser uncovering Howe's fraud before she was arrested. The press extended her victims a modicum of sympathy, describing their plights while also reminding the reader that they deserved their pain for trusting a woman with their money. Howe stood trial in Boston and was ultimately convicted (although not of fraud, but soliciting money under false pretences—for claiming that a Quaker charity was backing the venture). She spent three years in prison, and when she got out, in classic scammer fashion, she tried the whole thing again. Next, Howe opened up a new Woman's Bank on West Concord Street in Boston. She kept the scheme going from 1884 to 1886, offering depositors seven percent interest and gathering at least fifty-thousand dollars (USD), although historians think the number might be far higher. This time, however, Howe was never prosecuted. After being caught and closing down her bank, she gave up the game and returned to fortune-telling and doing astrology readings for twenty-five cents each. She died in 1892, at the age of sixty-five, no longer wealthy, but still notorious enough to warrant an obituary in the New York Times that read:

> For three months she had been living in a boarding and lodging house, carefully keeping from those whom she met the knowledge that she was the notorious Mrs. Howe of Woman's Bank memory.

In spite of her crimes, Sarah Howe is not a household name. It is not called a Howe scheme, it is a Ponzi scheme. While Ponzi and Howe were certainly held accountable for their actions in the end, their examples have not stopped others from carrying out similar schemes in the hundred years or so since then.

Most recently—and perhaps most notable of all—was the Ponzi run by Bernard Madoff, who again used new investor funds to pay existing investors in his investment company. It is widely thought that Madoff ran the biggest Ponzi scheme in financial history, worth around sixty-five billion dollars (USD). In 2008, Madoff was convicted for his scam and sentenced to one-hundred-and-fifty years in prison for various financial crimes, including securities fraud and money laundering. He died earlier in April 2021 at the age of eighty-two in a federal prison hospital in Butner, North Carolina.

The son of European Jewish immigrants, Madoff was born in New York in 1938. He founded a brokerage firm in 1960, which eventually became Bernard L. Madoff Investment Securities, where he served as chairman until his arrest by the US Federal Bureau of Investigation (FBI) in December 2008. Madoff also served as chairman of the Nasdaq Stock Market (NASDAQ) during the early 1990s, and Madoff Investment Securities was at one point the stock market's biggest market-maker. It was at this firm that Madoff built his broker-dealer and property-trading businesses over more than four decades. But it was the firm's clandestine investment management and advisory unit that became the focus of the fraud investigation.

The firm was located on the eighteenth and nineteenth floors of the Lipstick Building in Manhattan. But according to two of the firm's whistle-blowers employees, Madoff ran the investment advisory business from a separate floor, the seventeenth, with one of the employees confirming that Madoff kept the financial records of this business tightly secured. It was from this floor—with a distinctly concealed entrance—that Madoff managed to draw affluent investors into his Ponzi scheme. Ultimately, the scheme was a rather straightforward one. Madoff simply created an account in which his investment firm collected funds from clients and from which the same money was used to pay those clients who wanted to liquidate their holdings. The specific investment strategy he marketed to investors was the collar, also known as the spilt-strike conversion. Typically a position will consist of the ownership of 30–35 S&P 100 stocks, most correlated to that index, the sale of out-of-the-money 'calls' on the index, and the purchase of out-of-the-money 'puts' on the index, a Madoff hedge fund offering memorandum explained. The sale of the 'calls' is designed to increase the rate of return, while allowing upward movement of the stock portfolio to the strike price of the 'calls'. The 'puts' funded in large part by the sales of the 'calls', limit the portfolio's downside.

The strategy allowed Madoff to conceal his scam, avoid further scrutiny from investors, and provide investors and other interested parties with an explanation of how he managed to attain specific rates of return consistently, year after year. And by confining his portfolios to only blue-chip stocks, Madoff could easily obtain historical trading data to reverse engineer which trades his firm would have to trade in order to achieve a state of return for his client accounts. For instance, once he had decided that in November 2008, all his clients' accounts would be up one percent, then he would backwards—figuring out which stocks he would have had to trade in order to make one percent. Madoff or Frank DiPascali (who oversaw the Ponzi scheme's operation) would enter trades that never happened, with real prices, into an old IMB AS/400 computer he used for his advisory business and by then he had a track record. Then using a simple spreadsheet such as Excel, more than two-thousand-and-three-hundred client accounts were updated automatically—dividing among all the accounts the gains from the 'trades' that amounted to 'profits' of one percent.

Ultimately Madoff's Ponzi scheme unravelled when the global financial crisis prompted an attempted withdrawal of some seven billion (USD) by customers from his funds. Previously, Madoff simply paid clients who were requesting withdrawals using money he had deposited from new clients. But with little new money flowing in by November 2008, Madoff failed to cover the volume of withdrawal requests. Despite having received hundreds of millions of dollars in financial backing from friends, it was too little, too late. With credit drying up at banks, it proved impossible for Madoff to obtain the needed funding to meet the mountain of redemption requests. He thus told DiPascali to use the remaining two-hundred-and-thirty-four million dollars (USD) in the Ponzi Scheme account to pay favoured clients and relatives, before advising his sons,

Mark and Andrew, to pay company bonuses ahead of schedule from the two-hundred million dollars (USD) worth of company assets—explaining to them that his asset—management business was 'one big lie'. Madoff's sons reported him to authorities on 10 December 2008, and he was arrested the following day. Investigators found that Madoff had not made even one trade in many years. And instead of executing his spilt-strike conversion strategy as he had marketed to his clients, he simply deposited investors' funds in a Chase bank account and paid other customers seeking to cash out with those funds. He also provided clients with falsified account statements, showing completely fictionalised scenarios of investment returns being generated. Madoff was sentenced—as I said—to one-hundred-and-fifty years in prison and ordered to forfeit one-hundred-and-seventy billion dollars (USD) in assets, representing the amount of funds deposited by investors that were later disbursed to other investors. Others involved in the scheme also suffered greatly, not least his sons, who faced a civil lawsuit filed in October 2009 by Irving Picard, the court-appointed trustee for the liquidation of Bernard Madoff Investment Securities, for almost two-hundred million dollars (USD). Two years to the day following his father's arrest, Mark Madoff was found to have committed suicide. Less than three years later, Andrew had died from cancer. And by June 2017, a settlement was reached on the sons' estates for more than twenty-three million dollars (USD).

Despite being decades apart, however, the similarities between the two schemes run by Ponzi and Madoff are quite remarkable. Both offered their customers guarantees of consistently high returns with little risk, irrespective of market conditions; both survived for extended periods of time by their creators pretending that they were too complex in nature to explain and that revealing too much would erode returns as a result of competitors entering the market; and ultimately, both collapsed when the number of investors wishing to remove their money was too much for the schemes to cover their requests.

5.9 Herstatt Bank and Globalisation

In June 1974, Herstatt Bank, a relatively small German bank, was closed by regulators on account of large losses in the foreign exchange market and murky accounting statements. The bank was one that few outside the vicinity of Köln would have heard of. However, because of the manner in which foreign exchange trades were conducted, many other banks essentially had their money locked up at the failed Herstatt Bank. This episode changed the way these trades were settled and encouraged a rethink of the scope of bank regulation.

The bank was specialising in serving high-net-worth clients. This was not a very well-known financial institution, and it was the 35th largest bank in the country, a mid-sized family-owned bank. It was not particularly well managed. Iwan Herstatt had allowed the foreign currency division to operate with substantial freedom. This unit was run by a recognised expert in foreign exchange markets, Daniel Dattel. For Dattel, the end of the Bretton Woods system had created new trading opportunities in foreign exchange markets since the value of more currencies floated freely against each other. Iwan Herstatt was not aware of the risks taken by the foreign currency division. Regulators had produced critical reports of Herstatt Bank's situation based on factors like its reserves, difficulties with expansion, and tips provided by others in the same banking circles as Herstatt. By the spring of 1974, several banks were refusing to work with Herstatt. Many banks started to report large foreign currency losses. Herstatt Bank faced particularly large losses which its foreign currency division tried to cover up by falsifying financial statements. It was the questionable financial reporting that wrecked efforts to rescue the bank. Its banking licence withdrawn by the financial supervisor, Herstatt Bank failed on 26 June 1974. The bank was estimated to have lost four-hundred-and-seventy million marks in foreign exchange trades. This was in relation to a bank with total assets of approximately two-point-four billion marks and deposits of three-hundred million.

The failure of such a small bank in Germany turned out not to be a strictly local problem. Herstatt's currency operations linked it with several much larger banks. Because of differences in time zone, on the day of its demise Herstatt Bank received millions of deutschmarks from trades in Europe before it had to deliver amounts due to these same counterparties in US dollars in New York time. When the bank was closed at the end of the German business day, counterparties in America were unable to receive payment for their trades though they had already sent payment for their half of the trade before the end of the German business day. Many counterparties faced large losses. American banks were particularly affected. One of the banks was Seattle First National Bank, which had delivered twenty-two-point-five million dollars (USD) in West Germany marks to Herstatt Bank just hours before the bank's closure. The list of affected banks included Chase Manhattan Bank and Citibank as well as some European banks. The German regulators did not envision these international consequences before the failure of the bank. The knock-on effects of the failure were not limited to banks with direct exposure to Herstatt. Banks adopted new measures to limit future losses, with destructive effects on the existing system for global payments. New York banks delayed the settlement of payments with one another until their accounts were sufficiently in credit. The New York Clearing House also introduced a one-day settlement period by allowing a payment to be recalled on the morning of the day after the payment was released. In response to the risk that payments from American firms could be recalled, European banks sent payment orders to clearing houses that were conditional on receiving the counter-value in another currency in a different market. The financial system was fractured by such nervousness about settlement risk. Interest rates on US dollars in Europe rose relative to rates in the United States. The global payment system was stalling. Bank was reporting that payments which would have taken just five minutes to execute in the past were taking half a day now. Smaller banks were particularly affected. The risk of loss in the settlement process of a transaction is still known as 'Herstatt risk' today.

Herstatt Bank's failure triggered a reconsideration of the nature of bank supervision. German regulators were unable to get an accurate picture as to the extent of Herstatt's losses, in part because some of these were at the bank's Luxembourg subsidiary. They had also overlooked the international repercussions of closing the bank when they did. So, Herstatt Bank's collapse led to a rethink of the regulatory structure with a greater emphasis on international cooperation.

At the international level, this gave rise to the creation of the Basel Committee on Banking Supervision in 1975 within the existing Bank for International Settlements. The Basel Committee was formed to reduce gaps in bank supervision caused by international borders, and by extension the Basel Committee will draft the future Basel Accords, important waypoints in the globalisation of banking regulation. Of practical importance, a new real-time settlement system was introduced globally. This ultimately culminated in the creation of CLS Bank, which settles global foreign exchange transactions.

5.10 The Dotcom Bubble

The mid-1990s saw a worldwide, unprecedented growth in the information technology and telecommunications sectors. The cost of sending and storing information declined sharply. The massive adoption of personal computers and the spread of the World Wide Web revolutionised industry, trade, finance, and services. Ambitious entrepreneurs put together plans to launch online businesses, and venture capitalists were eager to finance them, lured by their potential profitability.

The dotcom bubble coincided with the longest period of economic expansion in the United States after World War II. Inflation and unemployment were declining, and economic growth and productivity increased substantially. From October 1998 onwards, markets cheered the seemingly endless IPOs of dotcom firms without paying much attention to the viability of their business models: a financial bubble was inflating. Most of the internet start-ups would never generate any revenue or profit. Encouraged by financial analysts, retail and institutional investors avidly purchased over-the-counter equities in anticipation that they would sell them for even higher prices. Liquidity was abundant, as the Federal Reserve had cut interest rates after the collapse of hedge fund Long-Term Capital Management in 1998. The effect was dramatic.

The dotcom bubble or information technology bubble was triggered mainly by speculation and substantial funding for these new internet start-ups, investments in dotcoms (named as such for the.com online top-level domain [TLD] used by such companies) boosted the NASDAQ Composite Index (COMP) from 751 in January 1995 to a peak of 5,048.62 on 10 March 2000. But the bubble eventually burst in March 2000, with many companies failing to even come close to fulfilling their promise. As such, the NASDAQ fell more than seventy-five percent between March 2000 and October 2002, thus wiping out almost five trillion dollars (USD) in market value.

During this time, several of the most hyped tech companies ended up declaring bankruptcy, such as Pets.com, eToys.com, etc. That said, others managed to survive and enjoy phenomenal growth to stand as some of the world's biggest companies including Amazon, eBay, and Cisco.

The proliferation of the World Wide Web (WWW) during the latter half of the 1990s ushered in a new era of internet-based companies, keen to capitalise on the wave of hype and anticipation the online world was expected to offer. Indeed, with the internet being widely heralded as one of the biggest technological break thoughts of the time, it is perhaps no surprise that so many companies and investors wanted to capitalise on the hysteria that abounded.

Arguably, the bubble began with the first public issuance of shares from an internet company—the web browser developer Netscape, which staged its initial public offering on 9 August 1995. The company provided, among other things, a new web browser, a programming language for web animation (JavaScript), and the ability to save certain browser information through cookies. But despite operating at a loss and having no discernible revenue streams, Netscape went public—and did so with considerable success. The stock was listed at $28 on the first morning of the offering but soon hit fifty-eight-point-twenty-five dollars (USD) on that day meaning that its market capitalisation sat above two-point-five billion dollars (USD). The success of Netscape's IPO was hugely influential in encouraging other internet start-up founders to take their own companies public. And investors flocked to fulfil their funding needs. Indeed, it soon became apparent that the frenzy to profit from this perceived internet boom meant that investors largely ignored the traditional fundamentals of these new tech companies, such as the price-to-earnings ratio, the debt-to-equity ratio, or the amount of free cash flow. Instead they punted on likely future performance and growth potentials as well as brand awareness and website-traffic metrics. Many start-ups did not even have established business models and could not demonstrate cash-flow generation, meaning that investing in them was a highly speculative endeavour that was not based on robust valuation models for the most part.

As such, most companies that issued shares through IPOs during the dotcom era ended up being excessively overvalued. It was this overvaluation that ultimately culminated in a massive bubble of dotcom stocks. By 1999, the price-to-earnings ratio of the NASDAQ Composite Index had astonishingly surpassed 90. Most dotcom companies were operating at net losses, spending heavily on advertising and brand awareness and offering their products and services for free or at sizeable discounts, hoping that their eventual growth would enable them to charge more profitable rates further down the line. This growth over profits mentality also resulted in more than a few tech companies spending excessively and irresponsibly on such unnecessary luxuries as employee vacations, cutting-edge business facilities, and dotcom parties to celebrate the launchings of new products and services.

The actions of the Federal Reserve System during the mid-1990s also played a significant role in exacerbating the dotcom craze, specifically by lowering interest rates and thus incentivising more borrowing by tech start-ups, as well as significantly lowering capital-gains tax rates. This only further encouraged venture capital firms and other investors to more liberally speculate in the burgeoning sector. It became clear that the mood towards technology stocks was beginning to change drastically, as investors realised that most tech start-ups were unable to become profitable anytime soon. Just as the monetary loosening during the mid-1990s supported the formation of the dotcom bubble, so, too, did the tightening that occurred in early 2000 contribute to the bursting of the bubble.

5.11 Cryptocurrencies and Decentralised Finance

It is undeniable that the evolution of money has a fascinating history (Ferguson 2019), and the birth of the Bitcoin network transformed society's concept of the subject into something altogether new. In its simplest form, money is simply information, sometimes coupled with physical items, that is traded for goods found or produced by humans. One of the earliest versions of money stems from ancient Mesopotamia (3,200 B.C.) when people used tablets to account for certain types of goods like grain, meal, and malt. The reason individuals developed an accounting system is because physical items could get too cumbersome to show wealth to others for credit. For example, if a person had six months' worth of grain in storage, it was easier to show someone from a distant village a ledger of the goods rather than transporting the grain itself. The first ledger entry system created by the Mesopotamians was called pictographic tablets. The Mesopotamians were the first to introduce the concept of a 'general ledger', which summarised an individual or group's financial information in a log. In Mesopotamia about five-thousand years ago, this was a single-entry accounting or single-entry bookkeeping. Essentially the primary bookkeeping record in a single-entry bookkeeping is the cash book, which is similar to a checking account register except all entries are allocated among several categories of income and expense accounts.

Thousands of years later, during the Renaissance period, the general ledger transformed into a different system called double-entry bookkeeping (see Chapters 2 and 4). The double-entry system was first documented centuries ago by Luca Pacioli, whose portrait is also painted in the picture of the Virgin (the *Brera Madonna*), as I have illustrated in Chapter 4. Pacioli is also painted in another portrait by Jacopo de Barbari dated around 1500, where he is probably demonstrating a theorem by Euclid written in an open book. The painting portrays the friar and the mathematician with a table filled with geometrical tools. In this painting the tools are the main subjects matter: the slate, the chalk, the square, and the compass, a dodecahedron model. A rhombicuboctahedron, half-filled with water is suspended from the ceiling, something that also Leonardo da Vinci illustrated in his '*Divina proportione*' in 1509. This again reminds the importance of Fibonacci numbers (see Chapter 4).

It is from those daily advancements in knowledge that the modern financial systems started to be based on the double-entry system created more than six-hundred years ago. Double-entry systems grew because trade swelled beyond borders, so people needed a way to maintain records that were far more trustworthy than the single-entry accounting ledgers. Leveraging single-entry accounting would not work well when dealing with people who are thousands of miles away. The new method helped facilitate lending and rather than a simple general record, a double-entry bookkeeping protocol required financiers to record a corresponding and opposite entry into two separate categories called debit and credit. Throughout history, ledgers were used to record economic transactions and property ownership. A ledger is, therefore, often referred to as the 'principal book', and entries can be recorded in stone, parchment, wood, metal, and with software as well. Ledgers were used for centuries, but the shared ledger system became popular in 1538 when the Church kept records. The double-entry bookkeeping system allows an entity to record a total of what is owed and what is owned (Assets = Liabilities + Equity). Alongside this, double-entry accounting keeps a record of what the entity spent and earned. Traditionally this system has two corresponding and equal sides that people call 'debit' and 'credit'. Historically, the left side was used for debit entries and the right side for credit. In Florence, the bank run by the Medici family (see Chapter 2) adopted the double-entry bookkeeping to keep track of the many complex transactions moving through accounts. This enabled the Medici Bank to expand beyond the traditional banking activities of the time. *Nostro* and *Vostro* are variations on the Italian-Latin words that mean 'Ours' and 'Yours', respectively. Modern retail banking is based since then on this assumption where both depositors and retail banks maintained ledgers of their account balances.

The ledger kept by the depositing customer is called a *Nostro* ledger; the bank kept the corresponding *Vostro* ledger.

One of the biggest issues with the double-entry system is trusting the human and fallible bookkeeper, messenger, or accountant (see Chapter 4). When computers came around, ledger systems became far more advanced and people tried to push the double-entry system to the next level. The problem with creating something more advanced than the double-entry accounting system was the notorious 'Byzantine generals problem' or the 'Byzantine Fault'. In essence, the Byzantine generals' problem is an allegory in the field of computer science, which tells a story of two generals (there can be more than two) planning to attack an enemy city. The generals tell both armies to attack from each side of the enemy's castle, the east side and the west side. The issue at hand is a timing or synchronisation problem coupled with trust, because both armies need to attack simultaneously. Now the two generals split a group of messengers but the only way the messengers can communicate is by entering via the enemy castle. The Byzantine generals' problem is not being able to trust the message from the messenger, as it may not be valid or truthful. Essentially, when a distributed ledger is being shared among computing systems people cannot trust which system or server (node) is trustworthy, compromised, or functioning with a failure to detect.

However, on 31 October 2008, an anonymous person(s) released a paper that solved the Byzantine Fault dilemma. That Halloween, when Satoshi Nakamoto released Bitcoin into the world, he distributed a very innovative form of money that utilised Professor Yuji Ijiri's triple-entry accounting system introduced in 1999. The process involves the basics of double-entry bookkeeping, but includes secure and verifiable cryptography. Instead of the debit and credit entries, the underlying assets are kept in one place that is verifiable by the two parties exchanging. In other words, in a triple-entry bookkeeping all the accounting entries are cryptographically validated by a third entry by hashing and a nonce. Nakamoto white paper says that with the triple-entry bookkeeping system, the entries are both congruent, but the infrastructure also adds a third entry into the ledger's validation process, which again is cryptographically sealed. Fundamentally, hashing or cryptographic hash function (CHF) is a mathematical function of arbitrary size we call a 'message'. A nonce is an arbitrary number that is used one time when the message is concealed in plain text. In the Byzantine general tale, one army sends a message (CHF) over the other general with a nonce. The other general then must decipher the CHF with some partial knowledge cryptographers call a 'hast target'. All the general has to do is hash the CHF and the nonce, as well as make sure everything corresponds with the hast target. If everything is valid, the two generals have easily synchronised the timing of an attack, without having to doubt the message system or massagers.

Nakamoto's software leverages the Hash-cash system (which is a proof-of-work system used to limit email spam or denial-of-service attacks and it was proposed in 1997 by Adam Back) which bolsters the security of the underlying infrastructure by utilising cryptographic hashes. Hash-cash is used for Nakamoto's proof-of-work (PoW) which is basically a blob of data that is difficult and expensive to produce. Nakamoto's Bitcoin leverages the proof-of-work SHA256. It is nearly impossible or extremely hard to falsify, destroy, or edit one or a few lines in the constant SHA256 ledger system. As the proof-of-work continues to build, it becomes extremely expensive and very time consuming to attack. The advantages of triple-entry bookkeeping are huge. For example, it offers a concept that is near trust-less, if one removes trusting the autonomous system. Auditing, reconciliation, and transparency are all reconsidered notions when it comes to trusting the books. Satoshi told people on numerous occasions that he solved the Byzantine generals' problem. The proof-of-work chain is a solution to the Byzantine generals' problem Nakamoto told James A. Donald on 13 November 2008.

In January 2009 the first working example of triple-entry accounting was born with Bitcoin. For the first time in history, individuals and organisations had access to a medium of exchange that was not controlled by one individual or a group of people, not issued by a government or central bank, and had zero corporate backings. Moreover, due to the innovation of triple-entry accounting and a transparent blockchain, anyone can verify the ledger, unlike central banks printing funds behind closed doors. A decentralised network validates transactions. Once confirmed, all transactions are stored digitally and recorded in a public 'blockchain', which can be thought of as a distributed accounting system. Bitcoin relies on a social contract that people as participants all agree upon, which includes: no confiscations, censorship resistance, digital scarcity, and all of these rules can be verified by the public at any time.

Bitcoin's current worth and future rest partly in the hands of the Bitcoin core maintainers, a group who are chosen by their peers and are often vague about their whereabouts. A loose network of donors pays most maintainers' salaries. The maintainers—successors to Bitcoin's mysterious creator known as Satoshi Nakamoto—must ensure that the software remains compatible with the latest versions of operating systems like Windows or MacOS and that it keeps up with transaction volumes. Software needs more care and feeding than many people think, and Bitcoin Core is no different. In a normal tech company, software developers would be organised into an established hierarchy with managers, job descriptions, and performance reviews. If it were publicly traded, investors would receive standardised disclosures about its finances, operations, and management. Crypto disclosures to investors are contained not in regulatory filings but in white papers, message boards, and in a code repository on GitHub, the Microsoft Corp.-owned website where Bitcoin Core is stored. Maintainers and other software developers discuss high-priority code tweaks and personnel matters in a weekly chat room that is public. Because it is open-source, anyone with a GitHub account can propose changes to Bitcoin Core. However, what sets maintainers apart from other developers is their ability to approve those changes and move them into the GitHub repository. There the changes become effective once users download software updates that are released every six months or so. New maintainers are chosen in an ad hoc votes after sometimes heated debates in the chat room. Developers type ACK 'acknowledge' to support a candidate, or NACK to oppose one.

It is undeniable that Bitcoin is the leading cryptocurrency, but there are nearly two-thousand others. The many other digital currencies are primarily online currencies. This has contributed to a surge of interest in cryptocurrencies. The initial euphoria—as often—has been accompanied by a proliferation of fraud, largely in the form of pump-and-dump schemes. Changes in technology and the current development of crypto regulations have made it easier to conduct such schemes. As I have illustrated in this chapter, pump-and-dump operations, which fraudulently manipulate prices by disseminating false information, have existed in economic contexts since at least the 1700s (think of the South Sea Company). Specifically a pump-and-dump scheme is a sort of fraud in which the perpetrators amass a commodity over time, inflate its price artificially by disseminating false information (pumping) and then sell what they have accumulated to unwary buyers at a higher price (dumping). Once the perpetrators have fraudulently inflated the price, it usually declines, leaving purchasers who made their decision based on misleading information at a loss.

In the world of cryptocurrencies, self-organised teams of individuals carry out online pump-and-dump operations.[13] The pump group ethos is simple: buy low, sell high. It is a form of speculation. The implication is that investors outside the pump group will see the rapidly rising price and rush to buy in, anxious not to miss the next Bitcoin-style gold rush. But the reality is a bit more complex. Easy wealth is always the founding principle of a pump group, whether it is presented in terms that seem reasonable or ridiculous. These groups are promoted heavily on Facebook, Instagram, and Twitter as both ads and general posts, but they almost exclusively operate on semi-anonymous messaging services like Discord and Telegram. The whole scam works like this: first an organiser grows their group to an acceptable size (two thousand seems to be the minimum) through promoting and by spamming join links. Next, they will find an unheard-of-coin and direct everyone to buy it, driving the price up. Commonly called altcoins (or less politely in cryptocurrency financial jargon: 'shit-coins'). These alternative cryptocurrencies are easy to make and generally worthless. The organiser sets a 'target price', and then it is basically a free-for-all, as participants decide on their own when to sell. In most established groups, the pumping process itself is surprisingly well-organised. Group leaders provide specific instructions to their members that include the exact time a pump will occur (translated into multiple time zones), what exchange the pump will take place on, what the 'target' inflation price is, how the pump signal[14] will be provided (some group say they use images instead of text, to counter bots), and a number of other helpful tips and tricks. After the pump signal is given, group members flood the chosen exchange, buying up as much of the coin as they can for cheap. Members are also expected to promote the coin on social media in order to create buzz around it, which is intended to attract new investors to the currency. Members of these groups sometimes even create fake celebrity tweets or fabricate news stories in order to affect the price of a coin. Members are instructed to 'dump' the coin—meaning, sell it as quickly as possible—once the coin reaches a pre-set 'target' price, in order to make a profit, however, the market usually collapses long before then due to panic and general volatility. For example, in January 2018 Big Pump Signal announced the pump of the day would be GVT, a four-month-old Russia-based altcoin created by an apparently product-less company called Genesis Vision. The pump-and-dump took place on the cryptocurrency exchange Binance. Thirty-four seconds before the pump signal was given for GVT in the general chat room, the coin was trading approximately at twenty-nine-point-twenty-two dollars (USD) according to data collected by CoinMarketCap. Immediately afterwards, it began to rise in value. Four minutes and sixteen seconds after the pump signal, it was at thirty-five dollars (USD), and at nine minutes and sixteen seconds post-pump-signal it had reached its peak at forty-five-point-forty-one dollars (USD). Anyone who invested immediately and dumped right at the peak could have potentially earned a fifty-five-point-fifty-one percent return on their investment. In other words, if a participant invested the equivalent of one-thousand dollars (USD) immediately after the signal dropped and happened to randomly guess when the peak would be and sold exactly then, they would have made one-thousand-five-hundred-and-fifty-five dollars (USD) (minus the 0.1% trading fee charged by Binance and any fees for withdrawing their money from the exchange). This is the best scenario possible, but it is an unlikely outcome for the average investor.

5.12 Centralised Finance

In December 2018, Gerald Cotten, the founder of Canada's largest crypto exchange at the time, QuadrigaCX went on a trip to India with his new bride, Miss Jennifer Robertson. There Cotten suffered from Crohn's disease, and fell ill. Unfortunately, his health took a turn for the worse and he passed away shortly after being admitted to a hospital. A month later, QadrigaCX announced his passing in a statement credited to his girlfriend, Miss Robertson.

Here is where the story gets strange. In the months leading to Cotton's death, customers had been complaining they could not get their money out of the exchange and were waiting weeks, if not months, to receive funds. On 28 January 2018 the exchange went offline for 'maintenance'. Soon after, a court filing revealed that QadrigaCX owed customers $190 million and what seemed to be the big kicker at the time: no one knew how to access the exchange's reserves. His widow stated in court that while she had Cotten's laptop, it was encrypted, she was never given the password or recovery key and Cotten was the only person with control of QuadrigaCX's cold storage system. In other words, access to somewhere around one-hundred-and-ninety million dollars (USD) in cryptocurrency potentially vanished with Cotten's death. Or so it seemed.

QuadrigaCX was started by Gerald Cotten and Michael Patryn in Canada in 2013, focusing on local trades of Bitcoin. With a small staff, they expanded in 2014 to open a Bitcoin ATM in Vancouver, but had trouble raising funds and ran out of money in 2015 after a failed attempt to go public and list on the Canadian Securities Exchange. By 2016, plans to go public were abandoned, the legal counsel was let go and all of the other directors had resigned from QuadrigaCX, creating a one-man show with Cotten alone running the business.

According to reports, Cotton ran the company from his laptop, from no permanent office. But the company grew despite its rocky start as the price of Bitcoin surged in 2017 from one-thousand dollars (USD) to nearly twenty-thousand dollars (USD). People wanted a way to get in on the action, and the company grew to three-hundred-and-fifty-thousand customers trading over a billion dollars in assets. When Bitcoin crashed in 2018, customers wanted to cash out what they could, and that is where the trouble really began.

Surely to understand how so many people trusted a company that was a one-man show with their money, it is important to know who that man was. Mr. Gerald Cotten was an early cryptocurrency evangelist and part of a Vancouver group in 2013 that referred to itself as the 'Vancouver Bitcoin Co-op'. On the surface, he seemed like a 'nice Canadian guy' who was an expert on cryptocurrency and believed in the power of Bitcoin, and cryptocurrency in general, to be a transformational technology for finance. Cotten did not seek the spotlight and was not known as a public figure. However, QuadrigaCX was often a sponsor of local crypto educational events and charities such as the Indian orphanage that he said was the reason for his December 2018 visit. At the time QuadrigaCX's business skyrocketed it was still difficult for most people to invest in cryptocurrency, and the company had the advantage of being one of the first to market. Cotten's evangelism and knowledge of Bitcoin was clear, and some of the company's success can be attributed to his early efforts to appear to care more about helping people understand and see the potential of Bitcoin than turning a profit.

The lack of a plan for access to QuadrigaCX's cold storage wallets seemed especially strange because it came to light that Cotten had changed his will in the month before he went to India. Customers who had been waiting on funds that were locked in QuadrigaCX accounts immediately started to cry foul, questioning if Cotten was really even dead.

While many people think Bitcoin is anonymous, it is not entirely true. Blockchain technology relies on there being a public ledger of all transactions—as I have previously explained—that can be verified and viewed by anyone, anywhere. To put it simply: you cannot necessarily tell from that ledger that a particular person (such as Cotten) transferred Bitcoin to another person (such as Robertson). However, you can view that at a certain time and date this specific wallet address transferred this amount of Bitcoin to this other wallet. So even if no one could access the cryptocurrency within QuadrigaCX's wallets in order to give money back to customers, the crypto would still exist there. In the coming months, six Bitcoin wallets were identified as linked to QuadrigaCX, but they were nearly empty.

After the revelation the cold storage wallets that were supposed to contain QuadrigaCX's reserves contained a small fraction of the $190 million, accounting firm Ernst & Young followed with another bombshell report in June 2019. It detailed how Cotten transferred millions of dollars in crypto out of customer accounts and into other exchanges, which he then used to fund his lavish lifestyle and personal trading activities. The trading activities were massive—the report detailed that between 2016 and 2018, Cotton transferred 9,450 Bitcoin out of the exchange's accounts. He had many fake accounts within QuadrigaCX, including one under the name Chris Markay, who was not only an alias but the single biggest user on the platform. The massive deposits Markay seemed to be making on QuadrigaCX were just as fake as he was, and Cotten (as Markay) used these fake funds to buy very real Bitcoin from other customers. He lost one-hundred-and-fifteen million dollars (USD) under these aliases, according to a report from the Ontario Securities Commission that detailed just where the money went. He also lost twenty-eight million dollars (USD) on external exchanges and spent approximately twenty-four million dollars (USD) on real estate, vehicles, travel, and other personal expenses. It was hard to nail down where all the money went; there was very little documentation. While exact figures may never be known, what was crystal clear at this point was that QuadrigaCX was a Ponzi scheme. The report begins:

> The downfall of crypto asset trading platform Quadriga CX resulted from a fraud committed by Quadriga's co-founder and CEO Gerald Cotten. Clients entrusted their assets to Quadriga, which provided false assurances that those assets would be safeguarded. In reality, Cotten spent, traded and

used those assets at will. Operating without any proper system of oversight or internal controls, Cotten was able to misuse client assets for years, unchecked and undetected, ultimately bringing down the entire platform.

From almost the moment the news came out that Cotten had died, long before the explosive report from Ernst & Young, theories started circulating online that Cotten was still alive and had faked his own death. Despite the fact there is an official death certificate, some are unconvinced. There is a typo in the death certificate. Cotten had cultivated skills from years of illicit activities in covering his tracks. He knew how to create fake identities and owned planes and a boat he could use to escape. There is ample evidence pointing to the idea that Cotten was indeed planning an exit scam and that he was a con artist.

In less than a week in November 2022, the cryptocurrency billionaire Mr. Sam Bankman-Fried went from industry leader to industry villain, lost most of his fortune, saw his thirty-two billion dollars (USD) company plunge into bankruptcy and became the target of investigations by the Securities and Exchange Commission and the Justice Department. Mr. Bankman-Fried was once compared to titans of finance like John Pierpont Morgan and Warren Buffett, but his empire collapsed in one week after a run on deposits left the crypto exchange, FTX, with an eight billion dollars (USD) shortfall, forcing the firm to file for bankruptcy. The damage rippled across the industry, destabilising other crypto companies and sowing widespread distrust of the technology. Besides some Twitter posts and occasional texts to reporters, Mr. Bankman-Fried, thirty years old, has said little publicly, and he offered limited details about the central question around him: whether FTX improperly used billions of dollars of customer funds to prop up a trading firm that he also founded Alameda Research. The Justice Department and the SEC are after this relationship. This is because Alameda had accumulated a large margin position on FTX, essentially meaning it had borrowed funds from the exchange. The size of the position was in the billions of dollars.

Mr. Bankman-Fried's fall has stunned the crypto world. Despite the billions that venture capital firms put into the company, FTX had none of those outside investors on its board. In the Bahamas, Mr. Bankman-Fried led a sometimes cloistered existence, surrounded by a small coterie of colleagues, some of whom were in romantic relationships with other FTX employees. He and his colleagues lived together in a penthouse in Albany, a six-hundred acre oceanside resort on the island of New

Providence in the Bahamas. The circle of colleagues numbered about fifteen. The relationship between Alameda and FTX was the root of Mr. Bankman-Fried's downfall. He founded the trading firm in 2017 and rented offices in Berkeley California, not far from where he had grown up as the son of Stanford Law professors. Soon the company made millions of dollars exploiting inefficiencies in the Bitcoin market. In 2019, Mr. Bankman-Fried relocated the company to Hong Kong, a friendlier regulatory environment. He moved with a small band of traders and went on to start FTX, a marketplace for crypto investors to buy, sell, and store digital assets.

FTX and Alameda were closely linked. Alameda traded heavily on the FTX platform, meaning it sometimes benefited when FTX's other customers lost money, a dynamic that critics called a conflict of interest. Alameda provided crucial liquidity and injections of capital that enabled other customers to complete transactions on the exchange. Alameda was run by Ms. Ellison, but Mr. Bankman-Fried was also involved, contributing to the decision-making on big trades, a person familiar with the company's inner workings said. At times, there did not appear to be much of a firewall between the businesses. Alameda was supposed to operate out of a separate office, but it seems that it was not the case.

Mr. Bankman-Fried moved FTX to the Bahamas in 2021, drawn by a regulatory setup that allowed him to offer risky trading options that were not legal in the United States. On the exchange, investors could borrow money to make big bets on the future value of cryptocurrencies. Mr. Bankman-Fried built an ambitious philanthropic operation, invested in dozens of other crypto companies, bought stock in the trading firm Robinhood, donated to political campaigns, gave media interviews and offered Elon Musk billions of dollars to help finance the mogul's Twitter takeover. Perhaps Mr. Bankman-Fried's most ambitious aim was to shape crypto regulation in Washington, where he testified to Congress and met with regulators. He also used his growing influence in the capital to criticise his biggest rival, Mr. Zhao (the chief executive of the rival exchange Binance) in private meetings. A former investor in FTX, Mr. Zhao still owned a large amount of FTT, a cryptocurrency that FTX invented to facilitate trading on its platform. On 6 November 2022, Mr. Zhao announced on Twitter that he was selling the FTT, spooking customers who rushed to withdraw their FTX deposits.

When FTX collapsed, Mr. Zhao initially agreed to buy the exchange in what would have amounted to a bailout and a first time ever private lender of last resort effort in crypto finance. But soon the deal fell through, after Binance found problems in the company's financials. In a Signal group chat that included Mr. Bankman-Fried and other FTX representatives, Mr. Zhao posted a note 'Sam, I am sorry', he wrote, 'but we will not be able to continue this deal. Way too many issues. CZ'. Mr. Bankman-Fried scrambled to line up new financing. The investigation found out that five-point-eight billion dollars (USD) out of fourteen-point-six billion dollars (USD) of assets on the balance sheet at Alameda Research, based on then-current valuations, were linked to FTX's exchange token, FTT. Both firms were founded by Bankman-Fried and FTT token was essentially created from thin air by FTX, inviting questions about the real-world, open market value of FTT tokens held in reserve by affiliated entities.

5.13 Conclusions

This chapter is showing the other side of the coin of speculation activities, namely the circumstances arising from excessive risk-taking or mispricing of financial risk. This can trigger a financial crisis. Indeed, financial crises represent clear evidence of the negative outcomes of uncertainty if this latter is not managed in a responsible manner. Broadly speaking, the responsibility feature gives rise to two different questions, namely which entity should be responsible for preventing market failures and within which legal framework it should operate in terms of government regulation or soft law and self-regulating approaches. For example, the lack of stringent financial regulation in relation to crypto exchanges might have led to the disastrous collapse of FTX in 2022 and consented to its founder Mr. Bankman-Fried to defraud many investors. In light of this, if crypto exchanges were regulated as traditional stock exchanges, the FTX's collapse would have never occurred. I shall argue that this is wishful thinking because still a manipulation of funds could occur by unscrupulous third party brokers (see Chapter 7). Furthermore, I claim that the possible tightening up of financial regulation is unlikely to limit the inevitable systemic risk consequences of the same economic system. More financial regulation does not necessarily equate to better regulation or to a safer economic environment. In fact, in a post-crisis regulatory environment, and even more evidently in a post-pandemic scenario since 2022–2023, the emergence of self-regulation enacted by private actors such as market operators and institutional organisations, and the expansion of 'regulatory networks' that are often criticised for their lack of accountability and legitimacy are over-complicating the law-making process. There is a need for a 'Global Administrative Law' capable of providing national standards traditionally governed by administrative law at the international level, thereby enhancing the democratisation of decision-making processes, protecting individual rights, promoting transparency, and enforcing the accountability of 'regulatory networks' such as the Basel Committee on Banking Supervision.

The main question is still whether the market and its operators can govern uncertainty and provide the economic system with reliable answers. However, in a closed system, uncertainty is one of the four structures of the market—as I said in Chapter 4—and it directly relates to money-making processes. For this reason, the role of uncertainty must not be underestimated because it is a central idea for profit realisation, and it is important for the activation of a spontaneous mechanism of market re-generation (autopoiesis). Financial markets are complex entities. This means that financial systems are open systems and communicate with their environment, although they are characterised by an operational closure by which structures of the environment cannot be imported inside the system. This idea is challenging, and it gives rise to a new role for law-making where the system itself develops and enacts its own regulation. Specifically, the idea of fragmented knowledge is Ladeur's central point of assertion to recognise the end of a centralised stock of knowledge administrated by the public state. As opposed to a Westphalian model of legislation, modern society is characterised by the 'a-centric' creation of order, and no central planner is contemplated within this new framework. For Ladeur, this means recognising a 'network of networks'. In other words, society is no longer based on hierarchical forms of power, but on heterarchical relationships aimed at creating, rather than individualism, a spontaneous process of cooperation. For this reason, one side-effect of such cooperation is the establishment of a collective order which is the product of self-organisation behaviours in society; so the law becomes merely a secondary instrument of integration that is no longer characterised by its authoritative conception as a form of mediation of consensus. Indeed, the dynamic evolution of regulatory regimes has contributed to the exponential growth of hybrid models of regulation. For instance, a new hybrid model of the law has consented to the exponential growth of swaps and derivatives contracts. The International Swaps and Derivatives Association (ISDA) has played a major role in the rise of derivatives by creating standard contracts and adapting them to different legal systems around the world. The ISDA was formed to develop templates for derivative instruments that would be enforceable in multiple jurisdictions. This is a direct example of the critical role that the law is playing in shaping the future, and indirectly in allowing private organisations discretionary power to determine market practices. The same example can be found in sovereign debt, with the International Capital Market Association (ICMA), which, in 2014, published a new standard of *pari passu* clause for inclusion in the terms and conditions (CACs) of sovereign debt securities, and an updated version of the aggregated collective action clauses for the terms and conditions of sovereign notes. A very good example of the application of those principles comes from the restructuring deal that Argentina reached with its foreign bondholders in early August 2020 in the form of a bond exchange offer that was approved overwhelmingly by its foreign bondholders. Aggregated CACs became the market standard as embodied in the model promulgated in 2014 by the ICMA and earlier-generation CACs based on series-by-series voting essentially only strengthened the hand of potential holdout creditors. Those are standard contractual terms to ensure the legal enforcement of financial obligations.

Hybrid models of regulation were not endorsed in 1630 during the Tulip Mania in Amsterdam, but the self-regulation aspect of market crises was already experimented. For example, at the time of the Dutch Golden Age and the Tulip Mania, the Dutch government was disinterested in intervening and the courts resolved not to get involved either, interpreting the speculation as a form of gambling beyond the law. With that the tulip mania came to an end. By contrast, sometimes the active role of the lawmaker has been the trigger for new financial innovations such as at the time of the Mississippi Bubble when in an effort to regulate the stock market, the Paris *Bourse* had its origins in a royal decree from 1724. Other times, the same occurrence of a financial turmoil has paved the way to revolutionary ideas from a regulatory prospective such as in the case of the Great Depression of 1929 when the Glass–Steagall Act was enacted in 1933 to separate commercial banking from investment banking. The Federal Deposit Insurance Corporation was also created at the same time. Similarly, the collapse of Herstatt Bank in Germany in 1974 led to the setting up of the Basel Committee on Banking Supervision at the international level. As this chapter has demonstrated, the law as well as a financial turmoil can be progressive and they can either legitimise or give rise to new financial innovations. Nonetheless, we shall never be too complacent to regulate all market dangers away because a perfect market equilibrium is not an intimate quality of financial markets.

Relevant financial crises

Date	*Financial crisis or important speculators*
1630	Tulip Mania in Amsterdam
1720	South Sea Company Bubble
1721	John Law gave rise to the Mississippi Bubble
1815	Napoleon is defeated at Waterloo and Nathan Rothschild speculates on gilt market on the London Stock Exchange accumulating a fortune
1820s	Sovereign bonds were issued by several newly independent countries following Latin America's successful revolt against Spanish colonial rule. After the course of just a few short years the sovereign bond boom of the early 1820s turned to bust
1820s	Self-proclaimed Scottish nobleman Gregor MacGregor launched one of the most audacious and elaborate frauds of all time, tricking thousands of British citizens into investing in 'Poyais', a territory in Central America which turned out to be entirely fictional
1879	Sarah Howe in Boston set up the Ladies' Deposit to help invest money for women. This is the first form of 'Ponzi Scheme' before the actual Charles Ponzi in 1920
1920	Charles Ponzi establishes the so-called 'Ponzi Scheme' and defrauds many American investors
1929	Great Depression in the United States
1990s	Dotcom Bubble, which coincided with massive growth in Internet adoption
2008	Madoff perpetrated one of the 'biggest' stock and securities fraud in American history
1974	Herstatt Bank collapses
2018	Gerald Cotton, the founder of Canada's largest crypto exchange at the time, QuadrigaCX, apparently 'dies' in India and defrauds investors
2022	Cryptocurrency billionaire Mr. Sam Bankman-Fried went from industry leader to industry villain, lost most of his fortune, saw his $32 billion company (FTX) plunge into bankruptcy

Notes

1. Mayer's family name derived from the red (*rot*) shield on the house in the ghetto in which his ancestors had once lived.
2. Rothschild family, the most famous of all European banking dynasties, which for some two-hundred years exerted great influence on the economic and, indirectly, the political history of Europe.

The house was founded by Mayer Amschel Rothschild (born 23 February 1744–died 19 September 1812).

3. The Darien Scheme originated by the invention of William Paterson whose other major claim to fame was the foundation of the Bank of England. He made his first fortune through international trade, travelling extensively throughout the Americas and West Indies. Upon his return to his native Scotland, Paterson sought to make his second fortune with a scheme of epic proportion.
4. The *Asiento de Negros* (Negroes' Contract) was introduced by Charles I of Spain in 1518. It was a monopoly granted for the supply of slaves to work in the American Spanish colonies. Over the years France, Portugal, and Britain had entered into this lucrative contract, as had a number of individual Spaniards. Granted to Britain by the Treaty of Utrecht in 1713, it required the supply of 4,800 slaves annually over the next thirty years. As it so happened, the contract did not prove very profitable, and led to the so-called War of Jenkins Ear between Spain and Britain in 1739. Britain terminated the contract in 1750, by which date some 450,000 Africans had been transported to South America by the *Asiento*. Essentially, the *Asiento* was an agreement between the Spanish crown and another party—be it a sovereign power or a private person—whereby a monopoly was granted for the supply of African slaves to work in the American Spanish colonies. An agreed sum was paid to the Spanish crown for this privilege, and the contract clearly stipulated the number of male and female slaves which had to be delivered for sale in the American markets. The first *asentista* (contractor) was a Genoese company which agreed to supply one-thousand slaves over an eight-year period. The Black African Slave Trade across the Atlantic was begun in 1502. Beginning as a trickle, it developed into a torrent. It was estimated that in total some eight to seventeen million Africans were transported to the New World by 1870. Slavery had been a fact of life since the earliest civilisations, but the transatlantic trade was particularly inhuman, if only because of the dreadful conditions endured—and often not endured—by the slaves on their outward voyage. Taken mostly from West and Central Africa, they were set to work in the Caribbean Islands, and in the colonies on the mainland of South and North America. The demand for such labour, much

increased with the opening of cotton, sugar, and other plantations, reached a peak of six million during the eighteenth century. This traffic in misery was part of the 'Triangle of Trade' whereby European merchants would exchange manufactured goods for captured slaves, transport them to the New World, and then return to their home ports with sugar, cotton, or other crops. If slaves survived the voyage, they were sold off like animals. Families were broken up, and men, women, and children were made to work long hours in plantations or down the mines. In Britain, this vile trade was not brought to an end officially until the politician William Wilberforce succeed in persuading Parliament to ban it in 1807.

5. When sailors returned from abroad they could not always get hold of their salary and so many sailors sold that right onto others in return for some quick cash.
6. Today Guardian Royal Exchange PLC is one of the largest composite insurers in the United Kingdom, with a portfolio including life insurance, private motor and household insurance, health care, property, and marine business. Guardian Royal Exchange was created in 1968 from the merger of two venerable insurance institutions, Royal Exchange Assurance and the Guardian Assurance Company. Royal Exchange was founded in 1720 and was one of the first two insurance companies to receive legal status by Royal Charter.
7. The company was formed in 1720. Established by Royal Charters granted in June 1720 (marine business) and April 1721 (fire and life insurance). It became a subsidiary of the Sun Alliance in 1965.
8. The Dow Jones Industrial Average (DJIA) or simply the Dow is a stock market index of thirty prominent companies listed on stock exchanges in the United States. The DJIA is one of the oldest and most commonly followed equity indexes. Many professionals consider it to be an inadequate representation of the overall US stock market compared to a broader market index such as the S&P 500. The DJIA includes only thirty large companies. It is price-weighted, unlike stock indices, which use market capitalisation. Furthermore, the DJIA does not use weighted arithmetic mean. The value of the index can also be calculated as the sum of the stock prices of the companies included in the index, divided by a factor, which is currently approximately 0.152. The factor is

changed whenever a constituent company undergoes a stock split so that the value of the index is unaffected by the stock split.

9. Roosevelt was not actually sitting beside a fireplace when he delivered the speeches, but behind a microphone-covered desk in the White House. Reporter Harry Butcher of CBS coined the term 'fireside chat' in a press release before on of Roosevelt's speeches on 7 May 1933. The name stuck, as it perfectly evoked the comforting intent behind Roosevelt's words; as well as their informal, conversational tone. Roosevelt took care to use the simplest possible language, concrete examples and analogies in the fireside chats, so as to be clearly understood by the largest number of Americans.
10. The 100-days concept is believed to have its roots in France, where the concept of '*Cent Jours*' (Hundred Days) refers to the period of 1815 between Napoleon Bonaparte's return to Paris from exile on the island of Elba and his final defeat at the Battle of Waterloo, after which King Louis XVIII regained the French throne.
11. The Prohibition Era began in 1920 when the 18th Amendment to the US Constitution, which banned the manufacture, transportation, and sale of intoxicating liquors, went into effect with the passage of the Volstead Act. Despite the new legislation, Prohibition was difficult to enforce. The increase of the illegal production and sale of liquor (known as 'bootlegging'), the proliferation of speakeasies (illegal drinking spots) and the accompanying rise in gang violence and organised crime led to waning support for the Prohibition by the end of the 1920s.
12. The religious Society of Friends, also referred to as the Quaker Movement, was founded in England in the seventeenth century by George Fox. He and other early Quakers, or Friends, were persecuted for their beliefs, which included the idea that the presence of God exists in every person. Quakers rejected elaborate religious ceremonies, did not have official clergy and believed in spiritual equality for men and women. Quaker missionaries first arrived in America in the mid-1650s. Quakers, who practice pacifism, played a key role in both the abolitionist and women's rights movements.
13. Pump-and-dump groups organise the scams in plain sight on the Discover server (voice over internet protocol and text chat service) or Telegram (instant messaging app), making it possible for anybody to join the groups without prior consent. In pump-and-dumps groups, there is a hierarchy of members and leaders (or

admins) who manage the group. Higher ranked members receive the notification that initiates the pump by disclosing the target coin a little earlier than lower ranked users. In this manner, the member has a greater change of purchasing at a cheaper cost and profiting more from the pump-and-dump scheme. Most groups are structure using an affiliation system, where members can move up the hierarchy by recruiting new members. The rating rises in proportion to the number of new members added to the group. In contrast, some organisations have a simplified hierarchical structure with just two levels: VIPs and common members. To join these organisations, a user must pay a charge, typically in Bitcoin between 0.001 and 0.1 Bitcoin.

14. 'Crypto pump signal' is a message intended to entice individuals to purchase a cryptocurrency so they can profit from the price manipulation caused by the sudden uptick in demand. After the pumping causes a significant price hike, which are called crypto dump signals, members start selling at a good profit.

Bibliography

Allan V, 'Gregor MacGregor, the Prince of Poyais' (11 July 2018) *History Today*.

Andrews M, 'County's 1920s land boom faded just as quickly as it had started' *Orlando Sentinel*, 12 December 1993.

Bernanke B S, *The Courage to Act* (Norton 2015).

Chancellor E, *Devil Take the Hindmost: A History of Financial Speculation* (Plume Books 2000).

Clark G, 'Debt, deficits, and crowding out: England, 1727–1840' (2001) 5 (3) European Review of Economic History 403–436.

Cutts R L, 'Power from group up: Japan's land bubble' (May-June 1990) Harvard Business Review.

De Graaf, B 'The price of security' in B. De Graaf (eds.) *Fighting Terror After Napoleon: How Europe Became Secure After 1815* (Cambridge University Press 2020).

De Roover R, 'The medici bank financial and commercial operations' (1946) 6 (2) The Journal of Economic History 153–172.

Ellis C, *The Partnership: The Making of Goldman Sachs* (Penguin 2009).

Ferguson N, *The Ascent of Money: A Financial History of the World* (Penguin 2019).

Flandreau M, Juan F, 'Bonds and brands: foundations of sovereign debt markets, 1820–1830' (2009) 69 (3) The Journal of Economic History 646–684.

Frank T, 'The financial crisis of 33 AD' (1935) 56 (4) The American Journal of Philology 336–341.

Galbraith J K, *The Great Crash, 1929* (Houghton Mifflin Harcourt, 2009).

Gauchet T, Christine H, 'Restoring credit in post-Napoleonic France: Settling French War claims' (2019) 27 (3) *War in History* 433–455.

Geithner T F, *Stress Test: Reflections on Financial Crises* (Broadway 2014).

Greenberg C L, *To Ask for an Equal Chance: African Americans in the Great Depression* (Rowman & Littlefield 2010).

Hamrick J T, et al., 'The economics of cryptocurrency pump and dump schemes' CEPR Discussion Paper No. DP13404.

Harold B, 'Secret bank records shine light on 1920s boom and bust' (27 January 2008) *Sarasota Herald-Tribute.*

Jones A W, 'Fashion in forecasting' (March 1949) *Fortune.*

Kindleberger C P, *Manias, Panics, and Crashes: A History of Financial Crisis* (7th edn. Palgrave Macmillan 2015).

Kindleberger C P, *A Financial History of Western Europe* (1st edn Routledge 2007).

King M, *The End of Alchemy: Money, Banking, and the Future of Global Economy* (Norton 2016).

Knowlton C, *Bubble in the Sun* (Simon & Schuster 2020).

Landau P, 'The hedge funds: Wall Street's new way to make money' (21 October 1968) *New York Magazine.*

Landau Peter, 'Alfred Winslow Jones: the long and short of the founding father' (August 1968) The Institutional Investor.

Loomis C, 'The Jones nobody keeps up with' (April 1966) *Fortune.*

Neal L, 'The financial crisis of 1825 and the restructuring of the British financial system' (1998) 80 (3) Review: Federal Reserve Bank of St. Louis

Novak M, *Daniel Defoe: Master of Fictions: His Life and Works* (Oxford University Press 2003).

Odlyzko A, 'Isaac newton, Daniel Defoe and the dynamics of financial bubbles' (2018) Financial History: The Magazine of the Museum of American Finance 18–21.

Oizumi E, 'Property finance in Japan: expansion and collapse of the bubble economy' (1994) 26 (2) Environment and Planning: Economy and Space.

Paolera G, Alan T, 'Sovereign debt in Latin America: 1820–1913' (2013) 31 (2) Revista De Historia Economica (Journal of Iberian and Latin American Economic History) 173–217.

Paulson H M, *On the Brink* (Hachette 2013).

Reed C, 'The Damn'd South Sea' (1999) Harvard Magazine.

Scott R, Knowlton C, 'How the Florida of the roaring twenties created modern America and triggered the Great Depression' (26 March 2020) History Unplugged Podcast.

Sicotte R, Catalina V, 'War and foreign debt settlement in early Republican Spanish America' (2009) 27 (2) Revista de Historia Economica (Journal of Iberian and Latin American Economic History) 247–289.

Silber K, 'The birth of hedge funds' (1 November 2010) ThinkAdvisor.

Strangeways T, *Sketch of the Mosquito Shore Including the Territory of Poyais* (Franklin Classics 2018).

Taylor B, 'The fraud of the Prince of Poyais on the London Stock Exchange' (18 November 2020) Global Financial Data.

Talyor B, 'Tiberius used quantitative easing to solve the financial crisis of 33 AD' (26 October 2013) Business Insider.

Tchernia A, *The Romans and Trade* (Oxford University Press 2016).

Tooze A, *Crashed: How a Decade of Financial Crises Changed the World* (Viking 2018).

The Economist, 'The King of con-men' (22 December 2012) *The Economist Newspaper*.

Walsh P, 'Writing the history of the financial crisis: lessons from the South Sea Bubble' (2012).

Woodman A J, *Tacitus, the Annals. Translated with Introduction and Notes* (Hackett 2004).

Working Papers in History and Policy (University College Dublin).

Wennerlind C, *Causalities of Credit: The English Financial Revolution, 1620–1720* (Harvard University Press 2011).

Yamey B S, 'Two-currency, Nostro and Vostro accounts: historical notes, 1400–1800' (2011) 38 (2) Accounting Historians Journal 125–143.

Zweig J, 'Great moment in hot stock tips' (8 August 2013) *The Wall Street Journal*.

CHAPTER 6

Short Selling: The Bears of the Market

Knowing what we know now, I believe on balance the commission would not do it again.The costs (of the short-selling ban on financials)appear to outweigh the benefits

Christopher Cox, former President of the SEC in 2008

6.1 Introduction

The previous chapters have illustrated that most investors buy and hold stocks to capitalise on long-term growth. This is called a 'long' position. When those purchases settle, the cash in the investor's account is reduced and stocks owned increased. When that investor sells stock, the opposite happens. But sometimes traders need to be able to short sell a stock too. That means they need to sell a stock they do not already own. Being able to short sell a stock is important for market efficiency. Not only does it reduce the trading costs and mispricing of derivatives, it also adds liquidity and improves price discovery on single stocks (Battalio and Schultz 2011).

However, under extreme circumstances of imminent financial crises, short selling practices can undermine markets' confidence and provoke a sudden decline in the securities of financial institutions unrelated to true price valuation. Indeed, financial institutions and particularly banks

D. D'Alvia, *The Speculator of Financial Markets*, Palgrave Macmillan Studies in Banking and Financial Institutions,
https://doi.org/10.1007/978-3-031-47901-4_6

are vulnerable to this crisis of confidence and panic counterparties in the conduct of their core business. Furthermore, speculative short selling attacks might put downward pressure on the entire stock market. It is for these reasons that governments and financial regulators have stepped in to curtail or ban short selling during times of market stress such as the Global Financial Crisis or more recently, at the onset of the Covid-19 pandemic as I will further explain in the conclusions by giving consolidating remarks.

This chapter is outlining salient cases of short selling transactions in order to highlight both positive and negative sides of this transactional practice. Indeed, short sellers are motivated to detect and explore negative news such as poor firm performance that investors have yet to be informed or unethical and opportunistic behaviours taken by managers at the cost of investors. In other words, short sellers are like 'detectives' of the capital markets, and they play an essential role. For example, as I will show in this chapter, James Chanos was short selling Enron Corp. before 2001, and indirectly he was able to signal to other investors the possible future collapse of the firm, but short sellers are often seen as a Cassandra, and investors tend to ignore their predictions. In fact, in Greek mythology, Cassandra was the Trojan beauty on whom the gods bestowed the gift of prophecy—and the curse that no one would believe her. She predicted the catastrophic events that resulted from the Trojan horse, but no one took her seriously. In some way, this is the investment establishment's attitude towards short sellers in today's treacherous stock market. Selling short is an 'art', and it might be expensive. In fact, selling a stock short implies, theoretically at least, that if the market moves against the short seller, the potential loss is infinite. For investors who buy a stock, the downside risk is limited to the purchase price, while the upside potential is infinite. It is just the opposite of a short seller. His upside is limited, while his downside is not. This gives the short seller a reason to do plenty of analysis. A short position must be watched every day and sometimes several times intraday.

This chapter will argue that short selling transactions have gained popularity and importance since the time of the Great Bear of Wall Street. Additionally, the rise of non-bank financial intermediaries and of hedge funds means that there is an increase in short positions in the stock market. In fact, many hedge funds use a combination of longs and shorts to insure against large losses when markets fall. There are also event-driven funds that may short a stock for a few days because of an expectation of bad news. Then there are funds that specialise in short selling—mutual funds like Grizzly Short Fund and the Prudent Bear Fund for individuals or Kynikos Associates for institutions. Investors who have a pessimistic view of the market or who have a significant long position and want to balance it may put some money in a fund that goes short.

6.2 The Great Bear of Wall Street

At the time of the American Civil War (see Chapter 3) a new generation of speculators appeared. Indeed, many old-fashioned speculators in the early years of Wall Street largely depended on social and political contacts, as I have also shown in the first case of stock cornering in Chapter 3. By contrast Jacob Little, who was the bear of his day relied only on his ability to predict future price moves of stocks based on rumours and upon his knowledge of the way the stock market worked.

Little was born in the early 1800s in Newburyport (MA) and was the son of a respected local shipbuilder. He went to New York as a teenager in 1817, worked as a clerk for a stockbroker, and in 1822 started his own firm with seven-hundred dollars (USD) that he managed to save from his earrings. Wall Street historian Henry Clews, writing in 1888, asserted that Little made and lost nine fortunes. Other stock market historians credit Little as having made and lost only four fortunes over the course of his life. Legend was growing, but what is certain is that Little was making his money as a short seller. He was the bear of his day, and the first prominent short seller in the history of Wall Street: a tactic that has since made fortunes for generations of speculators. During Little's time, a stock could be shorted because stock market rules allowed for future delivery of stock certificates. Today, the shares must be borrowed from a broker, who is paid a fee and interest. In addition, all dividends that are paid while the stock is shorted are paid to the owner, not the borrower.

Specifically, short selling stocks is an investment strategy in which the short seller bets that a stock will decline in value. In short selling, an investor borrows stock shares that they believe will drop in price, sells those borrowed shares at market price, then buys back the shares at a lower price. To complete the short sale, the investor returns the shares to the original lender and profits the difference between the buy and sell prices. Short selling is a short-term stock trading strategy. If the stock does fall in price, investors can yield sizable profits, but they can experience unlimited losses if the price rises. In a short sale, the short seller essentially sells shares they do not own.

Short sellers hope that the stock price drops to purchase the stock back at a lower price and profit the difference. If the price of the stock rises and the short seller buys the shares back at a higher price, they lose money on the trade. When the price of the stock rises, short sellers may hold out in the hopes that it will decrease; since short sellers must eventually repay the broker, they risk losing more money. When the share price increases, it is possible that the broker might issue a margin call, requiring the short seller to put even more money into the brokerage account or close out the trade by repurchasing the stock at the current higher price. As it can be seen, short selling is a form of speculation where market speculators short sell by identifying what they believe is an overpriced stock so they can profit off its decline. Short selling speculation is a highly risky investment strategy and for this reason might require hedging. Most investors who short sell shares are hedgers. Hedgers take a short position on a stock simply to offset the risk from other long position investments. Rather than profit off a short sale, hedgers want to minimise potential losses or protect gains on other long position investments in their portfolio. For instance, hedging is a common investment strategy for many hedge funds.

Little was historically the first short seller ever. He was one of the richest men in New York, and in the entire United States. However, he was knocked off not long after the important crash of 1837, which was caused by President Andrew Jackson's campaign against the existence of the national central bank of the United States. He ordered the withdrawal of US banknotes from circulation on the grounds that they had 'no intrinsic value' and, unlike gold, are 'liable to great and sudden fluctuations, thereby rendering property [values] insecure'. He feared that a monetary system based on paper money (as opposed to gold) would be manipulated by unscrupulous politicians, speculators, and foreign financiers. On a personal level, President Jackson was suspicious of bankers because he had lost a great deal of money years earlier in an unsuccessful, highly leveraged real estate speculation. Jackson was a major landowner and wanted to maintain the stability of land prices. The result of his policy was a sharp curtailment of credit, which was magnified when English investors (a major source of capital at that time) lost interest in the US capital market. Inevitably, liquidity on Wall Street evaporated and prices plunged. What could have been a temporary setback grew into a nearly devastating financial crisis as Jackson successfully 'destroyed' the Bank of the United States, the nation's central bank at the time. It would not be replaced by another central bank until 1913, when the modern

Federal Reserve system was created. Without a strong currency overseen by a respected national bank, confidence in American financial markets collapsed, both at domestic level and abroad.

In the 1840s, Wall Street was gripped by a devastating bear market, which was in many ways worse than the Great Depression of the 1930s (see Chapter 5). During this period, Little profited handsomely by repeatedly selling short as stock prices continuously plummeted. It was the time that he became known as the 'Great Bear of Wall Street'. One of the most interesting operations as a short seller occurred in 1837, when Little sold short shares of Erie Railroad stock. 'The higher the price went, the more Erie he sold' writes Edwin Lefevre in Reminiscences of a Stock Operator (1923). As the stock price of Erie Railroad edged higher, fellow traders took turns estimating how much Little would lose—a couple of million overnight (equivalent to billions today), they all agreed. Indeed, a group of rival stockbrokers decided to stage a corner against Little. The syndicate of speculators purchased virtually all of the available stock of Erie Railroad in the belief that Little was unaware of their actions. Among them there was also Daniel Drew another famous speculator. Then, confident they had cornered the stock, they demanded delivery of the shares that they believed Little had sold short.

However, Little had taken precaution. Far from losing millions, Little had exploited a loophole, enabling him to buy bonds in London and convert them into cheap stock to cover his audacious short sale. The Erie syndicate had forgotten about the existence of these bonds, which had been sold by the railroad in London a few years earlier. In a dramatic move, Little walked into the Erie offices carrying a bag filled with convertible bonds, and demanded his stock, which the company delivered as it was legally obliged to do. Little's opponents incurred large losses and suffered the indignity of knowing they had been tricked. It was 'one of the greatest of what we would [now] call arbitrage coups of all time' says Professor Geisst.

Eventually, Little was blindsided by the Panic of 1857. This stock market crash and bear market that followed were caused by overexpansion by businesses throughout the country following the California Gold Rush. When it became clear in 1857 that many Western mining shares were supported by hot air and no substance, many banks in the Western states collapsed, which triggered further bank failure back east, which in turn caused a panic in European financial markets. The result was a severe bear market in the United States and Europe. Little did not see it coming.

Instead of being short, was long (he had purchased huge amounts of stock, much of it 'on margin') meaning he had borrowed money to do so. This leverage causes a magnification of profits when stock prices increase, but also asserts equal force in the opposite direction when stock prices decline. As stock prices plummeted, Little was crushed by margin calls, which are demands from lenders for additional money to compensate for the loss of value of the shares. Little could not cover his position and he was forced into bankruptcy once again. On this occasion was not able to bounce back. He died in 1865, a broken man, and a friend collected a fraction of what had been owed Little to give to his family.

6.3 From Tea Panic to Boston Tea Party

In Chapter 3, I have illustrated how the birth of the mutual fund in Amsterdam came just after one of the eighteenth century's largest financial crisis. In the early 1770s, surpluses of goods imported from the East led to falling commodity prices. The direct economic impact of these depressed prices was worsened by bank failures. Specifically, the financial crisis of 1772 was triggered when a London bank lost three-hundred-thousand pounds (GBP) on a trade that involved betting against the shares of the British East India Company. Another early example of short selling. The British East India Company was struggling through the oversupply of tea in Britain but was rescued by a one-point-five million pounds (GBP) loan from the British Government. The crisis of 1772, as it would become known, led to policies that would change the way tea from India was imported into America. It was a benign outcome but its severe political and military consequences helped make a new nation.

As I have anticipated, the firm at the centre of the crisis of 1772 was the British East India Company. The company was established in 1600 with a monopoly on British trade with India (see Chapter 3). It imported valuable spices, textiles, tea, and other products from India into Europe with increasingly diminished competition. However, the vast privileges it had, came at a cost, the company was required to pay the British government four-hundred-thousand pounds (GBP) annually to maintain its monopoly. Following a treaty where it received the right to tax Indian subjects directly in 1765, it also had to pay the Mughal Emperor in Delhi two-hundred-and-sixty-thousand pounds (GBP) a year. In addition to a hefty tribute to two states, the British East India Company also had extraordinary expenses. For one, there was the mounting cost associated with defending its rule in India as its private army grew to over fifty-thousand strong. The First Anglo-Mysore War of the late 1760s caused the company's expenses to surge to one-point-seven million pounds (GBP) from less than half that a few years earlier. Adding to the company's trouble, a famine in Bengal slashed the tax revenue it expected to collect in India. Despite all this, the firm was regularly increasing its dividend, from ten percent of paid-in capital in 1769 to twelve-point-five percent in 1771. Whatever the condition of East India Company, it was not the fuse that ignited the crisis of 1772 that recognition would go to Alexander Fordyce, a Macaroni[1] gambler.

An entrepreneurial Scottish man, Fordyce left the family hosiery business to try his luck in finance, becoming a speculator and banker in London. It was there that he rose from humble clerk to partner at the relatively young banking firm of Neal, James, Fordyce, and Down, founded in 1757. Fordyce was among those who noticed the troubles mounting at the East India Company. Sensing a chance to profit, he used his position at his firm to place massive bets against the East India Company by short selling its shares. In the end, Fordyce's bet provides ill-timed. The East India Company was ailing but the speculator was short the stock just as it bounced in value following the company's dividend increases. Dividend hikes are doubly troubling for short sellers because they can both boost the value of the stock and simultaneously make it more expensive to borrow. Those dividends were so costly for the East India Company though that Fordyce would later be proved right about its perilous health. However, this would only be realised by others after any chance for Fordyce to profit had evaporated. Following the dividend increases, the company's share price rose to two-hundred-and-twenty-six pounds (GBP) in May 1771 after having fallen to one-hundred-and-ninety pounds (GBP) late the previous year. From there, it mostly traded sideways for about a year before a modest rise in the spring of 1772. That increase in the share price, of just around five percent was enough to force a margin call. Fordyce, whose position lost money as the stock rose, was asked by his lenders to put up ten percent more cash to make up for his losses, something he was unable to do. With that, Fordyce was bankrupt. In the end, the speculator's short position of somewhere around one million pounds (GBP) resulted in losses which exceeded one-hundred-and-fifty-thousand pounds (GBP) and were likely close to twice as high. Last minute requests for loans were not fruitful and Fordyce was unable to find a rescuer. It was the end not just for Fordyce but for his firm too. Neal, James, Fordyce, and Down closed on 10 June 1772 just a day after Fordyce fled to France leaving behind debts of perhaps two-hundred-and-fifty-thousand pounds (GBP).

The failure of Neal, James, Fordyce, and Down kicked off a series of bank runs in Britain, leading to the collapse of at least two dozen other banks. At least ten financial firms in London failed within a week. The crisis damaged those banks with the most speculative investments; one of these was the Ayr Bank in Scotland, formally known as Douglas, Heron & Co.. In fact, Scotland was particularly affected by the meltdown, in part because Fordyce's firm was a large buyer of the short-term debt of Scottish firms, buying up £4 million in bills over the previous five years. In the ensuing credit crunch, a dozen banks in Edinburgh closed as did a few others in provincial Scotland. Ayr Bank, which supplied Neal, James, Fordyce, and Down with financing was among the largest victims of the crisis of 1772. It was a terrific loss to Scottish banking being the largest bank in Scotland at the time and a creative one too. In response to whispers concerning its health, the bank offered a one-hundred pounds (GBP) reward to anyone who found the sources of rumours about the bank's solvency. Surely, a one-thousand pounds (GBP) reward would have done more to dispel the gossip. It was all for naught thought as the firm closed on June 25th following a bank run, just two weeks after Fordyce's firm was shut. Like Neal, James, Fordyce, and Down, it was unable to find an emergency lender. It was very nearly too big to rescue; the bank had liabilities of one-point-twenty-five million pounds (GBP) comprised forty percent of total Scottish bank assets and twenty-five percent of the country's bank deposits. Among the factors contributing to the bank's end was the curious nature of its equity capital. As part of the way it was established, the Ayr Bank's investors were given credit lines by the bank in an amount equal to their paid-in capital. This blurred the line between debt and equity capital and made the bank more leveraged. The arrangement also meant that many of the firm's shareholders were bankrupted by its collapse, having lost a lenient lender as well as their equity investment. Given that banking firms did not have limited liability in the eighteenth century, shareholders in firms like the Ayr Bank lost more than the value of their shares and had to make good on their banks' losses by liquidating personal property if necessary.

The crisis had wider economic consequences as well. The failure of the banks meant that Britain's nascent money markets froze. Great difficulty was encountered by merchants and industrialists trying to obtain short-term credit. This in turn caused trade to fall; imports to England and Scotland fell fourteen percent from 1772 to 1773. Because many long-term projects were financed on the rolling of short-term debts, many investments in infrastructure like toll roads and canals, booming in Britain at the time, were put on hold. Predictably given the financial and economic conditions, the credit crunch led to a notable rise in bankruptcies.

Rather curiously, George Colebrooke, the Chairman of the East India Company itself, was another of the casualties. He was a failed speculator himself, and like Fordyce went bankrupt and fled to France, not exactly the most obvious hiding place for runaway tycoons today but evidently so in the eighteenth century. The philosopher David Hume wrote in a letter to Adam Smith in June 1772:

> We are here in a very melancholy situation: continual bankruptcies, universal loss of credit and endless suspicions ... even the Bank of England is not entirely free from suspicion... the Carron Company is reeling, which is one of the greatest calamities of the whole; as they gave employment to near 10,000 people

The crisis also has the distinction of being the first major banking panic faced by the Bank of England, which was then eighty years old. It was at very least the largest financial panic since the collapse of the South Sea Bubble fifty years earlier (see Chapter 5) and many at the time thought this an even bigger crisis. The Bank of England did not see itself in those days as a lender of last resort. Though it did extend credit, it did so sparingly with an eye on its own capital. It did not save the Ayr Bank nor did it adjust interest rates, keeping its discount rate steady at five percent through the crisis (Kosmetatos, 2018). Nonetheless, by allowing precious metals to be drawn against securities posted as collateral, the Bank of England did provide crucial support. The panic was no doubt felt most acutely in Britain but it had international repercussions too. The financial system of neighbouring countries were also affected, particularly Sweden and Netherlands. In other great mercantile and financial centre of Northern Europe, Amsterdam, the crisis took a similar shape to that in Britain. The country was faced with dwindling credit. Events there came to a head with the failure of the Anglo-Dutch bank Clifford and Sons, which had a history longer than even that of the Bank of England. The situation improved when the city of Amsterdam set up a cooperative fund backed by the Bank of Amsterdam and other Dutch banks to stem the crisis.

In Britain, there was still another problem, namely that of the East India Company, the very company whose perilous position helped set the stage for the pandemonium. Faced with a glut of tea and all the other problems I have previously mentioned, the firm was facing a cash shortage. To provide some breathing room, the directors of the company cut its dividend to six percent in late 1772, validating Fordyce's investment thesis but offering him no other consolation. While the share price tumbled by a third over the next few months, the move occurred far too late for Fordyce. As in Holland, the authorities in Britain resorted to government intervention, enacting policies that would have far reaching and perhaps unforeseen consequences. Among the legislation passed to save the ailing trading company was the Tea Act of 1773. Under the Act, intended to address the tea glut in Europe, the East India Company was allowed to directly ship and sell tea to the American colonies without taxation and without middlemen, giving them preferential access to a new market. This valuable concession was accompanied by a loan of one-point-four million pounds (GBP) at a low four percent rate provided to the company by the Bank of England.

The measures worked in stemming the crisis though, at least in Europe where the economic situation improved in 1773. However, in America, where the Tea Act would have extraordinary political consequences, the situation was only beginning to deteriorate. In the British colonies, economic conditions were already weak given the reduced trade and unavailability of credit caused by the banking crisis. This caused great harm to the agrarian elite in the Southern colonies as they relied most on credit and the trade in cash crops like tobacco. Indeed, many of America's founding fathers were heavily reliant on credit from English and Scottish bankers who were now unable to simply roll over their obligations. Some regarded the imminent revolt in the colonies as a violent attempt at debt cancellation. The Irish poet Thomas Moor will say:

> Those vaunted demagogues, who nobly rose; From England's debtors to be England's foes; Who could their monarch in their purse forget; And break allegiance but to cancel debt.

The crisis of 1772 had its more memorable effect in the Northern colonies however. In Boston, merchants were protesting the Tea Act, which in their view was a direct threat to their livelihoods. Prior to the Tea Act, much of the tea in the colonies was smuggled from the Netherlands to avoid taxation. With tea able to be imported tax-free by the East India Company, not only the smugglers but even legal importers were facing ruin. In revolt, merchants and other protesters disguised as Mohawk Indians boarded three ships, the Dartmouth, Eleanor, and Beaver, and tossed nearly 350 chests of tea into the frigid Boston Harbour. That event in December 1773 only decades later became known as the Boston Tea Party, but its ramifications revealed themselves far more immediately.

6.4 Hamilton, and the Panic of 1792 in the United States

In 1792, Philadelphia was both the capitol and the financial centre of the United States. Consequently, it is not surprising that politics and finance intermixed to create the nation's first financial panic and the first time the government stepped in to save the markets from themselves.

Alexander Hamilton, the first Secretary of the Treasury, laid the foundations of the American financial system. Alexander Hamilton's father was James Hamilton, a drifting trader and son of Alexander Hamilton, the laird of Cambuskeith, Ayrshire, Scotland. His mother was Rachel Fawcett Lavine, the daughter of a French Huguenot physician and the wife of John Michael Lavine, a German or Danish merchant who had settled on the island of St. Croix in the Danish West Indies. In March 1776, through the influence of friends in the New York legislature, Alexander Hamilton was commissioned a captain in the provincial artillery. He organised his own company and at the Battle of Trenton when he and his men prevented the British under Lord Cornwallis from crossing the Raritan River and attacking George Washington's main army, showed conspicuous bravery. In February 1777 Washington invited him to become an aide-de-camp with the rank of lieutenant colonel. In his four years on Washington's staff he grew close to the general and was entrusted with his correspondence. He was sent on important military missions and, thanks to his fluent command of French, became liaison officer between Washington and the French generals and admirals. Despite Alexander Hamilton's close connections with George Washington, he was never a freemason. The myth seems to stem from a painting entitled 'The Petition' by John Ward Dunsmore which depicts a meeting of American Union Lodge. The Lodge met to consider a petition to create a

General Grand Lodge for the United States with George Washington as the General Grand Master. The artist decided to take some artistic licence and included Hamilton, a non-mason, in the painting.

George Washington was elected as Master of a Lodge, but there is no evidence that he ever presided as such. Alexandria Lodge n. 39 of Pennsylvania asked the Grand Lodge of Virginia for a new charter. Washington was an Honorary Member of this lodge. When the Grand Master signed the Virginia charter, Washington's name appeared in the place where the Master's normally would. While serving as President, Washington was elected but never installed as Master of Alexandria Lodge n. 22. Even though his civic duty kept him from attending the lodge, he held Freemasonry in the utmost regard and was buried with full Masonic Honours.

When Hamilton became Secretary of the Treasury on 11 September 1789, the nation's finances were negative. Government bonds were in default, and they were trading at twenty-five percent of face value. Hamilton planned to follow in the footsteps of John Law (see Chapter 5), and reduce the amount of government debt by allowing it to be converted into equity. The President of the Bank of the United States, or the First Bank of the United States, was chartered for a term of twenty years by the US Congress on 25 February 1791. The bank was part of Alexander Hamilton's plan for stabilising and improving the nation's credit by establishing a central bank, a mint, and introducing exercise taxes. Opposition to the bank was led by Thomas Jefferson and James Madison who thought the bank was unconstitutional and created an unnecessary centralisation of power. Hamilton modelled the Bank of the United States on the Bank of England. The bank could be a depository for collected taxes, make short-term loans to the government, and could serve as a holding site for incoming and outgoing money. Nevertheless, Hamilton saw the main goal of the bank's activities were commercial, not public. The Bank of the United States had $10 million in capital, of which two million dollars (USD) was subscribed by the US government. The eight million dollars (USD) in shares sold to the public (twenty-thousand shares at four-hundred dollars (USD) a share) were sold in July 1791. To understand how large the Bank of the United States was, the revenues of the Federal Government were only four-point-four million dollars (USD) in 1791, so the capitalisation of the Bank of the United States was twice that of the Federal Government's revenues. Also the combined ten million dollars (USD) in equity capital would make the

Bank of the United States larger than all, other early American banks and insurance companies combined. Even still, the order book for the new shares was oversubscribed.

Like many share offering of the time, it was arranged to allow investors to pay in their capital over time. Investors only had to give up twenty-five dollars (USD) to reserve the option to purchase a full share by making further payments of three-hundred-and-seventy-five dollars (USD) spread out over instalments. The options acquired for twenty-five dollars (USD) were called 'scrip' and they began to be traded among investors. The public was also given the right to pay with funds other than cash. In fact, only one-fourth of the share price needed to be paid in gold but up to three-fourths of the price could be paid by exchanging government bonds for shares.

In the summer of 1791, there was a bubble in the price of Bank of the United States. The options purchased for twenty-five dollars (USD) quickly doubled in value and kept rising. They were traded actively in New York though the New York Stock Exchange would only be formed a year later. In the end, prices for the scrip came crashing down and the government, at Hamilton's direction, chose to purchase government bonds to prevent the crash from affecting the prices of other securities. In all, about two percent of the total government debt, or over five-hundred-and-sixty-thousand dollars (USD) was repurchased providing liquidity to those needing to sell assets during the bust. With this crisis averted, the Bank of the United States launched late in 1791 and almost immediately began to add meaningfully to the money supply of the country. The bank issued banknotes and raised deposits to discount commercial paper, that is, to advance funds against short-term bills and receivables as a form of financing. Some were sceptical of the bank's prudence as its banknotes began to proliferate as far away as Boston while the bank was headquartered in Philadelphia. This prompted many to redeem their banknotes and deposits in exchange for precious metal specie reserves kept at the bank. Reserves at the Bank of the United States fell from over seven-hundred-thousand dollars (USD) in December 1791 to two-hundred-and forty-four-thousand dollars (USD) in March the following year. Seeing that it had expanded too rapidly this caused the bank to begin restricting credit. The volume of short-term bills on the bank's balance sheet fell from almost two-point-seven million dollars in January 1792 to under two-point-one million dollars (USD) two months later. From the Treasury, Hamilton urged a slower contraction, but the bank, along with others, began restricting credit quickly. It would help trigger yet another panic.

The expansion and contraction of the balance sheet of the Bank of the United States affected speculation in its own shares and other securities. At the heart of the frenzy was William Duer, an English-born New York based speculator. Duer was Hamilton's friend and a member of the Continental Congress, the Americans' governing body during the War of Independence. He became governor of Hamilton's recent creation, the 'Society for Establishing Useful Manufacturers' and raised five-hundred-thousand dollars (USD) for that new company. Duer also served as Hamilton's undersecretary at the Treasury.

Very late in 1791, Duer organised a pool along with Alexander Macomb, a wealthy land speculator who had purchased the largest piece of property from the state of New York, and with other owners of shares in the Bank of the United States. They were known as 'The Six Percent Club' since shares in the Bank of the United States paid a six percent dividend. Their goal was to try and corner the market before the next distribution of shares in July 1792 and sell the shares to European investors at a profit. Duer and the others bought the shares on time, in essence buying options, rather than buying full shares, so they could maximise their profit through leverage. The Bank of the United States finally opened in December 1791, and made use of its capital by making loans and issuing banknotes. This increased the money supply and helped to feed new speculation in bank shares and US six percent bonds. The wild ride in shares of the Bank of the United States continued. Shares in the Bank of the United States rose from five-hundred-and-twenty-eight dollars (USD) to seven-hundred-and-twelve dollars (USD) in 1792 as the Bank of the United States prepared to open branches in Boston, New York, Charleston, with other cities to follow. Duer got also others to invest with him, reportedly including a madam from one the city's brothels, who probably kept the money hidden in one of the well-worn beds, and co-signed notes with merchants to raise capital. Duer even withdrew two-hundred-and-ninety-two-thousand dollars (USD) from the treasury of the Society for Establishing Useful Manufacturers for personal investment and expenses to allow him to buy even more shares, an act that would later lead to his downfall.

With the shares overvalued, a number of short sellers formed a 'bear raid' to push the stock price lower. The bears were led by Governor George Clinton of New York, an ally of Thomas Jefferson who was opposed to the Bank of the United States and to Alexander Hamilton. Anything Clinton could do to embarrass the Bank or cause it to fail would help Jefferson and his cause. Clinton and his clique sold short all the stock they could to Duer. By March 1792, the banks started to face a credit crunch. Clinton and his clique began to withdraw large amounts of money from the city's banks to create a credit shortage. Moreover, it was springtime when farmers began withdrawing money from the banks to pay for the crops they were planting. Oliver Wolcott, the comptroller of the currency, had discovered the deficiency of two-hundred-and-ninety-two-thousand dollars (USD) at the Society for Establishing Useful Manufacturers, which Duer acknowledged, and demanded repayment. Wolcott called upon the US attorney in New York to sue Duer for the long overdue debt. Duer appealed to Alexander Hamilton to intercede on his behalf, but Hamilton refused, and on 9 March 1792, Duer failed to meet payments on some of his loans and Duer's paper pyramid collapsed. With Duer and his pool no longer able to buy shares in the Bank of the United States, the price of the stock began a precipitous decline. On 23 March, Duer took refuge in the New York city jail. Duer was soon joined in jail by two other members of the 'Six Percent Club'. Walter Livingston (who is buried at Trinity Churchyard near Wall Street), who had consigned over two-hundred-thousand dollars (USD) of notes signed by Duer, and Alexander Macomb, who defaulted on five-hundred-thousand dollars (USD) in stock he had purchased from the bears. By April, with the Six Percent Club defaulting and the price of Bank of the United States collapsing, the country suffered its first financial panic. This delighted Secretary of State Jefferson, Governor Clinton and his allies, who were opposed to Hamilton's attempt to centralise the finances of the United States. They could turn the panic into political capital which they would use to undercut Alexander Hamilton. In response to the crisis, many banks tightened their credit, and in March and April, money began flowing to farmers to provide funding for their crops. Cash reserves at the Bank of the United States decreased by 34% prompting the bank to not renew nearly twenty-five percent of its outstanding thirty-day loans. In order to pay off these loans, many borrowers were forced to sell securities they had purchased, which caused the price of stocks to fall sharply. The price of Bank of the United States half shares collapsed and the price of stock in the Society for Establishing Useful Manufacturers fell too in 1792. Duer had perpetrated the young nation's first financial panic and stock market crash, and he paid the price by spending the rest of his life in debtor's prison where he died on 7 March 1799.

For a second time, Hamilton and the Society for Establishing Useful Manufacturers authorised the government to buy up government bonds to support their price and slow the collapse in prices. On 26 March with only Jefferson dissenting the commission authorised one-hundred-thousand dollars (USD) in open market purchases of securities to offset the credit crunch that was occurring. Hamilton also had his own Bank of New York lend to merchant and securities dealers against their bond holdings, albeit at a higher interest rate, so to avoid liquidation of these holdings from further depressing prices. With these measures, a recovery accelerated and financial conditions quickly picked up from their April nadir. Stock prices also began to rise again. However, activity in the government bond markets fell and would not return to their speculation-induced levels for years. Trading volume in bonds fell from over seven-point-eight million dollars (USD) in 1791 to two-point-six million dollars (USD) in 1793 and would reach a low of one million dollars (USD) until 1799. Despite all this, economic effects were minimal and optimism soon returned.

6.5 The 1907 Knickerbocker Crisis in The Name of Two Brothers

Established as a bank in 1884, the Knickerbocker Trust Company was the firm whose near collapse triggered the panic of 1907 in the United States. It had grown rapidly in the preceding decade. In just the ten years before the crisis, the bank grew from ten million dollars (USD) in deposits to sixty-one million dollars (USD). This growth occurred under the leadership of the Bank's then President, Charles Tracy Barney. Knickerbocker was a New York city based trust company. New York trust companies operated like banks, as a financial intermediary offering deposit accounts. Depositors could request withdrawals of their balances on demand. However, trust companies differed from ordinary banks in two respects; they did not offer the kind of payment and check-clearing services that other banks offered and because they were not integral entities in the nation's payment system and thus saw fewer transactions, they generally held less cash on reserve. Whereas a post-crisis commission found that New York banks had averaged a twenty-five/twenty-seven percent ratio of cash reserves to deposits, reserve ratios for trusts were more like five percent.

So how does the bank get into trouble? The story involves two brothers and their plan to corner the market of shares of the United Copper Company. Otto and Augustus Heinze, along with another prominent business partner, attempted to buy enough shares that other potential buyers, such as those who needed to cover short positions, would have to pay a premium. As the two speculators bought up all the shares they could, prices surged. However, insufficient shares were purchased to successfully corner the market; the short sellers, the brothers tried to squeeze had no trouble buying shares at lower prices from others with which to cover their short positions. Prices for the shares fell precipitously, reversing their earlier gains as the Heinze brothers bought the shares, and the price eventually fell further, to a fraction of their initial value. The plan had failed and Otto and Augustus Heinze incurred large losses; among the lenders believed to be financing their scheme was the Knickerbocker Trust.

As soon as news of the failed scheme spread, banks associated with the Heinze brothers suffered bank runs as depositors feared the losses would be too great for those who lent the speculators money to survive. In actuality, though the Heinze brothers had asked Charles Barney for financial backing for their venture, the Knickerbocker Trust had not lent them money. However, Barney was viewed as closely associated with the brothers and so many suspected the trust was among their lenders anyway; there was a run on the bank. On 22 October 1907, the Knickerbocker Trust experienced eight million dollars (USD) in withdrawals, exhausting the trust's reserves. Police had to be called in to handle the crowds and the bank shut early that day, just pass noon, leaving many depositors waiting outside in line.

Charles Barney was not financially ruined. Despite his resignation from Knickerbocker Trust he still had an estimated two-point-five million dollars (USD) in assets over and above liabilities. But personally he was disgraced. On the morning of 14 November 1907, Barney was in his bedroom on the second floor of his house, with two windows facing 38th Street. He was accustomed to eating breakfast here and then conducting business by telephone before dressing in late morning. On this particular morning before 10:00 AM only one single shot fired could be heard from Barney's room. The wife ran into the room and saw Barney standing. As she approached her husband, he fell to the floor and she cradled his head in her lap. Barney had shot himself in the abdomen with a thirty-two calibre revolver. The wife later told the police that pistols were kept on every floor of the house for protection.

Fearing that the run would spread another banker took action. While John Pierpont Morgan believed that the Knickerbocker Trust was insolvent and thus not worth saving, the crisis began to spread to other trust companies. There was also a run on the Trust Company of America and this did worry Morgan, the city's preeminent banker. A spreading crisis meant that no bank would be trusted. A measure of trust between financiers and the stability of the markets in those days was the rate offered on loans backed by shares of stock. Data from the New York Times shows that when the Knickerbocker Trust closed on 22 October 1907, the rate offered on loans backed by stock collateral soared from nine-point-five percent to about one-hundred percent in two days. Unlike the Knickerbocker Trust, the Trust Company of America was solvent but experienced a run throughout the day following Knickerbocker's closure. With the cooperation and assistance of other lenders, the Trust was able to liquidate its assets without a disorderly fire sale that day. Then on 24 October 1907, Morgan led a consortium of banks in his library which arranged a loan of over $8 million for the Trust Company of America. This was followed by other action taken by the US Government and John D. Rockefeller, thus by organising these actions, JP Morgan halted the worst of that financial crisis. The Knickerbocker Trust would actually survive the panic of 1907 but only remaining closed to customer withdrawals for several weeks. However, its name would not survive and the firm was acquired by another trust company a few years later.

The panic of 1907 and the run on the Knickerbocker Trust led to the creation of the Federal Reserve System and Senator Nelson Aldrich started an inquiry into the monetary systems of other countries. The commission ended up publishing a series of papers over the period from 1909 to 1912. Some described the central banks and monetary and financial systems of other countries, including not just those of large nations like Germany and United Kingdom, but also Belgium, Canada, and Sweden. Other products of the Commission's work included some, no doubt interesting, papers on 'The history and methods of the Paris *Bourse*' and one on 'Seasonal variations in the relative demand for money and capital in the United States'. They may not all sound equally fascinating but in the end many of Commission's ideas were incorporated into the creation of the Federal Reserve in 1913.

6.6 Black Wednesday, and the Man Who Broke the Bank of England

On 1992, George Soros became one of the most famous currency traders in the world. This was thanks to his timely and brave bet against the Bank of England on what became known as 'Black Wednesday'. With costs of around three-point-three billion pounds (GBP), Britain's central bank was unable to defend itself from an attack in the currency market. Soros made about one billion dollars (USD) in profit as a result.

Soros born in Budapest in the Kingdom of Hungary in August 1930. The son of a prosperous and non-observant Jewish family, had his upbringing disrupted by the Nazis' arrival in Hungary in 1944. The family split up and used false papers to avoid being sent to concentration camps. In 1947 they moved to London. Soros studied philosophy under Karl Popper at the London School of Economics, but he abandoned his plans to become a philosopher. He joined the London merchant bank Singer & Friedlander. In 1956 he moved to New York City, where he worked initially as an analyst of European securities and rapidly made his mark. In 1973 Soros established the Soros Fund (later Quantum Endowment Fund), a hedge fund that subsequently spawned a range of associated companies. His daring investment decisions caused the funds to grow rapidly, but not all his gambles succeeded. He correctly foresaw the worldwide stock market crash of October 1987—but wrongly predicted that Japanese stock would fall hardest of all. Soros's status as an almost mythical financier was established in September 1992 when the British government devalued the pound sterling. Through his Quantum group of companies, Soros had sold billions in pounds during the days preceding devaluation, much of it purchased with borrowed money. Afterwards Soros bought back pounds, repaid the money he had borrowed, and made a profit of about $1 billion in only one month. The gambit earned him the nickname 'the man who broke the Bank of England'.

Could a repeat of the Soros score happen today? Traders can certainly position to profit if the euro currency unravels, but Soros' bet benefited from the insular nature of the Bank of England in the early 1990s. Central Banks today work much more quickly and collectively than in the past to avoid knock-on effects. Indeed, crisis today can emerge rapidly and central banks have moved to the forefront being in charge of financial stability in addition to their monetary stability mandates. Coordinated actions among central banks and more global prospective in adopting monetary policies can help in today's terms to avoid another speculation on currencies. Indeed, interest rate divergence is what helped Soros' trade a winner in 1992.

September 1992 was a month international money managers will not easily forget. It all started from the wrecked European Exchange Rate Mechanism (ERM)[2] that was set up in March 1979 by the then-members of the European Economic Community to keep the various European currencies relatively stable against one another. Essentially the ERM's purpose was to reduce exchange rate variability and stabilise monetary policy across Europe before introducing a common currency; it would eventually be known as the euro. Relatively narrow fixed trading rangers were established within which the prices of eleven European currencies were supposed to fluctuate. But the system could work only if the various countries coordinated their economic policies. In one nation had, say higher inflation than another, there would be greater strain on the system. Differences in interest rates also would strain the system. When differences in interest rates and inflation rates among the eleven got out of line, the central banks had to intervene to buy and thus support the weakening currency against speculators and currency hedgers. In former times, powerful central banks could usually frustrate speculators. They did so by simply buying massive amounts of the weaker currency and flooding the market with the stronger currency. But times were different when Soros and the others went short the weakest currencies. Firstly, while central banks can mobilise tens of billions of dollars, trading in foreign currency markets runs to a trillion dollars a day. Hence, the ERM might make sense politically, but it is economically dangerous. Secondly, going short a currency can be done in a number of ways. The simplest is to borrow money, say, Italian lira, and convert the borrowed money into, say, deutsche marks at the fixed rates. Then the speculator waits for the lira to drop sharply against the deutsche mark, buy in the now cheaper lira to repay the debt and pocket a lot of extra deutsche marks. This is what Soros did.

At first, Britain declined to join the ERM when it originated. Later on, it adopted a semi-official policy that shadowed the Deutsche Mark. In October 1990, the country decided to join the ERM, preventing its currency from fluctuating more than six percent in either direction by intervening in the currency markets with countertrades. When Britain joined the ERM, the rate was set to two-point-ninety-five deutsche marks per pound sterling with a six percent permissible move in either direction. The problem was that the country's inflation rate was high, and interest rates were over thirteen percent. The country's economic boom was far into a period of unsustainable growth. This set the stage for a bust period. Currency traders saw these underlying problems and began shorting the pound. Specifically, they bought one currency, such as the mark, using the pound. This allowed them to profit as the pound fell in value by comparison to the other currency. George Soros was one of these bearish currency traders. He amassed a short position of more than ten billion dollars (USD) worth of pounds.

The UK's prime minister and cabinet members approved the spending of billions in pounds. This was an attempt to contain the short selling by speculators. Then the British government announced that it would raise its interest rates from ten percent to fifteen percent. This was to try to attract currency traders looking for greater yield on their currency holdings. But the currency speculators did not trust the government would make good on these promises; they continued shorting the pound. After an emergency meeting among top officials, the United Kingdom was ultimately forced to withdraw from the ERM to let the market revalue its currency to more appropriate, lower levels. Afterwards the country was thrown in a recession. Many British citizens began referring to the ERM as the 'Eternal Recession Machine'. While the government lost a lot of money, some politicians are glad the ERM disaster occurred, since it paved the way for more conservative policies that would ultimately be credited for reviving the economy. Black Wednesday is well known as the day that Soros broke the Bank of England and made over one billion dollars (USD).

6.7 The Enron Scandal

Enron Corp. was founded in 1985 by Kenneth Lay in the merger of two natural-gas transmission companies, Houston Natural Gas Corporation and InterNorth, Inc.; the merged company, HNG InterNorth, was renamed Enron in 1986. After US Congress adopted a series of laws to deregulate the sale of natural gas in the early 1990s, the company lost its exclusive right to operate its pipelines. With the help of Jeffrey Skilling, who was initially a consultant and later became the company's chief operating officer, Enron transformed itself into a trader of energy derivative contracts, acting as an intermediary between natural-gas producers and their customers. The trades allowed the producers to mitigate the risk of energy-price fluctuations by fixing the selling price of their products through a contract negotiated by Enron for a fee. Under Skilling's leadership, Enron soon dominated the market for natural-gas contracts, and the company started to generate huge profits on its trade.

Skilling also gradually changed the culture of the company to emphasise aggressive trading. He hired top candidates from MBA programmes around the country and created an intensely competitive environment within the company, in which the focus was increasingly on closing as many cash-generating trades as possible in the shortest amount of time. One of his brightest recruits was Andrew Fastow, who quickly rose through the ranks to become Enron's chief financial officer. Fastow oversaw the financing of the company through investments in increasingly complex instruments, while Skilling oversaw the building of its vast trading operation.

The bull market of the 1990s helped to fuel Enron's ambitions and contributed to its rapid growth. There were deals to be made everywhere, and the company was ready to create a market for anything that anyone was willing to trade. It thus traded derivative contracts for a wide variety of commodities—including electricity, coal, paper, and steel—and even for the weather. An online trading division, Enron Online, was launched during the dotcom boom (see Chapter 5), and by 2001 it was executing online trades worth about two-point-five billion dollars (USD) a day. Enron also invested in building a broadband telecommunications network to facilitate high-speed trading.

As the boom years came to an end and as Enron faced increased competition in the energy-trading business, the company's profits shrank rapidly. Under pressure from shareholders, company executives began to rely on dubious accounting practices, including a technique known as 'mark-to-market accounting', to hide the troubles. Mark-to-market accounting allowed the company to write unrealised future gains from some trading contracts into current income statements, thus giving the illusion of higher current profits. Furthermore, the troubled operations of the company were transferred to so-called special purpose entities (SPEs), which are essentially limited partnerships created with outside parties. Although many companies distributed assets to SPEs, Enron abused the practice by using SPEs as dump sites for its troubled assets. Transferring those assets to SPEs meant that they were kept off Enron's books, making its losses look less severe than they really were. Some of those SPEs were run by Fastow himself.

In August 2001, Skilling abruptly resigned, and Lay resumed as the CEO. By this point the severity of the situation began to become apparent as a number of analysts began to dig into the details of Enron's publicly released financial statements. In October 2011 Enron shocked investors when it announced that it was going to post a six-hundred-and-thirty-eight million dollars (USD) loss for the third quarter and take a one-point-two billion dollars (USD) reduction in shareholder equity owing in part to Fastow's partnerships. Shortly thereafter the Securities and Exchange Commission began investigating the transactions between Enron and Fastow's SPEs. Some officials at Arthur Andersen then began shredding documents related to Enron audits.

As the details of the accounting frauds emerged, Enron went into free fall. Fastow was fired, and the company's stock price plummeted from a high of ninety dollars (USD) per share in mid-2000 to less than twelve dollars (USD) per share by the beginning of November 2001. That month Enron attempted to avoid disaster by agreeing to be acquired by Dynegy. However, weeks later Dynegy backed out the deal. The news caused Enron's stock to drop to under one dollar (USD) per share, taking with it the value of Enron employees' pensions, which were mainly tied to the company stock. On 2 December 2001, Enron filed for Chapter 11 bankruptcy protection.

Enron Corp. was probably the 'best friend' that Wall Street's short sellers ever had. Some of these professional bears bet against the energy company's stock early in 2001 because they were detecting by instinct fraud. The principal lesson that Enron has taught investors is about the need to question glowing corporate forecasts of sales and earnings, to dig deeper into companies' financial statements, and to think twice before affording sky-high price-to-earnings multiples to stocks of businesses heavy on hype and light on specifics.

One of the few voices raised against Enron before 2001 was that of James Chanos, a well-known research-intensive short seller who headed Kynikos Associates in New York. Chanos publicly questioned other analysts' assumptions about Enron's true profitability and made the argument that the company was merely a disguised 'hedge fund' a high-risk trading operation that did not deserve the huge valuation investors had given it. But Chanos got little publicity, and most institutional money managers were far more interested in hearing the upbeat pronouncements coming from then Enron CEO Jeffrey Skilling and from the army of brokerage analysts covering the company. Still Chanos's warnings belie the line heard most often on Wall Street, as big investors and analysts tried to explain why they did not see Enron's collapse coming. Led by a handful of professional sceptics, more investors did short Enron stock as 2001 wore on. But those bets rose relatively slowly, and even by September 2001 after Skilling had resigned and the share price was crumbling a modest thirteen-point-eight million Enron shares (less than two percent of the total outstanding) had been shorted, according to New York Stock Exchange data. In November 2001, as bankruptcy neared, short selling of Enron stock soared. But the 'big money' would have been made by shorting the stock at eighty dollars (USD) early in 2001, and holding that bet rather than shorting it at ten dollars (USD) in November. This because the profit on short sale is the difference between the price at which borrowed stock is sold and the price at which shares are bought back to repay the loan.

6.8 Lehman Brothers, and the 'Big Short'

Lehman Brothers' stock was selling at eighty-six dollars (USD) a share in February 2007, giving the company a market capitalisation of nearly sixty billion dollars (USD). For the year, the company reported a new record high net income, over four billion dollars (USD). In January 2008, Lehman Brothers was the fourth-largest investment bank in the United States. In March, immediately after Bear Stearns (the second-largest holder of mortgage-backed securities, right behind Lehman Brothers) almost collapsed, Lehman stock dropped by almost fifty percent. In June, the company reported a quarterly loss of two-point-eight billion dollars (USD), its first quarterly loss since being spun off from American Express way back in 1994.

By the end of 2008, Lehman Brothers Holdings Inc. had vanished from the investment banking landscape, the largest corporate bankruptcy filing in US history (with six-hundred-and-nineteen billion dollars (USD) in debt).

Lehman Brothers began with humble beginnings in the mid-nineteenth century, 1844 to be exact. It was started in Montgomery, Alabama by Henry Lehman, a Jewish immigrant from Germany. From being a dry-goods and general store, Henry's brothers—Mayer and

Emanuel—joined him, giving birth to Lehman Brothers in 1850. During the 1850s, Lehman began to become a major commodities trading company, specialising in the key cotton market. The company's shift from commodity trading to investment banking began in 1906 when it partnered with Goldman Sachs on an initial public offering. Between 1906 and 1926, Lehman was involved in underwriting nearly a hundred new equity issues, including those of such notable companies as F. W. Woolworth, Studebaker, and Macy's department stores.

The history of Lehman Brothers mirrors how investment banking's changed and developed in the United States' economy. The company managed to pursue and even thrive through major national upheavals such as the Civil War (see Chapter 3), both world wars, and the stock market crash of 1929 (see Chapter 5), and the resulting Great Depression. Going through a myriad of changes, spin-offs, and mergers, the company developed into a commodities brokerage and ultimately into one of the largest investment banks in the world.

Lehman Brothers was acquired by Shearson/American Express in 1984 for a reported three-hundred-and-sixty million dollars (USD). American Express owned Lehman Brothers from 1984 to 1994, at which time it spun the company off via an initial public offering, which attracted more than three billion dollars (USD) in new capital. The repeal of the Glass–Steagall Act (see Chapter 5)—which previously prevented banks from simultaneously conducting investment and commercial banking business—enabled Lehman Brothers to expand greatly by offering both services. Lehman Brothers prevailed after the horrors of 9/11 and continued as a dominant force in the investment banking industry. By 2007, Lehman had grown to become the fourth-largest investment banking firm in the country. Much of its growth and profitability came from huge investments in mortgage-backed securities (MBSs). Ironically, those very same instruments ultimately led to the company's downfall. Lehman Brothers was deeply invested in mortgaged-backed securities by the time the mid-200 s rolled around. The housing boom led to an over-abundance of both MBSs and collateral debt obligations (CDOs) being created and, by 2007, Lehman was the largest holder of MBSs.

It is undeniable that since the advent of securitisation, people who make the loan (namely, the lenders) are no longer at risk if the borrower fails to repay. Let me explain in plain terms: in the old system, when a homeowner paid their mortgage every month, the money went to their local lender. And since mortgages took decades to repay, lenders were careful. In the new system, lenders sold mortgages to investment banks. The investment banks combined thousands of mortgages and loans (including car loans, student loans, commercial mortgages, and credit card debt) to create complex derivatives called collateralised debt obligations or CDOs. The investment banks then sold the CDOs to investors. Now when homeowners paid their mortgages, the money went to investors all over the world. The investment banks paid rating agencies to evaluate the CDOs, and many of them were given a triple-A, which is the highest possible investment grade. This made CDOs popular with retirement funds, which could only purchase highly rated securities. This system was ticking time bomb. Lenders did not care anymore about whether a borrower could repay, so they started making riskier-loans. The investment banks did not care either, the more CDOs they sold, the higher their profit. And the rating agencies, which were paid by the investment banks, had no liability if their ratings of CDOs proved wrong because in the end they were issuing only a mere opinion. In the early 2000s there was a huge increase in the riskiest loans, called subprime. But when thousands of subprime loans were combined to create CDOs, many of them still received triple-A ratings. The investment banks actually preferred subprime loans, because they carried higher interest rates. This led to a massive increase in predatory lending. In fact, borrowers were needlessly placed in expensive subprime loans, and many loans were given to people who could not repay them. All the incentives that the financial institutions offered to their mortgage brokers were based on selling the most profitable products, which were predatory loans. Suddenly hundreds of billions of dollars a year were flowing through the securitisation chain. Since anyone could get a mortgage, home purchases and housing prices skyrocketed. The result was the biggest financial bubble in history. By 2008, home foreclosures were skyrocketing and the securitisation food chain imploded. Lenders could no longer sell their loans to the investment banks. And as the loans went bad, dozens of lenders failed. The market for CDOs collapsed, leaving the investment banks holding hundreds of billions of dollars in loans, CDOs, and real estate they could not sell.

There was another ticking bomb in the financial system, AIG the world's largest insurance company, was selling huge quantities of derivatives called credit default swaps (CDS). For investors who owned CDOs, credit default swaps worked like an insurance policy. An investor, who purchased a credit default swap paid AIG a quarterly premium. If the CDO went bad, AIG promised to pay the investor for their losses. But unlike regular insurance, speculators could also buy credit default swaps from AIG in order to bet against CDOs they did not own. The basic principle in insurance is that you can only insure something you own. For example, if I own a property, I own a house. I can only insure that house once. The derivatives universe essentially enables anybody to actually insure that house. So, an investor can insure that, somebody else could. Hence, it is like if fifty people might insure my house. What happens is, if my house burns down, now the number of losses in the system becomes proportionally larger.

Since credit default swaps were unregulated, AIG did not have to put aside any money to cover potential losses. Instead, AIG paid its employees huge cash bonuses as soon as contracts were signed. But if the CDOs later went bad, AIG would be on the hook. People essentially were rewarded for taking massive risks. In good times they generate short-term revenues and profits, and, therefore, bonuses. But that is going to lead to the firm to be bankrupt over time. That is a total distorted system of compensation. AIG's Financial Products (AIGFP) division in London issued five-hundred billion dollars (USD) worth of credit default swaps during the bubble, many of them for CDOs backed by subprime mortgages. The four-hundred employees at AIGFP made three-point-five billion dollars (USD) between 2000 and 2007. Joseph Cassano, the head of AIGFP, personally made three-hundred-and-fifteen million dollars (USD). In 2007, AIG's auditors raised warnings. One of them was Joseph St. Denis, resigned in protest after Cassano repeatedly blocked him from investigating AIGFP's accounting. In 2005, Professor Raghuram Rajan, then the chief economist of the International Monetary Fund delivered a paper at the Jackson Hole Symposium, the most elite banking conference in the World. The title of the paper was essentially 'Is Financial Development Making the World Riskier?' and the conclusion was it is. Rajan's paper focused on incentive structures that generated huge cash bonuses based on short-term profits, but which imposed no penalties for later losses. Rajan argued that these incentives encouraged bankers to take risks that might eventually destroy their own firms or even the entire financial system. It is very easy to generate performance by taking on more risk. So what you need to do is compensate for risk-adjusted performance.

Lehman Brothers' biggest competitor—Bear Stearns—failed first. A Federal Reserve-backed deal enabled JP Morgan Chase to buy out the company in 2008. The deal, though, made Lehman's future uncertain. Lehman was already in weakened state after depending on repos for daily funding. The company sought to boost market confidence through equity fundraising in the early summer of 2008. However, the move proved less reassuring when, in September, Lehman reported an anticipated third-quarter loss of nearly four billion dollars (USD). On top of this, it reported a five-point-six billion dollars (USD) loss in toxic asset write-downs. Lehman's stock plummeted some seventy-seven percent in the first seven days of September 2008. Richard Fuld—the CEO at that time—attempted to save face in front of investors and keep the doors open by using multiple tactics, including a spin-off of the company's commercial real estate assets. Nonetheless, investors saw Lehman for what it was: a sinking ship. The clear signal that investors were running came with the swelling of credit default swaps on Lehman's debt, as well as with the backtracking of major hedge fund investors. The final straw dropped by 15 September 2008 when, after attempted buyout rescue deals by both Bank of America and Barclays fell through. Lehman Brothers was forced to file for bankruptcy, an act that sent the company's stock plummeting a final ninety-three percent. When it was all over, Lehman Brothers—with its six-hundred-and-nineteen billion dollars (USD) in debts—was the largest corporate bankruptcy filing in US history. Following the bankruptcy filing, Barclays and Nomura Holdings eventually acquired the bulk of Lehman's investment banking and trading operations. Barclays additionally picked up Lehman's New York headquarters building. Lehman's collapse was a major contributor to the domino effect of multiple financial disaster that eventually became the Global Financial Crisis of 2008. For example, Lehman Brothers triggered the collapse of the world's largest insurance company, AIG. The global recession costed the world tens of trillions of dollars, rendered 210 millions of people unemployed across the world, and doubled the national debt of the United States. The destruction of equity wealth, of housing wealth, the destruction of income, of jobs. This is just a hugely expensive crisis, but one short seller hugely profit from it: Michael J. Burry.

Michael J. Burry grew up in San Jose, California. He studied economics and pre-med at UCLA and earned his medical degree at Vanderbilt University School of Medicine in Tennessee. After moving back to California to do his residency at Stanford, Burry would dabble in financial investing on nights off duty. Soon, without finishing, he left school to start his hedge fund, which he called Scion Capital. Michael Burry was always awkward and anti-social, leading him to later self-diagnose himself with Asperger's syndrome. And though he was exceptionally brilliant, Burry had few friends and was not yet established in investment circles when he embarked on his career. Burry stated that his investment style is built upon Benjamin Graham's and David Dodd's 1934 book 'Security Analysis' the core text for value investing, saying: 'All my stock picking is one-hundred percent based on the concept of margin of safety'.

Accordingly, he was among the first to call the dotcom bubble (see Chapter 3) by analysing overvalued companies with little revenue or profitability. He began shorting those stocks immediately, quickly earning extraordinary profits for his investors. Burry returned fifty-five percent in the first year (2001) even though the S&P 500 fell almost twelve percent. The market continued to decline dramatically over the next two years, yet Burry's fund returned sixteen percent (compared to the twenty-two percent fall of S&P 500) and fifty percent (S&P rose twenty-eight percent), making him one of the most successful investors in the industry at the time. As a result, by the end of 2004, he was managing six-hundred million dollars (USD) and turning investors away.

In 2005, Burry's focus turned to the subprime market. Through his analysis of mortgage lending practise and bank balance sheets in 2003 and 2004, he began to notice significant irregularities in this market, correctly predicting that the housing bubble would collapse as early as 2007. He saw the riskiness of the subprime market as millions of borrowers with low income and no assets bought homes with enormous leverage, in many cases, making no down payments for mortgages that they could not afford when interest rates would eventually rise. Yet the banking system was valued as if these mortgages were all solid, as I have explained before. Burry realised this would be unsustainable long term and that the credit products based on these subprime mortgages would plummet in value as soon as higher rates replaced the original rates. This conclusion led him to short the housing market by convincing Goldman Sachs and other investment banking companies to sell him credit default swaps (CDS) against subprime deals he saw as vulnerable. In short, sell positions on the assumption that housing prices will drop. However, as prices continued surging, Burry's clients grew nervous and frustrated as he continued his short plays using derivatives. Unfortunately or, instead, fortunately in retrospect, when they demanded to withdraw their capital, Burry simply refused the investors' pleas (by placing a moratorium on withdrawals from the fund), angering his clients even more.

Eventually, Burry's analysis proved correct: in 2007, the market started to turn in his predicted direction as more insiders understood the system's risks. Then the dominoes began to drop, with Bear Stearns, Lehman Brothers, AIG, and the rest of the financial system behind them. Burry's bet paid off, earning him a hefty personal profit of one-hundred million dollars (USD) and more than seven-hundred million dollars (USD) for his remaining investors. Scion Capital documented returns of 489.34% between its 1 November 2000 founding and June 2008. In contrast, the S&P 500 returned under three percent including dividends over the same period. Warren Buffet called Dr. Burry 'Cassandra', a Trojan priestess from Greek mythology who delivered true prophecies but, just like Burry and his warnings about the housing bubble, was never believed. Yet the most lucrative bet against the housing bubble was made by Paulson. His hedge fund firm, Paulson & Co. made twenty billion dollars (USD) on the trade between 2007 and 2009 driven by its bets against subprime mortgages through credit default swaps, according to The Wall Street Journal.

6.9 Terror Trader for a Fistful of Euros

On 11 April 2017, three bombs were ready to detonate when the players of Borussia Dortmund, one of Germany's best soccer teams, pulled into L'arrivee Hotel & Spa, on the outskirts of Dortmund, Germany. Dortmund was set to play AS Monaco and hoped to move a step closer in Champions League.

The German media debated who would design to attack such a German institution as soccer. Founded in Drtmund in 1962, the German Bundesliga is among the most popular and profitable leagues in the world. The team, known as DVB in Dortmund, is the city's most cherished icon and one of its few bright spots. Almost the entire city centre was obliterated during World War II. On *Westenhellweg*, Dortmund's pedestrian shopping street, it is impossible to walk more than a few feet without seeing the BVB logo. The city loves soccer so much that in 2009 it was selected to become the home of the German Football Museum. Its four floors hold hundreds of items and one unlikely clue to what motivated the attack: a display showing BVB's publicly traded shares, with a green line tied to the team's wins and losses that zigs up and mostly down from 2000 to 2015.

In 2000, Dortmund became the first and only club in Germany to list itself on the stock exchange, in an effort to compete with top-tier teams in signing expensive players. From 1995 to 2017, average player salaries in the Bundesliga almost tripled. Going public gave Dortmund about one-hundred-and-forty million Euros to secure its roster. Shortly after the attack, BVB's lawyer got an email from a man named Rudolf, a Dortmund fan and sports stock trader in the Austrian town of *Bad Ischl* claiming that something strange took place on the day of the attack. Indeed, on that day, someone had purchased 60,000 BVB put options—a wager that the shares would fall below a certain price by a certain date. Such purchase would have been only explainable if the buyer would have expected the stock value to go down very rapidly. This kind of drop would have not happen if Dortmund lost a game. It would require something more serious, like losing players, or the entire team, in a terror attack. Indeed, most short sellers are just looking for shares they expect to fall and trying to profit from the downward spiral. The classic example is Jim Chanos—as I have illustrated in the previous section—who shorted Enron Corp. stock before the company collapsed in 2001. But it is not unheard of for someone to try to create a catalyst to sink stocks. For instance, in 2018, Bill Ackman was in the game as an activist short seller. This means looking into businesses, building a thesis, creating a massive short position, and then publishing their reports for the rest of the market to decide on. A compelling enough report will kick start the decline in the shares they are holding and result in big wins. This can be a good technique to wipe out dodgy companies, or overinflated businesses.

Investigators contacted Commerzbank AG, the German bank whose subsidiary, Comdirect processed the options. Dortmund was not a commonly traded stock, so purchasing forty-thousand Euros worth of BVB derivatives was unheard of. Put options are high-risk. They decrease value as they approach their expiration date, in this case in June, and can depreciate dramatically if the stock price rises. Even more suspicious, one of the purchases had been made online only a few hours before the bombing, using an IP address at L'Arrivee Hotel. Interviews with employees revealed that a twentysomething man with a Russian accent had checked in two days before the attack and insisted on a room with a view of the entryway. It was not the man's first visit to the hotel: he would spend the night at L'Arrivee in early March, more than a month before the attack. Investigators soon identified the man as Sergej Wenergold, a 28-year-old German citizen living in the southern city of *Torrenburg am*

Neckar. For a week, investigators hid outside Wenergold's apartment. He worked as an electrician and he had no criminal past and no connection to far-right, far-left, or Islamic extremists. He was not a soccer fan, and he did not seem to need money. He had a stable income and no apparent gambling problem or debts. Still he was the only suspect. On 21 April 2017, ten days after the attack, police surrounded his car as he arrived at work and arrested him. Initially, Wenergold denied that he carried out the attacks. But as time dragged on, he admitted that he had built and set off the bombs and purchased the put options. He claimed he had not wanted to kill anybody, but merely to create the illusion of an Islamist terror attack. The idea for the plot, he later testified, came to him while watching coverage of the 2015 Paris spree. After the killings, he looked at the valuations of French companies and saw that the share prices had gone down, even though the attack did not target anything economic. Hence, he thought if there was an attack that explicitly targets a company, then its stock value would go down as well. If Wenergold shorted Dortmund and simulated an Islamic terror raid against the team, he figured, he could make money. Losing one game might not have a dramatic effect on it. Potential fatalities were only avoided because one of the devices, which were filled with metal pins, was placed about a metre off the ground and therefore too high to be fully effective, according to the German prosecutor's statement. Dortmund's share price did fall from five-point-seventy-three Euros per share on 10 April to five-point-sixty-one Euros per share after the attack on 11 April. It dropped only two percent, and the share price quickly rebounded to five-point-seventy-one Euros the following day, leading Wenergold to sell most of his options the next day at a loss. Still according to investigators, Wenergold could have made as much as five-hundred-and-seventy-thousand Euros in the unlikely event that BVB stock hit zero in the immediate aftermath of the attack. But his scheme did not pan out due to the limited injuries reported and the fact that management had already announced a new date for the quarterfinal.

6.10 GameStop, and the Bad Fate of Short Sellers

On 14 October 2021, the Securities and Exchange Commission released a 'Staff Report on Equity and Options Market Structure Conditions in Early 2021', specifying the conditions that allowed GameStop Corp.'s stock to go from seventeen dollars (USD) to roughly over three-hundred dollars (USD) over the course of January 2021 for no particular reason.

With more than five thousand stores, GameStop is a video game chain where customers can buy, sell, and trade their games, consoles, and gaming accessories. In 2021, GameStop's stock has soared to unbelievable heights. It became clear quite quickly that much of the activity was driven by day traders, many of whom had clubbed together on Reddit (one of the world's largest online communities) and other platforms to drive the stock up. Some did this to make money; but a large portion of them appear to have done it to hurt short sellers, who had placed heavy bets that the price of GameStop shares would fall. Suggested factors include anger of some investors towards Wall Street hedge funds for their role in the financial crisis of 2007 and 2008 or the general democratisation of the stock market coupled with the ability of retail traders to communicate instantaneously through social media. Specifically, professional managers of Wall Street, in particular hedge funds and investment funds did bet that GameStop's stock would crater. It was easy to see the downside for GameStop, a company that had closed seven-hundred-and-eighty-three stores in two years because more game and console sales were happening online an through its competitors—Walmart, Target, Best Buy, and Amazon especially since the inception of the pandemic in 2020.

The subreddit r/wallsstreetbets is an online community on Reddit. The community is known for discussion around meme stocks[3] and high-risk stock transactions. Observers congregating around r/wallstreetbets believed GameStop was being significantly undervalued, and with such a large amount of shares being short they could trigger a short squeeze by driving up the price to the point where short sellers had to capitulate and cover their positions at large losses. Those retail investors started to pump up the price of GameStop shares, and effectively trapped the short sellers in a short squeeze. The high price and volatility continued after the peak in late January 2021, and on 24 February 2021, the GameStop stock price doubled within a ninety minute period, and then averaged in the neighbourhood of two-hundred dollars (USD) per share for another month. On 24 March 2021, the GameStop stock price fell thirty-four percent to one-hundred-and-twenty dollars (USD) per share after earnings were released and the company announced plans for issuing a new secondary stock offering. On 25 March 2021, the stock recovered dramatically, rising by fifty-three percent. Even before the short squeeze, there had been interest in GameStop. Keith Gill, known by the Reddit username 'DeepFuckingValue' and the You Tube and Twitter alias 'Roaring Kitty' purchased fifty-three thousand dollars (USD) in call options on GameStop's stock in 2019 and saw his position rise to a value of forty-eight million dollars (USD) by 27 January 2021. Gill, a thirty-four years old marketing professional and Chartered Financial Analyst (CFA) from Massachusetts stated that he began investing in GameStop during the summer 2019, after believing the stock to be undervalued. He shared information regarding his investment on r/wallstreetbets providing regular updates on the investment's performance including times when the investment had plunged. According to Down Jones market data more than one-hundred-and-seventy-five million shares of GameStop were traded on 25 January 2021, the second largest total in a single day. According to the Financial Times a 'gamma squeeze' also took place in addition to the short squeeze: as traders bet on the rise of stocks by purchasing call options, and options sellers hedge their positions by purchasing the underlying stocks (here GameStop and the related securities) thereby driving their prices even higher.

Short sellers who had bet against GameStop suffered large losses as a result of the short squeeze. By 28 January 2021, Melvin Capital Management, an investment fund that heavily shorted GameStop had lost thirty percent of its value since the start of 2021, and by the end of January had suffered a loss of fifty-three percent of its investments. Citadel LLC and firm partners then invested two billion dollars (USD) in Melvin, while Point72 Asset Management's investment added seven-hundred-and-fifty million dollars (USD), for a total investment of two-point-seventy-five billion dollars (USD), before Melvin told CNBC that they covered (closed) their position on 26 January 2021, although the exact amount was not disclosed. Melvin ultimately shut down on 18 May 2022.

A short squeeze is not a new finance practice. This has happened before, most famously with Tesla stock, although this time the tone of the short squeeze was even violent. Indeed, this sentiment rose to new prominence during the height of the GameStop short squeeze when short sellers began shutting down their social accounts as mobs started to bombard them with death threats. For instance, Mr. Gabe Plotkin of Melvin Capital Management took the threats so seriously he had to hire security for him and his family. After taking massive hits to his short position on GameStop, he adapted his strategy but in May 2022 his firm failed.

The GameStop saga is reminding us that short sellers are exposed to a risk of short squeezing, which occurs when the shorted stock jumps in value due, for instance, to a sudden piece of favourable news. Short sellers are then forced to buy back the stock they had initially sold, in an effort to keep their losses from mounting. Purchasing the stock to cover their short positions raises the price of the shorted stock, thus triggering more short sellers to cover their positions by buying the stock. This can result in a cascade of stock purchases and an even bigger jump of the share price.

6.11 Conclusions

After implosions of institutions like Silicon Valley Bank, Signature Bank, and First Republic Bank during the 'March Madness' of 2023 (see Chapter 7), the profile of US regional banks further deteriorated and such market edge proved lucrative for some short sellers. Betting against regional lenders has netted about seven billion dollars (USD) in paper profits so far in 2023, as higher interest rates triggered liquidity concerns and led to the banking turmoil. US financial regulators have dealt relatively quickly with the banks that ran into trouble by providing liquidity assistance, but still some market operators urged the Securities and Exchange Commission (SEC) to impose a fifteen day prohibition on short sales to give time for work on restoring confidence (see Chapter 7). The SEC did not consider a short selling ban—this time—but such debate paved the way to call for more regulatory oversight of the practice of short selling. This because—as this chapter has illustrated—short sellers might specifically profit from banking crises. As opposed to the SEC, financial regulators across Europe and Asia initiated short selling bans to quell the market freefall, while exchanges enforced circuit breakers, extended trading holidays, and shortened trading hours.

By contrast, the SEC took a short selling ban position during the Global Financial Crisis of 2008 acting in concert with the UK Financial Services Authority. This was a temporary emergency action to prohibit short selling in financial companies to protect the integrity and quality of the securities market and strengthen investor confidence and restore equilibrium in markets. This ban was quickly imitated by the majority of other countries: some only banned 'naked short sales', in which the seller does not borrow shares to deliver them to the buyer during the settlement period; others also banned covered short sales, in which the seller protects himself by borrowing the shares. More recently, during the sovereign debt crisis of 2011–2012, regulators in most eurozone countries have reacted in the same way to share prices drops, especially those in the banking sector. The same occurred again in 2016, when both the Financial Conduct Authority in the United Kingdom and the Italian financial regulator (the CONSOB) banned short selling of shares in Italian bank Monte dei Paschi di Siena for at least three months. This measure was needed when Monte dei Paschi shares dropped around twenty percent in a single day.

Probably one of the best examples of short selling ban is during the Covid-19 pandemic in 2020 that has resulted in extreme volatility in equity markets across the EU and the world. In response, a number of market regulators across the EU have taken action using powers under Article 20 of the EU Short Selling Regulation (SSR—Regulation N. 236/2012). Specifically, regulators are empowered in the European Union under a detailed regulatory framework on short selling of shares and certain aspects of credit default swaps[4] (CDS) since 1 November 2012, under the EU Short Selling Regulation. The SSR applies to any person undertaking short selling of shares, sovereign debt, severing CDS and related instruments that are admitted to trading or traded on an EU trading venue. It also prohibits the entry into uncovered sovereign credit default swaps. The SSR does not relate to repos, securities lending, corporate and convertible bonds, although national regulators have powers under Articles 18 and 21 of the SSR to impose short selling restrictions on any financial instrument, if there is a serious threat to financial stability or to market confidence. The SSR requires holders of net short positions in shares or sovereign debt to make notifications once certain thresholds have been reached, as well as applying a blanket ban on uncovered short sales in shares.[5] Article 20 of the SSR also provides powers to national regulators to suspend short selling or limit transactions where 'exceptional circumstances' (meaning 'adverse events or developments which constitute a serious threat to the financial stability or to market confidence') exist. If an EU national regulator decides to impose such a temporary ban on short selling, that regulator is required to notify other EU regulators, the UK Financial Conduct Authority, and the European Securities and Markets Authority. National regulators will consider whether to apply that temporary ban in their own jurisdictions. The intention is to avoid short selling activity linked to particular shares moving to other jurisdictions where these shares are also traded. Equivalent provisions exist in the United States under Section 12 (k) (2) of the Securities Exchange Act of 1934 that empowers the SEC to issue emergency orders with immediate effect. On 24 February 2010, the SEC adopted a new rule to place certain restrictions on short selling when a stock is experiencing significant downward price pressure. This is an amendment to Regulation SHO[6] under the Securities Exchange Act of 1934. The Rule 201 imposes restrictions on short selling only when a stock has triggered a circuit breaker by experiencing a price decline of at least ten percent in one day. At that point, short selling would be permitted if the price of the security is above the current national best bid.

As it can be seen, few things are more predictable than loud demands for regulatory interventions to 'stop speculation' when stock market prices plunge. However, this argument has serious flaws. First, it is assumed that regulators know better than the market what the 'true valuation' of securities is, better than the thousands of investors who spend resources every day to also try to calculate such true valuations, so as to buy undervalued securities and sell overvalued ones. But if so, why don't the authorities that oversee security markets intervene even when prices rise above 'true valuations', before the market crashes? If we ban short sales to prevent unwarranted price drops, we should symmetrically ban 'excessive' purchases leading to unwarranted security market booms. Second, the empirical evidence that has accumulated over the years, especially in the last two decades, shows that the ban on short selling is neither able to support security prices, nor to make banks more stable. In a study published by Alessandro Beber and Marco Pagano in the Journal of Finance in 2013, short selling bans implemented over January 2008 and June 2009 did not go hand in hand with increases or lower drops in the prices of exchange, except in the United States in the two weeks following the application of the ban. An exception probably due to the simultaneous announcement of bank bailouts by the Federal Reserve. In other countries, where the bans were not accompanied by announcements of bank bailouts, or also targeted non-bank shares, or did not target bank share at all, the ban on short selling does not seem to have supported security prices. The estimates indicate that banning naked short sales did not have significant effects on share prices, and banning covered short sales even made them decrease. In light of this, lawmakers should subject short selling bans to specific conditions and parameter such as in the case of the United States in order to limit the discretionary powers of the financial regulator whose decisions might negatively influence the price of securities. This is a clear evidence that financial regulation might cause unintended consequences in the name of good purposes.

Relevant Financial Crises

Date	Financial Crisis or Important Speculators
1772	**Alexander Fordyce is the short seller of the East India Company in London**
1791	William Duer organised a pool along with Alexander Macomb and other owners of shares in the Bank of the United States to corner the market before the next distribution of shares in July 1792 and sell shares at profit to European investors. When shares overvalued, a number of short sellers formed a 'bear raid' to push the stock price lower. The bears were led by Governor George Clinton of New York
1800s–1900s	Jacob Little is the Great Bear of Wall Street in New York (US). One of the first short seller in capital markets in the United States
1907	Two brothers Otto and Augustus Heinze, along with another prominent business partner, attempted to buy enough shares that other potential buyers, such as those who need to cover short positions, would have to pay a premium. Prices surged. However, it was insufficient to corner the market. The short sellers, the brothers tried to squeeze had not trouble buying shares at lower prices from others to cover their short positions. The plan had failed and Otto and Augustus Heinze incurred large losses; among the lenders believed to be financing their scheme was the Knickerbocker Trust
1992	George Soros shorted the British Pound and 'broke' the Bank of England
2001	James Chanos is short selling Enron
2007–2008	Michael J. Burry shorted Lehman Brothers during the Global Financial Crisis making relevant profits
2017	Sergej Wenergold shorted Dortmund and simulated an Islamic terror raid against the football team. He figured, he could make money, if the value of share plummeted
2021	Short sellers who had bet against GameStop suffered large losses as a result of the short squeeze

Notes

1. A macaroni (formerly spelled maccaroni) was a pejorative term used to describe a fashionable fellow of mid-eighteenth-century England. Stereotypically, men in the macaroni culture dressed, spoke, and behaved in an unusually sentimental and androgynous manner. The term 'macaroni' pejoratively referred to a man who exceeded the ordinary bounds of fashion in terms of high-end clothing, fastidious eating, and gambling. The macaroni was a symbol of inappropriate bourgeois excess, effeminacy, and possible homosexuality, which was

then legally viewed as sodomy. However, many critics view the macaroni as representing a general change in the eighteenth-century English society such as political change, class consciousness, new nationalism, commodification, and consumer capitalism. The origin of the term 'macaroni' is when wealthy young British men traditionally took a trip around Europe upon their coming of age known as his Grand Tour. Italy was a key destination of these tours. During their trip, many developed a taste for maccaroni, a type of pasta little known in England then, and so they were said to belong to the Macaroni Club. They would refer to anything that was fashionable or *a la mode* as 'very maccaroni'.

2. The Exchange Rate Mechanism (ERM) created in 1979 laid the foundation for the later Economic and Monetary Union (EMU). The United Kingdom joined the ERM in 1990 (and left in 1992) but obtained an opt-out from joining EMU in return for agreeing to the next major Treaty amendment, the Maastricht Treaty, in 1991. The Maastricht Treaty (the Treaty on European Union) also created the three-pillared structure which included intergovernmental decision-making in foreign and security policy and justice and home affairs matters. This Treaty was controversial in the UK Parliament, because the Conservative Government under John Major had opted out its social policy provisions. In 1993 a confidence motion narrowly ensured parliamentary support for the Government's EC policy and the Treaty was subsequently ratified. The next Treaty amendment agreed in Amsterdam in 1997 included adoption of EU social policy provisions by the Labour Government of Tony Blair. Specifically, the Treaty of Amsterdam incorporated the Schengen provisions on the abolition of internal border controls and a common visa policy into the EU Treaties, with opt-outs for the United Kingdom and Ireland. On 1 January 1999 the single currency, the Euro, was adopted as the official currency of eleven of the fifteen EU Member States. This was initially adopted as a 'virtual currency' for commercial and financial transactions only. At the Helsinki European Council in December 1999, the EU agreed to open accession negotiations with several East European States, Cyprus and Malta, and recognised Turkey as an applicant state. Twelve European states adopted the Euro as a legal tender on 1 January 2002, and began to phase out their national currencies. Britain, Sweden, and Denmark did not join the single currency.

EMU was completed in 2002 when Euro coins and notes entered circulation for Eurozone States.

3. A meme stock refers to the shares of a company that have gained viral popularity due to heightened social sentiment. This social sentiment usually due to activity online, particularly on social media platforms. These online communities can dedicate heavy research and resources towards a particular stock. Meme stocks often have heavier discourse and analysis in discussion threads on websites like Reddit and posts to followers on platforms like Twitter and Facebook. Some believe that meme stock communities coordinate efforts to influence the prices of those shares, meme stock shareholders are often an unorganised set of independent individuals, each with their own investment views and preferences. Collectively, their independent actions have been shown to initiate short squeezes in heavily shorted names. As a result, meme stocks can become overvalued.
4. A credit default swap is a derivative contract which acts as a form of 'insurance' against the risk of credit default of a corporate or government bond. In return for a series of payments, the credit risk is transferred from the buyer to the seller. If the issuer default, the CDS seller pays the buyer the face value of the instrument. An uncovered or naked CDS is when the buyer of a CDS is not exposed to the credit risk of the underlying reference entity.
5. Naked shorting is the now-illegal practice of selling short shares that have not been affirmatively determined to exist. Ordinarily, traders must first borrow a stock or determine that it can be borrowed before they sell it short. In other words, naked short selling is where the seller has not borrowed the securities when the short sale occurs.
6. Regulation SHO is a set of rules from the Securities and Exchange Commission (SEC) implemented in 2005 that regulates short sale practices. Regulation SHO established 'locate' and 'close-out' requirements aimed at curtailing naked short selling and other practices. Regulation SHO requires broker-dealers to identify a source of borrowable stock before executing a short sale in any equity security with the goal of reducing the number of situations where stock is unavailable for settlement. Regulation SHO also requires firms that clear and settle trades to take action to close out failures to deliver by borrowing or purchasing securities of like kind and quantity. For short sale transactions, failures to deliver must be closed out by no later than the beginning of regular trading hours on the settlement

day following the settlement date. For long sale transactions or bona fide market making activities, failures to deliver must be closed out by no later than the beginning of regular trading hours on the third settlement day following the settlement date.

Bibliography

Battalio R, Schultz P, 'Regulatory uncertainty and market liquidity: The 2008 short sale ban's impact on equity option markets' (2011) 66 (6) The Journal of Finance, 2013–2053

Book J, 'What's the difference between Michael Burry and Alexander Fordyce?' (12 November 2019) American Institute for Economic Research

Bryan T, 'The Panic of 1792' (26 February 2016) Global Financial Data

Clews H, Niederhoffer V, *Fifty Years in Wall Street* (Wiley Investment Classics) (John Wiley & Sons 2006)

Cowen D J, 'The first bank of the United States and the Securities Market Crash of 1792' (2000) 60 (4) The Journal of Economic History, 1041–1060

Davis J, Wade Hand D, *Reflexivity and Economics: George Soros's theory of reflexivity and the methodology of economic science* (Routledge 2017)

Goodspeed T B, *Legislation instability: Adam Smith, free banking, and the financial crisis of 1772* (Harvard University Press 2016)

James N, 'Crisis chronicles: central bank crisis management during Wall Street's first crash (1792)' (9 May 2014) Liberty Street Economics, Federal Reserve Bank of New York

Kavoussi B, 'The panic of 1907: A human-caused crisis or a thunderstorm?' The Center for History and Economics

Kosmetatos P, *Financial contagion and market intervention in the 1772–3 credit crisis* (Cambridge Working Papers in Economic and Social History 2014)

Kosmetatos P, *The 1772–1773 British Credit Crisis* (Palgrave Macmillan 2018)

Lefevre E, *Reminiscences of a Stock Operator* (Albatross Publishers 2017)

Maccaro J, 'Jacob Little, Wall Street's First Tycoon' (18 February 2004) Working Money

Markham W J, *From Christopher Columbus to the Robber Barons: A Financial History of the United States 1492–1900* (Routledge 2022)

Mezrich B, *The Antisocial Network* (Grand Central Publishing 2019)

Moen J R, Tallman E, 'The panic of 1907' (4 December 2015) Federal Reserve History

New York Times, 'Funeral of Mr. Jacob Little' (1 April 1865)

New York Times, 'The convertible bonds: How Jacob Little manipulated matters years ago' (23 February 1882)

O'Neil W J, Morales G, *How to make money selling stocks short* (Wiley 2005)
Osnos P, *George Soros: A life in full* (Harvard Business Review Press 2022)
Parnes J, *Short selling for the long term: How a combination of short and long positions leads to investing success* (Wiley 2020)
Richard S, 'Alexander Hamilton: central banker and financial crisis manager' (2007) Financial History, 20–25
Richard S, et al., 'Alexander Hamilton, central banker: Crisis management during the US financial panic of 1792' (2009) 83 (1) Business History Review, 61–86
Rockoff H, 'Upon Daedalian wings of paper money: Adam Smith and the crisis of 1772' (December 2009) National Bureau of Economic Research
Robins N, *The corporation that changed the world: How the East India Company shaped the modern multinational* (Pluto Press 2012)
Sprague O M, *History of crises under the National Banking System* (Government Printing Office 1910)
Smith A., *An inquiry into the nature and causes of the Wealth of nations: A selected edition by Adam Smith* (Oxford University Press 1776)
Soros G, *The Alchemy of Finance: The new paradigm* (Wiley 2003)

CHAPTER 7

Conclusions

Michelangelo's Creation of Adam might only be a part of the Sistine Chapel ceiling, but something about this painting makes it stand out. It can be considered one of the most iconic images in European art history. It portrays more than the artist's bold point of view—it is no wonder that the painting, even while placed next to the Creation of Eve and the Congregation of the Waters, still makes the most famous section of the Sistine Chapel ceiling. In Michelangelo's time, most painters created their art in one specific way. Creation scenes were a common subject, but the Creation of Adam broke the boundaries that were set in the field of art and went out of the ordinary. Dominating the picture is a figure of God and a figure of Adam. Adam, located on the left side, is painted in somewhat relaxed fashion. This picture, in a sense, depicts more than the creation of the first man, in fact, it shows the very start of what would later become the human race. Adam's figure is curved as he stretches out to God, taking one's mind to the idea that man is made in the likeness of God himself. The way the two dominant figures relate and correspond to each other, one can almost see the closeness that Adam has with his creator. Michelangelo made the Creation of Adam in such a way that the figure of Adam echoes the figure of God, almost as if one is nothing but an extension of the other. God's form, in turn, is stretched out to reach Adam, and here is where one can find the most surprising of all

D. D'Alvia, *The Speculator of Financial Markets*, Palgrave Macmillan Studies in Banking and Financial Institutions,
https://doi.org/10.1007/978-3-031-47901-4_7

details. In fact, when in 1512, Michelangelo finally completed the fresco on the ceiling of the Sistine Chapel, the cardinals responsible for the care of the works stayed for hours watching and admiring the magnificent fresco. After the analysis, they reunited with the master, Michelangelo, and shamelessly fired: 'Do it again!'. Discontent was not aimed at all the work, but at a seemingly unimportant detail. Michelangelo had drawn the panel of the creation of man with the fingers of God and Adam touching each other. The cardinals asked that they not touch each other, but that the fingers of both should be separated, and that God's finger should always be stretched to the maximum, but that Adam's should contract in the last phalanx. A simple detail, but with an important meaning: God is there, but the decision to seek him depends on the man. If he wants, he will spread his finger, touch it, but if he does not want, he can spend his whole life without looking for it. The last phalanx of Adam's contracted finger thus represents free will. In light of this, this book would like to conclude with a message of hope. Beyond structural financial crisis and human mistakes or errors of perception in managing interest rate risks, legal risks, credit risks, financial risks, operational risks as well as liquidity risks, speculators and financial institutions have always a chance to act ethically in respect of the financial system at least to make the 'right choice' in a more secular meaning of the term. The story of the speculator has truly been a Via *Dolorosa*[1] during centuries as this book has illustrated in many instances. Despite an ethical act can undoubtedly generate trust in the system or at least produce some positive effects on the side of financial operators, the same possibility of restoring confidence in the face of an imminent financial crisis becomes a challenging activity that still requires specific answers.

To restore confidence is fundamental. A simple anecdote can help in further understanding the meaning of 'restoring confidence' in financial markets. On 10 June 2008, Dick Fuld, the soon-to-be infamous CEO of Lehman Brothers in New York, assembled his executive committee in response to a second-quarter earnings report registering nearly three billion dollars (USD) in losses. The purpose of the meeting was for everybody in Fuld's inner circle to weigh in on a single question. The question was not: 'How do we restructure the company in order to spin off our most toxic assets?' Nor was it: 'How can we increase our liquidity to address ballooning debts?' Nor even: 'With whom could we merge if it becomes necessary to avoid bankruptcy?' All these questions would be asked with increasing urgency. But, as far as Fuld was concerned, the more pressing question was: 'How do we restore confidence?'.

Confidence is among the most common and least interrogated terms in finance and economics. As the scene from the Lehman Brothers boardroom all too clearly demonstrates, financial operators often skip past the question of what confidence is, to ask how it can be manipulated. The same dynamic is seen today since the resolution of Silicon Valley Bank in March 2023. By that time, on 12 March 2023, the Secretary of the Treasury Janet L. Yellen, the Federal Reserve Board Chair, Jerome H. Powell, and the FIDC Chairman Martin J. Gruenberg, released a joint statement:

> Today we are taking decisive actions to protect the US economy by strengthening public confidence in our banking system. This step will ensure that the US banking system continues to perform its vital roles of protecting deposits and providing access to credit to households and businesses in a manner that promotes strong and sustainable economic growth. (...) No losses associated with the resolution of Silicon Valley Bank will be borne by the taxpayer. We are also announcing a similar systemic risk exception for Signature Bank in New York, which was closed today by its state chartering authority. (...) As with the resolution of Silicon Valley Bank, no losses will be born by the taxpayer.

As it can be seen, to restore confidence is fundamental. This was also understood by Fuld in 2008. Confidence was the endgame of a hypothetical publicity campaign designed to persuade the rest of the world to accept his version of reality. It became commonplace to characterise Fuld as a delusional recluse, who sabotaged Lehman's chance to get 'bailed out' like every other US investment bank by stubbornly refusing to admit how desperate the situation had become. But the villainisation of a few powerful individuals in the aftermath of a crisis is a common way financial operators and society at large avoid reckoning with a more troubling conclusion: there might be a systemic flaws in the structure of our financial system. Think of the witch trials in Chapter 1 or about John Law, Gregor MacGregor, John Blunt, Waddill Catchincs, George Merrick, Henry Flagler, Carl Fisher, Charles Ponzi, Sarah Howe, Bernie Madoff, Gerald Cotten, and Sam Bankman-Fried in Chapter 5 or Alexander Fordyce, Kenneth Lay, Charles Tracy Barney, Joseph Cassano in Chapter 6. This is a never-ending story, and some of our characters also committed suicide or ended their last days in despair and poverty. For the public opinion, they are the villain of financial markets, but still I claim that they are not the main responsible individuals to be blamed. I rather argue that such individuals are the 'victims' of financial markets. Indeed, the real conception that shall be blamed is our understanding of financial risk in terms of progress where within our culture excessive risk taking is synonym of higher profit making as I have illustrated in Chapter 4.

In the same fashion, Fuld—as I will shortly explain—is a simple actor or 'victim' of financial markets who pretends to restore confidence or better to manipulate its true meaning. Indeed, his plan to solve Lehman's problems by carefully massaging public perception was the conventional wisdom of the profession. He was right to insist that any difference between Lehman's exposure to toxic mortgage-backed securities and the exposure of their competitors was marginal. It was disproportionate amount of media attention that distinguished Lehman from the rest of the industry. Such coverage was, in Fuld's opinion, orchestrated by hedge fund managers such as David Einhorn who, by short selling Lehman's stock, positioned themselves to profit from public panic surrounding the bank (for more insights on short selling see Chapter 6). Lehman was being persecuted for misdemeanours afflicting every bank. While Fuld was likely right that hedge funds had suppressed Lehman's stock price with smear campaigns, his own team used analogous tactics to prop it up. The largest single-day gain in the company's history came on 18 March 2008, following a highly publicised quarterly earnings report. Erin Callan, who delivered the report via conference call to more than ten-thousand investors and journalists, reported that 'the fate of Lehman Brothers might hang in the balance'. Callan's statement revealed little that was not a matter of public record. Rather, subjective aspects of her demeanour—her easy tone, the casual way she handled pressing questions, her ability, in short, to disguise her awareness of what was at stake—were what interested the analysts. Such episodes explain why Fuld, in the ensuing months, doubled down on the strategy to 'restore confidence', repeatedly calling upon the most attractive, charismatic member of his management team to feign optimism in the face of sceptical reporters and, whenever possible, cable news cameras.

Finance is theatre—as this book has shown—and financial markets are its stage. In fact, both finance and theatre require the collective voluntary suspension of disbelief. When investors buy stocks, or even so much as make a bank deposit, one implicates himself in the illusion that a few slips of paper, a few drops of ink, or a few lines of code are interchangeable with parcels of land and weeks of labour. At the theatre, in exchange for our suspension of disbelief, we expect a concerted effort to produce verisimilitude. The narrative we pre-emptively consent to must be absorbing and at least minimally plausible. The demand for verisimilitude is what makes theatre risky. The audience reserves the right to stop pretending whenever they feel their feats of imagination are not being earned. They could decide at any moment that jeering the actors or hurling rotten tomatoes in superior entertainment. No matter how tight the script, no matter how well-rehearsed the cast, or expensive the production, there is still always a chance that it all goes terribly wrong.

Finance requires, in moments of crisis, the production of confidence in others by those who have none themselves. Confidence is finance's fourth wall. It is held up on one side by the convenience of money—and the public's passion for that convenience, which persuades them to trade their labour and property for greenbacks and bitcoins. It is held up on the other side by the producers of money, who naturally benefit from the public's passion for what they produce, but who must sustain the agreeable but ultimately fantastical illusion that money has any intrinsic value in the face of daily reminders that it does not. This book has shown that the financial system depends upon the plausibility of narratives of wealth and commerce performed by those best positioned to know those narratives: speculators. The normalisation of this deception is justified by a reasonable fear of the unknown. If the multitudes suddenly agreed that the financial system, global in scale and ever more interwoven in our daily lives, is not worthy of their confidence, what would be the result? It strains the imagination. From Karl Marx to John Maynard Keynes political economists believed that a wholesale rejection of the prevailing system of exchange would look an awful lot like revolution—with all the associated violence and suffering. What institutions or, for that matter, governments would survive a lifting of the veil over the theatre of global finance? Perhaps it is preferable to be lulled by the pleasant fictions of scrolling stock quotes, S&P ratings, and Fortune magazine rankings. But how long can confidence be sustained if there is widespread acceptance of the truth that a huge proportion of the financial wealth supposedly 'circulating' through the global economy is purely theoretical, reproducing itself automatically. According to John Maynard Keynes—for instance—economists habitually ignored or downplayed the centrality of confidence to market activity because it contradicted the profession's conventional models of economic behaviour, which assume that agents consistently make choices based on rational self-interest. As I have shown in Chapter 4, such models offer the illusion that uncertainty is calculable (a calculation that is, coincidently, often called a confidence interval), and that risk can be reliably managed. Keynes told a colleague in 1938:

> Generally speaking, in making a decision we have before us a large number of alternatives, none of which is demonstrably more 'rationale' than the others

Keynes believed that if businesses actually obeyed the prescriptions for rational behaviour upon which orthodox economic models are based, nobody would ever build, buy, barter, or bankroll anything. The human propensities towards hope, faith, even reckless gambling, have far greater effects upon enterprise than estimations of potential profit, which, in most cases prove inaccurate. 'A lot of proportion of our positive activities depend upon spontaneous optimism rather than on a mathematical expectation' Keynes wrote. And if that optimism falters 'leaving us to depend on nothing but a mathematical expectation, enterprise will fade and die'. The automation of capitalist accumulation is economic apocalypse. For Keynes, the 'state of confidence' involves assuming that the existing state of affairs will continue indefinitely even though we know from extensive experience that this is most unlikely. Confidence is what makes you continue to bet on black, even when you know you will inevitably see red. It spurs an irrational appetite for risk-taking. The 'state of confidence' aggregates many highly subjective and often only semi-conscious projections of the future. It is an amorphous variable, impossible to quantify or reliably account for, but liable to be the determining factor in the success of any investment decision, since abrupt and unpredictable shifts in the state of confidence can unsettle any sector of the economy or even the economy as a whole, almost instantaneously.

Confidence stands, simultaneously, as a synonym for certainty and uncertainty, and I would argue that every invocation of confidence in economics should be read with this paradox in mind, as this book has amply illustrated. Proclamations of confidence are frequently used as substitutes for substantive action and healthy self-reflection by financiers such as Flud, who are incapable of disinterestedly evaluating any alternative to the outcomes they ask others to be confident in. Similarly, in the name of confidence, financial regulators might take draconian measures such as in the case of fatal collapse of Lehman Brothers in 2008 or they might extend insurance to uninsured depositors as they did in 2023 for SVB. These actions have detrimental effects on the financial system. Financial regulation and supervision is many times inspired by good intentions, but it may generate unintended consequences because the banking system is fragile, and it is based on trust.

Confidence becomes an essential consideration because prices respond to even the smallest changes in perception. Keynes acknowledges the term's peculiar malleability by regularly placing its technical and colloquial invocations in close proximity. He wants to make clear that confidence cannot be quantified, reliably controlled, or pinned down with equations. Econometrics, he insists, is blind to the 'animal spirits'. Keynes does clarify how disruptive effects of swings in the state of confidence are magnified in economies dominated by large, concentrated financial centres—for instance, in the United States in 1929 and 2008 or in 2023 in the United States and Switzerland. The volatility of the US economy, which has been rocked by financial crisis with disconcerting regularity since the founding of the New York Stock Exchange, is directly attributable to the taste, and talent, in the United States for securitisation and propension to excessive risk-taking. Special Purpose Acquisition Companies are a case in point. Think about the exaggerated forward looking statements related to some high growth companies that constituted the targets of SPACs back in 2020.

Confidence enters macroeconomics through the stock exchange. In the absence of securities markets, Keynes explained, there is no object in frequently attempting to revalue an investment to which we are committed. The farmer cannot remove his capital from the farming business on a whim, then reconsider whether he should return to it later in the week. Before securities trading was common practice, the farmer's confidence, the shipper's confidence, and the realtor's confidence had no impact on the simple supply-and-demand logic that set the prices for their goods. But the stock exchange re-values many investments every day, and the revaluations give a frequent opportunity to the individual to revise his commitments. At the exchange, one can buy corn, even when corn is not in season (see Chapter 1), or one can buy flowers even when it is not blossoming season (see Chapter 5), or a stake in a building, even when no tenants are moving in or out (for example, the Florida land boom of the 1920s or the Japanese land bubble of 1988). Securities can be invented, amalgamated, contracted, or split. Under the pressure of constant negotiation, confidence becomes an essential consideration because prices respond to even the smallest changes in perception, changes that can be based on reliable information, compelling narratives, or abject rumours about specific companies, whole industries, or the entire economy. When corporations are motivated by and reliant upon stockholders, small changes in the state of confidence towards a single company can produce butterfly effects through the whole economy.

When Fuld proposed a publicity barrage with the intention of 'restoring confidence' in Lehman Brothers, he was conceding that a persuasive fiction, widely disseminated via the media, could relieve the firm of pressures from creditors, regulators, analysts, hedge funds, and investors more effectively than substantive strategies to reorganise and raise liquidity. However, as we consume more media, fluctuations in the state of confidence are likely to be even more extreme, and bank runs become quicker in the digital era as the collapse of Silicon Valley Bank has proved. Indeed, Silicon Valley Bank was dubbed the world's first twitter fuelled bank run. Social media had a very important influence on driving the bank run in a 24/7 mobile banking. For example, the forty-two billion dollars (USD) left SVB in a few hours on 9 March 2023. In the past, it would have taken some days or weeks to physically queue outside of the bank and to be informed about a possible collapse of a financial institution. Furthermore, information was sometime travelling at the speed of horses and sailing ships, as I have explained in Chapter 5 in the case of Nathan Rothschild. Today, the highs will be sustained by financial news outlets whose sources and audience are substantially identical, reinforcing the conventional wisdom as it recycles it. And the crashes will be both deeper and more sudden.

As I have anticipated before, one way of increasing confidence in financial markets is by operating according to ethical values (not necessarily religious values), and being able to demonstrate how governance, strategy, and decision-making has been informed by ethical principles is an issue which is squarely in the spotlight. Firms do not operate in a vacuum and their licence to operate depends on customers and stakeholders (including, importantly, regulators) being satisfied with their business approach. Building trust through an ethical framework and responsible business outlook is critical to sustainable success as well as to avoiding costly crises. While engendering trust through an ethical business approach demands an organisational mindset which is focused on achieving the right outcome, irrespective of legal or regulatory demands, complying with the rules and requirements which have been designed to deliver such outcomes is mandatory. Legal, regulatory, and societal expectations have been steadily increasing over recent years and a heretofore unseen volume of material now exists to help guide firms in the area of culture, conduct, and ethics. Indeed, I firmly believe that culture, conduct, and ethics are words which have come to pepper the regulatory lexicon. The importance of these intangible concepts and 'getting it right' has been clearly communicated, with myriad speeches and initiatives in the financial services sectors focusing on these issues. A sound ethical framework is something which can lay the foundations for, and strengthen, both the culture and conduct of an organisation. However, what is ethical has to be assessed in context, taking into account the nature of a firm's business, its customers, and its counterparties. Hence, values shall never be imposed by external third parties or regulators, but should be self-imposed by each individual firm and such values should reflect the business culture of such specific firm. Today, one venue where ethics in finance is seriously contemplated relates to sustainable finance.[2] For instance, by the end of June 2021 almost two-hundred billion dollars (USD) in sustainable bonds had been issued globally under the Green Bonds Principles established in 2014 by the ICMA.[3] On top of that, other sustainable financing, such as loans and equity capital, added up to seventy billion dollars (USD) in the first six months of 2021. The seismic shift in public opinion that sustainable business practices are crucial to address climate change and other environmental issues—as well as social injustice and poverty—has propelled sustainable finance from niche product status to global acclaim. Socially Responsible Investing is a concept that incorporates environmental, social, and governance (ESG) considerations and criteria into investment decisions, and it is one of the approaches adopted to promote the transition to a net zero economy. Sustainable finance is an emerging topic, but one that a compelling importance in the year to come. To this end, I argue that the primary responsibility to address climate change rests with governments rather than central banks. Clear mandates in the legal framework for central banks are key to sustain legitimacy. However, to the extent that climate change has consequences for price and financial stability, central banks within their mandate could or should adopt actions to address their impact. Hence, there is no need for a major legal reform, but at the same time there shall not be an active role of central banks to promote climate policies outside their traditional mandates related to monetary policy and price stability. The centrality of climate-related financial risks is also evidenced in a recent consultation issued on 6 July 2023 by the Basel Committee on Banking Supervision on revisions to the Core Principles for Effective Banking Supervision (2012). The consultation is reflecting developments in new risks, including climate-related financial risks and digitalisation. Specifically, climate-related financial risks can affect the safety and soundness of banks and have broader financial stability implications for the banking system. To this end, the consultation is proposing an amendment to require supervisors to consider climate-related financial risks in their supervisory methodologies and processes and to have the power to require banks to submit information that allows for the assessment of the materiality of climate-related financial risks. This also will require banks to have comprehensive risk management policies and processes for all material risks, including climate-related financial risks.

Financial markets are based on information, but sometimes the distorted use of such information has been capable of generating Ponzi schemes and errors of perception by investors and common people. As I have explained in Chapter 5, a Ponzi scheme involves a phony investment in which early investors are paid with the investments of later investors making the enterprise appear legitimate. But Charles Ponzi was neither the first nor the last, by far, to perpetrate this type of fraud. Ponzi schemes share some common characteristics. The high visibility and popularity of their apparently lucrative investment make them appear legitimate. Many Ponzi schemers also appear to be terribly selective in who is allowed to invest with them. For instance, Chapter 5 is documenting this approach when it is presenting the remarkable stories of Sarah Howe, Charles Ponzi, and Bernie Madoff. Investors begged these 'scam artists' to take their money. These individuals exploited a rampant fear of missing out on a golden opportunity.

The fear of missing out is another essential sentiment in financial markets. In fact, a common theme among Ponzi scheme victims is 'irrational exuberance', a term popularised by former Federal Reserve Chairman Alan Greenspan whereby people observe others making great profits from investments and determine that this means the investments are safe—even if there are no underlying reasons to support those conclusions. Irrational exuberance is nothing new and certainly was applicable as far back as during the tulip mania of the 1600 s in the Netherlands, when speculation in investments in tulip bulbs led to a dramatic market crash in 1637 (see Chapter 5). Whatever their differences, the same mistake is made by victims of all Ponzi schemes: putting money in an investment that is not completely understood. In a prison interview, Madoff, who stole fifty billion dollars (USD) from his victims, even had the chutzpah to blame his victims for their plight, indicating that if they had looked into his investment methodology, they would have seen that it was impossible to consistently earn the returns he claimed to deliver. So what have we learned since Ponzi was arrested more than one-hundred years ago? I guess, seemingly little. For instance, in 2020, the US law enforcement discovered sixty major Ponzi schemes, with victims investing three-point-twenty-five billion dollars (USD) in these totally fraudulent scams. And it is highly likely that the true number of Ponzi scams still being perpetrated is far greater.

Another clear example of Ponzi schemes or gambling today can be seen in crypto finance. Game theory (see Chapter 4) once again is useful to understand what happened in crypto finance between 2022 and 2023. Back in 2008, as I have explained, the job of an investment banker was not to win market share; it was to stay alive. And staying alive was not a zero-sum game; each bank was more likely to stay alive if its competitors did. The way to stay alive was not by convincing everyone that one particular bank was better than the competition. The way to stay alive was by convincing everyone that everything was fine, that the system was fine, in one word: confidence. Bad news for one bank was bad news for everyone. This same aptitude has been carried out in the banking industry during the March Madness of 2023 when Silicon Valley Bank tried and failed to raise two-point-twenty-five billion dollars (USD) in new funding to cover losses on its bond portfolio, and had begun looking for a buyer to save it. The same approach can be seen in the present and future crypto industry today. Between 2022 and 2023, crypto finance has suffered a crisis in confidence, with falling asset prices, contagion, rapid deleveraging, and bankruptcies of prominent firms. To restore confidence is difficult. Some prominent firms turned out to be scams and Ponzis, and it is reasonable to assume that there will be more in the future. There seems to be a very wide range of risk management practices and some prominent firms are probably much safer than others. However, it is still in the long term interest of managers of crypto firms to assure that people are confident that none of the 'big crypto business' are a scam. In other words, in crypto there is still a sort of half-understood imperfect equilibrium of mutually assured destruction. If everyone joined together to generously praise each other's projects, they would bolster overall confidence in the crypto financial system, and all of their projects would attract investors and do well. If one person said the opposite and discredit a competitor, this might harm the market as a whole. For example, one interesting crypto project is OlympusDAO, whose basic premise is that if everyone buys its tokens and do not sell them, then everyone would make money—whereas if one sells tokens, he would lose money (because tokens would go down as he sells them) and so would everyone else. The game theory of crypto is obvious, but Olympus was right to emphasise it. This idea is close to the core of crypto, but it has not been followed since May 2022 when TerraUSD (an algorithmic stablecoin) also known as UST and its sister token, Luna, crashed sending their prices to near zero. This has generated a panic selling and financial turmoil. Since then, the cryptocurrency industry has long struggled to convince regulators, investors, and ordinary customers that it is trustworthy. For instance, one of Mr. Bankman-Fried's priorities in Washington was to pass a bill giving the Commodity Futures Trading Commission authority to regulate the largest cryptocurrencies. Such a law would have provided FTX and other trading platforms with a smoother path to regulatory compliance in the United States and a deeper pool of potential investors. The FTX's collapse in 2022 killed the bill's opportunity. Since then, following the FTX bankruptcy more regulators have criticised crypto, and opinions on the matter tend to be extreme. The crypto industry still has congressional supporters in Washington, but the collapse of FTX has kicked off investigations by the SEC on how FTX improperly used customer funds to prop up Alameda Research, and this has remarkably changed the course of history for cryptocurrency exchanges. When the cryptocurrency market experienced a two trillion dollars (USD) crash in May 2022, FTX offered financial lifelines to several collapsing firms. Its fall has rippled through the industry. Lenders such as BlockFi and Genesis have suffered loss in the aftermath of FTX's collapse. By the end of 2022 crypto lending services have suffered extreme losses. The biggest three—BlockFi, Voyager, and Celsius—have all now collapsed. The basic on how this happened is similar. Crypto lenders were taking customer deposit in return for some preposterous yield. To make money while paying out that preposterous yield, lenders needed to invest customer funds in something that pays an even more preposterous yield. Those investments naturally involved a high level of risk, often a frightening amount of it. The details vary, but the technique is the same. For example, Celsius was making under-collateralised loans to crypto trader and investing in dubious yield farming projects. Hence, if there is a downturn in crypto prices, that high-risk, high-yield investment suffers. Customers panic and demand their money back. But their money is in risky assets that have lost most of their value, or which might be illiquid, or both. At that point, the choice is bailout or bankruptcy.

With the three big crypto lending platforms plus FTX in bankruptcy, it barely needs saying that centralised finance or CeFI, has fared poorly during this crypto crash. Yet decentralised finance, or DeFI, has held up fine. DeFI and lending protocols are mostly chugging along. This makes sense because most things in DeFI are just pieces of software that match lenders with borrowers or buyers with sellers (see Chapter 5); they usually do not hold customer funds, as centralised exchanges do. The critical element in centralised exchanges like FTX is that somebody—either the operator of the central limit-order book or an independent intermediary like a brokerage—takes custody of users funds. That provides certainty that when the exchange matches an order, each party will settle. If buyers or sellers could renege, they would do so whenever it was to their advantage, rendering the exchange unreliable and useless. Decentralised exchanges, by contrast, require no custody thanks to the blockchain-based innovation of the automated market maker. An exchange attracts liquidity providers, which deposit tokenised assets into a smart contract. A smart contract is a piece of code stored simultaneously on thousands of computers that use the blockchain to agree on the same result each time the code runs. Collectively, the assets in this smart contract provide an inventory for traders who swap them at prices determined by a formula also contained in the smart contract. For this service, traders pay a small fee on each trade, providing revenue to the exchange and a return to the liquidity providers. Because smart contracts are publicly visible, the funds within them are easy to audit. Because they cannot be altered by any one person (assuming the underlying code is strong), the money is impossible for any one person to steal. No actor assumes custody, and there is not risk of theft by a rough manager. This system requires investors to trust bits of public code rather than potentially culpable humans. If FTX were a US stock exchange rather than a cryptocurrency exchange, regulations would have required user funds to be held by an outside custodian and orders routed through a brokerage, but it would have been equally possible—and illegal—for a bad actor, working for the custodian, to misappropriate funds. In other words, operational risk as well as erroneous perceptions cannot be prevented and anticipated not even by the law, policymakers, supervisors, and lawmakers.

This is true especially if one reflects on the counteracting measures that for centuries have been implemented by governments and regulators. Nonetheless, very few regulations are effective and very few times the regulator is able to anticipate the course of the events. In other words, the regulator is often acting either too early or too late. Both circumstances are negative because they might produce over-regulation making markets sterile, and they might be the product of prejudice by taking the risk of enacting rules that sometimes are not even needed or at least are no more effective to prevent markets' dynamics that are already consumed because based on euphoria or speculative mania. Finally, regulation can also produce an unexpected result that is a paradox. By virtue of regulating more a specific sector, indirectly it is produced more legitimisation. Examples of this phenomenon can be seen both in crypto finance and SPACs. In respect of the former, I argue that we should separate unequivocally traditional finance from decentralised finance and centralised finance. This is done to preserve financial stability, and avoid serious threats to consumers' protection. As claimed by Professor Allen, both decentralised finance and centralised finance have 'shadow financial' functions, and they constitute a direct example of shadow banking 2.0. In one of the last Bank for International Settlements (BIS) bulletin issued on 12 January 2023, the BIS has provided a clear view on how centralised finance and decentralised finance can exacerbate the standard risks in traditional finance. The risks stemming from digitalisation have been also recently addressed in a consultation issued on 6 July 2023 by the Basel Committee on Banking Supervision on revisions to the Core Principles for Effective Banking Supervision (2012). In particular, digitalisation is changing both customer behaviours and the way that banking services are provided. The emergence of new products, new entrants, and the use of new technologies present both opportunities and risks for supervisors, banks, and the banking system. Specifically, the consultation is proposing a reform of the operational risk and operational resilience because banks are increasingly relying on third parties for provision of technology services, which creates additional points of cyber risk as well as potential system-wide concentrations. To this end, supervisors should be able to access relevant information and review the overall activities of the banking group, including those undertaken by service providers.

To this end, I argue that crypto trading and crypto markets are not like traditional finance. Finance and financial services exist to support the 'common good', namely a purpose that crypto trading lacks. Crypto trading tries to emulate traditional finance, but it is a complex system of finance that emulates high levered and opaque finance as I have shown, namely the outcomes that society wants less of. In other words, crypto trading is gambling where crypto traders bring money—fiat currency—into a casino or online gambling game and convert the winnings or losses back into money. To this end, centralised finance and decentralised finance are not 'real' finance, they are a pure gambling activity that shall be regulated by gamble laws. Notwithstanding the temptation to issue lenient new rules and financial legal frameworks on centralised finance and decentralised finance, financial regulators globally should resist such temptation to avoid the possible integration of crypto finance into real and traditional finance. Indeed, if such move is consented by the enactment of new banking regulation applicable to crypto finance, then the risk of systemic contagion would be real too. I argue, therefore, that in order to provide individual investor protection regulation, the application of existing securities regulation to crypto finance would serve the purpose, and this would also avoid a further legitimation of crypto finance or assimilation of the same to traditional finance. This because already under the existent securities regulation framework the vast majority of crypto exchanges and crypto assets would simply be unable to comply with registration requirements. In other words, the imposition of a de facto ban could be a first step in providing consumers with protections. Nonetheless, as also anticipated in the recent consultation by the Basel Committee on Banking Supervision—in July 2023—regulators and supervisors should be dynamic to respond to financial innovations, and especially to design consumers' protection regimes. For example, an investor protection regulatory framework is desirable for specific crypto assets such as stablecoins that are destined to become a new means of payment for retail users. Indeed, it is likely that stablecoins will be abandoned by qualified investors because of their high-risk profile and low-profitability (see Silicon Valley Bank where Circle Internet Financial Ltd deposited three-point-three billion dollars (USD) of its about forty billion of USD Coin reserves at the bank). It is undeniable that crypto finance is an industry in continuous evolution, but still it is not recognised as an asset class, and there is always an increasing trend towards centralisation as argued by Charles Goodhart, Rosa Lastra, and Hilary Allen. Indeed, stablecoins are gravitating around fiat currency and safe assets. This is reducing competition and it is bringing once again traditional finance in the spotlight. Another case in point is the new crypto exchange EDX Markets, an institutional-only exchange (ie retail orders are intermediated by brokers) launched in June 2023 and backed by firms including Citadel Securities, Fidelity Digital Assets, and Charles Schwab Corp. It will offer trading in four cryptocurrencies: Bitcoin, Ethereum, Litecoin, and Bitcoin Cash, and unlike existing crypto-trading platforms such as Coinbase Global Inc. and Binance Holdings Ltd., it offers a 'non-custodial' model, meaning that it does not hold clients' digital assets during trading. This to avoid conflict of interest and possible mismanagement of funds such as in the case of FTX. This is a way to trade crypto while almost completely rejecting the crypto financial system. This is bringing the structure of traditional finance to assets of crypto finance. It seems that traditional finance learned nothing from the crypto financial system except that it did not work. Which is a useful lesson.

In relation to SPACs, the Securities and Exchange Commission in the United States initiated a reform in March 2022 in order to 'control' the supposedly SPAC bubble. Since then, the lack of approval of such reform has generated regulatory uncertainty that has in turn disrupted the SPAC market and generated a negative market sentiment towards SPACs. Hence, SPACs were not a bubble per se—alike the South Sea Company in Chapter 5—due to their 'perverse' corporate mechanisms as some would like to claim, but SPACs were targeted by unreasonable doubts raised by the Securities and Exchange Commission without the enactment of proper and certain rules. Furthermore, if the proposed changes are eventually approved, then the de-SPAC phase (see Chapter 3 for further remarks on the meaning of the de-SPAC) will get closer to an IPO qualification rather than an M&A transaction, especially considering the proposed co-registrant role of the target company and the reform of the safe harbour. Essentially this is another instance where the approval of such SPAC reform will generate an important legitimisation of SPACs by allowing SPACs to even become the new IPO 2.0. The SPAC reform would also constitute the first remarkable change of the Securities Act 1933 and Securities Exchange Act 1934, one-hundred years after their enactments. This would be a historical moment if ever approved, and it would reshape the future of securities law in the United States.

Finally, I would like to point out two remarkable financial innovations, that might serve the purposes of traditional finance in the near future, namely tokenisation and artificial intelligence. Tokenisation is the conversion of physical assets or financial instruments into digital tokens on a blockchain network. This has been gaining significant attention recently. With blockchain technology acting as the foundation for this ground-breaking concept, it enables a secure, decentralised platform for creating, exchanging, and trading digital tokens. Tokenisation has the potential to transform financial markets and democratise investment opportunities, ultimately revolutionising the global economy. Blockchain technology presents a secure and transparent framework for tokenisation. By employing a decentralised ledger, blockchain networks facilitate the creation and management of digital tokens representing physical assets or financial instruments. These tokens can be traded, exchanged, or utilised in various transactions without the need for intermediaries such as banks or brokers. Tokenisation of blockchain technology has the potential to reshape financial markets by creating new, more accessible, and easily tradable financial assets. This can result in several substantial shifts in the financial landscape. For example, tokenisation facilitates fractional ownership, allowing investors to buy and sell portions of assets such as real estate, art, or private equity. This expands investment opportunities to a broader audience, promoting financial inclusion and wealth generation. Tokenisation enhanced market liquidity and it can release liquidity in previously illiquid asset classes, enabling more efficient trading and price discovery. This can lead to reduced transaction costs and improved market efficiency. Tokenisation also allows for the establishment of entirely new markets and investment opportunities. For example, tokenised assets can be aggregated into diverse portfolios or investment products, offering unique risk-return profile for investors. As it can be seen, tokenisation is revolutionising how assets and financial markets are perceived. By capitalising on security, transparency, and efficiency of blockchain technology, tokenisation holds the potential to transform financial markets and democratise investment opportunities. The economic impact of tokenisation is far reaching, with the potential to bolster economic efficiency, create jobs, promote financial inclusion, and foster innovation and entrepreneurship. However, the emergence of tokenisation also introduces regulatory challenges, as policymakers must adapt to this new financial landscape and ensure efficient protections are in place for investors and the broader economy. As tokenisation continues to gain traction, it is essential for businesses, investors, and regulators to understand and adapt to this emerging trend. By embracing the potential of tokenisation and working collaboratively to address its challenges, new economic opportunities can be unlocked and drive sustainable growth in the global economy. The future of finance lies in the integration of tokenisation and blockchain technology, and those who are prepared to navigate this new landscape will be at the forefront of a financial revolution. For example, think of the financial turmoil experienced by pension funds in the United Kingdom in October 2022 following Kwasi Kwarteng's mini-budget reform. That event was important in terms of financial stability and the Bank of England had to intervene with a promise to buy up to sixty-five billion pounds (GBP) of government debt. Specifically, pension funds invested in liability driven investment (LDI). The funds had essentially being invested in complex derivatives using long-dated government bonds as collateral—assets pledged as security to back up a financial contract. In the market turmoil after the mini-budge, the value of UK government bonds fell sharply as investors began to lose faith in the credibility of Truss administration to run a sustainable tax and spending policy. This meant a rise in yields—which move inversely to bond prices—in a reflection of the increased cost of government borrowing. As a result pensions funds invested in LDI schemes faced rolling 'margin calls' as the value of the bonds they had pledged as collateral collapsed. The funds then moved to sell other long-dated bonds they held to cover the cash demands, which in turn led to further selling pressure in the bond market in a self-reinforcing downward spiral. If pension funds' collateral would have been tokenised then it is likely that the process to meet such margin calls would have possibly been more efficient and quicker, probably avoiding the need for a formal intervention of the Bank of England and a possible turmoil of financial markets.

Finally, if human beings are emotional and irrational as I have further explained in Chapters 4, 5, and 6, then one way to avoid at least the emotional bit is by virtue of introducing artificial intelligence (AI) in providing investment advice. In fact, AI uses natural language processing (NLP) to comb through millions of articles and identify changes in public sentiment using more data than humans. Traditionally a financial advisor used to be expensive, but a robo-advisor is cheaper and more accessible. For example, Q.ai is an investment app that allows for one-tap investing guided by artificial intelligence, and it provides users with automated financial advice by using powerful deep-learning technology to make trades on behalf of investors. AI can conduct investment analysis and perform risk management functions by selecting securities based on their investment risks. As always the risk is managed to optimise returns. In some way, as I said, people are suggestible, and the news cycle can be particularly persuasive for an investor who might sell shares following market sentiment. AI resists those impulses. Thanks to the AI's NLP capabilities, it is possible to quickly comb through millions of articles and other content sources to identify the changes in public sentiment. Nonetheless, hallucinations might still be possible. For instance, OpenAI's ChatGPT has triggered a new global race in artificial intelligence. The chatbot is part of a wave of so-called generative AI—sophisticated systems that produce content from text to images—that has shaken up Big Tech and is set to transform industries and the future of work too. Despite its sudden burst in popularity, the technology has serious limitations and potential risks that include spewing misinformation and infringing on intellectual property. To this end, ChatGPT risk factors are starting to be included in securities offering documents. This is showing that artificial intelligence is still growing and developing, so only time will tell what it will be capable of in terms of investment advice as it advances. As this book has shown, I do not believe that new technological evolution will necessarily bring new issues to solve, because human beings are still those who are posing the questions, and therefore creating the problems to be solved. The difference will be seen only when artificial intelligence will be able on its own to raise new issues that require new answers. For the time being, I argue that the future of regulation, supervision, and policymaking shall be focused on the awareness that financial operators and the financial industry need to be prepared to provide new answers to old issues. For instance, the custodial issue in decentralised finance—as I said—can face the same issues of traditional finance if the funds are managed by a third independent party broker who tends to misbehave. Hence, supervision of financial markets is required, but cannot definitively solve the issue that is subjective and based on actual behaviours of market operators. Hence, disaster myopia is more real than ever. Also the liquidity mismatch in the case of crypto lenders do not differ from traditional liquidity risks that commercial banks have experienced for millennia, etc. Hence, tighter liquidity requirements can be a solution in conjunction with reporting.

As this book has shown, it is not important the form that finance can take or the goods or assets that might become the subject of speculation. Proper answers are essential to provide investors with adequate protections, but at the same time financial operators shall figuratively re-join their finger with God as in the Creation of Adam of the Sistine Chapel in Rome, and take a step in making the financial system a more ethical venue to serve the 'common good'. The re-discovery of such civic and moral virtue might allow eventually human begins to progress and evolve as well as to establish financial stability to stand firm tendentially for ever.

Notes

1. The Via *Dolorosa* has been part of Christian pilgrimages for centuries and plays a big part in discussions about Stations of the Cross as well as Christian traditions about where Jesus went in Jerusalem during the Passion Week. The Via Dolorosa sometimes called 'the way of suffering' is a route located in the Old City of Jerusalem which follows the route that Jesus is believed to have walked on his way to be crucified. The route follows the traditional 14 Stations of the Cross, beginning with a place where Christians have traditionally believed Pilate condemned Jesus to death (the Lion's Gate near what used to be a Roman fortress) and ending at a spot which is believed to hold the tomb where Jesus was buried (the Church of the Holy Sepulchre). The last location, the Church of the Holy Sepulchre is a large building containing multiple chapels and levels and contains the last five stations (located in different areas). The first historical reference to the Via *Dolorosa* is from the medieval period. Over the years, different Christians have suggested alternate sites for some of the 14 spots on the route, in the same way that some Christians have suggested alternate steps in the Stations of the Cross.
2. Notwithstanding, the higher emphasis on sustainable finance in recent years, the first steps can be traced back to almost thirty years ago when it became clear that a unique role in order to drive greater sustainability across the global economy will fall to the financial services industry. In 1991, the United Nations Environment Programme (UNEP) Financial Initiative was launched when a small group of commercial banks, including NatWest, joined forces with the UNEP. In May 1992, in the run up to the Rio Summit that year, the so-called Banking Initiative engaged a broad range of financial institutions, including commercial banks, investment banks, venture capitalists, asset managers, and multi-lateral development banks and agencies in a constructive dialogue about the link between economic development and environmental protection—the birth of Sustainable Finance. In early 2005, the United Nations Secretary-General Kofi Annan invited a group of the world's largest institutional investors to help develop the Principles for Responsible

Investment (PRI). One year later the PRI were launched at the New York Stock Exchange. Designed by investors for investors to aid the implementation of ESG issues into investment practice, the number of PRI signatories has grown from the initial one-hundred to now over three-thousand (half the world's institutional investors, representing over one-hundred trillion dollars (USD) of assets under management). Subsequently, the Principles for Responsible Banking (PRB) was launched in September 2019 at the United Nations Headquarters in New York City during the UN General Assembly, are unique framework for ensuring that signatory banks' strategy and practice align with the vision set out by the Sustainable Development Goals and the Paris Climate Agreement in 2015. Specifically, under the Paris Agreement government are required to determine, submit, and update their nationally determined contributions to achieve climate goals. This gives rise to key questions regarding the supportive role of central banks and bank supervisors. Nonetheless, the primary responsibility to address climate change shall rest with governments, and therefore, there should be clear mandates in the legal framework for central banks engaging with climate change and sustainability related policies to establish legitimacy. The Principles for Responsible Banking are designed to specifically cover the lending and underwriting activities of the banking world, complementing the UN-Supported Principles for Responsible Investment. One-hundred-and-ninety-seven banks, a third of the global banking industry, have so far joined the PRB. The signatory banks commit to taking three key steps, which enable them to improve their impact and contribution to society: analyse their current impact on people and planet; set targets where they have the most significant impact, and implement them; publicly report and progress. Finally, in 2012 and today applied by one quarter of the world's insurers, the Principles for Sustainable Insurance (PSI) designed a global roadmap to develop and expand innovative risk management and insurance solutions that help promote renewable energy, clean water, food security, sustainable cities, and disaster-resilient communities.

3. The Green Bond Principles (GBP) are voluntary process guidelines that recommend transparency and disclosure; and promote integrity in the development of the Green Bond market by clarifying the issuance process. The transparency and disclosure recommended by the Principles are also intended to provide the informational basis for

the market to increase capital allocation to environmentally beneficial purposes without any single authority or gate keeper. The GBP are intended for broad use by the market. They provide definitions of the recognised types of Green Bonds. Generally the Principles assist all participants by moving the market towards standard disclosures and reporting which will facilitate transactions.

Index

D. D'Alvia, *The Speculator of Financial Markets*, Palgrave Macmillan Studies in Banking and Financial Institutions,
https://doi.org/10.1007/978-3-031-47901-4

SPRINGER NATURE

GPSR Compliance

The European Union's (EU) General Product Safety Regulation (GPSR) is a set of rules that requires consumer products to be safe and our obligations to ensure this.

If you have any concerns about our products, you can contact us on ProductSafety@springernature.com

In case Publisher is established outside the EU, the EU authorized representative is:

Springer Nature Customer Service Center GmbH
Europaplatz 3
69115 Heidelberg, Germany

The manufacturer's authorised representative in the EU is Springer Nature Customer Service Centre GmbH, Europaplatz 3, 69115 Heidelberg, Germany. If you have any concerns regarding our products, please contact ProductSafety@springernature.com

Printed and bound by CPI Group (UK) Ltd, Croydon, CR0 4YY
01/10/2026
02225852-0004